W9-CLM-751

DYNASTY

TOM HOLLAND

DYNASTY

The Rise and Fall of
the House of Caesar

Doubleday

New York · London · Toronto
Sydney · Auckland

All rights reserved. Published in the United States by Doubleday, a division
of Penguin Random House LLC, New York. Originally published in
hardcover in Great Britain by Little, Brown, an imprint of Little, Brown
Book Group, a Hachette UK Company, London, in 2015.

www.doubleday.com

DOUBLEDAY and the portrayal of an anchor with a dolphin are
registered trademarks of Penguin Random House LLC.

Jacket design by Michael J. Windsor
Jacket photography (clockwise from upper left) Nero © DEA Picture
Library/ Getty Images; Augustus © E+/ Getty Images; Tiberius © Musée
Saint-Raymond, Toulouse, France / Bridgeman Images; Claudius and
Caligula © DEA Picture Library Getty Images
Author photograph © Charlie Hopkinson

Library of Congress Cataloging-in-Publication Data

Holland, Tom, author.
Dynasty : the rise and fall of the House of Caesar / by Tom Holland.
pages cm
Includes bibliographical references and index.
ISBN 978-0-385-53784-1 (hardcover)—ISBN 978-0-385-53790-2 (eBook)
1. Rome—Politics and government—30 B.C.–476 A.D.
2. Rome—History—Empire, 30 B.C.–476 A.D.   3. Emperors—Rome.
I. Title.
DG270.H65 2015
937'.070922—dc23
2015026911

MANUFACTURED IN THE UNITED STATES OF AMERICA

1 3 5 7 9 10 8 6 4 2

First United States Edition

For Katy
'at simul heroum laudes et facta parentis
iam legere . . .'

CONTENTS

ACKNOWLEDGEMENTS

As ever with my books, I owe a huge debt of gratitude to numerous people for their help. To my various editors, Richard Beswick, Gerry Howard, Frits van der Meij and Christoph Selzer, for their support, assistance and advice. To Iain Hunt, for all the care and patience he has brought to disentangling the knots of my manuscript – maps, timelines, end notes and all. To Susan de Soissons, the finest and kindest publicity director a writer could hope to have. To Patrick Walsh, best of agents, and everyone at Conville and Walsh. To Guy de la Bédoyère, Paul Cartledge, Catharine Edwards, Llewelyn Morgan and Andrew Wallace-Hadrill, for generously bringing to bear the full illuminating light of their scholarship on my manuscript, and exposing many an error. To Dan Snow, who more than made up for distracting me from the politics of the first century AD during the 2014 Scottish independence referendum campaign by reading a first draft of *Dynasty*, to invaluable effect. To Jamie Muir, who (as he has done ever since I wrote *Rubicon*) read each successive chapter as I printed it off – and then went the extra mile by accompanying me deep into the Teutoburg Forest. To Gareth Blayney, for his beautiful illustrations of ancient Rome, and for agreeing to bring all his talent to bear on the cover of this book. To Sophie Hay, for her kindness, generosity and enthusiasm, her photographs, her companionship on the road trip to Nemi and Spelunca, and her careful tracking of my Twitter avatar's evolution. To Laura Jeffrey, for her whole-hearted enjoyment of the plumbing on Caligula's pleasure-boat. To Stephen Key, for selflessly negotiating the roads between Rome, Nemi and Spelunca on behalf of Sophie, Laura and myself. To Mattia Buondonno, for his ebullient hospitality at Pompeii. To Charlie Campbell, for providing me with the opportunity to hit a six, bowl the Crown Prince of Udaipur, and play at Lord's – and thereby feel for myself what it must have been to rank as *Augustus*. To my cats, Edith and Tostig, for only periodically sitting on my keyboard. To my beloved wife, Sadie, for living these past years with the Caesars as well as me. To my younger daughter, Eliza, for (oh so perversely) choosing Nerva as her favourite emperor. To my elder daughter, Katy, to whom with all my love I dedicate this book.

MAPS

The Julians and Claudians

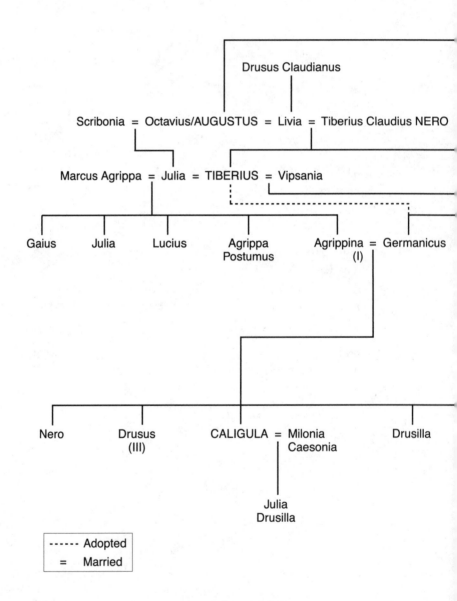

Julius Caesar

Drusus Claudianus

Scribonia = Octavius/AUGUSTUS = Livia = Tiberius Claudius NERO

Marcus Agrippa = Julia = TIBERIUS = Vipsania

Gaius   Julia   Lucius   Agrippa   Agrippina = Germanicus
                                Postumus   (I)

Nero   Drusus   CALIGULA = Milonia   Drusilla
              (III)   Caesonia

                                    Julia
                                    Drusilla

------ Adopted
  =   Married

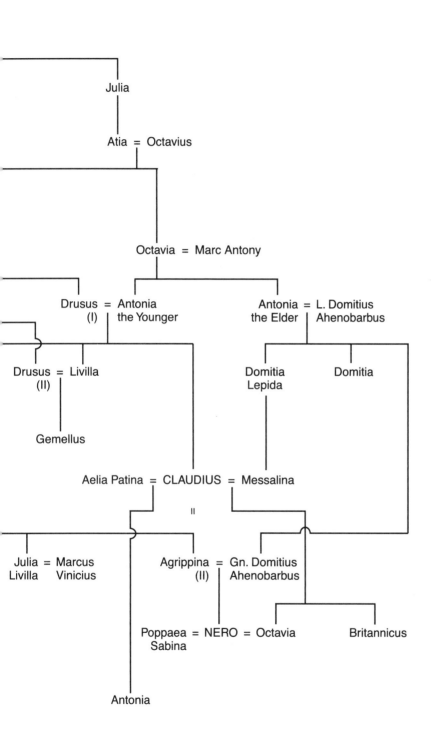

Julia

Atia = Octavius

Octavia = Marc Antony

Drusus = Antonia
(I)   the Younger

Antonia = L. Domitius
the Elder   Ahenobarbus

Drusus = Livilla
(II)

Domitia
Lepida

Domitia

Gemellus

Aelia Patina = CLAUDIUS = Messalina

II

Julia = Marcus
Livilla   Vinicius

Agrippina = Gn. Domitius
(II)   Ahenobarbus

Poppaea = NERO = Octavia
Sabina

Britannicus

Antonia

PREFACE

AD 40. It is early in the year. Gaius Julius Caesar Augustus Germanicus sits on a lofty platform beside the Ocean. As waves break on the shore and spray hangs in the air, he gazes out to sea. Many Roman ships over the years have been lost to its depths. Strange monsters are rumoured to lurk in its grey waters, while beyond the horizon there lies an island teeming with savage and mustachioed head-hunters: Britain. Perils such as these, lurking as they do on the very margins of civilisation, are fit to challenge even the boldest and most iron-willed hero.

The story of the Roman people, though, has always had about it an aura of the epic. They have emerged from dim and provincial obscurity to the command of the world: a feat like no other in history. Repeatedly put to trial, repeatedly surviving it triumphant, Rome has been well steeled for global rule. Now, seven hundred and ninety-two years after her founding, the man who ranks as her emperor wields power worthy of a god. Lined up alongside him on the northern beach are rank upon rank of the most formidable fighting force on the planet: armour-clad legionaries, catapults, battlefield artillery. The Emperor Gaius scans their length. He gives a command. At once, there is a blaring of trumpets. The signal for battle. Then silence. The Emperor raises his voice. 'Soldiers!' he cries. 'I command you to pick up shells. Fill your helmets with the spoils of the Ocean.'[1] And the legionaries, obedient to their emperor's order, do so.

Such, at any rate, is the story. But is it true? Did the soldiers really pick up shells? And if they did – why? The episode is one of the most notorious in the life of a man whose entire career remains to this day a thing of infamy. Caligula, the name by which the Emperor Gaius is better known, is one of the few people from ancient history to be as familiar to pornographers as to classicists. The scandalous details of his reign have always provoked prurient fascination. 'But enough of the emperor; now to the monster.'[2] So wrote Gaius Suetonius Tranquillus, a scholar and archivist in the imperial palace who doubled in his spare time as a biographer of the Caesars, and whose life of Caligula is the oldest extant one that we possess. Written almost a century after the Emperor's death, it catalogues a quite sensational array of depravities and crimes. He slept with his sisters! He dressed up as the goddess Venus! He planned to award his horse the highest magistracy in Rome! Set against the background of such stunts, Caligula's behaviour on the Channel coast comes to seem a good deal less surprising. Suetonius certainly had no problem in explaining his behaviour. 'He was ill in both body and mind.'[3]

But if Caligula was sick, then so too was Rome. The powers of life and death wielded by an emperor would have been abhorrent to an earlier generation. Almost a century before Caligula massed his legions on the shores of the Ocean and gazed out to Britain, his great-great-great-great-uncle had done the same – and then actually crossed the Channel. The exploits of Gaius Julius Caesar had been as spectacular as any in his city's history: not only two invasions of Britain but the permanent annexation of Gaul, as the Romans called what today is France. He had achieved his feats, though, as a citizen of a republic – one in which it was taken for granted by most that death was the only conceivable alternative to liberty. When Julius Caesar, trampling down this presumption, had laid claim to a primacy over his fellow citizens, it had resulted first in civil war, and then, after he had crushed his domestic foes as he had previously crushed the Gauls, in his assassination. Only after two more murderous bouts of slaughtering one another had the Roman people finally been inured to their servitude. Submission to the rule of a

single man had redeemed their city and its empire from self-destruction – but the cure itself had been a kind of sickness.

Augustus, their new master had called himself, 'The Divinely Favoured One'. The great-nephew of Julius Caesar, he had waded through blood to secure the command of Rome and her empire – and then, his rivals once dispatched, had coolly posed as a prince of peace. As cunning as he was ruthless, as patient as he was decisive, Augustus had managed to maintain his supremacy for decades, and then to die in his bed. Key to this achievement had been his ability to rule with rather than against the grain of Roman tradition: for by pretending that he was not an autocrat, he had licensed his fellow citizens to pretend that they were still free. A veil of shimmering and seductive subtlety had been draped over the brute contours of his dominance. Time, though, had seen this veil become increasingly threadbare. On Augustus's death in AD 14, the powers that he had accumulated over the course of his long and mendacious career stood revealed, not as temporary expediencies, but rather as a package to be handed down to an heir. His choice of successor had been a man raised since childhood in his own household, an aristocrat by the name of Tiberius. The many qualities of the new Caesar, which ranged from exemplary aristocratic pedigree to a track record as Rome's finest general, had counted for less than his status as Augustus's adopted son – and everyone had known it.

Tiberius, a man who all his life had been wedded to the virtues of the vanished Republic, had made an unhappy monarch; but Caligula, who had succeeded him in turn after a reign of twenty-three years, was unembarrassed. That he ruled the Roman world by virtue neither of age nor of experience, but as the great-grandson of Augustus, bothered him not the slightest. 'Nature produced him, in my opinion, to demonstrate just how far unlimited vice can go when combined with unlimited power.'[4] Such was the obituary delivered on him by Seneca, a philosopher who had known him well. The judgement, though, was not just on Caligula, but on Seneca's own peers, who had cringed and grovelled before the Emperor while he was still alive, and on the Roman people as a whole. The age was a rotten one: diseased, debased, degraded.

Or so many believed. Not everyone agreed. The regime established by Augustus would never have endured had it failed to offer what the Roman people had come so desperately to crave after decades of civil war: peace and order. The vast agglomeration of provinces ruled from Rome, which stretched from the North Sea to the Sahara, and from the Atlantic to the Fertile Crescent, reaped the benefits as well. Three centuries on, when the nativity of the most celebrated man to have been born in Augustus's reign stood in infinitely clearer focus than it had done at the time, a bishop named Eusebius could see in the Emperor's achievements the very guiding hand of God. 'It was not just as a consequence of human action,' he declared, 'that the greater part of the world should have come under Roman rule at the precise moment Jesus was born. The coincidence that saw our Saviour begin his mission against such a backdrop was undeniably arranged by divine agency. After all – had the world still been at war, and not united under a single form of government, then how much more difficult would it have been for the disciples to undertake their travels.'[5]

Eusebius could see, with the perspective provided by distance, just how startling was the feat of globalisation brought to fulfilment under Augustus and his successors. Brutal though the methods deployed to uphold it were, the sheer immensity of the regions pacified by Roman arms was unprecedented. 'To accept a gift,' went an ancient saying, 'is to sell your liberty.' Rome held her conquests in fee; but the peace that she bestowed upon them in exchange was not necessarily to be sniffed at. Whether in the suburbs of the capital itself, booming under the Caesars to become the largest city the world had ever seen, or across the span of the Mediterranean, united now for the first time under a single power, or in the furthermost corners of an empire whose global reach was without precedent, the *pax Romana* brought benefits to millions. Provincials might well be grateful. 'He cleared the sea of pirates, and filled it with merchant shipping.' So a Jew from the great Egyptian metropolis of Alexandria, writing in praise of Augustus, enthused. 'He gave freedom to every city, brought order where there had been chaos, and civilised savage peoples.'[6] Similar hymns of praise could be – and were – addressed to

Tiberius and Caligula. The depravities for which both men would end up notorious rarely had much impact on the world at large. It mattered little in the provinces who ruled as emperor – just so long as the centre held.

Nevertheless, even in the furthest reaches of the Empire, Caesar was a constant presence. How could he not be? 'In the whole wide world, there is not a single thing that escapes him.'[7] An exaggeration, of course – and yet due reflection of the mingled fear and awe that an emperor could hardly help but inspire in his subjects. He alone had command of Rome's monopoly of violence: the legions and the whole menacing apparatus of provincial government, which existed to ensure that taxes were paid, rebels slaughtered, and malefactors thrown to beasts or nailed up on crosses. There was no need for an emperor constantly to be showing his hand for dread of his arbitrary power to be universal across the world. Small wonder, then, that the face of Caesar should have become, for millions of his subjects, the face of Rome. Rare was the town that did not boast some image of him: a statue, a portrait bust, a frieze. Even in the most provincial backwater, to handle money was to be familiar with Caesar's profile. Within Augustus's own lifetime, no living citizen had ever appeared on a Roman coin; but no sooner had he seized control of the world than his face was being minted everywhere, stamped on gold, and silver, and bronze.* 'Whose likeness and inscription is this?' Even an itinerant street-preacher in the wilds of Galilee, holding up a coin and demanding to know whose face it portrayed, could be confident of the answer: 'Caesar's.'[8]

No surprise, then, that the character of an emperor, his achievements, his relationships and his foibles, should have been topics of obsessive fascination to his subjects. 'Your destiny it is to live as in a theatre where your audience is the entire world.'[9] Such was the warning attributed by one Roman historian to Maecenas, a particularly trusted confidant of Augustus's. Whether he really said it or not, the sentiment

---

* The earliest portrait of a living Roman on a Roman coin seems to have been of Julius Caesar. It was minted in 44 BC – the year, not coincidentally, of his assassination.

was true to the sheer theatricality of his master's performance. Augustus himself, lying on his deathbed, was reported by Suetonius to have asked his friends whether he had played his part well in the comedy of life; and then, on being assured that he had, to have demanded their applause as he headed for the exit. A good emperor had no choice but to be a good actor – as too did everyone else in the drama's cast. Caesar, after all, was never alone on the stage. His potential successors were public figures simply by virtue of their relationship to him. Even the wife, the niece or the granddaughter of an emperor might have her role to play. Get it wrong, and she was liable to pay a terrible price; but get it right, and her face might end up appearing on coins alongside Caesar's own. No household in history had ever before been so squarely in the public eye as that of Augustus. The fashions and hairstyles of its most prominent members, reproduced in exquisite detail by sculptors across the Empire, set trends from Syria to Spain. Their achievements were celebrated with spectacularly showy monuments, their scandals repeated with relish from seaport to seaport. Propaganda and gossip, each feeding off the other, gave to the dynasty of Augustus a celebrity that ranked, for the first time, as continent-spanning.

To what extent, though, did all the vaunting claims chiselled into showy marble and all the rumours whispered in marketplaces and bars approximate to what had actually happened in Caesar's palace? To be sure, by the time that Suetonius came to write his biographies of the emperors, there was no lack of material for him to draw upon: everything from official inscriptions to garbled gossip. Shrewder analysts, though, when they sought to make sense of Augustus and his heirs, could recognise at the heart of the dynasty's story a darkness that mocked and defied their efforts. Once, back in the days of the Republic, affairs of state had been debated in public, and the speeches of Rome's leaders transcribed for historians to study; but with the coming to power of Augustus, all that had changed. 'For, from then on, things began to be done secretly, and in such a way as not to be made public.'[10] Yes, the old rhythms of the political year, the annual cycle of elections and magistracies that once, back in the days of the Republic, had delivered to ambitious Romans the genuine opportunity to sway their city's fate, still endured – but as a largely irrelevant sideshow. The cockpit of power lay elsewhere now. The world had come to be governed, not in assemblies of the great and good, but in private chambers. A woman's whisperings in an emperor's ear, a document discreetly passed to him by a slave: either might have a greater impact than even the most ringing public oration. The implication, for any biographer of the Caesars, was grim but inescapable. 'Even when it comes to notable events, we are in the dark.'[11]

The historian who delivered this warning, although a close contemporary of Suetonius, was immeasurably his superior as a pathologist of autocracy – indeed, perhaps the greatest there has ever been. Cornelius Tacitus could draw on an intimate understanding of how Rome and her empire functioned. Over the course of a glittering career, he had spoken in the law courts, governed provinces, and held the highest magistracies to which a citizen could aspire; but he had also demonstrated a canny, if inglorious, instinct for survival. The dynasty that ruled Rome as he came of age was no longer that of Augustus, which had expired amid a welter of blood back in AD 68 – but it was potentially no less murderous for that. Rather than stand up to its exactions, Tacitus had opted to keep his head down, his gaze averted. The crimes of omission in which he felt himself complicit seem never entirely to have been cleansed from his conscience. The more he came to stand at a distance from public life, the more obsessively he sought to fathom the depths of the regime under which he was obliged to live, and to track how it had evolved. First he narrated the events of his own youth and adulthood; and then, in his final and greatest work, a history that has been known since the sixteenth century as *The Annals*, he turned his gaze back upon the dynasty of Augustus. Augustus himself, and his fateful primacy, Tacitus chose to analyse only in the most oblique manner: by focusing, not upon the man himself, but rather upon his heirs. Four Caesars in succession accordingly took centre stage: first Tiberius; then Caligula; then Caligula's uncle, Claudius; and finally, the last of the dynasty to rule, Augustus's great-great-grandson, Nero.

His death it was that marked the end of the line. Again and again, membership of the imperial family had been shown to come at fatal cost. By AD 68, not a single descendant of Augustus remained alive. Such was the measure of the story that Tacitus had to tell.

And of something else as well: the challenge of telling the story at all. Mordantly, in the first paragraph of The Annals, Tacitus spelt out the problem. 'The histories of Tiberius and Caligula, of Claudius and Nero, were falsified while they remained alive out of dread – and then, after their deaths, were composed under the influence of still festering hatreds.'[12] Only the most diligent research, the most studied objectivity, would do. Painstaking in his efforts to study the official records of each emperor's reign, Tacitus made equally sure never to take them on trust.* Words, under the Caesars, had become slippery, treacherous things. 'The age was a tainted one, degraded by its sycophancy.'[13] The bleakness of this judgement, bred as it was of personal experience, ensured that Tacitus's bitter scepticism ended up corroding all that it touched. In The Annals, not a Caesar who claimed to be acting in the best interests of the Roman people but he was a hypocrite; not an attempt to stay true to the city's traditions but it was a sham; not a fine-sounding sentiment but it was a lie. Rome's history is portrayed as a nightmare, haunted by terror and shadowed by blood, from which it is impossible for her citizens to awake. It is a portrait of despotism that many subsequent generations, witnessing the dimming of their own liberties, have not been slow to recognise. Wherever a tyranny has been planted on the ruins of a previously free order, and whenever specious slogans have been used to mask state-sanctioned crimes, it has been remembered. The dynasty of Augustus still defines the look of autocratic power.

That it should so haunt the public imagination comes, then, as little

---

* The recent discovery in Spain of a decree issued under Tiberius has shed intriguing light on Tacitus's methods. There can be no doubt that he had detailed knowledge of its wording; nor that he fully appreciated the degree to which it expressed, not the truth, but rather what those who had composed it wished to be taken for the truth.

surprise. When people think of imperial Rome, it is the city of the first Caesars that is most likely to come into their minds. There is no other period of ancient history that can compare for sheer unsettling fascination with its gallery of leading characters. Their lurid glamour has resulted in them becoming the very archetypes of feuding and murderous dynasts. Monsters such as we find in the pages of Tacitus and Suetonius seem sprung from some fantasy novel or TV box-set: Tiberius, grim, paranoid, and with a taste for having his testicles licked by young boys in swimming pools; Caligula, lamenting that the Roman people did not have a single neck, so that he might cut it through; Agrippina, the mother of Nero, scheming to bring to power the son who would end up having her murdered; Nero himself, kicking his pregnant wife to death, marrying a eunuch, and raising a pleasure palace over the fire-gutted centre of Rome. For those who like their tales of dynastic back-stabbing spiced up with poison and exotic extremes of perversion, the story might well seem to have everything. Murderous matriarchs, incestuous power-couples, downtrodden beta males who nevertheless end up wielding powers of life and death: all these staples of recent dramas are to be found in the sources for the period. The first Caesars, more than any comparable dynasty, remain to this day household names. Their celebrity holds.

All of which, it is as well to admit, can be a cause of some embarrassment to historians of the period. Tales of poison and depravity, precisely because so melodramatic, have a tendency to make them feel uncomfortable. The more sensational a story, after all, the less plausible it is liable to seem. The truth of the allegations laid against the Julio-Claudians – as the dynasty of Augustus is conventionally known by scholars – has for this reason long provoked disagreement. Could Caligula, for instance, really have been as mad as Suetonius and other ancient authors claimed? Perhaps, rather than insane, his more flamboyant stunts had simply been garbled in the transmission? Was it possible, for instance, that behind the seeming lunacy of his order to pick up seashells there was in fact a perfectly rational explanation? Many scholars have suggested as much. Over the years, numerous theories have been proposed. Perhaps – although no source mentions it – there had been a mutiny, and Caligula was looking to punish his soldiers by giving them some demeaning task? Or maybe he wanted them to look for pearls, or else for shells that he could then use to ornament water features? Or perhaps *concha*, the Latin word for 'shell', was in fact being used by Caligula to signify something quite different: a kind of boat, or even the genitals of a whore? Any of these suggestions are possible; none of them is definitive. Like a vivid dream, the episode seems haunted by the sense of some unfathomable logic, some meaning that all our efforts to understand it are doomed never quite to grasp. Such is often the frustration of ancient history: that there are things we will never know for certain.

None of which need necessarily be cause for despair. Known unknowns are not without their value to the historian of the first Caesars. The question of what precisely Caligula might have been getting up to on that Gallic beach will never be settled decisively; but what we do know for certain is that Roman historians did not feel that it particularly needed an explanation. They took for granted that ordering soldiers to pick up shells was the kind of thing that a bad, mad emperor did. The stories told of Caligula – that he insulted the gods, that he took pleasure in cruelty, that he revelled in every kind of sexual deviancy – were not unique to him. Rather, they were a part of the common stock of rumour that swirled whenever a Caesar offended the proprieties of the age. 'Leave ugly shadows alone where they lurk in their abyss of shame':[14] this po-faced admonition, delivered by an anthologist of improving stories during the reign of Tiberius, was one that few of his fellow citizens were inclined to follow. They adored gossip far too much. The anecdotes told of the imperial dynasty, holding up as they do a mirror to the deepest prejudices and terrors of those who swapped them, transport us to the heart of the Roman psyche. It is why any study of Augustus's dynasty can never simply be that, but must also serve as something more: a portrait of the Roman people themselves.

It is also why a narrative history, one that covers the entire span of the Julio-Claudian period, offers perhaps the surest way of steering a path between the Scylla of flaccid gullibility and the Charybdis of an overly muscle-bound scepticism. Clearly, not all stories told about the early Caesars are to be trusted; but equally, many of them do provide us with a handle on what most probably inspired them. Anecdotes that can seem utterly fantastical when read in isolation often appear much less so with the perspective that a narrative provides. The evolution of autocracy in Rome was a protracted and contingent business. Augustus, although ranked by historians as the city's first emperor, was never officially instituted as a monarch. Instead, he ruled by virtue of rights and honours voted him in piecemeal fashion. No formal procedure ever existed to govern the succession; and this ensured that each emperor in turn, on coming to power, was left with little option but to test the boundaries of what he could and could not do. As a result, the Julio-Claudians presided over one long continuous process of experimentation. That is why I have chosen in this book to trace the entire course of the dynasty, from its foundation to its final bloody expiration. The reign of each emperor is best understood, not on its own terms, but in the context of what preceded and followed it.

And all the more so because the study of the period, as is invariably the case with ancient history, can sometimes resemble the frustration of listening to an old-fashioned car radio, with various stations forever fading in and out of audibility. If only, for instance, we had the account by Tacitus of Caligula's actions on that beach by the Channel – but alas, we do not. Everything that *The Annals* had to report about the years between the death of Tiberius and the halfway stage of Claudius's reign has been lost. That Caligula, the most notorious member of his dynasty, should also be the Julio-Claudian for whose reign the sources are the patchiest is almost certainly not a coincidence. Although two thousand years of repetition might give us the impression that the narrative of the period has long since been settled, in many cases it has not. It remains as important, when studying ancient history, to recognise what we do not know as to tease out what we do. Readers should be aware that much of the narrative of this book, like the pontoon bridge that Caligula once built between two promontories in the Bay of Naples, spans turbulent depths. Controversy and disagreement are endemic to the study of the period. Yet this, of course, is precisely its fascination. Over the past few decades, the range and vitality of scholarly research into the Julio-Claudians have revolutionised our understanding of their age. If this book manages to give readers even a flavour of how exciting it is to study Rome's first imperial dynasty, then it will not have failed in its aim. Two millennia on, the West's primal examples of tyranny continue to instruct and appal.

'Nothing could be fainter than those torches which allow us, not to pierce the darkness, but to glimpse it.'[15] So wrote Seneca, shortly before his death in AD 65. The context of his observation was a shortcut that he had recently taken while travelling along the Bay of Naples, down a gloomy and dust-choked tunnel. 'What a prison it was, and how long. Nothing could compare with it.' As a man who had spent many years observing the imperial court, Seneca knew all about darkness. Caligula, resentful of his brilliance, had only narrowly been dissuaded from having him put to death; Claudius, offended by his adulterous affair with one of Caligula's sisters, had banished him to Corsica; Agrippina, looking for someone to rein in the vicious instincts of her son, had appointed him Nero's tutor. Seneca, who would ultimately be compelled by his erstwhile student to slit his own veins, had no illusions as to the nature of the regime he served. Even the peace that it had brought the world, he declared, had ultimately been founded upon nothing more noble than 'the exhaustion of cruelty'.[16] Despotism had been implicit in the new order from its very beginning.

Yet what he detested Seneca also adored. Contempt for power did not inhibit him from revelling in it. The darkness of Rome was lit by gold. Two thousand years on, we too, looking back to Augustus and his heirs, can recognise in their mingling of tyranny and achievement, sadism and glamour, power-lust and celebrity, an aureate quality such as no dynasty since has ever quite managed to match.

'Caesar and the state are one and the same.'[17]

How this came to be so is a story no less compelling, no less remarkable and no less salutary than it has ever been these past two thousand years.

*Guard, preserve and protect the way things now stand: the peace we
enjoy, and our emperor. And when he has done his duty, after a life
that I pray may be as long as possible, grace him with successors whose
shoulders will prove as sufficient to support the burden of our global
empire as we have found his to be.*

— Velleius Paterculus (c. 20 BC–c. AD 31)

*The stain of the wrongs committed back in ancient times by these men
Will never fade from the history books. Until the very end of time,
The monstrous deeds of the House of Caesar will stand condemned.*

— Claudian (c. AD 370–404)

Roman World in 44 BC

0 100 200 300 400 500 miles

0 200 400 600 800 km

BASTARNIANS

Caucasus Mts.

Danube

Black Sea

ARMENIA

Tomis

PANNONIA

ILLYRIA

MACEDONIA
Philippi

ASIA MINOR

Tigris

Carrhae

Brundisium

GREECE

Aegean

Euphrates

Actium

Antioch
SYRIA

Athens

CRETE

Mediterranean Sea

JUDAEA
Jerusalem

Alexandria

EGYPT

Nile

Red Sea

I

PADRONE

1

CHILDREN OF THE WOLF

The Making of a Superpower

The story of Rome began with a rape. A princess, a consecrated virgin, was surprised and ravished. Various accounts were given of the fateful assault. Some said that it happened in her sleep, when she dreamed that a man of miraculous beauty led her down to a shady river bank, and abandoned her there lost and alone. Others claimed that she was seized in the middle of a thunderstorm, while collecting water from a sacred grove. One story even told of a mysterious phallus which sprang up from the ashes of the royal hearth and took, not the princess, but her slavegirl. All were agreed, though, on the resulting pregnancy; and most – a few curmudgeonly revisionists aside – had no doubt that the rapist was a god.* Mars, the Spiller of Blood, had planted his seed in a mortal womb.

Two god-like boys were duly born of the rape. These twins, the offspring of their mother's shame, had no sooner been delivered than they were dumped into a nearby river, the Tiber. Still the

---

* Two historians, Marcus Octavius and Licinius Macer, claimed that the rapist had been the girl's uncle, who then, 'to conceal the result of his criminal action', killed his niece, and handed her newborn twins over to the swineherd.

3

wonders did not cease. Swept along on the floodwaters of the river, the box to which the two babies had been consigned eventually ran aground below a steep hill named the Palatine. There, in the mouth of a cave, beneath the dripping, fruit-laden branches of a fig tree, the twins were discovered by a she-wolf; and the wolf, rather than devouring them, licked them clean of mud and offered their hungry mouths its teats. A passing swineherd, witnessing this miraculous scene, came clambering down the slopes of the Palatine to their rescue. The she-wolf slunk off. The two boys, rescued by the swineherd and given the names Remus and Romulus, grew up to become peerless warriors. In due course, standing on the Palatine, Romulus had seen twelve eagles: a sure sign from the gods that he should found, there on the summit of the hill, the city which ever afterwards bore his name. It was he who ruled Rome as its first king.

This, at any rate, was the story told centuries later by the Roman people to explain the origins of their city, and the sheer glorious scale of their martial achievements. Foreigners, when they learnt of it, certainly found it all too plausible. That Romulus had been fathered by Mars, the god of war, and suckled by a she-wolf appeared – to those brought into bruising contact with his descendants – to explain much about the Roman character.[1] Even a people like the Macedonians, who under Alexander the Great had themselves conquered a vast empire, almost to the rising of the sun, knew that the Romans were a breed of men quite unlike any other. One brief, opening skirmish, fought to indecisive effect in 200 BC, had been enough to bring this home. Five centuries and more had passed since the age of Romulus – and yet there still clung to the Romans, so it appeared to their opponents, something of the chilling quality of creatures bred of myth. The Macedonians, retrieving their dead from the battlefield, had been appalled by the shambles they discovered there. Bodies mutilated and dismembered by Roman swords had soaked the earth with blood. Arms with the shoulders still attached, severed heads, reeking puddles of viscera: all bore witness to a pitch of violence more bestial than human. No blaming the Macedonians, then, for the panic they had felt that day, 'when they discovered the kind of weapons and the order of men they had to face'.[2] A dread of lycanthropes, after all, was only natural in civilised people. The wolvish nature of the Romans, the hint of claws beneath their fingernails and of a yellow stare behind their eyes, was one that people across the span of the Mediterranean, and far beyond, had learned to take for granted. 'Why, they admit themselves that their founders were suckled on the milk of a she-wolf!' Such was the desperate rallying cry of one king before his realm too was dragged down to ruin. 'It is only to be expected that they should all of them have the hearts of wolves. They are inveterately thirsty for blood, and insatiable in their greed. Their lusting after power and riches has no limits!'[3]

The Romans themselves, of course, saw things rather differently. It was the gods, they believed, who had granted them their mastery of the world. The genius of Rome was for rule. Yes, there might be those who excelled in other fields. Who, for instance, could rival the Greeks when it came to the shaping of bronze or marble, the mapping of the stars or the penning of sex manuals? Syrians were pre-eminent as dancers; Chaldaeans as astrologers; Germans as bodyguards. Only the Roman people, though, possessed the talents sufficient to conquer and maintain a universal empire. Their achievements brooked no argument. When it came to the sparing of the subjected, and the crushing of the haughty, they reigned supreme.

The roots of this greatness, so they believed, reached back to their very beginnings. 'The affairs of Rome are founded upon her ancient customs and the quality of her men.'[4] From the earliest days, the measure of the city's prowess had been the readiness of her citizens to sacrifice everything in the cause of the common good – even their lives. Romulus, building a wall around his foundation and ploughing a furrow, the *pomerium*, to hallow all that lay within it as ground sacred to Jupiter, king of the gods, had known that more was needed to render Rome truly inviolable. So Remus, his twin, had willingly offered himself up as a human sacrifice. Jumping across the boundary, he had been struck down with a shovel; 'and thereby, with his death, he had consecrated the fortifications of the new city'.[5] The primal earth and mortar of Rome had been fertilised by the blood of the war god's son.

Remus was the first to die for the good of the city – but certainly not the last. Five kings followed Romulus on the throne of Rome; and when the sixth, Tarquin the Proud, proved himself a vicious tyrant more than deserving of his nickname, his subjects put their lives on the line and rose in rebellion. In 509 BC, the monarchy was ended for good. The man who had led the uprising, a cousin of Tarquin's named Brutus, obliged the Roman people to swear a collective oath, 'that they would never again allow a single man to reign in Rome'. From that moment on, the word 'king' was the dirtiest in their political vocabulary. No longer subjects, they ranked instead as *cives*, 'citizens'. Now, at last, they were free to show their mettle. 'They began to walk taller, and to display their abilities to full advantage – for it is the nature of kings that they will hold good men in more suspicion than the bad, and dread the talents of others.'[6] No longer was there any need, in a city liberated from the jealous gaze of a monarch, to veil its citizens' yearning for glory. The measure of true achievement had become the praise of the Roman people. Even the humblest peasant, if he were not to see himself reflected in the mirror of his fellows' scorn, was obliged to shoulder his duties as a citizen, and prove himself a man – a *vir*.

Virtus, the quality of a *vir*, was the ultimate Roman ideal, that lustrous fusion of energy and courage which the Romans themselves identified as their chiefest strength. Even the gods concurred. In 362 BC, a century and a half after the downfall of Tarquin the Proud, a terrifying portent afflicted the centre of Rome. Below the Palatine, in the level expanse of paved ground known as the Forum, a great chasm opened up. Nothing could have been more calculated to strike terror into Roman hearts. The Forum was the very hub of civic life. It was where statesmen addressed the people, where magistrates dispensed justice, where merchants hawked their goods, and where virgins

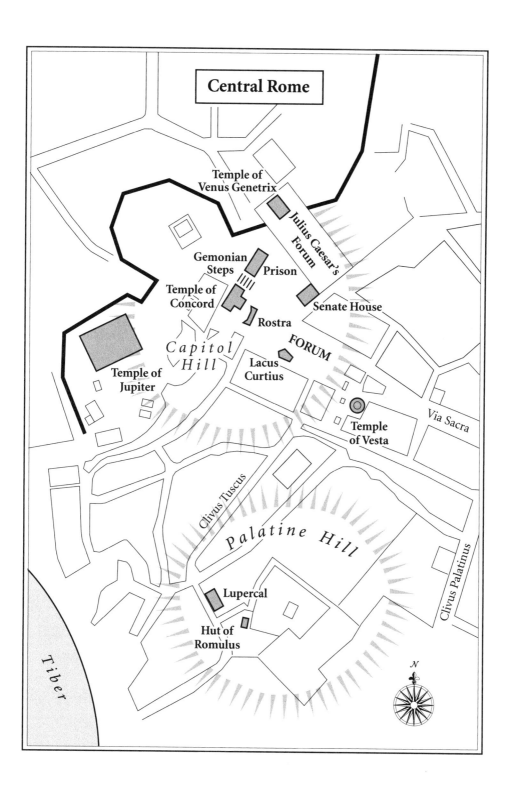

Central Rome

Temple of
Venus Genetrix

Julius Caesar's
Forum

Gemonian
Steps

Prison

Temple of
Concord

Senate House

Rostra

FORUM

*Capitol
Hill*

Lacus
Curtius

Temple of
Jupiter

Via Sacra

Temple
of Vesta

Clivus Tuscus

Palatine Hill

Clivus Palatinus

Lupercal

Hut of
Romulus

Tiber

N

consecrated to the service of Vesta, the goddess of the hearth, tended an eternal flame. That a gateway to the underworld had opened up in a place so fundamental to Roman life clearly betokened something terrible: the anger of the gods.

And so it proved. A sacrifice was demanded: 'the most precious thing you possess'.[7] What, though, was Rome's most precious possession? The question provoked much scratching of heads – until at length a young man named Marcus Curtius spoke up. Manliness and courage, he told his fellow citizens, were the greatest riches possessed by the Roman people. Then, arrayed in full armour, he climbed onto his horse, spurred it forward and made straight for the abyss. Over its edge he galloped. He and his horse plunged together into its depths. The chasm duly closed. A pool and a single olive tree were left to mark the spot, abiding memorials to a citizen who had perished that his fellows might live.

So highly did the Roman people prize this ideal of the common good that their name for it – res publica – served as shorthand for their entire system of government. It enabled the blaze of an individual citizen's longing for honour, his determination to test body and spirit in the crucible of adversity and emerge from every ordeal triumphant, to coexist with an iron sense of discipline. The consequences of this, for the Republic's neighbours, were invariably devastating. By 200 BC, when the Macedonians experienced for the first time the wolf-like savagery of which the legions were capable, Rome was already mistress of the western Mediterranean. Two years previously, her armies had delivered a knockout blow to the one power that had presumed to rival her for the title: a metropolis of merchant-princes on the coast of North Africa by the name of Carthage. Rome's victory had been an epochal triumph. The death struggle between the two cities had lasted, on and off, for over sixty years. In that time, war had reached the gates of Rome herself. Italy had been soaked in blood. 'The convulsive turmoil of the conflict had brought the whole world to shake.'[8] Ultimately, though, after a trial that would have seen any other people suing desperately for terms, the victors had emerged so battle-hardened as to seem forged of iron. Small surprise, then, that even the heirs of Alexander the Great should have found the legions impossible to withstand. King after king in the eastern Mediterranean had been brought to grovel before Roman magistrates. Weighed against a free and disciplined republic, monarchy seemed to have been found decisively wanting. 'Our emotions are governed by our minds.' So the ambassadors of one defeated king were sternly informed. 'These never alter – no matter what fortune may bring us. Just as adversity has never brought us low, so have we never been puffed up by success.'[9]

The man who spoke these words, Publius Cornelius Scipio, was certainly in a position to know. He was the epitome of success. His nickname, 'Africanus', bore stirring witness to his role as the conqueror of Rome's deadliest foe. It was he who had wrested Spain from the Carthaginians, defeated them in their own backyard, and then brought them to accept the most abject terms. A few years later, on the state roll of citizens, the name of Scipio appeared resplendent at the top of the list. This, in a society such as Rome's, was an honour like no other. Hierarchy was a defining obsession of the Roman people. All were officially graded according to a sliding scale of rank. The status of a citizen was calibrated with severe precision. Wealth, family and achievement combined to pinpoint precisely where, within the exacting class system of the Republic, each and every Roman stood. Even at the summit of society, status was ferociously patrolled. The highest-ranking citizens of all were enrolled in their own exclusive order: the Senate. This required of its members, in addition to riches and social standing, a record of service as magistrates sufficient to qualify them to be the arbiters of Rome's destiny. So sensitive, and so influential, were their deliberations that 'for many centuries not a senator breathed a word of them in public'.[10] As a result, unless a statesman could make his voice heard among their counsels, he might just as well have been dumb. Yet the right of a senator to speak to his fellows was not a given. The men called first in debate were always those who, by virtue of their pedigree, their moral standing and their service to the state, had accumulated the greatest prestige. *Auctoritas*, the Romans termed this quality – and the Republic, by placing Scipio first on the roll of its citizens, was granting its backing to the prodigious heft of his authority. The conqueror of Carthage had, by universal consent, 'attained a unique and dazzling glory'.[11] Even among the ranks of Rome's highest achievers, Scipio Africanus was acknowledged to have no rival. He was *Princeps Senatus*, 'the First Man of the Senate'.

Yet in this primacy lurked peril. The shadow cast by Scipio over his fellow citizens was one that could not help but provoke resentment. The guiding principle of the Republic remained what it had always been: that no one man should rule supreme in Rome. To the Roman people, the very appearance of a magistrate served as a reminder of the seductions and dangers of monarchy. The purple that lined the border of his toga had originally been the colour of kingship. 'Lictors' – bodyguards whose duty it was to clear a path for him through the crowds of his fellow citizens – had once similarly escorted Tarquin the Proud. The rods and single axe borne by each lictor on his shoulder – the *fasces*, as they were known – symbolised authority of an intimidatingly regal scope: the right to inflict both corporal and capital punishment.* Power of this order was an awesome and treacherous thing. Only with the most extreme precautions in place could anyone in a free republic be trusted to wield it. This was why, in the wake of the monarchy's downfall, the powers of the banished king had been allocated, not to a single magistrate, but to two: the consuls. Like a strong wine, the splendour of the consulship, and the undying glory that it brought to those who won it, required careful prior dilution. Not only could each consul be relied upon to keep a watchful eye upon the other, but the term of a consulship was set at a single year. The prestige enjoyed by Scipio, though, dazzled in defiance of any such limits. Even the grandest of the Republic's

---

* Lictors did not carry the axe within the limits of Rome itself. This symbolised the right of citizens to appeal against capital convictions.

elected magistrates were liable to find themselves diminished before it. The Senate House, as a result, began to sound with mutterings against the Princeps.

The truth was that glamour, in the Republic, had always been regarded with deep suspicion. Crow's feet and flintiness of manner were what the Roman people expected of their statesmen. The very word 'senator' derived from the Latin for 'old man'. The meteor of Scipio's career, though, had blazed from a scandalously youthful age. He had been appointed to the command against the Carthaginians in Spain when he was only twenty-six. He had won his first consulship a mere five years later. Even his elevation to the rank of *Princeps Senatus* had come at an age when other senators, far below him in the foothills of achievement, were still scrabbling after junior magistracies. Forging a dashing career of conquest before the jowls had begun to sag was, of course, what Alexander had so ringingly accomplished. Resentful senators were hardly reassured by this reflection. Alexander, after all, had been a foreigner – and a king. Renowned as he was for the god-like scale of his ambitions, it was unsettling to many senators that the self-promotion of such a troubling figure should have been aped by one of their own. Scipio, it was claimed, had been fathered on his mother by a snake; had won his victory in Spain thanks to the timely assistance of a god; had only to cross the Forum late at night for dogs to cease to bark. Princeps he may have been, but stories such as these implied a status that was off the scale.

And as such, intolerable. In 187 BC, when Scipio returned from a campaign in the East, his enemies were waiting for him. He was charged with embezzlement. Ripping up his account books before the full gaze of the Senate, Scipio indignantly reminded his accusers of all the treasure that he had won for Rome. It made no difference. Rather than risk the humiliation of conviction, the Princeps retired for good to his country estate. There, in 183 BC, he died a broken man. The fundamental principle of political life in the Republic had been brutally illustrated: 'that no one citizen should be permitted an eminence so formidable that it prevents him from being questioned by the laws'.[12]

Even a man as great as Scipio Africanus had found it impossible, in the final reckoning, to argue with that.

Wolf-bred the Romans may have been — but the future of the Republic, and of its liberties, appeared secure.

The Great Game

Or was it?

Scipio had submitted to the laws of the Republic — that much was true. Nevertheless, the sheer potency of his charisma hinted that the advance of the Republic to superpower status might not be without its pitfalls. Scipio's opponents had prided themselves on an obdurate provincialism. They took for granted that Rome's ancient customs were the best. Already, though, the limits of such conservatism were becoming apparent. Scipio was merely an outrider. The increasing tangle of Rome's diplomatic commitments, the incomparable proficiency of her legions, and her refusal to tolerate so much as a suggestion of disrespect combined to present her leading citizens with temptations of literally global scope. A century and more after the death of Scipio, the new darling of the Roman people had won for himself wealth and celebrity beyond the wildest dreams of earlier generations. Pompeius Magnus — 'Pompey the Great' — could boast a career that had fused illegality and self-aggrandisement to sensational effect. At the age of twenty-three, he had raised his own private army. A series of glamorous and lucrative commands had followed. Not for the man once nicknamed 'the youthful butcher'[13] the grind of a conventional career. Startlingly, he managed to win his first consulship — at the tender age of thirty-six — without ever having joined the Senate.

Even worse outrages were to follow. The proprieties of the Republic were trampled down in cavalier fashion. In 67 BC, Pompey was given a command that, for the first time, embraced the entire Mediterranean. A year later, he went one better by obtaining for himself *carte blanche* to impose direct rule over vast swathes of enticingly unannexed territory. The eastern reaches of Asia Minor, as the Romans called what is now Turkey, and the whole of Syria were gobbled up. Pompey was hailed as 'The Conqueror of all Nations'.[14] When he finally returned to Italy, in 62 BC, he came trailing more than glory in his wake. Kings were his clients and kingdoms his to milch. His legions owed their loyalty, not to the Republic, but to the man who had enabled them to asset-strip the East: their triumphant general, their *imperator*. As for Pompey himself, he had no time for false modesty: riding through the streets of Rome, he posed and preened in the cloak of Alexander the Great.

No one, not even the most embittered conservative, could deny his pre-eminence. 'One and all acknowledge his unrivalled status as Princeps.'[15] Unlike Scipio, Pompey did not owe this title to any vote of the Senate. Instead, like the incense he had brought back in groaning wagon trains from the East, his *auctoritas* hung dense over Rome, perfumed and intangible. The length and scope of Pompey's campaigning had made a mockery of the traditional rhythms of political life in the Republic. The prospect of sharing his commands with a colleague, or of having them limited to a single year at a time, had never crossed his mind. What was the Senate, that it should hobble 'the tamer of the world'?[16] Pompey had secured his victories, not despite, but because of his criminality. The implications were unsettling in the extreme. Laws that had served Rome well in the days of her provincialism were palpably starting to buckle now that she ruled the world. The same kings who crept and cringed in Pompey's train only served to demonstrate what dazzling pickings might be on offer to a citizen prepared to disdain the venerable safeguards against monarchy. Rome's greatness, long treasured by her citizens as the fruit of their liberty, now appeared to be menacing the Republic with the decay of its freedoms.

Except that Pompey, despite his muscle, had no wish to impose himself upon his fellow citizens at the point of a sword. Though he had always been greedy for power and fame, there were boundaries that even he flinched from crossing. A dominance that did not rest upon the approbation of his peers was a dominance not worth having. Military despotism was out of the question. Greatness, in the Republic, was nothing unless defined by the respect of the Senate and the Roman people. Pompey wanted it all. It was this that gave his enemies their chance. Though too intimidated by the resources available to the new Princeps to launch a prosecution against him, they could certainly deny him their co-operation. The result was paralysis. Pompey, to his shock and indignation, found his measures blocked in the Senate, his settlements left unratified, his achievements sneered at and dismissed. Politics as normal? So Pompey's enemies dared to hope. The one abiding constant of life in the Republic, it seemed, still held true. No one so overweening that he might not be taken down a peg or two.

A few of Pompey's chief rivals, though, when they studied the crisis afflicting their city, did so with a more pitiless and predatory gaze. No less than their fellow senators, they were prompted by the spectacle of a fellow citizen holding the gorgeous East in fee to bitter emotions of jealousy and fear; but what they could also recognise in it was the dawning of an intoxicating new age of possibility. No longer was a mere consulship to be reckoned the summit of a Roman's ambition. Appetite was coming to exceed the capacity of the Republic's institutions to sate it. Prizes on a global scale now appeared tantalisingly within reach: 'the sea, the land, the course of the stars'.[17] All it needed was the nerve to reach out and seize them.

In 60 BC, as Pompey's enemies continued to snarl and snap at the heels of the great man, two of Rome's most formidable operators were plotting a manoeuvre of momentous audacity. Marcus Licinius Crassus and Gaius Julius Caesar were men whose envy of the Princeps was exceeded only by their determination to emulate him. Both had good cause to set their sights high. Crassus had long sat like a spider at the heart of a monstrous web. A proven general and a former consul, his *auctoritas* was nevertheless a thing of shadow as well as brilliance. Like Pompey, he had recognised that the surest wellsprings of power in Rome were no longer the traditional ones. Although perfectly at home on the stage of public life, his true genius was for pulling strings from behind the scenes. Rich beyond the dreams of anyone in Rome, and displaying consistency only in his infinite capacity for opportunism, Crassus had employed his seemingly inexhaustible wealth to ensnare an entire generation of men on the make. Most, once they accepted his credit, then found it impossible to clear the interest. It took a man of rare political talent to break free and emerge as a player in his own right.

Such a man was Caesar. In 60 BC, he was forty years old: the scion of an ancient but faded family, notorious for his profligate dandyism and massively in debt. No one, though, not even his enemies – of whom there were plenty – could deny his talents. Charm fused with ruthlessness, dash with determination, to potent effect. Although clearly the inferior of Crassus, let alone Pompey, in terms of resources and reputation, what Caesar could offer the two men was a firm grip on the official reins of power. In 59, he was due to serve as one of the two elected consuls of the Republic. Clearly, with the combined backing of Pompey and Crassus behind him, and with his own ineffable qualities of cool and resolve to draw upon, he would be able – however illegally – to neutralise his consular colleague. The consulship would become, in effect, that of 'Julius and Caesar'.[18] He and his two allies would then be able to ram through a whole hit-list of measures. Pompey, Crassus, Caesar: all were likely to profit splendidly from their three-headed partnership.

And so it proved. Subsequent generations would distinguish in the birth of this 'triumvirate' a development as fateful as it was ominous: 'the forging of a conspiracy to take captive the Republic'.[19] In truth, the three dynasts were doing nothing that political heavyweights had not been busy at for centuries. Business had always been conducted in Rome by the fashioning of alliances, the doing-down of rivals. Nevertheless, the consulship of Julius and Caesar did indeed constitute a fatal waymark in her history. When Caesar's heavies emptied a bucket of shit over the rival consul, beat up his

15

lictors, and strong-armed the wretched man into effective retirement, it heralded a year of illegalities so blatant that no conservative would ever forget or forgive them. That the deals forced through by Caesar served the interests of his two allies quite as much as his own did not prevent the consul himself from being held principally to blame. His foes were now viscerally committed to his destruction. Caesar, no less passionately, was committed to the pursuit of greatness.

Understandably, then, he had made sure while still consul to book for himself the most splendid insurance policy possible: a governorship of tremendous scope. In the spring of 58, Caesar headed north to take command of three whole provinces: one in the Balkans, one directly on the northern frontier of Italy, and one on the far side of the Alps, in southern Gaul. Here, he could reckon himself secure from his enemies. It was forbidden for any magistrate of the Roman people to be brought to trial – and Caesar's term as governor had been set at a constitutionally outrageous five years. In due course, it would end up double that.

The junior partner of Pompey and Crassus Caesar may have been – but neither had succeeded in leveraging their alliance to more promising effect than the new governor of Gaul. A decade's worth of immunity from prosecution was only the start. Equally priceless were the opportunities offered for glory-hunting. Beyond the Alps, and the limits of Roman power, lay the wilds of *Gallia Comata*, 'Long-Haired Gaul'. Here dwelt teeming hordes of barbarians: spike-haired, semi-nude warriors much given to sticking the heads of their enemies on posts and downing their liquor neat. For centuries, they had embodied the Republic's darkest nightmares; but Caesar – boldly, brilliantly, illegally – had no sooner arrived in Gaul than he was looking to conquer the lot. His campaigns were on a devastating scale. A million people, so it was said, perished over their course. A million more were enslaved. For a decade, blood and smoke were general over Gaul. By the end of Caesar's term as governor, all the tribes, from the Rhine to the Ocean, had been broken upon his sword. Even the Germans and the Britons, savages on the edge of the world whose prowess was as proverbial as it was exotic, had been taught respect for Roman arms. Meanwhile, back in the capital, Caesar's fellow citizens thrilled to the lavishness of their new hero's generosity, and to the sensational news of his exploits. Caesar himself, rich in fame and plunder, and with an army of battle-seasoned legions at his back, had won for himself by 50 BC an *auctoritas* fit to rival that of Pompey. His enemies in the Senate, counting down the days until he finally relinquished his governorship, knew now more than ever that they could not afford to miss their chance.

To Caesar, the conqueror of Gaul, the prospect of being harried through law courts by a crew of pygmies was intolerable. Rather than suffer such a humiliation, his intention was to move seamlessly from provincial command to a second consulship. To achieve this, though, he would need allies – and much had changed during his absence from Rome. The triumvirate had only ever been as strong as its three legs – and, by 50 BC, one of those legs was gone. Four years earlier, Crassus had left for Syria. Desperate to follow the trail blazed by Pompey and Caesar, he had secured a command against the Parthians, the one people in the Near East still presumptuous enough to defy Roman hegemony. The expedition had promised pickings splendid enough to satisfy even Rome's most notoriously avaricious man. The Parthians ruled an empire that was fabulously wealthy. It stretched from the Indian Ocean, that 'pearl-bearing sea',[20] to the uplands of Persia, where, it was confidently reported, there stood a mountain made entirely of gold, to Mesopotamia, where untold luxuries – silks, and perfumes, and aromatic drinking-cups – were available in its teeming markets.

Unfortunately, though, the Parthians were not only rich, but underhand. Rather than stand and fight, they preferred to shoot arrows from horseback, repeatedly wheeling and retreating as they did so. The invaders, ponderous and sweaty, had found themselves helpless against this womanish tactic. In 53 BC, trapped on a baking plain outside the Mesopotamian border town of Carrhae, Crassus and thirty thousand of his men had been wiped out. The eagles, silver representations of the holy bird of Jupiter which served each legion as its symbol and its standard, had fallen into enemy hands. Together with Crassus's head, they had ended up as trophies at the Parthian court. To dare, it turned out, was not always to win.

As for Rome, the damage inflicted upon her by the defeat at Carrhae was even more grievous than had at first appeared. A body-blow had been struck which threatened the stability of the entire Republic. With Crassus gone, the field of players in the great game of Roman politics had narrowed at a perilous moment. It was not only conservatives, resolved to preserve the fabric of the state's functioning and its traditions, who felt threatened by the brilliance of Caesar's achievements. So too did his surviving triumviral partner, Pompey the Great. As Caesar and his enemies in Rome manoeuvred with increasing desperation for advantage, both were in direct competition for the support of the Princeps. This, although it played to the great man's vanity, also left him feeling subtly diminished. Caesar or Caesar's enemies: the terms of the most excruciating choice that Pompey had ever been obliged to make were being defined for him by his erstwhile junior partner. That being so, the rupture between the two men was, perhaps, in the final reckoning, inevitable. In December of 50 BC, when one of the two consuls for the year travelled to Pompey's villa outside Rome, presented him with a sword, and charged him to wield it against Caesar in defence of the Republic, Pompey replied that he would – 'if no other way can be found'.[21] This reply alone helped to ensure that it would not. Caesar, given the choice whether to submit to the law and surrender his command, or to stand firm in defence of his *auctoritas* and declare civil war, barely hesitated. Not for him the self-restraint of a Scipio. On 10 January, 49 BC, he and one of his legions crossed the Rubicon, a small river that marked the frontier of his province with Italy. The die was cast. 'The kingdom was divided by the sword; and the fortune of the imperial people, who had the sea, the land and the whole world in their possession, was inadequate for two.'[22]

Holding Out for a Hero

The aptitude of the Roman people for killing, which had first won them their universal dominion, was now unleashed upon themselves. Legion fought with legion, 'and the world itself was maimed'.[23] The war launched by Caesar's crossing of the Rubicon would last for more than four years and sweep from one end of the Mediterranean to the other. Not even the defeat of Pompey in open battle, and his subsequent murder and decapitation while on the run from his victorious rival, could bring the conflict to an end. From Africa to Spain, the killing went on. Pompey, 'his powerful trunk left headless on a beach',[24] was only the most prominent of the multitudes consigned to foreign dust. The inheritance of tradition and law that had once joined the Roman people in a shared unity of purpose meant nothing to soldiers who now looked for reward, not to antique notions of the common good, but to the commander who rode at their head. Captives were flung from walls or else had their hands cut off. The corpses of freshly slaughtered Romans were used by other Romans to build ramparts. Legionaries, as though they were mere Gauls, set the heads of their countrymen on pikes. To such a pass had the bonds of citizenship come.

That rival wolfpacks should have fallen to savaging one another came as no great surprise to those across whose lands they were snapping and snarling. Provincials had long had their own take on the origins of their masters. They understood better than the heirs of Romulus themselves what it meant to be bred of a wolf. Stories that to the Roman people had always been a cause of pride took on a very different light when seen through the eyes of the conquered. Hostile spin had increasingly served to blacken Rome's native traditions. It was said that Romulus, standing on the Palatine, had seen not eagles but vultures, passing on their way to feast on carrion; that the first Romans were 'barbarians and vagrants';[25] that Remus, rather than selflessly offering up his own life for the good of the city, had in fact been murdered by his brother. 'What sort of people, then, are the

Romans?'[26] This question, long demanded by those who hated and feared them, was one to which the Romans themselves could no longer provide a confident answer. What if their enemies were right? What if Romulus had indeed murdered his brother? What if it were the fate of the Roman people to repeat the primordial crime of their founder until such time as the anger of the gods had been satisfied, and all the world been drowned in blood? Fratricide, after all, was not easily appeased. Even soldiers brutalised by years of conflict knew that. In the spring of 45 BC, as Caesar advanced across the plains of southern Spain to confront the last of the armies still in the field against him, his men captured one of the enemy. The prisoner, it turned out, had slain his own brother. So revolted were the soldiers by this crime that they beat him to death with clubs. One day later, in a victory that finally ranked as conclusive, Caesar wrought such slaughter on his opponents that thirty thousand of his fellow citizens were left on the battlefield as food for flies.

The ruin inflicted on Rome, though, was not to be measured solely by the casualty figures. Untold damage had also been done to the vital organs of the state. Caesar himself, whose genius was of a thoroughly unsentimental nature, could recognise this more clearly than anyone. The Republic, he scoffed in an indiscreet moment, was 'a mere name – without form or substance'.[27] Nevertheless, even though he had made himself undisputed master of the Roman world, he was still obliged to tread carefully. The sensibilities of his fellow citizens were not lightly offended. Many, amid the tempest-wrack of the age, clung to the reassurance provided by their inheritance from the past like drowning men to flotsam.

On his return to Rome from the killing fields of Spain, Caesar duly opted to throw money at the problem. He wooed the Roman people with spectacular entertainments and the promise of *grands projets*. Public feasts were held at which thousands upon thousands of citizens were lavishly wined and dined; a cavalcade of elephants lumbered through the night with torches blazing on their backs; a plan was drawn up to reroute the Tiber. Meanwhile, Caesar worked to conciliate his enemies in the Senate – not so easily bought – with flamboyant displays of forgiveness. His willingness to pardon opponents, to back them for magistracies and to flatter them with military postings was a thing of wonder even to his bitterest foes. He graciously ordered to be restored the same statues of Pompey which had been toppled and smashed by his partisans.

Yet there was, in this same exercise of clemency, more than a whiff of what made so many of his peers resent and detest him. Merciful he may have been – but mercy was properly the virtue of a master. Caesar felt no call to apologise for his dominance. Penetrating intelligence combined with the habits bred of long achievement and command to convince him that only he had the solving of what appeared otherwise an insoluble crisis. The traditions of the Republic, shot through as they were with the presumption that no one citizen should establish permanent supremacy over his fellows, were plainly difficult to square with this conviction. Caesar had not won himself the mastery of Rome only to share it now with men whom he despised. Accordingly, looking to veil what otherwise ran the risk of appearing nakedly despotic, he did what Roman policy-makers, no matter how radical or bold, had invariably done when faced with a challenge: he looked to the past. There, mouldering in the venerable lumber-box of the Republic, was to be found a precedent potentially well suited to Caesar's needs. Provision for a citizen to exercise supreme authority over the Roman people during a time of crisis did in fact already exist. *Dictator*, the post was called. Caesar duly dusted the office down. Only a single adjustment was required to tailor the dictatorship to his requirements: the antique scruple which decreed that no citizen be trusted with it for longer than six months naturally had to go. Already, before leaving for Spain, Caesar had been appointed to the position for ten years. Early in February 44, he went one better. By a decree of the Senate, he was appointed 'Dictator For Life'.

Here, for citizens hopeful that the antique virtues of their people might be renewed, and the wounds of civil war healed, was a

portentous and chilling moment. Functional Caesar's new office may
have been – but that was precisely what rendered it so ominous. It
was not only the Dictator's peers, their prospects of attaining the
political heights now definitively blocked until such time as Caesar
should die or be removed, who were liable to find it baneful. So too
were all those left nervous and bewildered by the calamities that had
overwhelmed their city. Perpetual dictatorship implied perpetual
crisis, after all. 'The Roman people, whom the immortals wish to
rule the world, enslaved? Impossible!'[28] Yet clearly it was possible. The
favour of the gods had been lost. The golden threads that linked the
present to the past seemed snapped. The providence that had
brought Rome her greatness now appeared suddenly insubstantial
and delusory, and the city itself, that seat of empire, diminished.
Perpetual dictatorship denied to the Roman people what, ever since
Romulus first climbed the Palatine, had seemed their birthright: self-
confidence.

Even Caesar himself, perhaps, was prey to a certain anxiety. No
matter how contemptuous of the Republic and its traditions he had
grown, he did not scorn the aura of the wondrous that clung to his
city. Beyond the Senate House and the crowded jumble of the Forum,
he had used the riches plundered from Gaul to build a slimline second
forum; and here, in the centre of the city's most cutting-edge development, he had opened a portal onto the fabulous prehistory of
Rome. A temple clad in the brightest marble, the building caught in
its sheen haunting and primordial reflections. Once, before the
Republic, before the monarchy, before even Remus and Romulus
themselves, there had been a Trojan prince; and this Trojan prince
had been the son of Venus, the goddess of love. Aeneas, as befitted a
man with immortal blood in his veins, had been entrusted by the
gods with a truly awesome destiny. When Troy, after a ten-year siege,
had finally fallen to the Greeks and gone up in flames, Aeneas had
been undaunted. Lifting his aged father, that one-time paramour of
Venus, up onto his shoulders, and gathering together a crowd of
fellow refugees, he had made his escape from the burning city.

Eventually, after numerous adventures, he and his band of Trojan adventurers had arrived in Italy. Here he had put down new roots. It was from Aeneas that the mother of Remus and Romulus was descended. This meant that the Romans too ranked as his descendants – as 'Aeneads'.[29] Caesar's new temple, dedicated to the divine mother of the Trojan prince, was, then, for his battered and demoralised countrymen, an opportunity to be reassured as to their splendid pedigree.

It was also something more. Venus was, in the opinion of Caesar, doubly his ancestress – his *genetrix*. His family, the Julians, laid claim directly to her bloodline. The son of Aeneas, they reported, had called himself Julus: a genealogical detail which, naturally enough, they regarded as clinching. Others were not quite so certain. Even those who did not openly dispute it inclined to the agnostic. 'At such a remove, after all, how can one possibly state for certain what happened?'[30] Caesar himself, though, with his temple to Venus Genetrix, was brooking no argument. The Romans were a chosen people – and he the definitive Roman.

That Caesar was indeed a man whose talents outsoared 'the narrow confines common to man',[31] and whose energies, however monstrous, possessed an almost divine power, was a truth so self-evident that not even his bitterest foes could deny it. The temple to Venus Genetrix, by holding a mirror up to Caesar himself as well as to the vanished age when gods had slept with mortals, eerily blurred the boundary between the two. Approach its steps, and there, next to the steady plashing of two fountains, stood a bronze statue of his horse.* This remarkable beast, which had front hooves exactly like the hands of a man, could only ever have been mounted by a hero – and sure enough, 'it had refused to let anyone else ever ride it'.[32] Then, inside the temple, glittering amid its shadows, waited the reminder of another epic aspect of Caesar's career. Back in 48, midway through the

---

* The statue was originally of Alexander's horse. Caesar had brought it to Rome from Greece, and replaced Alexander's head with his own.

civil war, he had met with the ruler of the one Greek monarchy permitted by the Republic to subsist in a nominal, if enervated, independence: Cleopatra, the Queen of Egypt. Caesar, never one to look a gift-horse in the mouth, had promptly got her pregnant. This exploit, which had provided his enemies with no end of prurient sniggers, was now cast by the temple in its proper, glorious light. It was why, sharing the temple of Venus Genetrix with a statue of the goddess herself, there stood a gilded bronze of Cleopatra. Just as Aeneas, that father of the Roman people, had lived in an age when heroes slept by right with queens amid the convulsions of great wars and the wreckage of nations, so too, it was revealed, did the contemporaries of Caesar. Dictator though he was, he ranked as something more as well. That he was dismissive of the Republic rendered him, in his own opinion, only the more, not the less, antique. It confirmed him as a hero of ancient epic.

On 15 February, a few days after Caesar's appointment as 'Dictator For Life', came the perfect opportunity to put this conceit to the test. The date was a potent one, both joyous and haunted. As adrenaline-fuelled as any in the Roman calendar, it was simultaneously stalked by the dead, who had been known to mark the festival by rising from their graves and roaming the streets. The crowds for it built early. People milled through the Forum, or else gathered on the far side of the Palatine, below the cave where Remus and Romulus had long, long before been fed by the she-wolf: the 'Lupercal'.* In the mouth of the cave, below the branches of the sacred fig tree, oiled men known as *Luperci*, naked save for a loincloth of goatskin, stood shivering in the winter breeze. Also made of goatskin were the thongs they held in their hands, and which women in the crowds below, many of them stripped to the waist, would invariably blush to see waved in their direction. Naturally, it took a certain physique to carry off a

---

* Varro, the most learned of Roman scholars, explained that the she-wolf was to be identified with a goddess named Luperca. In Latin, '*lupa pepercit*' meant 'the she-wolf spared them'.

loincloth – and especially so in February. Most of the men, sure enough, were strappingly young. Not all, though. One of the *Luperci* was almost forty – and a consul, no less. The spectacle of a magistrate of the Roman people 'naked, oiled and drunk'[33] was one fit to appal all those concerned for the dignity of the Republic. Not that the consul himself greatly cared. Marc Antony had always enjoyed tweaking the noses of the uptight. Still ruggedly handsome, even in middle age, he was a man who valued his pleasures. More significantly, though, he had a seasoned eye for a winner. So well had Antony served Caesar in Gaul and during the civil war that he had come to rank as the Dictator's chief lieutenant. Now he was going to perform another service. Antony knew that Caesar was waiting on the far side of the Palatine Hill, sat on a golden throne in the Forum. No time to delay, then. All was ready. Goats had been offered up in sacrifice, and a dog. Their blood had been smeared across the foreheads of two young boys and then immediately wiped clean; the two young boys, as they were obliged to do, had burst out in wild laughter. Time to go. Time to celebrate the Lupercalia.

As the men in their skimpy loincloths fanned out from the Lupercal and began running round the spurs of the Palatine, their course was one that plunged them deep into the mysteries of their city's past. Whipping half-naked women as they sped by, bringing down the goat-thong lash so hard that blood was left beading the welts, the *Luperci* were acting in obedience to an oracle given two centuries before. 'The sacred goat must enter the mothers of Italy.'[34] If not, then every pregnancy was doomed to end in stillbirth. This was why, at the Lupercalia, women would offer themselves up willingly to the lash. Better broken skin, after all, than penetration by a goat of a different kind. Yet the origins of the Lupercalia were older by far than the oracle. Running into the Forum, the *Luperci* approached a second fig tree, one that marked the political nerve centre of the city, the open space where the Roman people had always traditionally met in assembly: the *Comitium*. Here the Senate House stood; and here, at the founding of the Republic, was where a speaker's platform, the *Rostra*, had first been raised. Already, even then, the Comitium had been fabulously old. There were some who claimed the fig tree which stood beside the Rostra to have been the very one beneath which Remus and Romulus had been nursed by the she-wolf, magically transplanted there from the Palatine by a wonder-worker back in the time of the kings. The confusion was telling. The memories that the Roman people had of their past were a swirl of paradoxes. Now, as the *Luperci* ran with their goat-skin thongs from one fig tree to another, those same paradoxes were being brought thrillingly to life. On a day when the human mingled with the wolvish, the carnal with the supernatural, the anxiety-racked Rome of Caesar's dictatorship with the phantom city of the kings, who could tell what might not happen?

Antony, running with the rest of the *Luperci* down the length of the Forum, came to a halt before the Comitium. Here too Caesar's workmen had been busy. The site of the Senate House, incinerated during a riot eight years earlier, was still covered in scaffolding. Other monuments, many of them fabulously ancient, had been flattened to make way for a gleaming level pavement. The Rostra, demolished along with much else, had been rebuilt complete with stylish polychrome cladding. This, as Antony approached it, was where Caesar sat waiting. Dictator of the Roman people, it was only fitting that he should preside over the Lupercalia enthroned amid building works and shining marble, public markers of his resolve to renovate the state. Which did not mean, of course, that he aimed to set it upon wholly new foundations – quite the contrary. What better day than the Lupercalia, when the youth of Rome ran like wolves, to remind the Roman people that the wellsprings of their history were more primordial by far than the Republic? As token of that, Caesar himself had come to the festival dressed in the ancient costume of the city's kings: purple toga and calf-length boots in fetching red leather. And now Antony, reaching the Comitium, halting directly in front of the Dictator, stepping up to the Rostra, held forward all that was needed to complete the ensemble: that ultimate symbol of monarchy, a diadem entwined with laurel.

A few desultory rounds of applause greeted the gesture. Otherwise all was leaden silence. Then Caesar, after a pause, pushed the diadem away – and the Forum echoed to tumultuous cheering.

Again Antony pressed the diadem on the Dictator; again the Dictator refused it. 'And so the experiment failed.'[35] And Caesar, rising to his feet, ordered that the diadem be presented to Jupiter – 'for Rome would have no other king'.[36]

He was correct. Despite the palpable inadequacies of their battered political order, and notwithstanding the many calamities that had left the Republic a broken, bleeding thing, the Roman people would never permit a mortal to rule over them as king. The word remained one 'they could not bear so much as to hear'.[37] Caesar, by laying claim to a perpetual dictatorship, and putting his fellow senators so utterly in the shade, had signed his own death warrant. Exactly one month after the festival of the Lupercalia, on the 15th or 'Ides' of March, he was struck down beneath a hail of daggers at a meeting of the Senate. The leader of the conspiracy, and its conscience, was a Brutus, descended from the man who had expelled Tarquin and ended the monarchy. Brutus and his fellow assassins, who killed Caesar in the name of liberty, devoutly believed that his death would be sufficient to save the Republic. Others, clearer-sighted, were more despairing. They feared that the murder of Caesar solved nothing. 'If a man of his genius was unable to find a way out,' one such analyst asked, 'who will find one now?'[38] What if the crisis had no solution? What if Rome herself were finished?

And perhaps more than Rome. In the fretful days and weeks that followed Caesar's assassination, evidence of a seemingly cosmic doom was to be seen in the skies. The days began to darken. The sun was lost behind a bruised and violet gloom. Some, like Antony, believed that it was turning its gaze away in horror 'from the foul wrong done to Caesar'.[39] Others, more bleakly, dreaded retribution for the crimes of the entire age, and the onset of an eternal night. These anxieties intensified yet further when a comet was seen burning in the sky for seven days in a row.* What did it mean? Once again, there was a variety of opinions. Already, in the immediate wake of Caesar's death, crowds of angry mourners had set up an altar to him in the Forum; and now, as the fiery star streaked across the sky, a conviction gathered weight that the soul of the slain Dictator was ascending to heaven, 'there to be received among the spirits of the immortal gods'.[40] Others, though, were unconvinced. Comets, after all, were baneful things. Readers of the future, practised in the interpretation of such wonders, had no doubt that a sign of fearful portent was being given. An age was passing, the world nearing its end. One soothsayer, warning that it was forbidden humanity to know the full scale of the horrors that were fast approaching, and that to reveal them would cost him his life, delivered his prognostications even so – and promptly dropped dead on the spot.

Meanwhile, in Rome, in legionary camps and in cities across the empire, hard men spoke fine words and methodically planned for war.

And wolves, in lofty cities, made the nights echo with their howls.

---

* No fewer than nine of the sources which mention this comet date it to the week of Caesar's funeral games – which, if true, would immeasurably have added to its impact.

2

BACK TO THE FUTURE

A Tide in the Affairs of Men

Late one January, a decade and a half before the soul of the murdered Caesar blazed across the skies of Rome, a girl was born destined herself to become a god.[1] Even in the womb, the immortals had been keeping careful watch over her. Pregnancy was a perilous business. Only supernatural oversight could guarantee success. Right from the moment of conception, the unborn child had been growing under the protection of a succession of deities. As she finally emerged into the world from her squatting mother, to be raised aloft by the midwife, washed clean of blood and then given her first taste of milk, various goddesses were still on hand to keep track of her progress: Levana, Rumina, Potina.[*]

The gods, though, were no longer alone in deciding whether the infant would survive. 'The ten long months of tedious waiting'[2] endured by her mother were over – and now the girl had passed into the power of her father. A Roman was made, not born. A baby in its first week of life was a nameless, rightless thing, 'more like a plant

---

[*] Levana derived from the Latin for 'to lift', *levare*, and presided over the raising of a child by the midwife immediately after birth.

than a human being' until the loss of her umbilical cord.[3] Whether in that time she would be acknowledged or exposed and left to die was the decision of her father, and her father alone. No man in the world held quite such authority over his offspring as a Roman.* The absolute rule denied a consul was readily ceded by children to their father. A son might come of age, marry, win the utmost glory and honour, and yet still remain under the *patria potestas*, 'paternal control'. A father's power over his child was literally one of life and death. This did not mean, however, that it was widely exercised. Just the opposite. Absolute power was combined, in the Roman parenting ideal, with mercy, forbearance and devotion. 'What father, after all, is in a rush to lop off his own limbs?'[4] Even the disposal of an unwanted newborn, though perfectly legal, tended to be shrouded in secrecy. It spoke of poverty, or adultery, or perhaps deformity in the child. Invariably, it was a matter of shame.

There was to be no rejection that January, though. Eight days after the girl's birth, at a ceremony which combined solemn rituals of purification with joyous partying, she was finally given a name: Livia Drusilla.† Her father could well afford to raise her. Marcus Livius Drusus Claudianus boasted a name as distinguished as any in Rome. From his own father, a famously principled statesman who in his day had been the city's foremost champion of the poor, he had inherited connections that spanned the whole of Italy.[5] The name of 'Livius Drusus', in a time of upheaval and civil conflict, had considerable heft. It was not, though, the only one to which the infant Livia Drusilla was heir. In Rome, where the great game of dynastic competition was at least as much about forging alliances as foiling rivals, adoption was a widely practised tactic. It was considered perfectly legitimate for the son of a skilful politician to be adoptive rather than natural – and such

---

* Although, as the Romans themselves were graciously prepared to acknowledge, the Galatians ran them a close second.
† A boy, for reasons that even the Romans found mysterious, would be given his name after nine days.

a man was Drusus Claudianus. It was his last name that revealed as much. Legally the son of Livius Drusus though he had ended up, he had not abandoned the memory of the house into which he had been born. That he was called 'Claudianus' marked him out, not just as someone adopted, but as the scion of a family as celebrated and formidable as any in Rome.

The fame of the Claudians was as ancient as the Republic itself. Attius Clausus, the founder of the dynasty, had migrated to Rome from the Sabine hills a few miles to the north of the city a mere five years after the expulsion of Tarquin the Proud. Less than a decade later he had become consul. From that moment on, the Claudians had never ceased to dominate the magistrate lists of the Republic. Staggeringly, they had even managed to secure five dictatorships. The name of the most celebrated Claudian of them all, an iron-willed innovator and reformer by the name of Appius Claudius 'the Blind', was stamped across the very plains and valleys of Italy. In 312 BC, at a time when the Republic was looking to secure its still precarious control of the peninsula, he had ordered the building of a mighty road southwards from Rome. Known as the Via Appia, this was ultimately extended as far as Brundisium, the great port on the heel of Italy which served as the gateway to the East. Such a feat of engineering, the mooring which bound Rome to her wealthiest provinces, was precisely the kind of accomplishment which best illustrated, in the opinion of foreign observers, 'the greatness of her empire'.[6] Who were the Claudians to disagree?

Having the most famous road in the world named after one's ancestor was, in the carnivorous struggle for magistracies that formed the essence of political life in Rome, a priceless advertisement. The hold of the Claudians on the people's affections was formidable and self-perpetuating. Glory in war and prodigality in peace kept their name permanently burnished. Attius Clausus, arriving in Rome back in the first decade of the Republic, had come trailing a great band of clients with him, and this power of patronage, swelling over the succeeding centuries, translated for the Claudians into a peerless election-winning machine. Webs of obligation enmeshed the generations. Whether it was a favour done to a family on the make or an aqueduct built to benefit the whole of Rome, the Claudians had a rare talent for making offers that others could not refuse. It kept them *nobilis*, 'well-known'. Men from humbler backgrounds, who found nobles such as the Claudians a near-insuperable obstacle on the road to their own advancement, could only fume. The glamour of the nobility inspired envy and resentment in equal measure: 'All those born of noble family have to do is sleep for the Roman people to bestow upon them every kind of perk.'[7]

This, though, was an exaggeration. If nobility brought advantage, it also brought brutal pressure. No one became a senator, still less a consul, by right of birth. Even a Claudian had to win election. Boys raised on tales of Appius Claudius could hardly help but feel a monstrous burden of expectation. And not only boys. Girls too were rigorously schooled in the duty owed their ancestry. Naturally, there could be no question of them ever running for the consulship, commanding an army or building a road. As women, they had no political rights at all. Yet they too were expected to have aspirations. *Virtus* was not just for men. A girl, when she stood in the hallway of her father's house and saw there wax masks of her ancestors suspended from the wall, their eyeballs made of glass, their gaze blank and impenetrable, their appearance eerily lifelike, was no less liable to feel haunted by their example than a boy.

The annals of the Claudians were filled with the deeds of women. One, a virgin consecrated to the service of Vesta, and therefore sacrosanct, had fearlessly ridden in her father's chariot to protect him from enemies who were looking to drag him down; another, anxious to demonstrate that 'her rectitude was of the most old-fashioned kind',[8] had done so in spectacular fashion by pulling a boat single-handed up the Tiber. Showing off her virtue, though, was not all that the young Livia could look forward to in adulthood. The decades prior to her birth had seen a subtle shift in the status of noble women. Whereas once they would have passed into the power of a husband on marriage, increasingly they were kept under the *patria potestas*. The prime loyalty of a Roman wife remained to her father's line. A Claudian matron, possessed of the steely self-assurance that had long been her family's birthright, was rarely content with a merely ornamental role. Rather than serve meekly as an appendage to her husband, she tended to operate to a distinct agenda. Even as her brothers strutted and fretted upon the public stage, she could be a player behind the scenes. More than many senators, she stood at the heart of things. Slapped down by a woman of status, even a former consul might feel obliged to hold his tongue.*

In the first decade of Livia's life, authority of this order still counted for much. Far from intimidating them, the monstrous shadows cast by Pompey and Caesar only encouraged in the Claudians an opportunism regarded as excessive even by the standards of the time. The head of the family, Appius Claudius Pulcher, was both implacable and shameless in his pursuit of Claudian interests. Content that the gods alone merited his respect, he paid obsessive attention to oracles and the entrails of animals, while behaving towards his fellow citizens with such arrogance and rapacity as to end up a byword for both. Entrusted on the eve of the civil war with reform of the Senate, he expelled swathes of his colleagues for vices of which, as his furious opponents did not hesitate to point out, he himself was invariably the most notorious exemplar. Not even his effrontery, though, could compare with that of his younger brother. Blending hauteur and demagoguery to ground-breaking effect, Publius Clodius brought gangsterism to the very heart of Rome. Paramilitaries passionately loyal to him squatted out in the Forum, menaced his rivals, and even at one point took to chanting aspersions on Pompey's masculinity. Meanwhile, as Clodius's street-gangs roamed the city, his sisters padded like restless cats from

---

* The great orator Cicero records a five-word put-down delivered to him by Servilia, who was both the former mistress of Julius Caesar and the mother of Marcus Brutus, Caesar's most eminent assassin. 'I bit my tongue,' Cicero records.

marriage to marriage, working their own magic in the family cause. The eldest, the dark-eyed and brilliant Clodia Metelli, was Rome's undisputed queen of chic. The mingled devotion and dread which she inspired in her admirers was a fitting measure of the reputation secured by her family in the face of Pompey's dominance and the gathering might of Caesar. 'When injured, they resent it; when angered, they lash out; when provoked, they fight.'[9] Even in the mood of crisis that preceded the crossing of the Rubicon, the power of the Claudians retained its allure of menace.

Nevertheless, it came at a price. In an era dominated by upstart warlords, the ferocity required of the Claudians to maintain their ancestral primacy struck a perturbing and scandalous note. The legacy they were fighting to defend could not help but end up tarnished by it. Increasingly, the pride of the Claudians in their lineage was cast by their adversaries as something altogether more sinister: 'a timeless and inborn arrogance'.[10] Antique Claudians of previously unimpeachable reputation began to be painted by chroniclers in melodramatic colours as rapists and would-be kings. Achievements were counterpointed with monstrous crimes. Long-forgotten figures of scandal gained a lurid new prominence. Set against the ruggedly pious builder of the Appian Way, for instance, was his grandson, who, informed on the brink of a naval battle that the sacred chickens would not eat, had ordered them dumped into the sea. 'If they won't eat, let them drink,'[11] he had sneered – and promptly lost his fleet. Then there was his sister who, delayed while riding through the streets of Rome by a milling crowd of citizens, had lamented in a piercing voice that her brother was not around to lose a second fleet. Monsters of insolence such as these, in the age of Clodius and his sisters, loomed ever more grotesquely in the public imagination. No one could deny the range and extent of Claudian prowess; but increasingly the history of the family was cast by their enemies as a record of darkness as well as light. For every benefactor of the Roman people, it seemed, there had been a Claudian trampling and treading them down.

Better arrogance, the Claudians themselves might have retorted, than mediocrity. Yet even they, when the firestorm of civil war finally swept down upon Rome in 49, found it impossible to maintain their traditional independence of action. Already, three years before Caesar's crossing of the Rubicon, Clodius had been murdered in a brawl on the Appian Way. Appius Claudius, torn between backing Pompey and backing Caesar, frantically sought guidance from the gods, and then resolved his dilemma by dying before battle could be joined. Livia's father, who at the time of her birth had been a partisan of Caesar, kept his head down, quietly nurturing his resentment of his erstwhile patron's ever more excessive dominance. When the Dictator was murdered, Drusus Claudianus publicly approved the deed. The conviction of Caesar's assassins that by killing him they had set Rome's time-hallowed political order back on its feet might almost have been designed to appeal to a Claudian. The times, though, remained confused. The heavens were dark, after all, and a comet was blazing through the sky. Nothing could be taken for granted. Only by husbanding their full strength could the Claudians hope to reclaim their rightful place in the affairs of the Roman people. That, at any rate, was how Drusus Claudianus read the situation. Accordingly, he drew up a plan. He would marry off his daughter.

Livia herself by this stage was more than ready for such a step. She was in her mid-teens, after all, and time was getting on. Many aristocratic girls were married off as young as twelve. A nubile daughter was too priceless an asset for a noble to delay putting her to dynastic purposes for long. Drusus Claudianus, though, had preferred not to hurry things. His eye was fixed on a particular prize. For many generations now, the descendants of Appius Claudius had consisted of two distinct offshoots. One of his sons, Claudius Pulcher, had fathered the line to which Drusus Claudianus himself belonged, and which, in the first decade of Livia's life, had so fixated and appalled the Roman people. The descendants of a second son, Claudius Nero, had been altogether more modest in their achievements. The last Nero to hold the consulship had done so all the way back in 202, at a time when Scipio had still been busy fighting Carthaginians. What, though, if the two lines were to be reunited? Only give Livia a Neronian husband, and the result would be a potent consolidation of Claudian resources. A generation which had flowing in its veins the mingled blood of both Pulchri and Nerones would be a formidable one indeed. The times being what they were, it was certainly worth a try.

And an eligible Neronian, by great good fortune, just happened to be ready to hand. Tiberius Claudius Nero was some two decades older than Livia, and well set on a promising career. He had enjoyed a good civil war. Correctly identifying Caesar as a winner, he had commanded a fleet, secured various honours, and been sent on the Dictator's business to Gaul. Now, on his return to Rome, he was offered Livia's hand. Tiberius Nero accepted it. He also took on board something else: the politics of his prospective father-in-law. With a disdain for consistency that marked him out as a true Claudian, the man who had basked in Caesar's favour now coolly stood up in the wake of his patron's murder to propose honours for his killers. This volte-face was only incidentally about the rights and wrongs of the assassination itself. Tiberius Nero was laying down a marker. Emerged at last from Caesar's shadow, Rome's most celebrated dynasty was back. The future, like the past, was being cast as Claudian.

Already, though, events were overtaking these hopes. As maids under the direction of her mother fussed around Livia, braiding her hair into the ferociously complex 'towered crown'[12] demanded by tradition of a bride, fresh and murderous novelties were brewing in the world beyond. To these, the bridegroom in his gleaming white toga, arriving at the house of his wife-to-be, was as yet oblivious. That danger might reach directly into the home of a great nobleman was a prospect too sinister and monstrous to contemplate. The house of even the humblest Roman stood directly under the protection of the gods. It was what defined him as civilised, as a man rooted to the city in which he lived. 'What more sacred than the house of a citizen, no matter his class – what more hedged about by every kind of religious safeguard?'[13]

To this question, a girl on her wedding day served as a notably reassuring answer. The six ornate tresses into which Livia's hair had been woven gave her the look of a virgin pledged in service to Vesta, the goddess of the hearth. Her veil, coloured saffron to match the one worn by the priestess of Jupiter, had been dyed by specialists using the same stamens of crocuses that would-be mothers sampled as an aid to fertility.[14] A divinely sanctioned fusion of virginity and fecundity: what more could a bridegroom want? Tiberius Nero, at the end of a wedding banquet hosted by his father-in-law, duly wrested Livia from her mother's arms and led her, as though taking her captive, to his own house on the Palatine. This pretended abduction of a bride harked back to an episode from the very beginnings of Rome. Once, in the reign of Romulus, when the original settlers of the city had found themselves lacking in women, they had stolen the daughters of the neighbouring people, the Sabines; and it was as a memory of that primal rape, perhaps, that a bride wore in her towering hairdo, interwoven with marjoram and flowers, a single spearhead. Yet though 'war and conflict had attended the earliest pairing of man and woman in Rome',[15] the arrival of his new bride into Tiberius Nero's home was greeted, not with foreboding, but with jokes, cheering and applause. Just as the stolen brides of the first Romans had bred a race of heroes, so Livia, it was trusted, would now perpetuate the Claudian line. She would do so as the guardian of her husband's hearth, its flame banked up every evening and rekindled every new day. Like the ramparts of Rome itself, the walls of a citizen's home stood inviolate and sacrosanct. As Tiberius Nero lifted his bride up into his arms and carried her over the threshold, Consevius, the god of conception, already had his eye on the couple. In 42 BC, on 16 November, Livia gave birth to a son. Like his father, the boy was named Tiberius Claudius Nero. In this tiny child, all the ambitions of the two great Claudian lines met and were joined.

But too late. Even as their son was being delivered, the hopes that had brought Livia into Tiberius Nero's marital bed lay in ruins. The brief year of their married life together in Rome had witnessed a reign of terror on a scale unmatched in the city's history. The days when its destiny could be swayed by the jostling for position among its leading families, and by their competition for magistracies and honours, had been terminated once and for all. Not merely put into the shade, as they had been by Caesar's dictatorship, many of the great dynasties of the Republic had suffered hideous mutilation. The violence unleashed against them had been both calculated and savage. Even as Tiberius Nero and Livia were blithely celebrating their nuptials, the adherents of the slain Dictator had been preparing to seize the initiative in the most brutal fashion imaginable. A year and a half of manoeuvring against Caesar's assassins had secured for them the mastery of the western provinces, and of Rome itself. Then, one night late in 43, almost a year to the day before the birth of Livia's son, whitened boards had appeared in the Forum. They carried the names of men charged with treachery to Caesar. Rewards were offered for their murder. 'The killers are to bring their heads to us.'[16] Among those proscribed had been Livia's father. Luckier than the 2300 reported to have perished, Drusus Claudianus had managed to slip the bounty-hunters and make his way east, where Brutus, still at liberty, was busy recruiting armies for the looming showdown.

Sure enough, the renewal of open civil war had not been long in coming. Early in 42, the defenders of Caesar's memory had formally consecrated their murdered patron as a god. Over the succeeding months, they had spent the riches purloined from the proscribed on legions of their own before finally, towards the end of the campaigning season, they crossed from Italy to Greece. Advancing into Macedonia, they had confronted their adversaries on a plain east of the city of Philippi. Two terrible battles had ensued. Victory in the death-struggle had ultimately gone to the adherents of Caesar. Brutus had fallen on his sword. The aristocracy, already scarred as a result of the proscriptions, had suffered a second lethal culling. 'In no other conflict did men possessed of the most illustrious names endure a bloodier toll.'[17] Among the dead, fallen like Brutus on his own sword in the wake of the battle, was Drusus Claudianus. The news reached Rome a few weeks later. Livia learned of her father's death as she was giving birth to his grandson.

That she was safe in Rome at all owed everything to Tiberius Nero's slippery opportunism. Sensing the way the wind was blowing, he had made sure to renew his old allegiance to the now deified Caesar. As a result, despite the ruin of her father's fortunes and the forfeiture of his property, Livia was able to deliver her son in surroundings befitting her rank. The Palatine, where Romulus had once built his thatched hut, was now easily the most exclusive district in Rome. The hut itself, reverently kept in a continuous state of repair, still stood above the cave of the Lupercal, but otherwise there was nothing on the hill that did not scream privilege. The Claudians, naturally, had long enjoyed a prominent position there. It was on the Palatine that Clodia Metelli had hosted the most fashionable soirées in Rome, and Clodius, after knocking through two already hefty mansions, based himself in flamboyantly imposing headquarters. Tiberius Nero, however much he may have mourned the slaughter of his class at Philippi, would have been reassured, as he paced his splendid house, that he had made the right call. Better a shift of loyalties, after all, than the loss of his property on the Palatine.

Yet even as his son was being raised up in the midwife's arms, he knew his fortunes now stood on precarious foundations. Memories of the proscriptions were still raw. The shock given to the self-assurance of Rome's elite was not easily suppressed. Nowhere, not even the most exclusive residence, could any longer be considered secure. The first victim of the proscriptions had been murdered in his own dining room, with his guests gathered all around him, in the innermost sanctum of his home. Bursting in on their quarry, the soldiers had shown no compunction in defiling this scene of hospitality. A centurion, drawing his sword, had decapitated the wretched host, then warned the other diners with a gesture of his blade that any fuss would see them suffer the same fate. Terrified, they had remained lying where they were until late into the night, as the headless corpse slowly stiffened beside them, and blood soaked through the couch onto the floor. What once had served as the marks of a citizen's greatness — a fine house, beautiful sculptures, a swimming pool — had become, during the frenzy of the proscriptions, the opposite: potential death warrants. Even Claudians had learned to dread the midnight knocking at the door. Always now, at the back of the mind, there lurked the dread of what might follow it: 'soldiers rushing in, the forcing of locks, menacing words, fierce looks, a glitter of weapons'.[18]

Clearly, then, to those of the nobility who had survived the carnage of the proscriptions and Philippi, and now found themselves stumbling out from their bolt-holes into an utterly transformed political landscape, the need to arrive at a permanent accommodation with their new overlords was a desperate one. Three men had claimed licence to rule the world as Caesar's avengers. Their compact was not, as the original triumvirate had been, a murky arrangement of the kind traditional among Roman power-brokers, but something altogether more revolutionary: a formal grant of absolute rule. Legally, the goal of the Triumvirs had been defined as 'the restoration of the Republic' – but no one was much fooled by that fine slogan. The Caesarian leaders had not waded through blood merely to abdicate their hard-won supremacy. In the wake of Philippi, the only resistance to them still to be found was in Sicily, where Pompey's son Sextus had established a rackety piratical regime. Otherwise, the authority of the Triumvirate was absolute. Yet its continuance could hardly be taken for granted. Triumvirs, as everyone was all too well aware, had a habit of falling out. The Roman upper classes, as they sought to set their fortunes back on a solid foundation, were accordingly faced with a potentially life-and-death decision: which member of the Triumvirate to back.

One could immediately be discounted. Marcus Aemilius Lepidus was an old associate of Caesar's whose impeccable pedigree and wide array of connections could not conceal his essential mediocrity. Demoted to serving as the watchman of Italy during the Philippi campaign, he was already on the way out. This left Rome and her empire divided, in effect, between two very different warlords. One, like Lepidus, was a noble of illustrious heritage and proven loyalty to Caesar: none other than the consul who had run with the *Luperci*, Marc Antony. His role in the proscriptions notwithstanding, there were many among the Roman elite who could not help but admire him. At Philippi, it was Antony's prowess as a general that had won the day. Amid the carnage of the battlefield, he had stripped off his cloak and draped it over Brutus's corpse. Resourceful, buccaneering and generous, his virtues were of a kind to which the Roman people had always warmed. He may have been a Triumvir – but Antony, to his erstwhile peers, offered at least the reassurance of familiarity.

Which was more than could be said for his partner in the rule of the world. Nothing, perhaps, better exemplified the upheavals and convulsions that had afflicted the Roman people since the murder of Caesar than the rise to dominance of the man born Gaius Octavius. His greatness served as a bitter reproach to the maimed aristocracy. His ancestry was sufficiently obscure that enemies could charge one of his great-grandfathers with having been 'a freed slave, a rope-maker',[19] and another an African perfumier turned baker – and be believed.* His childhood had been spent, not on the heights of the Palatine, but in a dusty town named Velitrae, some twenty miles down the Appian Way.† His brief career had consisted of a sustained and merciless assault on the most sacred traditions of the Republic. Eight months after the murder of Caesar, when barely nineteen, he had staged an abortive military coup. Ten months later, he had swept into Rome at the head of a private army. Consul when not yet twenty, legally appointed Triumvir, and commander alongside Antony of nineteen legions at Philippi, no one in his city's history had won for himself such power so fast, so young. Neither morality nor considerations of mercy had been permitted to stand in his way. While

---

* The enemy was Antony. In reality, the family was old and wealthy, but had only recently attained a degree of political prominence. Octavius's father was the first of his line to enter the Senate, and would have run for the consulship after serving a term of office in Macedonia had he not died while returning to Rome.
† The room which had served the young Octavius as his nursery was subsequently left with such a charge of the supernatural that anyone who tried to sleep in it would be hurled out through the doorway by invisible forces.

Antony had gazed in sorrow at his fallen adversary on the battlefield of Philippi, his youthful colleague had shed no tears. Instead, ordering Brutus's corpse decapitated, he had packed the head off to Rome. There, with pointed symbolism, it had been placed at the foot of the statue where Caesar had died.[20]

'The malice of those who have plotted against us, and who brought Caesar to his fate, cannot be mollified by kindness.'[21] With these words, the Triumvirs had justified their sanctioning of murder and civil war. To Gaius Octavius, the obligation to avenge Caesar had provided particular licence for his deeds. On the eve of Philippi, he had publicly sworn to build a temple in Rome to Mars the Avenger: a declaration that fighting in a civil war was not, to him, a crime, but an urgent and pious duty. The young man was the grandson of the Dictator's sister — but he was also something spectacularly more. Caesar, blessed with an eye for talent, and lacking a legitimate son of his own, had moved before his death to adopt Octavius as his heir. This, of course, was the same tactic that had seen Livia's father adopted by Livius Drusus: a perfectly legitimate expression of the perennial struggle of Roman nobles to maintain their lineage and entangle their peers in sticky webs of obligation. Adoption by Caesar, though, had provided Octavius with a leg-up like no other. The gawky eighteen-year-old from Velitrae had been graced with two priceless inheritances: his great-uncle's fortune and his prestige. Caesar's money had granted legions; his name, *auctoritas*. So potent were these bequests that they would prove to have lit in the teenage Octavius an ambition such as no young Roman embarking on his career had ever before thought to nurture: to win sole and permanent supremacy for himself. When it was subsequently confirmed that the comet seen above Rome had indeed been his adoptive father's soul streaking heavenwards, his legacy had become even more awe-inspiring. The young man once known as Gaius Octavius could now lay claim to a nomenclature of almost superhuman resplendence. For all that his enemies delighted in calling him 'Octavianus', he himself scorned the name. Not merely Caesar, he insisted on being known as Caesar *Divi Filius* — 'Son of a God'.

To the Roman elite, all this was liable to seem more sinister than splendid. Confronted by the chill and alien figure of the young Caesar, most nobles instinctively recoiled. Those who had survived the slaughter of Philippi tended to seek refuge, for want of any better alternative, in the train of Antony. Others faced a trickier choice. While Antony, in the division of the world that followed Philippi, had been granted responsibility for the East, the young Caesar had returned to Italy. Nobles such as Tiberius Nero, resident in Rome, found the Son of a God resident directly on their doorstep. With Antony far distant, and the young Caesar's murderousness in defence of his own interests a matter of all too public record, most opted, unsurprisingly, to keep their heads down. A few, though, did begin to plot. Feelers were put out to Antony's agents in Italy. Whispered schemes to restore the Republic began to circulate once again in exclusive circles. When Antony's brother, Lucius, became consul and spoke in unsubtle terms of freeing Rome from tyranny, hatred of the young Caesar and everything he represented burst into open flames. Nowhere did they blaze more violently than in Etruria and Umbria, celebrated and beautiful lands north of Rome, where rivers glided beneath towering crags on which stood ancient ramparts. One of these hill-towns, Perusia, now became the stronghold of Lucius and his army. Men from across Italy flocked to join them. Most were destitute, with only their lives left to lose; but not all, by any means. Some were senators – and among their number was Tiberius Nero.

In this desperate throw, he was accompanied by his wife and infant son. Roman women did not normally travel with their husbands to war, but the times were far from normal. The world had been turned upside down – and even male prerogatives were starting to fray. During the proscriptions, condemned men, as they hid out in attics or stables, had found themselves humiliatingly dependent on their wives. The shocking tale was told of one woman, notorious for her affairs, who had betrayed her husband to bounty-hunters, and then married her lover the same day. Many wives, though, had proven themselves both faithful and heroic. One, in a particularly hardy show of courage, had even braved a beating from Lepidus's heavies to beg for her husband's life. 'They covered you with bruises,' he recalled later in grateful admiration, 'but never broke your spirit.'[22] Other women, in an even more remarkable display of masculine resolve, had taken to the streets. Early in 42, at a time when the extortions of the Triumvirate were bleeding Rome dry, an entire delegation of them had marched on the Forum. Climbing on to the Rostra, their spokeswoman had boldly awakened memories of a murdered tradition: freedom of speech. Hortensia was the daughter of Hortensius Hortalus, one of the greatest orators of his day, whose fearlessness in eviscerating his opponents could be measured by the splendid riches it had won him: a dining table on which, for the first time in Rome, peacock was served; an incomparable wine cellar; a mansion on the Palatine. Now, speaking as men no longer dared to speak, his daughter had fearlessly arraigned the Triumvirs themselves. 'Why should we women pay taxes,' Hortensia had demanded, 'when we have no part in the honours, the commands, the rule of the state?'[23] To this question, the Triumvirs had responded by having the women driven from the Forum; but such was their embarrassment that they did eventually, with much bad grace, agree to a tax cut. The episode was one that Livia would doubtless have noted with interest. It taught a lesson fit for the times. Such were the evils to which Rome was prey that a woman might find herself obliged, just perhaps, to take the defence of her patrimony into her own hands.

Meanwhile, of course, it was to her husband that Livia looked to ensure their son the gilded future befitting a child with the mingled blood of two Claudian lines in his veins. It did not take long, though, for her confidence in Tiberius Nero to start appearing horribly misplaced. Signing up to an insurrection against the young Caesar did not turn out to have been a sensible move. Calamity followed fast upon calamity. Lucius's rebellion was crushed with predictable ruthlessness. Even though Lucius himself was pardoned, other senators were not so lucky. The young Caesar, as though offering up a blood-sacrifice to his deified father, had large numbers publicly executed on the Ides of March.[24] There could be no doubt, then, that Tiberius, despite managing to flee the sack of Perusia with his family, was in mortal danger. Arriving in Naples, he tried to instigate another uprising. It too was crushed. Taking to the countryside, the fugitive couple were almost betrayed by the crying of the infant Tiberius, and only just managed to evade the soldiers pursuing them. Making their escape to Sextus Pompey's pirate base in Sicily, they were greeted with such froideur that Tiberius Nero, prickly as only a Claudian down on his luck could be, ended up heading off east in a huff. Rebuffed in turn by Antony, he then managed briefly to find a bolt-hole in Greece, before being forced on the run yet again. As they made their escape through a forest, a fire broke out. Livia's dress was left charred. Even her hair was singed. Meanwhile, back in Rome, her husband had been officially proscribed and his house on the Palatine confiscated. As the mother of the heir to the Claudians, Livia was entitled, perhaps, to feel that enough was enough.

By the summer of 39, when a treaty patched up between the Triumvirs and Sextus Pompey provided exiles such as Tiberius Nero with an amnesty, Livia could have been left with no illusions as to the brute realities of the new order. She returned to a Rome in which her circumstances were sadly diminished. Even the fact that her husband had got her pregnant again failed to improve her mood. Tiberius Nero had proven signally unequal to Livia's hopes for herself and her heirs. There could be no disputing the courage she had shown in accompanying him on his disastrous travels. Ultimately, though, her loyalty was not to him but to her father's line. Blue-blooded, beautiful and not yet twenty, Livia knew that she still had plenty to offer a man. All it needed was a match worthier than Tiberius Nero.

Meanwhile, in the splendid mansion on the Palatine that had belonged to Hortensius Hortalus until its confiscation in the proscriptions, the young Caesar was also tiring of his spouse. Scribonia was a woman of frigid dignity – or, as her husband preferred to put it, with notable lack of gallantry, 'a wearing tendency to argue'.[25] She lacked what even her enemies were willing to grant that Livia possessed in abundance: charm and sex appeal. Nor, despite the fact that she came from a noble and powerful family, could Scribonia's pedigree possibly compare with that of a Claudian. To the young Caesar, whose status as the 'Son of a God' had made him seem only the more vulgar in the eyes of the authentic nobility, marriage into Rome's most celebrated family had everything to recommend it. He might be master of half the world – but he was still sensitive to the charge of being a parvenu. That Livia possessed physical attractions in addition to everything else merely confirmed him in his decision. By the autumn of 39, only a few months after her return from exile, he had made his move on the pregnant wife of Tiberius Nero.

The cuckolded husband himself, too demoralised by now to stand on his dignity any further, was so desperate to repair his fortunes that he almost forced Livia on the young Caesar. Adding to the mingled shock and delight with which the Roman people greeted the emerging scandal was the fact that Scribonia too was heavily pregnant. Only once she had given birth to a daughter, Julia, did her husband feel decently able to divorce her. By the autumn of 39, the young Caesar was betrothed to Livia. The wedding itself still had to wait. To marry a woman pregnant by another man was a step too offensive to propriety even for the son of a god. At last, though, on 14 January 38, Livia gave birth to her second child, a boy named Drusus. Three days later, she was married to the young Caesar. Tiberius Nero, playing the role of her dead father, gave his former wife away. Livia's return to the Palatine was formally sealed.

She was destined to remain there, its undisputed mistress, for the rest of her life. Her new husband understood full well what he had obtained by marrying her. 'He would never cease to love her, esteem her, stay true to her.'[26]

Livia, at any rate, was secure at last.

The Roman Spring

It was not only nobles who risked losing everything to the criminal and disorienting age presided over by the young Caesar.

Italy

0   50   100 miles
0 50 100 150 kms

Alps

• Ticenum

Rubicon

*Ligurian
Sea*

ETRURIA

UMBRIA

• Arretium

Perusia •

• Volsinii

Elba

⊙ Planasia

CORSICA

Fidenae •

Ostia •

Antium •

Rome •

Nemi •

Velitrae •

Spelunca

• Sulmo

Apennine Hills

A d r i a t i c   S e a

CAMPANIA

Venusia

Appian Way

Brundisium

Naples •

Beneventum •

SAMNIUM

Pandateria •

Capri •

SARDINIA

*T y r r h e n i a n
S e a*

M e d i t e r r a n e a n   S e a

• Rhegium

SICILY

Early in 41 BC, a few months after the bloodiest campaign in Roman history had exhausted itself at Philippi, a troupe of scarred and burly men headed south along the Appian Way. As they advanced up the slopes of an ancient volcano named Mount Vulture, they followed a standard topped by that ultimate bird of prey, the eagle. Farmers watching it pass might well have found themselves eyeing its silver beak and talons with trepidation. They knew what its arrival signalled. The young Caesar, with vengeance on the assassins of his adoptive father now secured, had faced a most invidious task on his return to Italy. Some 50,000 of his soldiers, battle-hardened veterans all, were looking to him expectantly for their reward. And what they wanted was the prize for which, more than any other, they had been willing to cross the seas and slaughter their fellow citizens: a plot of land.

Even before Philippi, the Triumvirs had earmarked territory around eighteen Italian cities for confiscation. These plans were necessarily on a massive scale. It has been estimated that at Philippi a quarter of all citizens of military age fought on one side or the other.[27] Now, with the return home of the victors, expropriation became the order of the day. Landowners across some of the most fertile regions of Italy learned to dread the appearance on their property of demobbed soldiers. 'Everywhere, in every field, such confusion!'[28] Villas, farm equipment, slaves, might all be seized. The larger the estate, the more scope there was for the surveyor, armed with his 'pitiless measuring-rod',[29] to divide it up and settle entire units at a time. Resistance was brutally crushed. Generally, though, like doves before the approach of an eagle, the dispossessed knew better than to fight back. Some were permitted to stay on as tenants. They were the lucky ones. Most were left with no choice but to bow their heads before the evils of the age, and leave their stolen homes. 'Fortune turns everything upside down.'[30]

The same spectres of larceny and violence that had brought terror to the nobility during the proscriptions were now general across Italy. While it was the prosperous lowland regions they stalked most menacingly, well-watered fields were not their sole temptation. On Mount Vulture, where wolves still haunted expanses of thick forest, and during summer the fields were baked by scorching winds, the poverty of the soil did not spare the locals from ruin. Too much else was at stake. No one concerned with the mastery of Italy could afford to neglect the spot. Already, 250 years before the arrival on Mount Vulture of the young Caesar's veterans, Roman settlers had established a colony on its flank. Venusia, planted on a crag midway between two ravines, had served Rome as a key forward post, her gateway to the south. Italy back then was still little more than a geographical expression, the Romans themselves merely one among a patchwork of peoples. Others could boast characters no less distinctive. There were the Etruscans, whose sway at one time had extended beyond their native Etruria as far south as Rome itself, and whose talent for reading 'auspices' – supernatural markers of the future revealed through the flight of vultures or the dietary habits of chickens – was unrivalled. There were the Marsians, near neighbours of the Romans up in the Apennine hills, whose singing could make snakes explode. There were the Samnites, whose ancestors in ancient times had been led by a mysterious ox to the harsh mountain fastnesses above Naples, and who for more than fifty years, back in the fourth century BC, had obdurately defied the southward thrust of the legions. In time, though, they and all the other peoples of Italy had been broken; and gradually, as Roman supremacy established itself throughout the peninsula, Italians had come to think of themselves as sharing a common identity. Venusia, raised to stand sentinel over the Appian Way as it left Samnium and descended towards the Adriatic, had begun to lose its founding purpose. The assurance it had once provided the Roman people, 'that it would block any hostile incursion',[31] had become redundant. No longer did it serve as a frontier town.

Let it fall into the wrong hands, though, and the city could still present a menace. It did not need ancient history to teach the young Caesar this. As recently as 91 BC, the people of Venusia had joined various other Italians, from the Marsians to the Samnites, in open rebellion against Rome. An independent state had been proclaimed. Its coins had portrayed a wolf trampled under foot by a bull. Yet, however savage the war had been before its final suppression, and however severe the fright it had given Rome, the insurrection itself had been bred less of hatred than of a snubbed devotion. The ambition of most Italians had been to share in Roman power, not annihilate it. To visit Venusia was immediately to understand why. Civic amenities rose everywhere. Baths, aqueducts, amphitheatres: none of these had come cheap. Italians, whether as soldiers or merchants, had profited splendidly from their mistress's conquest of the Mediterranean – which was why, when the Senate approved a proposal that people across the peninsula become full citizens of Rome, the insurrection had promptly collapsed. From that moment on, the whole of Italy had ranked as Roman.

By the time that the veterans of Philippi arrived in Venusia to evict the local landowners and divide up their fields into neat chequerboard plots, such an identity was all that most Italians had left them. Fifty years previously, in the wake of the great rebellion against Rome, many of the inhabitants of Venusia had been enslaved and scattered far and wide. The children of new arrivals had filled the city's leading school: 'the intimidating sons of intimidating centurions'.[32] Then, with the outbreak of civil war, an entire generation of young men had been conscripted. 'Curved sickles were straightened out and forged into swords.'[33] Many had perished in foreign fields. Those who returned did so with few loyalties save to their comrades and their generals. Now, like the blades of a giant plough, the surveyors of the young Caesar had arrived to slice up Venusia yet again. Few of the customs once characteristic of the region had been able to survive such repeated harrowings. 'So utterly have they deteriorated that everything which once made them distinctive – differences of language, armour, dress and so on – has completely vanished.'[34]

Even so, there were still some Italians who suffered the knowledge of this as a form of bereavement. One last firestorm of destruction remained to come. When Antony's brother Lucius raised the banner of armed opposition to the young Caesar in 41 BC and barricaded himself behind the walls of Perusia, the motives of those who flocked to him were various and confused. While a few, like Tiberius Nero, were inspired by dreams of restoring the Republic, and others, the vast majority, were men left impoverished and embittered by the appropriation of their lands, there were some whose dreams of a time before Rome, when their cities had been free, had life in them yet. Unlike in Venusia and Samnium, where the spirit of rebellion had been extinguished beyond all hope of resurrection, in the rich lands further north, and in Etruria especially, it still flickered faintly.

Not for long, though. The young Caesar was hardly the man to tolerate any challenge to his authority. The brutality with which he and his lieutenants crushed Lucius's uprising brought ruin to many an ancient and famous town. Some, like Perusia, were burned to the ground; others hit with fines so exorbitant that their citizens were forced to abandon them altogether. Ever more refugees were added to the bands of the dispossessed. Amid the blackened fields and bandit-haunted woods of Etruria, phantoms could easily seem a more vivid presence than the living. Survivors were left to mourn 'the devastated hearths of the Etruscans, that ancient race'.[35]

Yet where there was misery, there lurked opportunity as well. Cross the corpse-strewn hills from Perusia, and the traveller would come to a city blessed with what had become, amid the evils of the age, that most useful of attributes: a powerful patron. Arretium, which had lost its independence to Rome centuries before, had as its most prominent citizen a man who claimed descent from Etruscan royalty, no less. To the Roman nobility, the lineage of which Gaius Maecenas boasted was so contemptible as to border on the sinister; but Maecenas himself, a man much given to florid showmanship, felt no need to pander to the sneering of senators. The chaos that spelt doom to so many others had been the making of him. Restless and clear-sighted, he had glided with great facility to the heart of the new order. Backing the young Caesar as a winner right from the start, he had profited massively from his punt. Not everything stolen from the proscribed had gone to fund the triumviral war effort. Those sufficiently alert to the new wellsprings of power, provided they only had the talent and nerve to take advantage of them, had been able to drink deeply of spectacular riches.

Certainly, even his enemies had no doubt of Maecenas's ability. 'He was a man who, whenever the occasion required it, would literally never sleep – and who was as quick to see what needed to be done as he was skilled in achieving it.'[36] The young Caesar, in his resolve to win for himself impregnable dominance over his fellow citizens, had urgent need of such lieutenants. This was why, even as Etruria blazed, the fixer from Arretium enjoyed his ear.

The violence, the theft, the calculated atrocities: these, for a new regime desperate to establish itself upon a firm footing, had been unavoidable. But Maecenas, like his master, understood that arbitrary illegalities could never hope to secure its long-term future. His preening as the heir of Etruscan kings was not merely a calculated defiance of Rome's traditional power-brokers, to whom Arretium was a backwater best known for churning out cheap pots. It also served as a reassurance to the class of people who had borne the brunt of the appropriations: Italy's landowners. The young Caesar, now that he had settled his veterans, desperately needed to broaden his support. This, in light of what his return from Philippi had meant for Italy, might have seemed a grotesque hope. Yet so convulsive were the horrors of the age, so devastating the vicissitudes of civil war, so absolute the seeming abandonment of the world by the gods, that someone, anyone, was desperately needed now to offer Rome a ray of hope. A regime that could restore to a bruised and terrified people a measure at least of peace might be forgiven much. Even, perhaps, the circumstances of its own rise to power.

For most Romans, though – whether they lived in the city itself or in the towns and villages of Italy – the future seemed only to be darkening. Victory over Lucius had failed to clear the field of the young Caesar's enemies. On Sicily, Sextus Pompey remained as entrenched as ever, and certainly in no mood to do the heir of his father's nemesis any favours. Instead, posing as a favourite of the sea god, he amused himself by sporting an aquamarine cloak and throttling the shipping lanes. As a result, a further tightening of the screw was now added to the miseries consequent on blackened fields and military requisitions.

Thanks to a blockade of the grain ships that might otherwise have helped to feed a starving people, by 38 BC famine was gripping the land. Bands of murderous vagrants infested the roads. In Rome, where the slums seethed with refugees, hunger gave a desperate edge to the mood of misery and rage. Proposals for a fresh round of taxes, aimed at funding the destruction of Sextus, precipitated open rioting. The young Caesar was stoned in the streets. Only with difficulty did he escape the mob. Later, when the bodies of those killed in the clashes were slung into the Tiber, gangs of desperate thieves waded out and stripped them bare. Such were the straits, it seemed, to which the Roman people had been reduced. Nothing was left them save to scavenge corpses.

That Rome was doomed, that her streets might end up abandoned to beasts of prey, that the city itself be turned to ashes: these were fears some now openly acknowledged.

> *It is true: a harsh fate pursues*
> *the Romans, and the crime of fratricide,*
> *since the blood of blameless Remus*
> *was spilt on the ground – a curse on his heirs.*[37]

Well might the man who delivered this grim prognosis have felt a sense of despair. Quintus Horatius Flaccus – Horace – was a genial man; but he spoke for any number of Italians caught up in 'the cruel miseries of exile, the miseries of war'.[38] The son of a wealthy auctioneer from Venusia, he had fought at Philippi on the side of Caesar's assassins. Years later, veiling the horror of the carnage behind amused self-deprecation, he would describe how he had managed to escape the battle only by tossing away his shield and then relying on a supernatural mist; but in grim reality, he had seen enough of Roman slaughtering Roman always to be haunted by the experience. Certainly, after Philippi, he had lost his appetite for carrying on the fight. When an amnesty offered him the chance to head home, he seized it. The surveyors, though, had reached Venusia before him. His lands were gone.

Resistance, with the shadow of proscription still hanging dark over those who had fought for the Republic at Philippi, was out of the question. Horace duly joined the flood of those made homeless, and headed for Rome. Here, either by scraping together what remained to him of his patrimony or by tapping a powerful contact, he managed to secure for himself a post as an accountant in the government treasury. A living, to be sure – but a sorry comedown for a one-time landowner, even so. Horace, who combined his evident head for figures with a genius for self-expression, dared to explore in verse the fracturing of the age. Existence was precarious, and the worst might yet be to come. A world in which men could be evicted from their lands upon a whim was one in which no one, not even the seeming winners, stood secure. 'Let Fortune rage, then, and stir up fresh convulsions. How much worse will she make things than they already are?'[39]

A pointed question – and one which the young Caesar, who had murdered and extorted his way from out-of-town obscurity to the mastery of Italy, could hardly help but be haunted by himself. He knew from the scale of his ascent, none better, just how far he had to fall. Cornered by the starving mob, pelted with stones and filth, rescued only with difficulty from being torn to pieces, he had stared the precariousness of his dominance directly in the face. Yet only two years later, Fortune had once again confirmed the young Caesar as her favourite. In September 36, Sextus Pompey was trapped off the east coast of Sicily and his fleet destroyed. Although Sextus himself managed to escape, his power was broken for good, and within a year he was dead. Meanwhile, back in Italy, the young Caesar was being hailed for the first time in genuinely rapturous terms. 'All the towns gave him, at the age of twenty-eight, a seat among their gods.'[40] No spitting hatred now. Whereas Philippi had brought nothing but misery to Italy, the joy of the naval victory over Sextus was something in which everyone could share. Sicily with its rich fields was restored to the young Caesar's rule. Ships bringing food began to dock once again at Italian ports. The blockade was over for good. In Rome, a golden statue of the victor was placed by official vote of the Senate on a column adorned with appropriate naval décor. 'Peace, long ravaged by civil strife,' read the inscription on its base, 'he restored by land and sea.'[41]

At last, it seemed, enthusiasm for the new regime was starting to reach beyond those who had profited from it personally. The young Caesar, alert as ever to opportunity, moved with his customary deftness to encourage this trend. Conscious of how loathed the Triumvirate had become, and eager to hint at a brightening future, he began to pose with smooth shamelessness as the defender of all that he had spent so long attacking. Taxes were remitted, and documents from the dark days of the proscriptions burned with much ostentation. A few cosmetic powers were restored to the traditional magistracies of the Republic. Lepidus, long since neutered, was formally retired and packed off into exile. Meanwhile, the young Caesar himself began to hint that the Triumvirate itself should be retired.

Naturally, he avoided putting this fine-sounding sentiment into anything like action. Such a step, as yet, was out of the question. Even with Sextus and Lepidus both cleared from the board, there remained another player very much in the game. In the East, Antony showed no sign of losing his taste for power. Why would he? His appetites had always been on a swaggering scale. While the young Caesar, back in Rome, 'wore himself out with civil strife and wars',[42] Antony had been revelling in everything that the wealthy provinces and kingdoms of the eastern Mediterranean had to offer. Legions, riches, adulation: all were his. With the world now starkly divided between the two surviving Triumvirs, it was the younger man whose position still appeared the weaker. Yet in the glamour that was Antony's as the master of the East, there lay, perhaps, a weakness. And weakness, as countless others had learnt to their cost, was something that the young Caesar had a lethal genius for sniffing out.

Certainly, to a man of his proven murderousness, character assassination was a minor consideration. A decade on from the proscriptions, it was his rival's good name that he was now looking to dispatch. He knew the potency of rumour, 'which revels in filling people up with endless gossip, and blends equally what is true and not into a single song'.[43] Calumnies as shocking as they were colourful duly began to swirl through Rome. Antony's every action was cast in the worst possible light. His affectations, it was whispered, had degenerated into something monarchical, more appropriate to a silken Oriental despot than a magistrate of the Roman people. Corrupted by the soft temptations of the East, Antony had taken to urinating into a golden chamberpot. He blew fortunes on dinner parties. Most shocking of all, he had succumbed to the wiles of the Queen of Egypt. Picking up where Caesar had left off, Antony had bedded Cleopatra; but his resulting infatuation had got the better of him, and he was now little more than her plaything and her dupe. That he was married to Octavia, the sister of his triumviral colleague and an impeccably respectable matron, shamed him not a jot. Instead, in a calculated insult to the young Caesar, he had packed her off back to Rome. The truest insult of all, however, was to the dignity of the Roman people. Now, when the Queen wanted a foot-massage, it was Antony who obliged. The implications, to those who believed such stories, were sinister in the extreme. Who was to say how far Cleopatra's ambitions might not extend? What if Antony, in thrall to such a siren, should help her to the rule of the entire East? What if he should help her – horror of horrors – to the rule of Rome?

Articulated as it was with subtle and venomous brilliance, this image of Antony as a man seduced from all his natural loyalties began to take on a life of its own. Inevitably, the more damage was done to his reputation, the more brightly did his rival's shine by comparison. Particularly devastating was the contrast to Cleopatra presented by Livia, that dutiful heiress of the Claudian line. Her doting husband duly sought to rub it in. In 35, he secured permission to set up public statues of Livia, and Octavia too. He also won for the two women a privilege that was naturally out of the question for Cleopatra: formal sanctions against anyone offering them insult. These measures were passed readily enough. Livia, whose breeding and public displays of modesty were exemplary, was widely admired in senatorial circles. Nor were the nobility alone in seeing her as one of their own. Many

Italians did as well. Marcus Livius Drusus, her adoptive grandfather, had been their champion as well as the hero of the Roman poor. In 91 BC, he had sought to push through a law granting them citizenship. One evening, in the hall of his own house, an unknown assassin had struck him down with a shoemaker's knife. It was grief and fury at this murder of their champion that had done much to push the Italians into open revolt. Almost sixty years on, he remained widely cherished as a martyr. Livia, as his heir, was heir as well to his renown. Her presence next to the young Caesar, devoted and adoring, served as a growing reassurance to Italians that her husband too, despite the proscriptions, despite the expropriations, despite Perusia, might after all be on their side.

The surest boost to this reassurance, however, was the palpable improvement in his record. With his authority at last secure across the entire western half of Rome's empire, he now devoted skills once deployed in the cause of criminality to the restoration of law and order. Pirates were cleared from the seas and bandits from the hills of Italy. The one-time terrorist promoted himself as a dutiful public servant. Opportunism was replaced by a show of sober competence. As he had done since the beginning of his adventuring, the young Caesar displayed a keen eye for talent. Ability, not pedigree, remained the surest way to his favour. Upstarts continued to thrive. Senators might still roll their eyes at this; but for most citizens, relief that the worst seemed to be over, that the flood-tide of chaos appeared to be ebbing, outweighed even the pleasures of snobbery. For a decade now, ever since the Ides of March, the funeral games of the murdered Dictator had been raging. What mattered to the Roman people was no longer who won, but simply that there be a definitive winner. Bloodied and exhausted, they had grown too war-weary to care very much who ruled them – just so long as they were granted peace.

'Harmony enables small things to flourish – while the lack of it destroys the great.'[44] The man whose favourite saying this was knew well of what he spoke. Marcus Vipsanius Agrippa, who from the first appearance of the young Caesar on the political scene had ranked alongside Maecenas as the most trusted of his partisans, came from a background of staggering obscurity. 'Having such a son did not make the father any better known.'[45] Agrippa brushed all such condescension aside. Charmless and dour, his passion was for the reality rather than the appurtenances of power. Always one pace behind the young Caesar, the image of the honest deputy, as colourless and dull as his leader appeared refulgent, he rested content in the knowledge of just how much he was needed. Agrippa shared with the taskmaster he served so loyally an unspoken secret. The young Caesar was a hopeless general. Rumours of uselessness in battle had always shadowed him. At Philippi he had managed to lose his tent to the enemy while spending most of the campaign sick; in the war against Sextus he had suffered two resounding defeats. Agrippa, by contrast, was a natural. He it was whose speed of manoeuvre had served to bottle up the rebels in Perusia; who had equipped the young Caesar's fleet with metal claws fired from catapults; who had brought Sextus to ultimate defeat. Rugged peasant resolve and an eye for innovation: these were the very qualities that had first set Rome upon her path to greatness. Agrippa, far from cringing before the nobility, regarded himself as the authentic representative of his city's antique virtues. Aggressive in his humility, he was willing literally to plumb the depths in the service of the Roman people.

So it was, in 33 BC, that the conqueror of Sextus descended into the murk and filth of Rome's sewers. For generations, ambitious nobles had regarded the aedileship – the magistracy responsible for the city's physical infrastructure – as a mere stepping-stone to more glamorous postings; but Agrippa, already the second most powerful man in Rome, did not disdain its duties. He welcomed the chance to get his hands dirty. A vast workforce was set to emptying and scrubbing clean the sewers – after which, in a triumphant demonstration of how practical were the benefits to be had from the new regime, Agrippa had himself rowed along the central drain. Meanwhile, even as the city was being given this enema, other workmen were busy restoring the aqueducts and building a whole new one, the 'Aqua Julia'. 'In such quantities was water brought into Rome that it flowed like rivers through the city and its sewers. Almost every house was given cisterns and service-pipes, and fountains were everywhere.'[46] Feats of public service such as these were in the noblest, most muscular Roman tradition. Harking back to the heroic age of Appius Claudius, who had alternated winning battles with building roads, Agrippa was simultaneously working to usher in a new age – one that would see the city emerge cleansed of all its grime. Nothing was beneath his notice. Even barbers were recruited to the cause. Come a public holiday, and they would be sponsored to provide a free shave. Such was the future to which Agrippa, on behalf of his god-like leader, was guiding the Roman people: one scraped clear of all its stubble.

Even men with good cause to loathe the young Caesar – men who had fought against him at Philippi, men who had lost their lands – might recognise the appeal of such a programme. In 36 BC, at a party held to celebrate the defeat of Sextus, Horace had willingly toasted the victory, 'to the music of flute and lyre'.[47] His host that evening had been the subtlest and most valued of the young Caesar's advisors, a man as close as any to the heart of the regime. Where Agrippa was abrasive, Maecenas was perfumed and smooth, practised less at killing than at 'reconciling friends at odds'.[48] Horace, in offering this judgement, spoke from personal experience. Shortly after his arrival in Rome, broken and embittered, he had been introduced to the great man. Tongue-tied with nerves, he had barely been able to confess his circumstances. 'Nine months later, an order came, summoning me to be numbered among your friends.'[49] It was an offer not to be refused.

The relationship between the two men, although never one of equals, was soon affectionate and close. Maecenas combined an aptitude for intimacy with a connoisseur's eye for genius – and Horace offered him both. Inevitably, friendship with a power-broker of such intimidating influence came with strings attached. Travelling with Maecenas on the young Caesar's business, Horace would sometimes be obliged to turn a blind eye, to affect a diplomatic conjunctivitis; pestered by others to betray his friend's secrets, he would have no choice but to pose as 'a prodigy of silence'.[50] Yet the compromises were never simply one-way. Horace did not renounce his past; nor, though he paid affectionate tribute to Maecenas, did he permit himself to become his patron's shill. He remained too independent, too much his own man, for that. In an age when the reach of poetry might be great, and the needs of the regime served by Maecenas no less so, he signally failed to offer the young Caesar public praise. With Antony still in command of a host of legions in the East, and the menace of war louring increasingly heavy, too much hung in the balance. Like so many others, Horace had learnt the hard way the perils of nailing colours to a mast.

Maecenas, subtle and penetrating, understood this perfectly well. He knew that Horace, like the Roman people as a whole, could not, in the final reckoning, be brutalised into loyalty. Their hopes had to be met, their terrors eased. They needed to be wooed. What, then, did Horace want? The liberty for which he had fought at Philippi was dead – irrevocably so. His hopes now were more limited, and as solid as his own round paunch. 'These are the objects of my prayers. A plot of land – not so very large. A garden, a spring beside the house, its water ever-flowing, and a small wood on a slope.'[51] Such a dream was shared by many others across Italy: by those granted land, by those robbed of it. Now, with the great cycle of civil wars approaching at last its definitive climax, the yearning of the Roman people for peace was more desperate than ever. Victory, in the final reckoning, was likeliest to go to whichever of the two surviving warlords could satisfy it the best.

By 32 BC, the young Caesar was ready at last to go for broke. The war of words no longer sufficed. It was time to meet Antony in open battle. Not that the young Caesar actually named Antony as his opponent. He had no wish to cast the war as one fought against fellow citizens. Instead, it was Cleopatra, whose baneful powers of seduction had already made a slave of Antony and eunuchs of his followers, whom he selflessly pledged to destroy. This he did in a manner that was fast becoming the keynote of his regime: by blending nostalgia with innovation. Back in ancient times, so it was said, a declaration of war had always been accompanied by the ritual hurling of a spear. Particularly memorable was the one thrown by Romulus, which on landing had sprouted branches and turned into a tree. Although it lay beyond even the young Caesar to emulate that particular stunt, his revival of the ceremony did satisfyingly showcase him as the defender of antique Roman virtue. It was not, though, the only step he took. A far more radical measure had also been adopted: one that served to define him in a way quite without precedent. 'The whole of Italy swore loyalty to me of its own accord, and demanded me as leader in war.'[52] This claim, as it happened, was not entirely free of spin. The oath had in fact been the young Caesar's own idea, and very far from voluntary – but a masterstroke, even so. By appealing to the towns and villages beyond Rome for support, even before he had obtained a decree from the Senate, he potently signalled his ambition to fight as their champion. Back in the days of their revolt against Rome, the Italians had sworn a mass oath of loyalty to the cause of freedom. Now, en masse, they pledged their loyalty to the young Caesar. Less than a decade after his return from Philippi had wrought misery and upheaval across Italy, he could head back to war as its champion. When finally, in the spring of 31, he crossed the Adriatic to meet with the enemy in northern Greece, he took with him – in addition to his battleships and legions – a weapon that his rival could not hope to combat. No longer was he merely at the head of a faction. 'Leading the Italians into battle, with the Senate and the people, and the gods both of the household and the city,'[53] he had become something infinitely more potent: the face of the once and future Rome.

Granted, not everyone in Italy swallowed this. Some towns stayed faithful to Antony. Taxes imposed to fund the war effort resulted in much grumbling. In Rome there was even a full-blown riot. In general, though, people across Italy were content to hold their breath and wait. Infallible portents indicated that the crisis was ready to peak. The incineration by lightning of a two-headed snake, almost a hundred feet long, that had appeared in Etruria and caused enormous damage, was particularly noted. Sure enough, by summer it was clear that the fortunes of war were moving the way of the young Caesar. Antony, outmanoeuvred by Agrippa, was bottled up beside a promontory called Actium. In September, news reached Italy of a decisive development. Antony had launched a desperate attempt to force the naval blockade. Although he and Cleopatra had both made their escape, most of his fleet had surrendered. So too, a week later, had his legions.

The following spring, and the young Caesar was ready to wrap up his victory for good. Advancing on Egypt, he was met with barely a fight. First Antony perished by his own hand, then Cleopatra. The rule of her dynasty perished with her. Egypt was now the young Caesar's to do with as he wished. So too the world. For thirteen long years, ever since the Ides of March, it had been ravaged by wars and horrors so devastating that many had dreaded the complete collapse of Roman power, and the end of the world. Now at last the conflict was done.

'Time for a drink.'[54] Horace's relief, as he raised a toast to the defeat of Cleopatra and the victory of the young Caesar, was palpable. Maecenas, whose responsibility it had been during the months of his leader's absence abroad to maintain order in Italy, was no doubt delighted to sense it. He knew just what he had in his reflective and independent-minded friend: a mirror held to all those who, storm-tossed by the evils of the age, had somehow attained dry land. 'What are self-sufficiency and happiness? The ability to say: "I have lived."' Maecenas could not return to Horace the lands stolen from him: they were gone for ever. He could, though, make some recompense now that the regime he served was secure at last. Shortly after Actium had ensured that he would not, after all, be appearing on any proscription list of Antony's, he gave to his friend an estate just north of Rome, amid the Sabine hills. It was, in every sense, the answer to Horace's prayers. No wonder it seemed to the poet a place hallowed by the joy he took in it. It was peaceful, it was beautiful, it was everything that the decade he had just experienced was not. In the farm's fields, the crops grew with supernatural abundance; in its woods, the kids could roam without fear of the wolf, that beast of Mars. The gods, long absent from Italy, were back.

Or so Horace, and many, many others like him, now dared to hope.

The Spoils of Honour

'Conquering your neighbours was your chief preoccupation.'[55] So it was said of Romulus. Fighting foreigners, not themselves: this, everyone could agree, was the proper business of the Roman people. Naturally, in war as in peace, it was essential to respect legal niceties. Unprovoked aggression, while only to be expected from wild beasts and barbarians, was behaviour inappropriate to a civilised people. 'When we go to war, it is for the sake of our allies – or to uphold our empire.'[56] So it had always been. When Romulus attacked his neighbours, it had been with the resolve never to tolerate disrespect. Retribution for insult or injury had always been swift. One local king, ambushed and routed after presuming to raid Roman territory, had been cut down by Romulus himself. Here, in this slaying of a general by his opposite number, had been an exploit fit to illumine the succeeding ages. What more glorious feat of single combat could possibly be envisaged? Romulus, after stripping the blood-soaked armour from his foe, had borne it proudly back to Rome.

There was only one god worthy to receive the dedication of such a prize: Jupiter, the king of the gods himself. Hung at first from the branches of a sacred oak, the 'spoils of honour' had subsequently been moved into a temple custom-built for the purpose, the very first to be consecrated in the city. 'Here,' Romulus had decreed, 'was where, in days to come, anyone who emulates me by killing a general or a king with his own hands, shall lay the stripped arms – the "spoils of honour".'[57]

In the event, over the long and glorious course of Roman history, only a couple of other men had ever managed the feat. One was Cornelius Cossus, a cavalry officer who was supposed to have lived in the first century of the Republic, and the second a contemporary of Scipio Africanus by the name of Marcellus. The days when a commander would meet with his opposite number in single combat seemed to belong to a vanished age of heroes. Over time, the temple in which the 'spoils of honour' were stored had itself begun to crumble. Venerable though it was, it had long since been overshadowed. The steep hill on which it stood, across the Forum from the Palatine, had always been the seat of the gods. The Capitol was where, back in the golden age before history's beginning, Jupiter's father Saturn had established his throne. It was also where Rome's largest temple had been raised in the final decades of the city's own monarchy. Burned down in 83 BC, it had promptly been rebuilt on an even more grandiose scale. That it too was dedicated to Jupiter only served to emphasise the pokiness of Romulus's original temple. As Rome, in the terrible decade that followed the Ides of March, grew ever shabbier, so the city's oldest shrine seemed on the verge of collapse: 'roofless and dilapidated with age and neglect'.[58]

Yet all along, beneath the cobwebs and the dust, the temple had been sheltering a weapon with the potential to set kingdoms tottering. Stored inside the crumbling walls, alongside the 'spoils of honour' and a lightning bolt made of stone, lay an antique spear. It was this that the young Caesar, when declaring war on Cleopatra in 32 BC, had hurled in accordance with venerable custom.[59] Nothing could better have served to associate him with the martial virtues of Rome's founder. Heading off to war, he did so as a second Romulus. Meanwhile, back on the Capitol, workmen were moving in. Comprehensive repairs were begun to Rome's oldest temple. So comprehensive, indeed, as to rank as an almost total rebuild. The young Caesar knew better than to neglect the home front. The hammering and chiselling in the heart of the city provided a perfect accompaniment to the news coming in from Actium and Egypt. Even though the new Romulus was likelier, in truth, to pass a battle vomiting in his tent than engaging in hand-to-hand combat with enemy generals, that was beside the point. By 29, when he finally returned from the East with Antony and

Cleopatra both dead, and the whole world seemingly his, it was to a city in which the wellspring of Rome's martial traditions had been rebranded as his own.

It was not enough to be a victor. *Auctoritas*, that ineffable quality of prestige which served the Roman people as their surest measure of greatness, required a man to look and behave like a victor as well. The young Caesar, whose talents as an actor were no less formidable than his ambition, had long been sensitive to this. At Philippi, the prisoners-of-war had pointedly refused to salute him; at Perusia, the besieged defenders had mocked him as 'Octavia'.[60] By 38, he had had enough. Licking his wounds after a particularly humiliating reverse at the hands of Sextus, he had drawn a veil over his military inadequacies by means of one of his favourite and boldest expedients: beefing up his name.[61] A new one had begun to feature on his coins. Henceforward, these proclaimed, he was to be known as *Imperator Caesar* – 'Caesar The Victorious General'. Many commanders had been hailed as such on the field of battle, but none before had ever dreamed of making it so thoroughly and immodestly his own. Once Sextus was out of the way, the freshly minted Imperator Caesar had gone to great lengths to live up to his bold new nomenclature. In 35, he had headed across the Adriatic to the Balkans, there to test himself against bands of obstreperous barbarians named Illyrians. Two years of sporadic campaigning had enabled him to chalk up a succession of much-publicised victories. The tribes of Illyria had been variously ambushed, besieged and massacred. Some eagles captured a decade and more previously had been redeemed from captivity. Imperator Caesar himself had sustained a heroic wound to his right knee. Here, in the pacification of Illyria, had been a splendid appetiser for the even more glorious victories that were to follow. When, in the summer of 29, the conqueror of Egypt returned home from his settlement of the East, the refulgence of his *auctoritas* filled the whole world with its blaze. Imperator Caesar had become the sum of his name.

Italy, meanwhile, had been awaiting the conqueror with a degree of nervousness. Memories of his return from a previous civil war were still raw. As after Philippi, so after Actium the victor came trailing a monstrous number of land-hungry soldiers. His own recruitment drive and defections from his foes had combined to set him at the head of almost sixty legions. Such was the mood of anxiety that even Horace found himself pestered for inside information. 'Where does Caesar mean to give his soldiers the land he has promised them?'[62] The question weighed on everyone's mind. Given how brutally the returning hero had consolidated his power in the early years of his career, it could hardly have done otherwise. Yet the trepidation was to prove misplaced. The murderousness of the young Caesar's early career had been the measure of his weakness, not his strength. Now, with no foe left standing to oppose him, and the wealth of the East at his back, naked gangsterism no longer served his interests. The surest buttress of power he possessed was his *auctoritas* – and the surest buttress of that was his ability to serve the Roman people as the restorer and guarantor of peace.

That he had secured his greatness over the corpses of his fellow citizens was a truth no longer in anyone's interest to dwell upon. In January 29, six months before Imperator Caesar's return from the East, the Senate had formally approved his stupefying new first name. His status as the supreme exemplar of Rome's glory, the embodiment of the military virtues that had won her an empire and then come close to destroying her, was now official. The days when predatory noblemen waded through blood after dominance were over. Henceforward, there was to be only one. 'Let the better reign singly.'[63] On 13 August, this was made manifest in the most public way imaginable when Imperator Caesar finally entered Rome. Riding in formal procession through the city, pulled by four horses in a chariot ornamented with gold and ivory and followed by his army, he celebrated his martial prowess as only a Roman knew how.

The 'triumph', as this ritual was called, trailed a reassuringly venerable pedigree. Scholars traced its origins back to the very beginnings of Rome.[64] It was said that Romulus, after stripping his fallen adversary of the 'spoils of honour', had then blazed a trail by making his way into the city 'dressed in a purple robe and wearing a crown of laurel on his head'.[65] True or not, triumphs had long been serving the Roman people as waymarks on their road to empire. Scipio, Pompey and Julius Caesar had all celebrated them. None, though, could compare for sheer magnificence with the show now being put on by Imperator Caesar. Three whole days were required to celebrate the sweep of his victories. Illyria, Actium and Egypt: each was the focus of a separate triumph. 'The streets resounded to joy, games and applause.'[66] The climax came when the fabled riches of Cleopatra's kingdom, all the most fabulous pickings that the land of the pharaohs had to offer, were paraded before the crowds. Roman jaws collectively dropped. The exotic was not the only focus of the celebrations, though. Entering Rome on the morning of his first triumph, Imperator Caesar had been conducted into the city by the virgin priestesses of Vesta; riding through the streets, he had been followed by the leading magistrates of the Republic. Simultaneously ground-breaking and backward-looking, his triumphs – the first ever to be celebrated on three consecutive days – offered his fellow citizens both spectacle and reassurance. The Roman people recognised, as they were meant to recognise, that they were watching the ultimate in triumphs.

And when the processions were done, when the crowds had melted away and the gilded chariot been put into storage, what remained of those three remarkable August days were memories, and the sense of a new beginning. For all that they might enjoy a good triumph, the Roman people had had their fill of militarism. 'No son of mine will be a soldier.'[67] There were many, over the past twenty years, who had come to feel the same. Imperator Caesar understood this perfectly well. He could not possibly enjoy popular support while also keeping the military underpinnings of his regime exposed nakedly to view. Accordingly, even as the clamour and dazzle of his triumphs were filling the streets of Rome, measures were being taken to disperse his vast train of soldiers.

With the riches of conquered Egypt behind him, Imperator Caesar could well afford to throw money at the problem. No need for confiscations now. Instead, vast sums of money were spent on buying up land for thousands upon thousands of demobbed soldiers. Some were settled in Italy, others in colonies abroad. None of them made trouble; none of them cut up rough. No feat of governance on such a mammoth scale had ever before been attempted by a Roman statesman – still less pulled off. The achievement was welcomed, not surprisingly, with widespread and heartfelt gratitude. The promises of Imperator Caesar, it appeared, were not just specious talk. Peace, after all the horrors of civil war, was a prospect genuinely in view. 'The violent age of battle grows mild.'[68]

Not everywhere, though. The empire of the Roman people, bordered as it was by vast numbers of contumacious barbarians, could hardly afford to beat all its swords into ploughshares. Some legions, at any rate, were still needed to stand sentry. Gaul and Spain, Syria and Egypt, would certainly require garrisons. The Balkans too, despite the heroic performance of Imperator Caesar against the Illyrians, remained a festering source of trouble. Tribes of the kind who lurked beyond the Danube, bearded, shaggy-chested and armed with poisoned arrows, did not – as was the habit of civilised people – build cities and remain in them, but were instead forever on the move. In the summer of 29, even as Imperator Caesar was staging his triumphs in Rome, crisis was brewing in the badlands beyond the province of Macedonia. A tribe called the Bastarnians, who normally lurked in dank forests by the mouth of the Danube and were known, as a result, as the People of the Pine Trees, were heading southwards. Travelling in such numbers that they had even brought their wives and children with them, they were a patent menace. With their wagon train rumbling ever closer to Macedonia, the duty of the governor was clear. Even if the Bastarnians had no intention of actually crossing onto Roman soil, their temerity in approaching the frontier could not be allowed to go unpunished. The situation demanded a pre-emptive strike.

Such, at any rate, was the thinking of the governor himself. In marshalling his legions, ordering them to march out into the barbarian wilds and setting himself at their head, he was displaying the same dauntless spirit that had won the Roman people their empire in the first place. Romulus, no doubt, would have done the same. Yet back in Rome, the sudden flaring of war in the Balkans was signally unwelcome. Only one man was permitted to play at being Romulus – and it was not the governor of Macedonia. Thirty years earlier, when the deified father of Imperator Caesar had himself been the governor of a frontier province, his march northwards to stem a migration of barbarians had been the first step in his conquest of the whole of Gaul. No one needed any reminding of what had followed on from that. Yet Imperator Caesar was in a bind. He could not simply forbid a Roman aristocrat from doing what a Roman aristocrat was supposed to do. The dark days of the proscriptions, when his power had been naked and sanguinary, were past. He had no wish to rule as a despot. Do that, and he risked perishing as his deified father had done, beneath a hail of senators' knives. Hence his dilemma. Somehow, he had to find a way of securing the co-operation of the Senate, while at the same time denying its big beasts any taste of authentic power.

And indisputably, the governor of Macedonia ranked as a big beast. Marcus Licinius Crassus was the grandson and namesake of the billionaire whose manoeuvrings had done so much to make the political weather in the decade before the crossing of the Rubicon and the eruption of civil war. The grandson was very much a chip off the old block. He had negotiated the treacherous rapids of the age with skill, leveraging abrupt shifts of loyalty to great effect. Abandoning Sextus Pompey in the nick of time, he had transferred his support to Antony; then, just before Actium, he had jumped ship once again. Displaying an eye for business that would have done credit to his grandfather, Crassus had driven an impressively hard bargain. Imperator Caesar had agreed to reward him for his treachery with a consulship, and then, when his term of office was done, a province with its own complement of legions. Twenty-four years had passed since the death of his grandfather amid the sands of Carrhae, and the loss to the Parthians of his eagles. The humiliation of the defeat was still vividly felt by the Roman people – and by Crassus, especially so. Now, by blundering their way towards his province, the Bastarnians had presented him with the perfect opportunity to ease it. He would wipe clean the slate of his family's honour with barbarian blood.

The Bastarnians themselves, when they realised the full scale of the force that was advancing against them, responded with panic. Their king, a man named Deldo, sent envoys to Crassus, 'urging him not to chase them – since they had done the Romans no harm'.[69] Their pursuer, greeting the ambassadors with a smooth show of hospitality, offered them a drink – and then another, and another. The more inebriated the envoys became, the more he pumped them for information. The Bastarnians, it turned out, were hunkered down with their wagons beyond a nearby forest. Once he was certain of his quarry's dispositions, Crassus did not hesitate. Orders were given. Even though it was dark by now, his men began to advance.

Meanwhile, on the far side of the forest, it was becoming clear to the Bastarnian king that his envoys would not be returning. Then, as dawn broke, Deldo made out, beyond the blaze of watchfires, Roman scouts on the edge of the forest. Warriors with sheath-knives drawn and bow-strings of horsegut tautened almost to breaking point began to spill out from the ring of wagons. A hail of arrows, their tips dipped in venom, rattled down upon the Roman scouts. Some fell; others melted back into the forest. Bastarnian warbands, plunging into the murk, pursued them as they fled. Battle-cries of triumph sounded above the crashing of the undergrowth. None of the Bastarnians – and certainly not their king – paused to think they might be blundering into a trap.

That, though, was precisely what Crassus had set. The ambush, when it was sprung, proved devastating. The Bastarnian warbands were wiped out and their corpses left to fertilise the roots of the forest; their women and children were rounded up; their wagons put to the torch. A message of Roman greatness, written in blood and fire, was being sent far across the Balkans. Most glorious of all was the memorial to the victory won by Crassus himself. It was upon his sword and nobody else's that the king of the Bastarnians had perished. Deldo's armour, stripped from his corpse, constituted a trophy such as no Roman general had won in centuries. Crassus's soldiers, when they hailed him on the field of battle as *imperator*, were saluting him as well as something more: only the fourth man in their history to win for himself the 'spoils of honour'.

To Imperator Caesar, of course, the news could hardly have been less welcome. His triumphs, his building programme on the Capitol, his very name: all had been designed to establish him in the minds of the Roman people as the epitome of the victorious general. That another *imperator* might now parade through the streets of Rome with armour stripped from a barbarian chieftain, and place it in the same temple that he had been restoring with such expense and show, was an intolerable prospect. It directly menaced his *auctoritas*. As such, it was not to be borne. Nothing better demonstrated the embarrassment felt at Crassus's feat than the knee-jerk desperation of the attempt to stymie it. Imperator Caesar had long since mastered the art of veiling his own interests behind a smokescreen of often bogus tradition – and now he attempted the trick once again. Renovation of the ancient temple on the Capitol, it was abruptly announced, had turned up a remarkable find. Workmen had discovered an ancient linen corselet. Imperator Caesar himself, 'the restorer of the very temple, had seen it with his own eyes'.[70] An inscription on the corselet proved that it had belonged to none other than Cornelius Cossus, the second of the three heroes to have dedicated the 'spoils of honour' to Jupiter. Not only that, but it revealed a hitherto unsuspected fact. Cossus, contrary to what the annals and histories of the Republic had always claimed, had in fact been a consul when he won his famous trophy. Perhaps, then, in light of this revelation, there was a case for arguing that Crassus, as a mere governor, was not qualified to present the 'spoils of honour'?

In fact, there was not. That Crassus had been a governor rather than a consul when he slew the king of the Bastarnians did not alter the reality that he had been in sole command. Nevertheless, the waters had been successfully muddied. With Crassus absent in

71

Macedonia for at least another year, there was time enough for Imperator Caesar to neutralise any potential damage. There could certainly be no doubting now the urgency of the challenge that faced him. His *auctoritas* had to be rendered impregnable. So it was, throughout 28, that he renewed his efforts to cast himself as the defender of all that was noblest and best in the inheritance of the Roman people: 'the man who had given back to them their laws and rights'.[71] Any lingering traces of the terrorist he had once been, and of the criminality for which he had been notorious, were systematically erased. All unconstitutional measures enacted during the dark days of the proscriptions and the civil wars were solemnly rescinded; free elections to magistracies restored; eighty silver statues of himself, the height of upstart vulgarity, melted down. In their place, Imperator Caesar accepted no honour 'inconsistent with the customs of our ancestors'.[72] The man who in the early days of his career had sanctioned the murder of senators now sat in honour at their head. Gratefully, he received from them the venerable title once worn by Scipio Africanus: *Princeps Senatus* – 'First Man of the Senate'.

The graciousness of Imperator Caesar in restoring to the Roman people their abrogated liberties naturally deserved no less. And there was more to come. On 13 January 27, in a spectacular gesture of renunciation, the man who had extinguished the flames of civil war and won for himself the rule of the world informed the Senate that he was laying down all his powers. Henceforward, he was content to serve simply as what he had been for the past four years, an elected consul. 'The public welfare,' as he would later put it with sonorous modesty, 'I transferred out of my power into those of the Senate and the Roman people – to do with as they judged best.'[73] What the Senate judged best, after listening to Imperator Caesar with carefully rehearsed surprise, was to salute him as a hero in the noblest traditions of the Republic. Almost two decades earlier, at the feast of the Lupercalia, a panting and thong-clad Antony had presented the Deified Julius with a royal diadem; but now, when the Senate in their turn pressed a crown upon a Caesar, it was to honour him, not as the master, but as the servant of the Roman people. The 'civic crown' was a simple wreath of oak leaves which celebrated, as its name implied, the shared bonds of citizenship. Only a Roman who had saved the life of another in battle, 'slaying the adversary who had been threatening his fellow, nor ever giving ground',[74] was fit to be awarded it. Who more deserving, then, than the man who had kept the empire itself from implosion? Imperator Caesar, grateful to the Senate for the honour shown him, did not hesitate to accept it. The modesty of the award was precisely what rendered it so precious. Orders were given for it to be placed where all could see it: directly above Imperator Caesar's front door. There it was to hang perpetually – a reminder 'of the citizens he had saved'.[75]

What other noble could hope to compete with this – the mingled glory and humility of it? *Auctoritas* of such an order put every magistracy, every lineage, every battle honour in the shade. There were few in the Senate House, as they listened to Imperator Caesar declare himself 'a mild man, interested only in a quiet life',[76] who would have doubted that. To be sure, his claim to be restoring to senators their ancient licence to compete for honours was no mere sham. Had it been otherwise, their resentment of his regime would have smouldered with the same desperation that had proved so fatal to his deified father. Imperator Caesar needed their backing. The changes that he offered them were genuine. The Senate was to become what it had been before the civil wars: the surest path to high office. Elections were to be open. Competition was to be unconstrained. Imperator Caesar himself, far from merely allocating magistracies to his favoured candidates, would be obliged to canvass for them, and cast his vote just like everyone else. The pre-eminence of the Senate, it might have seemed to the more trusting of its members, had indeed been burnished and redeemed.

Yet even though the lustre of the Republic's ancient offices still burned brightly, the changed nature of the world inhabited by those who aspired to hold them was not easily ignored. Reminders of it loomed everywhere. Crossing the Forum that morning to hear

Imperator Caesar speak, senators had made their way past gleaming new monuments raised to the glory of the Deified Julius and his son: temples, statues, arches. Glancing up at the roof of the recently completed Senate House, it would have been impossible for them to miss a statue of Victory, her feet treading down the globe. Now, watching Imperator Caesar deliver his momentous address, they could see directly behind him a second statue of Victory, conspicuous on a pillar and surrounded by trophies pillaged from Egypt. For some, the intimidating glamour of it all proved too much. Displays of loyalty lurched into melodramatic excess. One senator, after yelling that he would rather die than outlive Imperator Caesar, rushed from the Senate House into the streets, where he began urging the crowds to swear the same. Even the Tiber seemed overcome. Bursting its banks, it flooded the low-lying districts of Rome – a clear sign from the gods that they intended Imperator Caesar 'to have the whole city under his authority'.[77] To primacy of such an order, the formal title of *Princeps Senatus* hardly did justice. No formal title could. The greatness of Imperator Caesar far outsoared the capacity of any single rank or honour to define it. Best, then, perhaps, to think of him simply as *princeps*: the 'first man' of Rome, and of the world.

Imperator Caesar, as ever, was having it both ways. His resignation of formal powers was no resignation of power. The carnivorous rivalries that had brought the Republic to ruin were not being unleashed anew. Aristocrats with famous names might compete for high office, just as their ancestors had done – but they would be doing so in the manner of captive tigers, padding around the confines of an ornate and splendid zoo. The response to the Princeps's speech from within the Senate House itself, minutely orchestrated as it was, made sure of that. Even as Crassus, in his winter quarters, was recovering from a second hard season of campaigning, measures were being taken to ensure that great dynasts like him would never again have the opportunity to go adventuring against barbarians. No sooner had the Princeps sat down after finishing his speech than pliant senators were rising and begging him not to abandon his military command. The

Princeps, stern and selfless, refused. The senators continued to beg. The Roman people still needed a guardian of their liberty. That being so, the placemen asked, would the Princeps not accept a command such as Pompey or his own deified father had once held, embracing a number of provinces and set at ten years? Nothing remotely contrary to tradition, nothing remotely smacking of monarchy, about that. The Princeps pondered this argument. Then, after due reflection, he acknowledged that the senators perhaps had a point. Reluctantly, dutifully, nobly, he shouldered the command.

Gaul and Spain, Syria and Egypt: these were the pick of the provinces awarded by a grateful Senate to Imperator Caesar. Together, they provided him with a force of over twenty legions. Henceforward, those who commanded them in the field would do so as his subordinates – his 'legates'. No more were men with famous names to go glory-hunting after 'spoils of honour'. Crassus himself, in Macedonia, was permitted to keep his province – but his wings had been decisively clipped. When he returned home in the summer of 27, the Princeps did not feel it worth the bother of denying him his triumph. Crassus duly paraded his trophies and prisoners through Rome. Enthusiasm for his exploits was widespread. Horace was just one of many to toast them.[78] There was no mention, though, of the 'spoils of honour', nor any visit paid to the tiny temple of Jupiter. Crassus, after his moment in the sun, faded from public attention. His days of campaigning were over. His successors as governor of Macedonia, although not appointed directly by the Princeps, were dull men, and obscure. One of them, it was true, did go so far as to launch an unprovoked attack on a nearby friendly king – but he was immediately hauled back to Rome, and put on trial for illegal adventuring. The Princeps himself deigned to appear as a witness for the prosecution. Governors after that made sure to stay well within the borders of Macedonia.

None of which meant that the Roman people were deprived of martial adventures to cheer. Quite the opposite. The Princeps took his provincial responsibilities very seriously. There remained a world still to be conquered and pacified, and he intended to prove himself worthy of this earth-shaking mission. Victories over barbarians were the necessary justification of his command. So it was that wars blazed along almost every frontier for which the Princeps had responsibility. His legates embarked on a programme of expansion without precedent in Roman history. Legions tracked the course of the Nile deep into Ethiopia; penetrated the remote desert sands of Arabia; tamed the bandits of the Alps. To people back in Rome, it began to seem that even the most remote and savage of nations might soon be brought to bow their necks. 'Caesar,' wrote Horace in a state of high excitement, 'is heading off against the Britons, to the very ends of the world!'[79] In fact, Caesar was not. He had a different target in mind. It was in Spain, where the tribes of the northern mountains had for two centuries defied the advance of Roman arms, that the Princeps, early in 26, took up personal command. Divine backing for this move was made spectacularly clear early on in the expedition, when a lightning bolt grazed the litter in which he was being carried, incinerating a nearby slave. That Jupiter was plainly keeping a personal eye on his favourite turned out to be just as well – for the campaigning did not play to the Princeps's strengths. So debilitating did he find the style of guerilla warfare favoured by the natives that, as was invariably his habit when in the field, he retired to his sickbed – whereupon the barbarians, in a spasm of fatal over-confidence, engaged in open battle and were brought to defeat. The ever loyal Agrippa then mopped up the rest. The Princeps himself, naturally enough, took all the credit.

The willingness of the Roman people to indulge him in this, to bring out the garlands and to crack open jars of wine on his return from Spain, mingled flattery with palpable nervousness. The health of the Princeps was shattered. Physicians diagnosed abscesses of the liver. Many feared the worst. 'While Caesar holds the world in his hands, I need have no fear of civil war or a violent death.'[80] So declared Horace, speaking the simple truth. Settled contentedly on his Sabine farm, he had no wish to lose the fruits of peace. Neither did the vast majority of his fellow citizens. Early in 23, when the Princeps grew so ill that his death was hourly expected, the whole of Rome held its breath. There were some, no doubt, in their yearning to be free of his dominance, who prayed for it; but there were many more who did not. The slender thread from which the stability of the world hung stood nakedly exposed. The Princeps, even as he tossed and sweated on his sickbed, drew his own conclusions. When eventually he recovered, redeemed from death's door by a vigorous course of cold baths, it was with the determination not to let the crisis go to waste. It was now much more apparent to him than before that widespread backing existed for his primacy. He moved fast to take advantage.

On 1 July 23, the Princeps announced that he was laying down his eleventh consulship. Once again, as had been the case four and a half years previously, a gesture of renunciation veiled what was simultaneously an entrenchment of his supremacy. The shadow-play that had characterised the original bargain struck between him and the Senate was now refined to yet further heights of ambivalence. Certainly, there was much in the terms of the new arrangement to delight upwardly mobile elements in the Senate. No longer would one of the two consulships be clogged up by the Princeps, year after year after year. Opportunities to secure Rome's pre-eminent magistracy were doubled overnight. The old days of the Republic, and of its most competitive traditions, did indeed appear restored. Naturally, though, this came at a price. The Senate had its own side of the bargain to meet. Awesome new powers were ceded to the Princeps. The right to summon senators whenever he wished, to present them with legislation, and to outrank even those governors who were not officially his legates: all these privileges were agreed and ratified. Four years previously, Imperator Caesar would not have dared to demand them. Now things were changed. His *auctoritas*, that thing of dazzling light and deepest, darkest shadow, had gained fresh muscle, fresh teeth.

A year later, when the ravages of hunger and plague led the people of Rome to riot, and to declare that only his appointment as Dictator would serve to redeem the city, the Princeps dismissed them in affronted terms. Falling to his knees, he tore and ripped at his clothes.

Time was when, coming to the Senate House, he had worn armour beneath his toga – but now, baring his chest, he begged the people to stab him rather than force him to be Dictator. Calculated these histrionics may have been, but his indignation was genuine. It no longer needed the example of his deified father to make him recoil from emulating it. Greatness such as he had won for himself was not to be constrained within the limits of any formal position. His power, like the perfume of the richest incense, had percolated to every nook, every cranny of the Roman state. No need, then, to offend tradition by desecrating it. What had he done, after all, if not make it his own? Now, when people gazed at the Princeps, they did not see the executioner of the Republic. Rather, they saw its embodiment. 'What is Caesar, if not the state itself?'[81]

Ever since the age of nineteen, when he had declared himself the avenging son of a god, the one-time Gaius Octavius had known that the surest reality lay in the eye of the beholder. What people could be persuaded not to see was quite as important as what they could. Marcus Crassus, desperate to redeem the disgrace of his grandfather's fate, had cornered a barbarian king and felled him with his own sword; but the Princeps, when he set out in September 22 directly for the eastern provinces, knew better than to trust to steel alone. The blaze of his reputation, fit as it was to overawe both the Parthians and his fellow citizens back home, was a surer weapon by far. Rather than risk the fate of Crassus by going to war, the Princeps opted instead to open negotiations directly with Phraates, the king of Parthia.

The gambit was unparalleled. No previous *imperator* had ever thought to settle a dispute with barbarians except by force of arms. Only a leader of god-like prestige could possibly have thought to fly in the face of such unyielding martial precedent – just as only a leader of god-like prestige could possibly have made it pay. Phraates, relieved to be treated as an equal by the bellicose and unpredictable superpower on his doorstep, duly accepted the offer of a negotiated peace. As a token of goodwill, he handed over precisely what the Princeps had travelled east to obtain: the eagles captured from Crassus at

Carrhae. A glorious achievement. What was the stripping of armour from some stinking Balkan chieftain to compare?

Returning to Rome after three years away, the Princeps made sure to rub the point home. On the sacred hill of the Capitol, where the first ever battle honours won by a Roman had been placed many centuries before, he ordered a small temple built. Here it was, for the while, that the standards were to be kept: a function designed, like its location, to echo that of the ancient temple of Jupiter.[82] The Princeps, with his customary blend of subtlety and precision, knew exactly the message that he was broadcasting to his fellow citizens. Although he might not have killed a rival general, he had won for himself the very ultimate in spoils of honour. Truly, he was the second Romulus – the founder anew of Rome.

On the day of the city's founding, twelve eagles had flown over the Palatine. The sign had been touched by an awesome, superhuman power, a power described by the Romans as *augustus*. Back in 27 BC, when the Senate had been pressing on the Princeps his globe-spanning provincial command, one of its members had seized on the word as the perfect adjective to describe him. Other senators, alert to the taste of Imperator Caesar for accumulating new names, had been pushing for him to be called 'Romulus' – but the entire Senate, the moment *augustus* was mentioned, had known at once that nothing else would do. The Princeps himself, reluctant to bear the name of a king, had concurred. So it had come to pass. Imperator Caesar, by official vote of the Senate, had been awarded the additional name of 'Augustus'. Less menacing than 'Romulus', it was also fantastically more impressive. '*Augustus* is what our fathers call anything holy. *Augustus* is what we call a temple that has been properly consecrated by the hand of the priests.'[83]

A man with such a name had no need of formal rank. Neither king, nor dictator, nor even consul, he was something infinitely more. The gods had given to Rome, in her hour of most desperate need, a touch of the divine. They had given her Imperator Caesar Augustus.

The God Father

During one of his periodic bouts of illness, the Princeps decided that he could do with a secretary. Casting around for a suitable candidate, his eye fell on Horace. Witty, personable and discreet, the poet appeared the perfect fit. Horace himself, though, was appalled. He had not escaped the grind of accountancy only to be chained to another man's ink and scrolls. Summoning all his immense reservoirs of tact, he duly made his excuses. He too, he explained to the Princeps, suffered from ill health. The offer, very regretfully, was one that he would have to refuse.

This rejection, coming as it did from someone who had fought on the losing side at Philippi, might have seemed a bold one. The aura of violence and menace that had clung to Augustus when he was a young man still lingered faintly. It could be hard for those of a certain generation to see the Princeps raise his hand in a gesture of salute, and not remember a story told of him as a triumvir: of how with his own fingers he had once gouged out the eyes of a suspected assassin. Times, though, had changed. Augustus himself had been anxious enough about the story explicitly to deny it. His youthful atrocities had long since served their purpose. Now that he had won for himself the mastery of the Roman state, he had no further need of cruelty. Displays of mercy better served his love of power. Augustus was perfectly content to tolerate what he no longer had cause to fear. In the temple to Venus Genetrix built by his deified father, the statue of Cleopatra still touched the shadows with a shimmering of gold. Iullus Antonius, the dashing and cultivated son of Antony, was brought up in Octavia's household and married off to a niece of the Princeps. Men who had fought for Pompey, who had commanded legions at Philippi, who kept statues of the Deified Julius's assassins in their homes, were encouraged to serve as consuls. Augustus had no interest in pursuing vendettas once his own security was no longer at stake. Horace could turn down the offer of a secretaryship and still retain his favour.

Indeed, the Princeps was widely known as a man who could enjoy a joke against himself. Meeting a young man who looked just like him, he asked, "'Tell me, was your mother ever in Rome?" "No," came the answer. "But my father was – often."'[84] Anecdotes such as these did wonders for the Princeps's image. It helped as well that he could give as good as he got. Augustus's sense of humour, like that of the vast mass of his fellow citizens, inclined to the raucous. Dwarves, cripples, people with gout: all prompted him to celebrated witticisms. Maecenas was joshed by the Princeps for his 'loose, effeminate and languishing style',[85] Horace for being fat. Augustus meant it all affably enough. That he addressed the poet as 'the very cleanest of pricks'[86] was a mark of affection, not contempt – and he was perfectly capable, in his dealings with those he cherished, of displaying sensitivity and charm. Yet there remained a toughness, an asperity about his character that reminded those with a taste for snobbery of the small-town conservatism from which he had sprung. Whether cheering on boxers in back streets, sporting a battered sunhat or roaring with laughter at the sight of a hunchback, Imperator Caesar Augustus retained just a hint of the provincial.

None of which did him any harm among the mass of the Roman people. It gratified them to think of the Princeps as a man without airs and graces. Intimate personal details, carefully leaked, helped to cast him as a citizen of honest, simple tastes. It was common knowledge that a man whose name served to place him midway between the earth and the heavens ate much like a peasant, that his bread was coarse and his wine of an unfashionable vintage. Divine appetites, even in the son of a god, were capable of causing bitter resentment. Augustus had discovered this the hard way. In the aftermath of Philippi, when the world had seemed abandoned by the gods, aping the absent immortals had become quite the craze among ambitious warlords. A former consul might think nothing of painting his body blue, putting on the fish's tail appropriate to a sea god and flopping around on all fours. Augustus, in the first throes of his passion for Livia, had staged a particularly provocative masquerade. At a time when Rome was in the grip of famine, he had held a drinking party to which all the guests had come dressed as immortals. The groom himself had starred as the golden and eternally youthful god of light and music, Apollo. Down in the streets of the starving city, outrage at the news had blended with bitterness and scorn. 'Yes, to be sure,' men had cried, 'Caesar is Apollo – Apollo the Torturer.'[87]

The people of Rome had particular reason to associate a god more commonly worshipped as the patron of prophecy and self-discipline with vicious cruelty. In the Forum, next to the sacred fig tree, there stood the statue of a pot-bellied man with a wine-sack on his shoulder. This was Marsyas, a satyr who had once challenged Apollo to a musical contest, been cheated of the victory that was rightfully his, and then been flayed alive for his presumption. Such, at any rate, was the version of the story told by the Greeks – but in Italy an altogether happier ending was reported. Marsyas, they claimed, had escaped the irate Apollo and fled to the Apennines, where he had taught the arts of augury to the natives and fathered the snake-charming Marsians. Rome was not the only city to commemorate him. Statues of Marsyas were to be found in public squares across Italy. For all that the satyr might be shown with leg irons on his ankles, he stood defiantly unchained. He had slipped the bonds of his divine master. So it was that he served Italians as 'a symbol of liberty'.[88]

Augustus, who in almost everything save his ambition was deeply conservative, had far too much respect for tradition ever to think of having such a venerable memorial removed from the Forum. Nevertheless, the statue of Marsyas was troubling to him on a number of levels. At Philippi, where his own watchword had been 'Apollo', that of his opponents had been 'liberty'. Not only that, but Marsyas was believed by his devotees to have been sprung from his would-be flayer's clutches by a rival god named Liber, an anarchic deity who had taught humanity to enjoy wine and sexual abandon, whose very name meant 'Freedom', and who – capping it all – had been worshipped by Antony as his particular patron. The clash between the erstwhile Triumvirs had been patterned in the heavens. Antony, riding in procession through Cleopatra's capital, had done so dressed

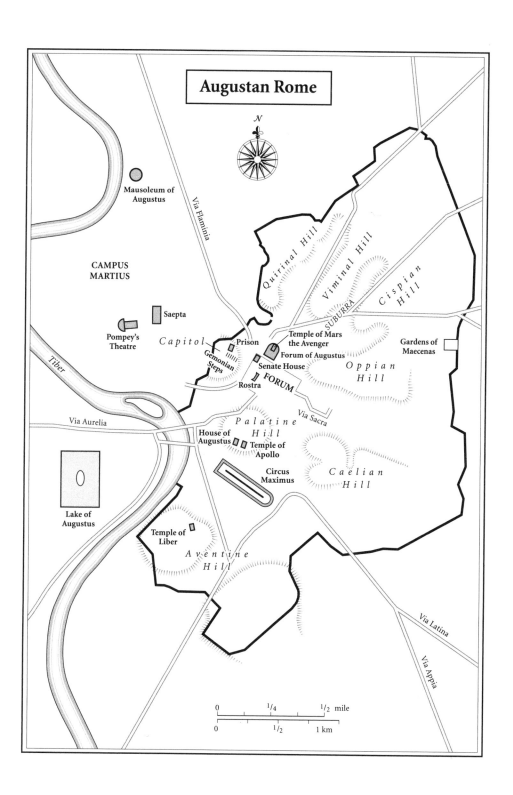

Augustan Rome

N

Mausoleum of
Augustus

Via Flaminia

CAMPUS
MARTIUS

Saepta

Pompey's
Theatre

Tiber

Capitol

Prison

Gemonian
Steps

Temple of Mars
the Avenger

Forum of Augustus

Senate House

FORUM

Rostra

Via Sacra

Quirinal Hill

Viminal Hill

Cispian Hill

SUBURRA

Oppian Hill

Gardens of
Maecenas

Via Aurelia

House of
Augustus

*Palatine
Hill*

Temple of
Apollo

Circus
Maximus

*Caelian
Hill*

Lake of
Augustus

Temple of
Liber

*Aventine
Hill*

Via Latina

Via Appia

| 0 | | 1/4 | | 1/2 mile |
| 0 | 1/2 | | 1 km | |

as Liber, 'his head wreathed in ivy, his body draped in a robe of saffron gold'.[89] Visiting Asia Minor, where in ancient times the contest between Apollo and Marsyas had been staged, he had been greeted by revellers dressed as satyrs. The night before his suicide, ghostly sounds of music and laughter had filled the Egyptian air; 'and men said that the god to whom Antony had always compared himself, and been most devoted, was abandoning him at last'.[90]

Meanwhile, back in Rome, the victory of Antony's conqueror had been Apollo's triumph as well. The patching-up of Jupiter's ancient temple on the Capitol had been as nothing compared to the stupefying redevelopment of the hill on the facing side of the Forum. In 36 BC, shortly after the defeat of Sextus Pompey, lightning had struck the Palatine. A god had spoken – but which god? Augurers sponsored by Rome's most eminent devotee of Apollo had dutifully served up the answer. For almost a decade, in obedience to their ruling, cranes and scaffolding had crowded the summit of the Palatine. Only by October 28 had the work finally been completed. The Roman people, just as they were meant to do, had gawped at it in awe. Planted on the hill above the Lupercal, next to where the hut once built by Romulus out of humble wood and thatch still stood in a state of improbable conservation, there now gleamed a monument built to the most advanced international standards. Raised on a massive marble pediment, adorned with doors of ivory, and crowned by a four-horse chariot made of bronze, 'the snow-white temple of brilliant Apollo'[91] made a literally dazzling addition to the Roman skyline. On one side of the Palatine it loomed over the Forum; on the other over the charred remains of an ancient temple of Liber.[92] That this had burned down in the same year as Antony's defeat at Actium only rammed the message home. Augustus, triumphant in all his enterprises, had backed a heavenly winner.

Nevertheless, he had not forgotten how easily the poor and starving had once been roused to curse him for impersonating Apollo. Even though the Princeps had never stinted in his devotion to the god of light, he knew better now than to parade his sense of identification at drunken dinner parties. Behaviour like that smacked altogether too much of Antony. Augustus preferred a perpetual play of radiance and shadow to be evident across his face. His image was as tightly controlled as it was charged with ambivalence. The portrait of him fashioned by sculptors offered to the Roman people a fitting reflection of the infinite subtleties and paradoxes of the man himself. In the jug ears of his statues it was possible to catch the glimpse of a thoroughly human Princeps: one whose eyebrows met above his nose, whose teeth were bad, and whose anxieties about his height were such that he wore platform heels. Yet he was a handsome man for all that; and it was his conceit, one that plenty were willing to flatter, that he had only to fix people with 'his clear and brilliant gaze'[93] for them to lower their eyes, as though before the sun. In his statues, the jug-eared Princeps appeared as beauteous as Apollo. Suspended midway between youth and maturity, between melancholy and triumph, between the mortal and divine, he was a Roman in every sense *Augustus*.

There was certainly to be no place in his portraits for the thinning hair and sagging jowls that once, in the heyday of the Republic, had served as the markers of high-achieving statesmen. What need for Augustus to emphasise his experience? All stood in awe of his achievements. He had accomplished more than any number of senators scored with wrinkles. The close association between ugliness and *virtus*, always cherished by conservatives, was hardly one to appeal to Augustus. The Princeps, rather than reining in his taste for self-promotion, aimed instead to mould tastes to the contours of his own. Never before in history had so many portraits of a single man been manufactured, disseminated and put on public display. A new orthodoxy was being marketed to the Roman people: that power should be good-looking. Evident to all those who gazed upon the statues of Augustus, it could increasingly be read as well in an even more prominent sphere: the fabric of the city.

Rome, although 'the seat of empire and of the gods',[94] had long presented a face woefully inadequate to her status as the capital of the world. Brown smoke from thousands upon thousands of workshops and hearth-fires hung in a pall over cramped shanty towns. Steepling apartment blocks shored up by brace-work clung precariously to the slopes of the city's hills. Blackened temples crumbled amid labyrinths of twisting and filthy streets. Compared to the gleaming cities of the East, where kings descended from the generals of Alexander the Great had burnished their capitals in swaggering fashion, Rome was a shabby and monochrome sprawl. So drab were its mud bricks and blotchy tufas that ambassadors from eastern monarchies, when they first began to arrive in the city, had found it hard to stifle their sniffs of disdain. Yet the lack of *grands projets*, which to Greeks appeared the symptom of a comical backwardness, had traditionally served the Roman people themselves as evidence of their liberty. Coloured marble, pompous avenues, urban planning: what were these, if not the prerogatives of kings? No one, in a free republic, could be permitted such sinister grandstanding. This was why, in the last feverish decade before the crossing of the Rubicon, the sudden appearance in Rome of a rash of grandiose monuments had served as portents of the Republic's ruin. Just as Julius Caesar had funded his own forum, complete with marble temple and statue of his horse, so had Pompey the Great put his name to the city's first theatre built of stone. These rival developments, set as they were against the squalor and decay general in the rest of the city, had glittered like gold fillings amid a mouthful of bleeding gums. Both had served the glory, less of the Roman people, than of their respective sponsors — and unsurprisingly so. To fashion out of an urban agglomeration as chaotic and ramshackle as Rome a capital worthy of a global empire was a project of renewal beyond anything that anyone had ever before attempted. Only a citizen possessed of limitless resources, infinite *auctoritas* and plenty of time could even think to embark upon it. Only a citizen, in short, like Augustus.

Naturally, the attentions lavished by the Princeps upon the city were hardly selfless. Nothing that he did ever was. His aim, as it had always been, was to wipe the floor with any hint of competition.

Even the dead were fair game. The heirs of Scipio Africanus, for instance, looking to remind the Roman people of their pedigree, had surmounted the processional way that wound up the side of the Capitol with a novel form of architectural showmanship: a colossal arch. Augustus, as only he could, now went decisively one better. Dominating the road that led from the Forum up to the Palatine, his own version was a perfectly judged exercise in putting even the most distinguished dynasties in the shade. Ostensibly dedicated to his birth father, who had died when the infant Octavius was only four, the monument nevertheless strongly hinted at an altogether more glamorous lineage. Rather than portraits of his mortal ancestors, the arch featured an astonishing statue of Apollo, complete with chariot and four horses, all carved out of a single block of stone. Subtly yet decisively, Augustus had cast the sniggering jokes about his parentage on their head. While the arch did not explicitly confirm the rumour reported of his mother, that nine months before his birth she had been visited while asleep in the temple of Apollo by a serpent, who had left on her body a miraculous 'mark in colours like a snake',[95] it did nothing to deny it. Such was the dimension of ambivalence in which Augustus always preferred to operate. Reluctant to offend Roman sensibilities by claiming Apollo as his father, yet perfectly content to make play with it, he was, as ever, having his cake and eating it.

The tightrope he walked in achieving this was necessarily precarious. It took a peculiar genius to pose as a being almost at one with the gods and simultaneously as a man of the people. Spectacular pretension was fused in Augustus with almost unearthly reserves of patience and self-discipline. The gleaming new temple of Apollo, even as it shed its lustre upon the Princeps's adjacent house, also opened up to ordinary citizens what had previously been the preserve of oligarchs. Libraries, courtyards and porticoes, annexed to the main body of the temple, now dominated the summit of the Palatine. Against such a backdrop, the private residence of the Princeps himself could not help but seem modest to the point of frugality. Even though

Hortensius, its original owner, had been notorious in his own lifetime for the effeminate character of his extravagance, trends had long since moved on. New markers of luxury now adorned the homes of the super-rich. At a time when Maecenas, that celebrated arbiter of taste, was busy introducing the heated swimming pool to Rome, the Princeps's house struck those familiar with top-end properties as 'notable neither for scale nor style'.[96] Not for him a tower of the kind that Maecenas had built as the centrepiece of his exquisite palazzo, a folly so steepling that it afforded its owner views of the distant Apennines. Augustus, a man wealthier than the Republic itself, did not need to demonstrate to anyone just how well endowed he was.

And in this, as he well knew, he was at one with the sentiments of the mass of the Roman people. 'While they may approve of beautifying public monuments, they have no time for private luxury.'[97] The self-made followers of Augustus, gorged as they were on the plunder of civil war, did not serve their leader's purposes by flaunting their appropriations. Maecenas, by virtue of his devotion to fashion, stood at risk of becoming unfashionable. His sprawling gardens next to one of the city gates had been built over a paupers' cemetery; his achingly modish topiary was fertilised by 'the bleached bones'[98] of the poor. Infinitely better qualified to serve as the public face of the new regime was the dour and hard-faced Agrippa. Despite himself having come from nowhere into possession of Antony's splendid mansion on the Palatine and entire territories overseas, he retained the crowd-pleasing image of a bluff peasant. Not hesitating to bait the nobility, he pressed for the nationalisation of privately owned works of art. Such treasures, he argued, were properly the Roman people's to enjoy. The Princeps himself, who had laboured so hard to seduce and reassure the aristocracy, was hardly the man to put such a proposal into action; but nothing that Agrippa ever said or did was without his master's sanction. Augustus, with his unparalleled nose for sniffing out advantage, had distinguished in the attitude of the upper classes to the masses a yet further source of profit. On the one hand, it was a point of principle among those committed to the noblest traditions of the Republic that it was 'for the Roman people to grant all powers, all commissions, all commands';[99] on the other, that these same Roman people were 'the bilge-water of the city'.[100] Here, amid the murk of such contradictory opinions, was ample opportunity for Augustus to consolidate his position yet further. Who better qualified than the Restorer of the Republic, after all, to realise the full potential of hypocrisy?

That it was indeed the Princeps, with his healing hands, who had salved the bleeding state back to health was a conceit that few, in the wake of the civil wars, had any great interest in disputing. When a golden shield listing Augustus's cardinal virtues was hung inside the Senate House, the inscription recorded that it had been placed there by *Senatus Populusque Romanus*, 'The Senate and the Roman People'. Yet this fine-sounding slogan, even as it proclaimed harmony between the city's elite and its masses, hinted as well at division. The commitment of Rome's citizens to the common good, so precious to them as an ideal, had been accompanied right from the beginnings of their city by a rival drumbeat. When Romulus, standing on the Palatine, witnessed twelve eagles passing overhead, he had been in competition with his twin. Remus, from his own vantage point just south of the Palatine on a summit named the Aventine, had seen a paltry six birds; and from that moment on, the rival destinies of the twin hills had been fixed. Just as the Palatine had always provided the city with its most exclusive hub of power, so did the Aventine serve as the stronghold of the disadvantaged, of the poor – of the *plebs*. Always, behind the civic unity which was the proudest boast of the Republic, there had throbbed the pulse of class resentments. The poor, sneered at by the upper classes as *plebs sordida* – 'the great unwashed' – had a long and proud tradition of standing up for their rights. Repeated attempts to crush their freedoms had been heroically resisted.

The most venerable monument to such resistance, built on the lower slope of the Aventine centuries before Antony had thought to co-opt it, was none other than the shrine of Liber. It commemorated an occasion way back in 494 BC when the plebs, oppressed by debt and the exactions of the rich, had staged a mass walk-out. Heading upriver from Rome, the strikers had camped on a hill overlooking the Tiber. Here, in a pointed retort to the institution of the consulship, they had elected two officials of their own – 'tribunes'[101] – to serve as guardians of their interests. The tribunes, the plebs had agreed, were to be regarded as sacrosanct. The life of anyone who laid so much as a finger on them was to be forfeit. Blood-curdling compacts to that effect had been sworn. The Roman upper classes, with great reluctance, had been brought to swallow these terms. Centuries on, and the tribunate had emerged to become one of the most potent offices in the entire Republic. It remained sacrilege to assault any citizen who held it. A tribune could impose the death penalty on those who challenged his authority; veto legislation of which he did not approve; summon the Senate and introduce measures of his own. Privileges of this order, freighted as they were by tradition and potentially awesome in their scope, could hardly help but pique the interest of the Princeps.

And sure enough, in due course, he had made his move. Laying down his consulship, he had reaped momentous compensation. Many of the most formidable powers ceded to him by the Senate in 23 BC, and which had served to buttress his primacy to such decisive effect, were those of a tribune: the *tribunicia potestas*. The plebs themselves, far from resenting this appropriation of their hard-won prerogatives by Rome's richest man, were instead confirmed in their view of him as their champion. It certainly came as no novelty to them that a man of high-class pedigree might wish to exercise the *tribunicia potestas*. A hundred years before, two grandsons of Scipio Africanus, Tiberius and Gaius Gracchus, had served as tribunes; more recently, the rumbustious career of Clodius Pulcher had been launched on the back of a tribunate. A palpable flavour of class warfare clung to the memories of all three men. Hostile elements in the Senate had been provoked to open violence by their agitating. Blood had flowed in the streets of Rome. Both the Gracchi brothers had been assassinated: Tiberius clubbed to death with a stool-leg and Gaius decapitated. As for Clodius, it was the riots following his murder by a political adversary that had led to the immolation of the original Senate House. Perhaps, then, among the ranks of the senators, there was a flutter of nervousness that Augustus, in laying down the powers of a consul, should have taken up those of a tribune.

If so, then they mistook their man. An operator as consummately sphinx-like as the Princeps had no interest in playing the demagogue. No matter that he had been endowed with the *tribunicia potestas*, he was not a tribune. The people's favourite, he offered himself as well to the Senate as their protector. Just how combustible the plebs might still be, and just how dependent the rich were upon Augustus to keep secure for them their swimming pools, their works of art and their exquisite topiary, had been made unsettlingly apparent to them in the wake of his departure from Rome. Between 23 and 19 BC, with the Princeps absent in the eastern Mediterranean, the city had seethed with factionalism and street fighting. Riots had flared. Murders had spiked. A consul had nervously requested extra bodyguards. Order had been restored only when the Princeps finally returned from the East, bringing with him in triumph the standards won back from the Parthians. The lesson had been well and truly rubbed home. 'When Augustus was absent from Rome, the people were fractious – and when he was present, they behaved themselves.'[102]

Guardian of the Senate and champion of the plebs: the Princeps was both of these, and more. For too long, the Republic had been its own worst enemy. Together, the greed of the mighty and the brutishness of the masses had brought it to the verge of ruin. Had the gods not sent Augustus to redeem Rome from the misery of the civil wars, then city and empire alike would surely have perished. The duty of the Princeps was clear: to stand guard over the Republic and protect it from itself. Revolution could not have been further from his mind. His heaven-sent responsibility it was to remind Senate and people alike of what they had originally been. Restore to them their ancient birthright of *virtus* and discipline, and his mission would be complete. 'The good man,' he once ringingly declared, 'is the one who has no intention of altering the traditional way of doing things.'[103] All that

Augustus had ever done, all the changes that he had ever made, all the manifold breaks with recent custom for which he had pushed, had aimed, not at novelty, but rather at the opposite: the return to the Roman people of their ancestral inheritance of greatness.

Once, the gods had graced Rome with their favours and their protection. Incense had perfumed the flames of sacrifice and veiled the sun with smoke; the blood of white oxen had spilled from axe-blows onto the earth; festivals of primordial antiquity had given order to the city's year. But then, over time, as the processions had come to be abandoned, so the rituals had been forgotten and the stones of the shrines grown mute. Horace had been only one of many to shudder at the sight of temples sharing in the general dilapidation of the city. 'The sanctuaries with their dark images stand ruined, befouled with smoke.'[104] Struggling to keep afloat during the difficult years that had followed his return from Philippi, haunted by his memories of citizen slaughtering citizen and impoverished by the loss of his lands, the poet had drawn the obvious conclusion. 'The gods, because neglected, have brought a whole multitude of evils on sorrowing Italy.'[105] Augustus, charged as he was by the heavens with purging the Republic of its sickness, fully concurred with this diagnosis. His repairs to the ancient shrine on the Palatine in which the 'spoils of honour' were kept had been only a start. Crumbling and roofless temples were an affront both to the gods and to the dignity of the Roman people: pustules upon the face of the city. Augustus, with the wealth of the world his to command, could well afford the necessary medicine. What had been decayed was to become pristine; what had been black was to become white; what had been mud-brick was to become marble. As the scaffolding came down from the temple of Apollo on the Palatine, so it went up across the rest of Rome. Even Livia, who sponsored the sprucing-up of a sanctuary on the Aventine much favoured by respectable matrons, got in on the act. As for the Princeps himself, he would end up funding the restoration of no fewer than eighty-two temples. If some were only given a lick of paint or a layering of stucco, then most were endowed with as handsome a makeover as the world's finest architects could provide. Entire mountains were levelled to provide them with the necessary supplies of stone. So, at any rate, ran the joke. It was beauty, not antiquity, that counted now. 'The temples of our ancestors were all well and good – but golden ones are more delightful. Majesty, after all, is what becomes a god.'[106]

And the gods themselves clearly concurred. By 17 BC, a decade on from the settlement that had seen Imperator Caesar named Augustus, it was evident that Rome had once again become a place hallowed by the favour of the heavens. 'The world was pacified. The rightful political order was restored. All stood easy and prosperous.'[107] As May turned to June, the Roman people were invited to celebrate a profound mystery: the turning of the centuries and the dawning of a new cycle of time. Entertainments were staged; chariot races held; lavish banquets thrown. First, though, for three days in succession, the gods were given their due of sustenance and blood; and by night, illumined by the torches which had been handed out free to the entire population of the city, the Princeps himself led the celebrations. To the Moerae, the three white-robed Fates who directed the city's destiny, he offered a sacrifice of lambs and goats; and then, to the goddess of childbirth, a gift of cakes. A golden age was being born – and just in case there was still anyone who had failed to take in the message, a poem composed specially for the occasion by Horace was sung on both the Capitol and the Palatine, with the aim of ramming it home. 'Grant riches, and progeny, and every kind of glory to the people of Romulus.'[108] Many who heard this prayer sounding out across the Forum, hymned by a choir of girls and boys of spotless probity, and framed by a skyline edged with gold and gleaming marble, would doubtless have reflected that the gods had already obliged. 'Truth, and Peace, and Honour, and our venerable tradition of Probity, and *Virtus*, long neglected, all venture back among us. Blessed Plenty too – why, here she is with her horn of abundance!'[109]

And still, over the course of the years that followed, it overflowed. Rome was fast becoming beautiful. The gods were not alone in being graced with home improvements. The Roman people, as they watched their native city grow ever less shabby, ever more resplendent, began to take for granted the apparently limitless coffers of their Princeps. His generosity seemed to know no bounds. When, for instance, the heirs of Pompey the Great found themselves too poverty-stricken to maintain the upkeep of their ancestor's great stone theatre, who should step in but Augustus? Other noble families too, knowing that they could not hope to compete in such stakes, had long since withdrawn from the fray. Whether it was building bath complexes on a scale vaster than any seen before, or renovating in an eye-poppingly sumptuous manner the hall in which the Roman people cast their votes, or else improving the city's roads, Augustus and his ever-loyal henchman Agrippa were the only show in town.

So selfless was the Princeps's concern for the good of his fellow citizens that even the memory of his own friends might be sacrificed to it. One such was Vedius Pollio, a financier who had done much to boost the tax efficiency of Rome's provinces in Asia Minor, and grown obscenely rich on the back of it. When he died in 15 BC, and left the Princeps the vast property that he had built on a spur above the Forum, Augustus had it ostentatiously flattened. The site was then given to his wife. Livia, no less conscious than her husband of her responsibilities towards the Roman people, had it rebuilt in splendid fashion, complete with colonnades and fountains, and presented to the delighted public. So, in the new age presided over by Caesar Augustus, was the selfish greed of plutocrats justly treated. 'An example had been well and truly made.'[110]

The death of Vedius, a one-time nobody who had profited from the carnage and upheavals of the civil wars to emerge as one of the wealthiest men in Rome, spoke of the passage of the years. Those who could remember a time before the crossing of the Rubicon, when citizens had contended with one another in a free Republic, were growing old. Late in 13 BC, when Lepidus passed away, many were surprised to discover that the former triumvir had not died years before. Formally stripped of his powers back in 36, and exiled to an obscure corner of Italy, he had spent two decades and more in wraith-like retirement. Only a single honour had been left to him: the office of *Pontifex Maximus*, the High Priest of Rome. Naturally, there was never any doubt as to his successor. The Roman people had long been pressing Augustus to strip Lepidus of the post; but the Princeps, sternly set against sacrilege, had refused. Now, in 12 BC, men and women from across Italy flocked to Rome to hail his election.

The new Pontifex, meanwhile, was moving with his customary eye for the main chance to turn the office to his own advantage. Tradition prescribed that he move into an official mansion in the heart of the Forum, where he could serve as guardian to the virgins who tended the eternal hearth-flame of the city. Augustus, who had not the slightest intention of abandoning the Palatine, instead settled upon a compromise as pious as it was self-serving: he had part of his house dedicated to the goddess Vesta. His private residence, connected as it already was to the great temple of Apollo, took on a new sheen of sanctity. Augustus himself moved one step closer to heaven.

The man who had once scandalised the guardians of Roman tradition by making himself consul at the tender age of nineteen was now in his fifties. Even as his statues continued to portray him as preternaturally fresh-faced, his wrinkles were growing deeper. Already, some of the closest partners of his youth were succumbing to age. Agrippa, exhausted by his labours, died only a few months after the election of Augustus as Pontifex; four years later, Maecenas was consigned to his grave. In his will, he requested his old friend to 'remember Horace as you do myself'[111] – and sure enough, when the poet too died fifty-nine days later, Augustus had him laid to rest near Maecenas's tomb.

Here, to a man notorious for his bouts of ill health, were ominous reminders of his own mortality; and yet, for all that, the Princeps did not die. Quite the opposite. Miraculously, as the decades slipped by, he seemed to be growing haler. Age, it turned out, agreed with him. Far from sapping his *auctoritas*, grey hair only burnished it. A veteran grown old in the service of his city: here was the kind of authority figure with whom the Roman people were instinctively familiar. In 3 BC, Augustus turned sixty. A few months later, he was elected consul for the first time in many years. Still, though, his fellow citizens were not done with paying him honour. In January, a delegation of plebeians travelled to his coastal retreat and begged him to accept a new title: 'Father of his Country'. Augustus refused. Then, on 5 February, all ranks of society came together to press the honour on him. When the Princeps, back in Rome, arrived at a theatre, everyone in the audience hailed him with the title. Shortly afterwards, at a meeting of the Senate, the assembled senators added their own voices. 'We join with the Roman people,' declared their spokesman, 'in saluting you as Father of our Country.' This time Augustus did not turn down the title. 'All that I ever hoped for,' he declared in a choked voice, 'I have now achieved.' And as he spoke, his eyes began to fill with tears.[112]

Imperator Caesar Augustus had embarked on his rise to power as the avenger of his deified father. 'That was his task, his duty, his priority.'[113] Now, forty years and more on, it was he who had become the father. Early that summer, on 12 May, the Princeps formally dedicated a building that, more than all the many others he had bestowed upon the Roman people, served as the monument to his extraordinary career. His temple to Mars the Avenger, vowed long before on the eve of Philippi, had been completed only after an inordinate length of time. Reluctant to stir up memories of his youthful confiscations of land, Augustus had shrunk from forcing through compulsory purchases. As a result, his agents had found themselves embroiled in any number of property disputes. Some owners had refused point-blank to sell. Strange angles, forced on the architect by this obduracy, had begun to appear in the outline of the development. Redesign had followed redesign. The delays had lasted years. In the end, Augustus's patience had snapped. He had ordered the temple finished, come what may. Even as the day of its dedication drew near, building materials were still being gathered up and paint slapped on. Yet no amount of last-minute hurry could impair its jaw-dropping impact. Augustus's great programme of renewal had achieved its supreme masterpiece. To a people whose descent from Mars was evident in the emergence of their city from backwoods obscurity to the rule of the world, he had paid his most splendid tribute: 'an achievement on a scale worthy of the god'.[114]

War had been the making of Augustus as it had been of Rome, and the Princeps did not shrink from acknowledging the fact. The duty he had owed his deified father was inscribed on the face of a gleaming new forum. Statues of the Julians, with Aeneas himself resplendent in the centre, stood positioned in a semicircle to one side of the temple of Mars the Avenger. Yet the drenching of Philippi in Roman blood was not the only vengeance commemorated in the great complex. So too was an altogether happier triumph. The standards lost by Crassus to the Parthians at last had a setting worthy of Augustus's feat in winning them back. Transferred from their makeshift home on the Capitol, they now adorned the inner sanctum of Mars's towering temple. No matter that it was Augustus who had redeemed them – the victory was one in which all the Roman people could share. Outside, gazing down from the front of the temple across the coloured flagstones of the Forum, a semi-naked Mars was portrayed with sword and spear in hand, his foot placed on the world. Augustus was not so vainglorious as to pretend that Rome's global sway was entirely down to himself.

Quite the opposite, in fact. Facing the statues of the Julians, on the far side of the Forum, was another half-ring of statues. In their centre stood Romulus, complete with the 'spoils of honour'; around him, forming a veritable hall of fame, all the many other heroes who had contributed to Roman greatness.[115] These, so Augustus declared, were the models who had served to inspire him in his service to Rome. His line of descent from them was quite as clear as that from the family of Julius Caesar. He embodied nothing alien, nothing remotely out of accord with the best of Roman practice. The same would doubtless be true of those 'who might follow him as Princeps'.[116] There had been no revolution. Rome past and Rome future: they met, and were reconciled, in the figure of a single man.

Imperator, Augustus, Father of his Country: the one-time Gaius Octavius was entitled to feel, as he presided over the dedication of his splendid new temple complex, that he had very little left to prove. Who now could reasonably doubt that he was, as he had always believed, the favourite of the heavens? 'You are the greatest ever Princeps.'[117] So Horace had written shortly before his death. This verdict had not been flattery – merely a statement of obvious fact. Augustus had given peace to his fellow citizens, reconciled them to the gods, and restored to them their hope.

Surely now nothing could go wrong?

3

THE EXHAUSTION OF CRUELTY

Back to Basics

Naturally, there were whisperings of scandal.

There always had been. Gossip was part of the air that citizens breathed. Wherever people gathered, they would pause and swap the rumours that passed for news. A story had only to be heard in the Forum for it to spread with remorseless inevitability out through the maze of the city's back-alleys, into workshops and narrow cul-de-sacs, and tiny, hidden squares where pigs rooted for garbage and fullers hung their washing out to dry. The Roman people had always had a puritanical streak. No vice was so private that it could be kept from them for long. Political life in Rome was not named *res publica* for nothing. The jeers and hisses of a crowd were sure to pursue even the most eminent of men caught up in any impropriety. Graffiti scrawled and scratched across the city served up to everyone who could read them such a relentless dishing of dirt that people fretted the sheer weight of it all might bring walls crashing down. Even the illiterate would shit on the monuments of those who had offended them. The Romans were a people with a rare genius for throwing mud.

No one, then, could possibly have stood at the head of their affairs for as long as Augustus had done, and not found his white toga marked along its hem with the occasional splash of filth. The sensational circumstances of his marriage to Livia remained vivid in the minds of his fellow citizens. A man capable of jumping someone else's pregnant wife was clearly capable of jumping anyone. Even though the precise details of his presumed affairs were hazy, Augustus's womanising was something widely taken for granted. Livia, far from making trouble, was said to have maintained her hold on her husband by turning a blind eye to his many adulteries, and keeping him well supplied with virgins. Friends of the Princeps, looking to extenuate this goatish behaviour, insisted that his affairs were the result of calculation, not of lust, and that he only ever bedded the wives of senators he wished to keep an eye upon. Others were not so sure. A man as promiscuous as Augustus was reputed to be seemed, to many citizens, lacking the self-control that was properly the mark of a Roman. Unchecked sexual appetites, while only to be expected in a woman – or, of course, a Greek – were hardly appropriate to a citizen steeled in the noblest traditions of the city. Energies devoted to sleeping around were better suited to serving the glory of the Roman people. Augustus's reputation as a serial adulterer, far from boosting the aura of his machismo, cast him instead in an effeminate and sinister light. No man could be reckoned truly a man who was the slave of his own desires. Playboys who chased after married women were well known to be womanish themselves. The Princeps, it was whispered, smoothed his legs by singeing off their hairs with red-hot nut shells.

A shocking detail, to be sure. Nevertheless, as Augustus himself appreciated, it could have been far worse. Compared to Antony, he had got off lightly. None of the allegations laid against him remotely began to compare with the deadly tidal wave of effluent that he himself had unleashed against his great rival. The damage done to his reputation was never critical. Indeed, the stories told of his effeminacy titillated less because they appeared plausible than because, in large part, they did not. Far from scorning the morals of those who slandered him, the Princeps shared them to the depths of his marrow – and the Roman people knew it. When Augustus let it be known that he wore clothes woven for him by his wife, no one thought to accuse the richest man in the world of hypocrisy for wearing homespun. Just as Livia had brought a touch of patrician class to his household, so also did she serve it as a living embodiment of antique virtues. As the partner of Augustus, no hint of adulterous passions ever attached to her. A woman who knew what it was to lose everything, she guarded her status as wife of the Princeps with a chaste and icy self-discipline. She understood full well that 'her looks, her words, her every action, were a focus of intense attention'.[1] Never seen in public without the *stola*, the long, voluminous and stiflingly cumbersome dress which served the Roman matron as the symbol of her modesty, Livia knew to perfection what her husband required of a woman. In private, she served as his closest confidante; in public, as a living emblem of piety and traditional values.

Admiration for the virtues associated by the Roman people with their stern and heroic past was the reverse face of their addiction to gossip. Wealth and pedigree had never served them as the exclusive determinant of status. 'The Romans did not think it proper that a man should be free to get married or have children merely as he pleased – nor that he should be permitted to live and indulge himself according to his own personal preferences and appetites.'[2] Surveillance in Rome was both relentless and officially sanctioned. Citizens had always been divided with great precision into classes – and behaviour unworthy of the class to which a man had been assigned would invariably see him demoted. The Princeps, as befitted his status at the summit of the pecking order, took this regulation of his fellow citizens very seriously indeed. The return of peace to Rome after the chaos and upheavals of civil war had also meant the restoration of state-determined hierarchies. In 28 BC, and then again twenty years later, Augustus submitted the entire civil population to a census. Not surprisingly, he kept a particularly beady eye on the top end of society. The census of 28 BC resulted in a wholesale slimming down of the Senate, which was then purged again in 19 BC. Mortifying though this naturally was for those expelled, it greatly enhanced the prestige of those who had made the cut. Augustus's ruthless streamlining boosted the dignity of the entire order. *Maiestas*, this was termed in Latin: the aura of majesty and greatness that, back in the days when a citizen's vote still counted for something, had been regarded as the prerogative of the Roman people as a whole. It was the Princeps himself, of course, who most formidably embodied *maiestas* – but not exclusively so. A Senate worthy to share with him in the heroic project of redeeming the Republic was a vital part of his purpose, after all. Not even Imperator Caesar Augustus could shoulder that particular burden alone.

Yet there remained a snag. The more exclusive an order the Senate became, the fewer senators there were to assist with the demands of a global empire. Clearly, then, it was essential to find an alternative reservoir of talent. The effective administration of the world required nothing less. Fortunately, even before establishing his regime, the Princeps had identified a possible solution. It was Maecenas, ever the trend-setter, who had blazed the trail. Immense though the responsibilities vested in him by Augustus had been, he had never held any official magistracy. Instead, rather than enter the Senate and compete for public office, he had rested content with the highest rank open to a private citizen: that of an *eques*, or knight. Once, back in the rugged early days of Rome, it was possession of a horse that had qualified a citizen to be registered among the city's elite; but that, of course, lay long in the past. Many knights, over the course of the previous century, had grown so fabulously rich on the back of empire that they had ended up boasting whole stables of thoroughbreds. With senators legally banned from dirtying their hands in the sordid business of overseas trade, the field had been left clear for equestrian financiers to gorge themselves on the wealth of Rome's new provinces. Then, amid the implosion of the Republic, the character of the order had begun to change. Plutocrats were joined by 'men made knights by the maelstrom of conflict'.[3] Officers who had fought on the winning side in the civil war; aristocrats from obscure Italian towns keen to better themselves; even, disconcertingly, the occasional son of a slave made good: all had come to sport the golden ring which marked a knight. Men such as these were the Princeps's kind of people. Tough and high-achieving, they constituted precisely what he needed: a ready officer-corps. Torn as he was between respect for the Senate as an order and a lurking suspicion of its individual members, Augustus could hardly help but warm to the new breed of equestrian. The hand of his friendship, as Maecenas could vouch, might bring many favours. Even as the Senate rejoiced in the brilliant and growing blaze of its *maiestas*, so, in the shadows, knights were quietly thriving. No longer, under Augustus, were commands and offices the sole preserve of elected magistrates. Gradually, obliquely, they were being privatised.

Such a policy, by its nature, could not possibly be acknowledged. Augustus himself, never appearing so conservative as when engaged in innovation, looked to the past as well as to the future. The more he broke with tradition by entrusting knights with public office, the more he masked the policy behind celebrations of their primordial purpose. Phantasmal cavalrymen in antique armour, charging down adversaries from the epic days of early Rome, haunted his imaginings. Those who betrayed this heritage were made to pay. When a knight was found to have cut off his two sons' thumbs, thereby invaliding them out of military service, the Princeps imposed on him an exemplary penalty. The wretched man was sold at public auction; then, bought by one of Augustus's proxies, he was banished in disgrace to the country. Nor was he alone in being expelled. Knights who failed to measure up to the exacting standards expected of them by the Princeps were quite as likely to be drummed out of their order as senators. Reviving a venerable custom, Augustus even subjected them to an annual inspection. Every 15 July, equestrians were obliged to parade through the streets of Rome, riding in serried ranks, as though just arrived from battle. Those with rewards for valour were expected to wear them. Those too old for the saddle were expected to come on foot. It was, most people agreed, 'a tremendous sight, and worthy of the greatness of Rome's dominion'.[4]

Not everyone, though. Some equestrians, even as they joined the parading of homespun, peasant virtues through the capital of the world, struggled to keep a straight face. Times had moved on. The hamlet of wooden huts and cattle byres ruled by Romulus was now a wonderland of gold and marble. 'We live in a civilised age. Rustic boorishness, of the kind displayed by our forefathers, is a thing of the past.'[5] So spoke a poet, youthful and chic, who had emerged in the second decade of Augustus's supremacy to become the toast of the city's *avant garde*: the authentic voice of Roman metrosexuality. His distaste for the life of the countryside so idealised by the Princeps was bred of personal experience. For all his urbanity and sophistication, there was a provincial quality to Publius Ovidius Naso – Ovid. He was not a native of Rome. Sulmo, a fat, lazy town some ninety miles east of the capital, was inhabited by a people who less than a century before had been enthusiastic participants in the Italian Revolt, and were notorious for the aptitude of their witches. Hemmed in all around by precipitous mountains, Sulmo was separated from the metropolis by forests teeming with wolves and bandits. Ovid's own family, although equestrian for several generations, had remained firmly based in their native town, big fish in a tiny pond. But then, as for so many others in Italy, everything had changed. With the rise to power of Augustus, dazzling new opportunities had opened up for families such as Ovid's. His father had seized on them with relish. Packing off his two sons to Rome, he had invested heavily in their education. When Ovid's elder brother died at twenty, Ovid himself was left alone to carry the burden of his father's ambition. 'The Senate House was waiting.'[6] The young man's heart, though, was never in it. 'I lacked both the physical toughness for such a career, and the aptitude. I flinched from the stresses of ambition.'[7] The stern demands placed on him by his father, the glorification by the Princeps of Rome's ancient past, the trumpeting of martial values – all left the young Ovid cold. It was not merely that he rejected them; he found them risible.

In this, he was recognisably of a new generation. Born a year after Julius Caesar's murder, Ovid had never known what it was to live in a free republic. Nor, though, did he have personal experience of the horrors endured by his elders: fighting amid foreign dust against fellow citizens; losing ancestral fields to strangers; watching cities burn. Rejoicing in the blessings of peace and prosperity brought by Caesar Augustus, Ovid knew what he had been spared, and was duly grateful for it. Yet he saw in them not a restoration of Rome's ancient and god-given order, but something very different: the essence of what it meant to be modern. 'The present,' he rejoiced, 'suits me down to the ground.'[8] In the cityscape fashioned by Augustus to serve as a mirror to the favour of the gods, and as a monument to the glory both of the Roman people and of himself, Ovid discovered a playground. The delight he took in it was exultant – but not of a kind to please the Princeps. His pastimes were altogether too edgy, too counter-cultural for that. When Ovid strolled up to Apollo's temple on the Palatine, or haunted the shady colonnades raised on the site of Vedius's palace, or visited the arches of Pompey's theatre, it was not to admire the architecture. He was scoping out girls.

To boast of this, as Ovid freely did, and to pose as a universal 'tutor in love',[9] was highly shocking to a moral and iron-willed people such as the Romans. Time was, long before Augustus brought in his own census, that a senator had been demoted for kissing his own wife in public. Only when startled by thunder, one venerable moralist had grimly joked, was it permissible for a woman to fall into the arms of her husband.[10] Standards had eased over the years; but the notion that a citizen might freely abandon a career of service to his fellows, devoting himself instead to the arts of the bedroom, retained its power to shock. Ovid, with almost wilful glee, paraded his scorn of what he mocked as priggish convention. 'Not for me our traditional virtues.'[11] Caesar Augustus, celebrating the greatest and most spectacular triumph ever witnessed in Rome, had ridden through the capital parading the trophies of victory won from the Queen of Egypt. Ovid, beating himself up for slapping his girlfriend, imagined her led bruised and pale in a very similar triumph, cheered on by watching crowds. 'Hooray for the brave, bold man – he's vanquished a girl!'[12]

A joke, as Ovid well knew, that could hardly fail to bring a smile to the lips of those sophisticated enough to grasp his meaning. Mockery of the great was as much a tradition in salons as it was in slums. Augustus, who affected to have restored freedom of speech together with all the other liberties lost during the civil wars, was hardly one to bother himself with the occasional fleabite. This did not mean, though, that poets – or anyone else – had licence to write whatever they liked. Appointed as he was by the gods to the great task of saving and regenerating the Roman people, Augustus could not possibly tip the wink at any corrosion of their ancestral values. A citizen was made, not born. A male, after all, was not necessarily a man. Just as Rome had hauled herself up from powerless obscurity to the rule of the world, so was it necessary for each and every Roman to be forged over the course of his life to the requisite standard of masculinity. Softness, both of body and spirit, was a perpetual menace. It had to be guarded against at all costs. Augustus had not blessed the city with monuments of dazzling beauty and polish only to see them become a cruising ground for lounge lizards. The fruits of peace would be worthless if all they bred was an epicene obsession with sex.

'Everything comes down to this: self-control.'[13] Which did not mean, of course, that a citizen was expected to live like a eunuch. Quite the contrary. A Roman penis was potent, masterful, prodigious. In a city where the phallus was everywhere to be seen, protecting doorways as a symbol of good luck, guarding crossroads or scaring off birds in gardens, ramrod size was much admired. A generously endowed man hitting the bath-house might well be greeted with 'a round of nervous applause'.[14] A citizen equipped with such a weapon, particularly a young one, 'in whom a degree of animal-spirits was natural',[15] could hardly be expected to keep it permanently sheathed. Even the sternest of moralists acknowledged this. Why else, after all, were there whores? A brothel was not so different from a latrine: dirty and disreputable, yes, but serving an essential purpose as a receptacle of human waste. A man could no more be expected to ignore his sexual needs than he could a full bladder. Not for nothing did the same word, *meio*, mean both 'urinate' and 'ejaculate'. A thrust or two, deep and quick, like the stabbing of a sword into the guts, 'right the way up to the hair and the hilt of the balls',[16] and the business would be done. Whether into the vagina, the anus or the mouth, it made no real difference – just so long as it was masterful. Nor did it greatly matter who took the penis thrust – man or woman, boy or girl – provided that one crucial qualification, one essential safeguard, was respected. Free-born Romans, male and female both: these were strictly, absolutely off-limits.

The taboo was as potent as it was ancient. Cleaving to it was how the Romans defined themselves as a people. They regarded purity, 'that chiefest prop of men and women alike',[17] not as a drab or passive virtue, but as something lambent, edged about by flame. Like the hearthfire which it was the sacred duty of every Roman wife to guard, it could not be extinguished without terrible sacrilege. This was why, of all the offences that an unchecked sexual appetite might prompt a citizen to commit, there was none so unsettling to his fellows as adultery. To cuckold a man was not merely to take possession of his wife; it was also to shaft the husband himself. Lurking in the stories whispered about Augustus's affairs with women from senatorial families was a bitter reflection on his dominance. No one, after all, could hope for recompense from the Princeps. Whatever the truth of the gossip, nothing better rammed home to men their impotence before his greatness than that it rendered him immune from the right of a cuckold to vengeance. This, as prescribed by tradition, was of a ferociously brutal order. The wife caught *in flagrante*, so one famously stern moralist had ruled, might be murdered on the spot.[18] The lover too, according to some – although others, more liberal, recommended simply castrating him, or perhaps shoving a mullet up his anus. The threat of violence, savage and potentially murderous, hung over every adulterous contact.

Or did it? There was, perhaps, for those up to speed with the times, something just a little bit provincial, just a little bit musty, about an antique sexual taboo. 'How like a rustic, to get upset when your wife cheats on you.'[19] So Ovid, a man with his finger on the pulse of high society, observed with practised smoothness. Yet if the cuckold who kicked up a fuss was a boor, then so too was the one who failed to a spoilsport. The various prohibitions and perils erected by custom in the path of the adulterer were liable to strike the seasoned connoisseur of erotic pleasure less as deterrents than as incentives, spicing up the fun. 'We always want what we're not allowed.'[20] Ovid, in offering this sage observation, was putting his finger on a mocking truth. Forbidden fruit tasted the sweetest. 'Prohibitions, trust me, only encourage bad behaviour.'[21] This, in a city as addicted to gossip as Rome, was a paradox that plenty were prepared to swallow. Speculation as to what might be going on in the city's most exclusive bedrooms naturally transfixed the public. That adultery was regarded by the upper classes as one tremendous game, in which the rules were there to be broken, and the measure of cool was to smuggle a lover into the marital bed, was widely taken for granted. No smoke without fire, after all. Proofs of the adulterous and effeminate character of Rome's fast set were everywhere to be seen. In the dandyishly loose way they wore their togas; in their clean nails, sprucely clipped nasal hair and sinister lack of body odour; above all, in the oiled sheen of their limbs. For a man to shave his armpits was, everyone could agree, simply good manners; but to do as Augustus was said to have done, and depilate the legs, was disgusting, plain and simple. Body hair was the mark of a man. Everyone knew, though, that adulterers cared nothing for that. Smooth skin, not a pelt, was what they brought to seduction. It was all most deviant and alarming. Even Ovid might sometimes be provoked to pontificate: 'Men are all such fashion-victims these days that, really, we can hardly blame women for feeling the pressure.'[22]

None of which stopped the poet himself from cheerily offering grooming tips to his male as well as his female fans. Ovid, though,

did not have the care of Roman morals in his charge. Frivolous metrosexuality, in the opinion of the man who did, was part of the
problem, not a solution. Augustus, who had brought order where
previously there was chaos, who had lavished on his fellow citizens
the riches of conquered kingdoms, who had transformed their city
into a capital of unrivalled beauty and splendour, did not care to
think that his labours might merely have contributed to a softening
of their ancestral virtues. Such a prospect was too appalling to be
borne. The Romans were either the heirs of their upright forefathers
or they were nothing. The Princeps's ambition was simple: that his
fellow citizens should be true to all that was best about their past.
They were the Romans: the lords of the world, the people of the
toga. This, in the mirror that he had set up to his fellow citizens,
fashioned out of monuments, and festivals, and all the various fruits
of peace, was the reflection that he wished them always to catch of
themselves.

Yet what if they caught something else? Perhaps there lay a warning in a recent scandalous development in the field of interior
decoration. In bedrooms across Rome, walls and ceilings were coming
to be lined with mirrors. Even beyond the limits of the city, out in his
rural retreat among the Sabine hills, Horace had signed up to the
craze. Notoriously, so had a billionaire by the name of Hostius
Quadra. The mirrors on his walls boasted a particularly distinctive feature: everything reflected in them appeared larger than it actually
was. 'So it was that the freak made a show of his own deviancy.'[23] As
one girl gave him a blow-job, and he licked out a second, so his anus,
in a hideous desecration of all that a Roman should properly be, was
shafted by a man with a giant cock – which, seen in the mirror,
appeared possessed of truly gargantuan size, 'larger than his capacity
to take'.[24] To groom, depilate and titivate like a woman was one thing;
but to be fucked like one was a hideous extreme of degradation. What
else was it, after all, but the willing surrender of everything that made
a Roman a man? In the grotesquely reflected couplings of Hostius
Quadra was to be caught the spectacle of a terrifying abyss, one into

which any citizen who surrendered to self-indulgence might end up sinking.

'Every part of me is given over to filth.'[25] The monstrous quality of this boast ensured that Augustus, when Hostius Quadra eventually came to be murdered by his own slaves, refused to have them punished. As a statement of the Princeps's disapproval, this could hardly have been more ringing. Another entrant had been added to his public hall of shame. Yet there was an irony to the billionaire's fate that Augustus himself no doubt found deeply troubling. By venerable tradition, the regulation of morals within a household was a matter for the citizen who stood at its head. It was not the business of anyone else to get involved. A Roman unable to control the behaviour of his own dependants barely ranked as a Roman at all. How, then, to judge a city in which it was slaves who punished the master? As one, it seemed, in which ancient certainties had been disconcertingly upended. In which fathers could no longer be trusted to discipline their children, nor husbands their wives. In which the morals of the Roman people required the regulation, not just of custom, not just of ancestral example, but – shamingly – of law.

A challenge that Augustus felt he could not duck. When Horace, looking to explain the implosion of the Republic, had identified the cause as a septic addiction to adultery, he had done so in total seriousness. Fond of a mirrored bedroom he may have been himself – but he had no doubt that the origins of the civil war, that supreme catastrophe, had lain in deviancy and licence. 'Such was the wellspring of the calamities that flooded our country, our people.'[26] What else, indeed, could it possibly have been? Everyone knew where the ultimate roots of crisis in a state lay: not in constitutional or social tensions, let alone in the unfathomable workings of finance, but in the degeneration of its morals. Seen in this light, the depravities of monsters such as Hostius Quadra served as an ominous warning. The pus had not been wholly drained from the body politic. Beneath the brilliant show of the city rebuilt by the Princeps, it was still festering and breeding. How, then, charged as he was by the gods with the salving of Rome back to health, could Augustus not enforce an iron-bitted cure? 'All very well wringing our hands – but we need measures to fit the crime.'[27]

So it was, soon after his return in triumph from the East, bringing with him the standards lost by Crassus, that the Princeps had made his move. In 18 BC, a law was passed that aimed to regulate the marital behaviour of the upper classes. The heroic early days of Rome, when men had wed only virtuous matrons, breeding vast numbers of infant citizens on them for the good of the Republic, were to be revived by means of legislation. Bachelorhood, social *mésalliances*, childlessness: all were severely penalised. Then, a few months later, came a law that poked its nose even more intrusively into the affairs of senators and equestrians. Adultery was made a public offence. Cuckolds were legally obliged to divorce their cheating wives. Those who did not, whether out of embarrassment or perhaps, more sinisterly, because they took a sordid pleasure in the business of their own humiliation, were to be charged with pimping. Adulterers, meanwhile, were to suffer swingeing financial penalties and exile to an island. Adulteresses too – and banned from ever again marrying a free-born citizen. Even their dress was to proclaim their shame. Not for them the *stola*, that emblem of womanly rectitude. 'When they step out, it is generally in a dark toga – to distinguish them from matrons.'[28] A bitter degradation. The toga was not only the dress of a male citizen; it was also the most distinctive costume worn by a whore. No longer deserving of the honour and respect due a Roman matron, the convicted adulteress was to be ranked legally with the lowest of the low: prostitutes, madams, even actresses. Like them, she was to take her place among the moral underclass, the dregs of society – the *infames*.

Smouldering resentment among the aristocracy, who viewed the legislation as an assault both on their own privacy and on Roman tradition, did nothing to affect the Princeps's resolve. He knew his duty. Long before the joyous moment in 2 BC, when by universal acclamation the title 'Father of his Country' was awarded to Augustus, his status had become self-evident. He was, in effect, 'a universal parent'.[29] Like the model of a father, he had chided, guided and loved the Roman people. Licence had been tamed. Effeminacy and adultery had been reined in. 'Households had been rendered chaste, cleansed of depravity, and all the stains of misbehaviour checked by custom and law.'[30] There certainly seemed no need for the Father of his Country, a few weeks after his tear-choked acceptance of the title, to dread 17 March, the annual festival of Liber. Once, when he had still been merely one of two rival warlords, things had been different. Back then, when the devotees of Antony's divine and disturbing patron celebrated the god's festival, bearing in wild procession through the streets a giant phallus, the menace to ancestral virtues would have been palpable. Horrified conservatives had been attempting to geld the worship of Liber ever since its first manifestation in Rome, almost two centuries before. It was all wine, and late nights, and debauch. Appetites, no matter how deviant, were satisfied without heed to propriety. Everybody slept with everybody else. A more scandalous mockery of Roman values it was hard to imagine. Yet now, with Antony long dead, and every citizen a dependant of the Father of his Country, it was mockery that stood defeated, Roman values triumphant. Two months after the festival of Liber, in the new forum that he had peopled with statues of the city's antique heroes and adorned with battle trophies, Augustus dedicated his great temple to Mars. Companion of legionaries in the line of battle, the rapist of Romulus's mother, swift and brutal in all that he did, the god offered as stern a model of masculinity as Liber did not. Of one thing, at any rate, the Roman people could be confident. Mars was not the kind to depilate himself.

Beyond the great wall which served the god's temple as a flood barrier, though, the tides of appetite surged on. In hallways and courtyards, and under the noses of stern fathers, secret assignations were still being made. Amid stifled laughter, those in the know continued to whisper reports of scandalous doings. Meanwhile, in the ancient forum, the statue of Marsyas, that servant of Liber, stood where he had always done: a symbol of licence at its most defiant.

'Set strictures on a person all you like, but the mind remains adulterous.' So observed Ovid, pushing as ever at the boundaries of what it was acceptable to say. 'You cannot regulate desire.'[31] Time would soon discover whether he was right or not.

Family Trees

One day, it was said, shortly after Livia's second betrothal, a remarkable event occurred. An eagle, swooping down over where she was sitting, dropped a white chicken into her lap. Even more astonishingly, the hen – which was perfectly unharmed – had a sprig of fresh laurel in its beak. An awesome portent, self-evidently. Bird and laurel were both duly removed for safekeeping to a Claudian estate just outside Rome, at Prima Porta, on a promontory above the Tiber. Here, the hen produced a brood of chicks, while the sprig of laurel, planted in one of the villa's borders, sprouted to luxuriant effect. The implication of the episode, as time went by and Livia's hold on Augustus tightened, appeared evident enough to most people: 'that she was destined to hold the power of Caesar in a fold of her robe, and keep him under her thumb'.[32]

To some, though, the mysteriously burgeoning bush hinted at a different meaning. The laurel was no ordinary tree. Lightning was powerless to strike it; its leaves served to fumigate spilt blood; it was sacred to Apollo. All of which made it a perfect emblem of Augustus – and sure enough, when the Senate awarded him the name in 27 BC, they also decreed that his house be publicly adorned with laurel, 'veiling the doors, wreathing the holy gates with a chaplet of dark leaves'.[33] Soon, it began to seem sacrilege for anyone else to sport it. As for Augustus himself, only the laurel dropped into Livia's lap would do. Celebrating his three great triumphs, the Princeps had held one of its branches in his hand, and been wreathed in its leaves.

The Julians and Claudians under Augustus

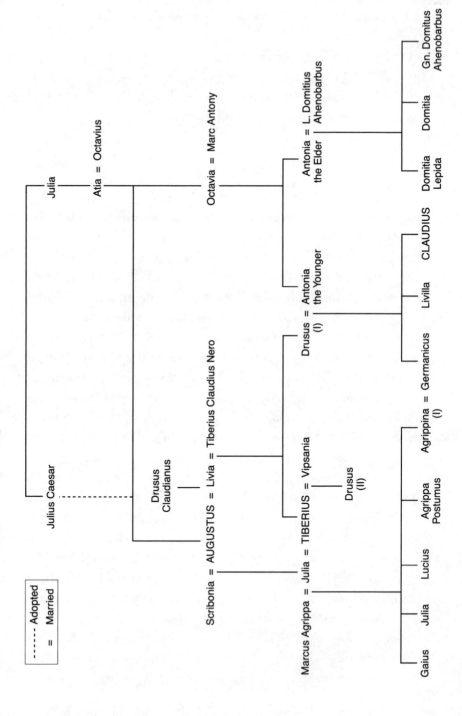

Compared to the blaze of such greatness, the glimmering of other men's victories inevitably came to seem as nothing. Crassus, after celebrating his own triumph, had vanished into obscurity. The days were passing when even the most blue-blooded of nobles could expect to ride through Rome crowned with laurel. It was those who stood closest to the Princeps who understood this best. Agrippa, although the greatest general of his generation, had consistently refused a triumph. He knew better than to upstage Augustus. 'Practised in obedience to that one man as he was, he aimed for the obedience of everybody else in turn.'[34] Between the traditional show of power and the reality, the gap was widening fast. Soon enough, even those who lacked Agrippa's acuity had been brought to recognise this. In 19 BC, a general by the name of Lucius Cornelius Balbus paraded through the streets of Rome in recognition of his victory over a tribe of Africans. It marked the end of an era. Never again would a private citizen celebrate a triumph.

Did this mean, though, that in the future only Augustus himself would have the right to the honour? Perhaps not. Something more than laurel, after all, had been dropped into Livia's lap. So full of squawking white chickens was the villa to which the original hen had been removed that it came to be known as 'The Coop'.[35] Clearly it was foreordained that Augustus should have many descendants. Nevertheless, a puzzle remained. Even though it was Livia who had welcomed the white hen into her lap, and she already had two sons, she seemed unable to give her second husband an heir. The older she grew, the clearer it became that Augustus was going to be left with just one child: a girl. Julia, his daughter by the cantankerous Scribonia, certainly provided him with a useful pawn in the great game of his dynastic ambitions; but a pawn was not enough. Augustus, like the head of any other household, required a male heir. So it was, taking a leaf out of his own great-uncle's book, that he had looked to his sister. Octavia, much admired and impeccably virtuous, had played a key role in the crisis that had led up to Actium. Married to Antony as a token of the compact between the two triumvirs, she had then

115

been rejected by him in favour of the Queen of Egypt, sent packing back to Rome and ignominiously divorced. Throughout it all she had maintained perfect dignity; and when, in the wake of her brother's victory over her erstwhile husband, she had consented to bring up the dashing young Iullus Antonius, Antony's son by an earlier wife, the Roman people were only confirmed in their admiration for her as a paragon of womanhood. The young Antonius had duly been raised alongside Octavia's children. Two of these, Antonia the Elder and Antonia the Younger, were his own half-sisters. The others were Octavia's by her first husband – and one of these children was a boy. Marcus Claudius Marcellus was handsome, charismatic, and touched by the mystique of his distant ancestor, the war hero who had once captured the 'spoils of honour': qualities more than fit to tickle his uncle's fancy. In 29 BC, the boy had ridden alongside the Princeps as he celebrated his triumph. Two years later, he had been given a taste of active service in Spain. Then, in 25 BC, had come the ultimate mark of favour: marriage to the fourteen-year-old Julia. Augustus, it seemed, had anointed his heir.

Time, though, would see him shrink from the implications of this decision. In 23 BC, as he was lying on his sickbed, he had slipped off his signet ring and pressed it into the palm, not of Marcellus, but of Agrippa. Augustus, who knew what it was to be plunged as a young man into the snake-pit of Roman politics, had clearly doubted his nephew's ability to survive and thrive in it as he had done. That, though, was hardly the limit of his anxieties. More than the future of his own household lay at stake, after all. Any heir of his would have a claim to the rule of the world. Yet here loomed a paradox. The bundle of powers and honours that Augustus had won for himself was nothing that could be passed on readily to a successor. Even to make the attempt would be to confirm what he had spent so long denying: the brute fact of his autocracy. No matter how battered and traumatised by civil war, the Roman people were not prepared to tolerate the rule of a king. Augustus was merely the first citizen of a free republic: such was the universal conceit. Only a man who shared in his prestige could hope, in the final reckoning, to succeed him as Princeps.

Marcellus, popular and glamorous though he was, did not yet rank as such a figure. Nor, as it turned out, would he ever. A few months after Augustus, defying the odds, had been successfully nursed back to health, Marcellus fell sick in his turn. Death, cheated of the uncle, claimed the nephew instead. Devastated, Octavia retired from all public appearances, and was said never to have smiled again. The Roman people shared in her grief. The memory of Marcellus, so promising, so lustrous, so young, would long be cherished. Perhaps, in the sheer scale of the public mourning, the glimpse was to be caught of a new age: one in which the blaze of Augustus's charisma, aureate and superhuman as it was, would serve to illumine every member of his family. What were the lilies and the bright flowers scattered in memory of Marcellus, if not a tribute paid to the radiant dawning of this light? Even in the blackness of death, the young man's profile appeared back-lit. The effulgence that haloed it was that of the *Domus Augusta* – the 'August Family' of the god-like Princeps.

All of which ensured that the widowed Julia, still only sixteen, could not possibly be left single for long. There was, in effect, a single candidate to hand. Augustus had already signalled as much back when he had given Agrippa his ring. 'Kill him or make him your son-in-law'[36] – such was the cheerily cynical advice of Maecenas. Augustus, who relied far too much on his old *consigliere* even to contemplate the first option, duly went for the second. Despite already being married to one of Julia's cousins, Agrippa obediently divorced her, taking the Princeps's daughter as his wife. The marriage, in the event, proved a great success. To Agrippa it served as public confirmation of his pre-eminent status, not merely as the deputy but the heir-apparent of Caesar. Augustus, meanwhile, was provided with a perfect opportunity to hedge his bets. Even as the laurel bush planted at Prima Porta flourished and spread, so was Julia doing her filial duty by giving birth to a succession of children. Two were girls: one named Agrippina after her father, and the second, with an even more notable lack of originality, Julia. But there was more — much more. In 20 BC, Julia had given Augustus his first grandson, a healthy young boy called Gaius. Three years later came a second, Lucius. The Princeps was ecstatic. No sooner had Lucius been born than he adopted both brothers. Now at last he had his sons.

Agrippa, whatever his private feelings, did not complain. He grasped perfectly how much brighter the prospects of Gaius and Lucius would blaze for bearing the name of Caesar. He knew too that he remained the heir presumptive. In 18 BC, he had even been granted a share of the *tribunicia potestas*, powers that were among the most formidable of those wielded by the Princeps. The road ahead appeared clear at last. When the Princeps died, Agrippa would step into his shoes; and when Agrippa died, Gaius Caesar. This, in a great family like the Julians, was how arrangements and alliances had always been fashioned. Far from promoting some sinister brand of hereditary monarchy, the Princeps's plans for his family were of a thoroughly traditional kind. The bonds of loyalty and obligation that Augustus saw as securing the future of Rome were such as any true-born citizen could value and respect. Who was there, ploughing the fields and tending the gardens only lately fertilised by civil bloodshed, to argue with that?

Not many, as it turned out. The Roman people's devotion to Marcellus turned out to have been no flash in the pan. When Agrippa, exhausted by his many exertions, died in 12 BC, the loss of the man whom Augustus had been banking upon to succeed him immediately won novel and eager attention for the next generation of the August Family. Fascination with the Princeps's grandchildren was widespread. There was certainly no lack of them. Julia, who had been pregnant when her husband died, had ended up giving birth to a third son: Agrippa Postumus, as he was inevitably known. It was his two older brothers, though, who were the real darlings of the Roman people. Although Gaius was eight and Lucius only five, anticipation of their future greatness served to cloak both boys in potent glamour. This was something new. Children had never before demanded much attention in Rome. Even the most precocious of debutants on the political stage – Scipio, Pompey, Augustus himself – had already come of age when they first made their entrance. It was the measure of the Princeps's aura that it continued to bathe all the members of his household – even the youngest – in its light. Enthusiasm for the two infant princes exceeded all expectations. Paraded whenever there was a requirement for the August Family to be seen, they embodied for the Roman crowds a winning combination of magnetism and boyishness. Here, in this popularity of theirs, was all that Augustus could possibly have hoped for. Adopted as the people's favourites, Gaius and Lucius offered to their grandfather a precious reassurance that heredity might after all be viable. The notion of a ruling dynasty, it seemed, was not entirely beyond the pale.

Except that Augustus himself still felt torn. In 6 BC, when the Roman people voted for the fourteen-year-old Gaius to become consul, he was appalled. Summoning an assembly, he berated them for their frivolity. The pleasure that he took in Gaius's popularity competed in his heart with sterner impulses. Just as he had shrunk from entrusting the rule of the world to Marcellus, so now he flinched from placing it irrevocably in the hands of an untempered boy. Augustus had not laboured for decades to restore the noblest and most exacting traditions of the Republic, only to make a mockery of them himself. The loss of Agrippa was painfully, bitterly felt. Yet how to replace him? His old comrade had possessed rare capabilities. Loyalty to the Princeps himself; flinty virtues of the kind that would have been familiar to Romulus; experience such as could only be forged at the head of legions, steeling mind and body alike in the service of Roman greatness: these had been Agrippa's qualities. What odds on finding a second such paragon? Impossibly long, it might have seemed.

And yet, as so often in the career of the Princeps, the gods appeared to be smiling on him. A solution to the problem of how best to meet the loss of his trusted deputy was staring him in the face. The obvious replacement could hardly have been more ready to hand: a perfect candidate to play Agrippa's role. From infancy, he had grown up a member of the August Family itself; and from the age of sixteen, when he had accompanied Augustus on his campaign in the wilds of northern Spain, he had devoted himself to the service of the Roman people. Seasoned in the business of both war and state, he was a man who had already achieved much on behalf of his fellow citizens. Now, it seemed, he was primed to achieve much more, in the service both of the Princeps and of Rome. There was really only a single drawback. Whereas Agrippa had always been Augustus's creature, from a background so humble that the disdainful nobility had scorned to attend his funeral, Livia's son Tiberius Claudius Nero was head of the most celebrated and brilliant family in Roman history. The son both of a Nero and of a Pulcher, the blood of the Claudians flowed doubly in his veins. Such a man had expectations that owed nothing to Augustus.

Livia's second marriage had not diminished one jot the loyalty that she felt to her ancestral line. Moving into her new husband's home, she had made sure to take her two boys with her. Tiberius and Drusus had grown up doubly privileged, as stepsons of the Princeps and as heirs to the incomparable traditions of their Claudian forebears. Naturally, there had been the odd indignity to swallow. Accompanying Marcellus in his stepfather's triumph, for instance, the young Tiberius had been obliged to ride on the left-hand, less prestigious side. Yet slights such as this were vastly outweighed by the advantages to be had from their mother's marriage to Augustus. Unlike most other heirs to the great dynasties of the Republic, Tiberius and Drusus did not have to kick their heels in the gilded cage of Rome. Instead, they were permitted to embark on careers of the kind that only a generation before would have been taken for granted as the birthright of their class. In the Alps, in the Balkans, in the forests and bogs of Germany, the two brothers won a succession of glorious victories. Of these, it was the accomplishments of Drusus that glittered the more brightly, those of Tiberius that were the harder-won. The younger brother, to whom charm came easily, had a talent never possessed by the elder for making himself loved; and yet

Augustus, who would often complain behind Tiberius's back of his 'austere and uncompromising disposition',[37] understood what it signified, and respected it. To serve as head of the Claudians was no light responsibility. Tiberius, who combined the hardiness of a natural soldier with the aptitudes and interests of a scholar, was uncompromisingly old-fashioned. The codes and standards of behaviour that had first set his people, back in the heroic days of Appius Claudius, on the road to the rule of the world, animated him in everything that he did. To Tiberius, the Republic that Augustus claimed to have nursed back to health was no fiction, no empty word, but rather the living essence of what it meant to be a Roman. The Princeps, who affected to believe the same thing, had no problem with this nostalgia for Rome's traditional order. Quite the contrary: it only confirmed him in his high regard for Tiberius as a man of principle. So it was, in the wake of Agrippa's death, that he had issued an order to his stepson. Take the action, Tiberius was instructed, that would signal to the world his new and favoured status. Divorce his wife; marry Julia; become not just the stepson but the son-in-law of the Princeps.

Yet there remained limits to what even Augustus could command. Licensed though he was as head of the August Family to meddle all he pleased in the marital arrangements of its various members, Tiberius hardly made for an easy puppet. While he had been left with no choice but to take Julia as his wife, he did not have to pretend that he liked it. Already married prior to Agrippa's death to his daughter, Vipsania, Tiberius had found the separation a wretched experience. The couple had been happy: Vipsania had given her husband both a son, named Drusus after his uncle, and her devotion. Tiberius, who normally made sure to keep his emotions on a tight leash, had found it impossible to conceal his agony at the separation. Chancing to meet with Vipsania some time later, he followed her with such a look of hangdog bereavement that orders came from on high to ensure that it never happened again. The causes of Tiberius's unhappiness, though, ran deeper than divorce from a much-loved wife. The role Augustus expected of him could not help but be profoundly humiliating to a Claudian. To lurk in the wings as a potential caretaker, and to hear in the cheers and applause that greeted a pair of untested boys whenever they appeared how much more popular they were than him, were no easy experiences for so proud a man. Illusions that on a distant frontier might conceivably have some life in them were hard to sustain in the presence of two princelings. Torn between his loyalty to Augustus and his contempt for the monarchy so patently embodied by Gaius and Lucius, Tiberius did not find Rome a happy place to be. Unsurprisingly, he preferred distant, dangerous frontiers. There, at any rate, the values that he prized still had a role to play. Not only that, but he did not have to spend time with his wife.

Which in turn was a great relief for her. Julia, strong-armed by her father into a third marriage, was as different from her dour and dutiful new husband as it was possible for two people brought up in the same household to be. True, she had quite fancied Tiberius once, back when she was still married to Agrippa – or so it was said. Julia was the kind of woman who attracted such gossip. Wilful, sophisticated and high-spirited, she was much loved for her generosity of spirit, and much admired for her intelligence and wit. Far from dismissing the rumours of adultery, she dared to mock the censoriousness of those who spread them. How could the stories that she had cheated on Agrippa possibly be true, she was once asked, when Gaius and Lucius looked so very like him? 'Why,' she answered, 'because I only ever take on passengers after the cargo-hold has been loaded.'[38] The joke, in light of everything that her father stood for, could hardly have been more shocking. It certainly helped to confirm all with a taste for boldness and subversion in their affection for her. The first woman to have the sacred blood of Augustus flowing in her veins, she was also the first to make play with what that might mean in practice. Not for Julia the hypocrisies with which Livia so soberly veiled herself. Scolded for not emulating her father's ostentatious frugality, she only laughed. 'While he may forget that he is Caesar, I never forget that I am Caesar's daughter.'[39]

Caesar himself, unsurprisingly, was not amused. When the Princeps declared that he had 'two wayward daughters to put up with, Julia and the Roman Republic',[40] his tetchiness was laid revealingly bare. The challenges of fatherhood were many. In his dealings with his fellow citizens, Augustus laid claim to the rights and responsibilities of a parent; conversely, in making arrangements for his daughter, he could never treat her as though she were merely his child. By keeping her in his marriage-bed, Tiberius was serving the needs of the Princeps no less surely than he did when off slaughtering barbarians. Augustus, who had briefly contemplated pairing Julia up with an obscure and inoffensive knight, so anxious was he to keep the mother of his heirs from ambitious paramours, had never knowingly failed to neutralise a problem. Tiberius and Julia both knew this well enough. In the first years of their marriage, the couple duly struggled to put a good face on matters. When Tiberius left for a provincial command in the Balkans, Julia went with him. Shortly afterwards, she gave birth to a son. On her husband's return to Rome, she joined with Livia in hosting a banquet for the leading women of the city in his honour, while Tiberius himself feasted the people on the Capitol. All might have seemed well enough.

But it was not. The fissure between the couple was widening all the time. Between the witty, quicksilver Julia and her husband, 'who ever since a child had been far too serious and austere for jokes', there was a natural lack of empathy.[41] Then came two bereavements in quick succession. First, they lost their son; then, as Livia and Julia were preparing a second banquet, this time in honour of Drusus's return from the front, news arrived from Germany. Drusus was dead. His horse had rolled on him, his leg had been crushed and gangrene had set in.* Tiberius, alerted to the news, had ridden hundreds of miles through barely pacified territory, accompanied by a single guide, and reached his brother just before he died. As a display of fraternal love,

---

* Or possibly he suffered internal injuries. 'He died on his way to the Rhine of some illness,' is Dio's helpful version of what happened (55.1.4).

it was worthy of the noblest traditions of their ancestors – and fittingly so, for Drusus too had been a great admirer of republican virtues. No effeminate extremes of mourning, then, for the bereaved Tiberius. Instead, as though walking through the landscape of some ancient annal, he escorted the corpse back to the capital on foot, dry-eyed, grim-set. Such were the obsequies appropriate to a Roman hero. 'It was not only in war that discipline had to be maintained, but in mourning as well.'[42] Yet everywhere, to Tiberius's disgust, the corpse of Drusus was greeted by wild displays of emotional incontinence. Even the soldiers wept. Arriving back in Rome, Tiberius's sense of living out of time, in a world neglectful of all that had made the city great, grew ever more oppressive. True to his heritage as a Claudian, he had laboured tirelessly in the cause of the Roman people, on remote frontiers, amid dripping forests, in rough-hewn camps – and yet the glory that this had won him was tarnished. In 7 BC he was granted a triumph, and a year later the grant of *tribunicia potestas* that Agrippa had once enjoyed: honours that Tiberius found so delusory as to seem mocking. The cheers that followed him as he rode in his triumphal chariot through Rome were faint compared to those that greeted the teenage Gaius; the awesome powers of a tribune did not inhibit his wife from looking down her Julian nose at him. Everything about his situation, to a man of his pride and prickliness, was insupportable.

In 6 BC, five years into his marriage, Tiberius finally snapped. The grant of *tribunicia potestas*, which to the outside world appeared the mark of his greatness, plunged him into despair. When Augustus, making clear that he had only ever approved it in the first place because he wished his son-in-law to shoulder the more tedious and demanding of his responsibilities, ordered Tiberius east on a diplomatic mission, he was met with a blunt refusal. Unused to taking no for an answer, the Princeps reiterated his instructions. Tiberius promptly went on hunger strike. He wished to lay down all his public offices, he announced. He wished to retire. Furious and baffled, Augustus demanded openly in the Senate that he change his mind.

Livia, even more appalled by her son's wilfulness, entreated him in private. Tiberius remained obdurate. Eventually, after a four-day standoff, it was Augustus who blinked first. As though to rub his victory home, Tiberius then promptly headed east – not as the deputy of Caesar, but as a private citizen. Settling on the Greek island of Rhodes, he there devoted himself to all the traditional pleasures of a dignified retirement: literary studies, chatting to philosophers, snacking on fish. Horace, taking possession of his Sabine farm, had done much the same, fashioning out of the delight that he took in his leisure joyous and immortal poetry: an affirmation that war was over, a celebration of the coming of peace. The statement being made by Tiberius, though, was a very different one. Claudians were hardly given to retiring from public life – and especially not to an island full of Greeks. That Rome's foremost general, 'the most eminent after Augustus of all her citizens', had now despaired of it offered sobering food for thought. A damning health-check had been delivered on the state of the Republic. Tiberius, by so ostentatiously doing nothing, had known full well what he was doing.

Yet in the event, he was barely missed. So furious had Augustus been in the immediate wake of the standoff with his son-in-law that it had literally made him ill. Nevertheless, for all his rage and perplexity, it turned out that he could cope perfectly manageably without Tiberius. Perhaps, had some pressing military emergency erupted, it would have been different; but all seemed well in Rome. The frontiers remained stable, the provinces at peace. Not only that, but Gaius and Lucius, schooled closely in the arts of governance by its greatest living practitioner, would soon be men. One year after Tiberius's departure for Rhodes, Gaius was honoured by the equestrians with an unprecedented rank: 'Princeps of Youth'. Simultaneously, he was inducted into the Senate, designated consul five years ahead, and given a major priesthood. In 2 BC, Lucius too was introduced by Augustus to the Senate, and proclaimed a 'Princeps of Youth'. '*Virtus*,' as Ovid put it, with a perfectly straight face, 'flourishes young in a Caesar.'[43]

The course of the future seemed set fair. Though Livia, mourning the death of her younger son and the disgrace of her elder, might despair of the prospects of the Claudians, those of the Julians seemed secure. In the villa at Prima Porta, the white chickens continued to lay their eggs, and the miraculous laurel tree still spread its branches. Father of his Country, Augustus was father as well of two brilliant princes. It seemed that his troublesome daughter and mulish son-in-law could both be put safely to the back of his mind.

The Arts of Love

August, 2 BC. The dog days of summer. In the hills beyond Rome, sheep and bullocks sought shelter from the scorching heat wherever they could find it, while men offered sacrifice to cooling springs. In the great city itself, narrow streets sweltered beneath the stench of brown smog. Caesar Augustus, concerned as ever for the well-being of his fellow citizens, had recently taken steps to complement the flow of water along the capital's aqueducts, and from the beautiful marble fountains erected decades earlier by Agrippa, by building a massive lake. Stretching some 1800 feet by 1200, it stood on the far bank of the Tiber, and was crossed by a spectacularly engineered bridge. Here, sparing no expense, the Princeps chose to celebrate the great events of the previous few months: his becoming the Father of his Country, and the dedication of his splendid temple to Mars. Out on the lake, entire squadrons of warships re-enacted the battle of Salamis, the heroic victory of 480 BC in which the Greeks had defeated a fleet of invading barbarians.

Echoes of a more recent victory were hard to miss. It was thanks to the rout of Cleopatra and her jabbering, animal-worshipping hordes at Actium that Augustus, for almost thirty years now, had been able to nurse the shattered Republic back to its present golden state of health. Nostalgia, though, was only a part of the Princeps's message. He was looking to the future as well. The barbarians defeated at Salamis had come from the same lands now ruled by the Parthians – and the time had come, so Augustus felt, for the eastern front to receive renewed attention. Tiberius, the man originally entrusted with the mission, had flunked the challenge; but Gaius Caesar, recently turned eighteen, was ready at last to take up the reins. The following year he would leave for the East. As spectators on the banks of the artificial lake cheered the splintering of timbers and the sinking of battleships, a stirring vision was being offered them of the future – one in which 'the final gaps in Caesar's rule of the world are plugged'.[44]

Not that all the audience were necessarily much interested in the Princeps's ambitions. Ovid, visiting the naval extravaganza, barely had eyes for the battle itself. He was there to ogle women. 'The crowds being what they are, there is someone for everybody's tastes.'[45] More than a decade and a half had passed since the criminalisation of adultery, but Ovid, the most fashionable poet in Rome, still dared to make titillating play with his taste for married women. No better time to satisfy it than the long, hot, lazy afternoons of summer. The half-closed shutters of a bedroom, the play of shadow and sunbeams, the soft-footed tread of some other man's wife, her long hair loose, her white throat bare, her dress thin and skimpy: Ovid was not afraid to pray publicly for 'the enjoyment of many such a siesta'.[46] Deliciously, seditiously, beyond the gleam of the war god's new temple and the forest of masts out on the Princeps's artificial lake, Rome still sheltered shrines to forbidden pleasure.

As Augustus would soon find out for himself. Shortly after his re-enactment of the battle of Salamis, near the same Rostra in the Forum from which he had originally proposed his laws against adultery, a crown of flowers appeared on Marsyas's head. Who had put it there? Gossip fingered a truly scandalous culprit: none other than the Princeps's own daughter. Rumour had been swirling around Julia for a long while – and now, in the hour of her father's apotheosis, it reached critical gale force. It was whispered that she had taken not one, but a whole multitude of lovers. That she had partied by night in the Forum, and stained the Rostra with her adulterous affairs. That she had sold herself to strangers beneath the statue of Marsyas. Not a law of her divine father, not a value, but she had disgraced it. That in itself was scandal enough – but there was worse. The rumours, fetid and unsourced though they were, hinted darkly at treason. Among Julia's lovers was the son of her father's greatest enemy. Sharing torchlit revels with Iullus Antonius, she had been paying honour to Liber, the patron of Antony. The insult to all that her father stood for, to all that he had achieved, could hardly have been more pointed. No wonder, when at last the news of Julia's escapades was broken to the Princeps, that the informers dared to hint at 'plots against his life'.[47]

As a young man, a terrorist barely out of his teens, the future Augustus had spared no one, shown no compunction, in securing his goal of absolute predominance. Decades had since passed, softening the memory of his youthful cruelty: 'He well deserves the name of father.'[48] Julia herself, as wilful as she was bold, had dared to imagine as Tiberius had done, that the Princeps might safely be crossed. A fatal mistake. Those with clearer insight into Augustus's nature knew better than to imagine that a leopard could ever entirely change its spots: 'I would certainly not describe as mercy what was actually the exhaustion of cruelty.'[49] Augustus's powers, as a father, were those of death as well as life. In the humiliation inflicted upon him by his daughter he found, as he had so often done before when confronted by setbacks, only an opportunity to entrench his greatness yet further. No one, after he had dealt with Julia and her lovers, was to be left in any doubt that the Father of his Country reserved the right to destroy as well as cherish those in his power. Rather than draw a veil over the scandal, he opted to expose the whole sordid business to the Senate. His voice raw with shock and horror, Augustus braved the hidden smirks of the listening nobility. A mortifying indignity, certainly – but all for long-term advantage. Senators were being exposed to a fact of political life long veiled behind the Princeps's show of patience and forbearance: that he could, if he so wished, annihilate anyone he pleased.

It was Iullus Antonius who paid the ultimate price. Whether his affair with Julia had been as scandalous as the gossip had it, let alone as sinister in its implications as Augustus seems to have suspected, no one could know for sure. The truth of his ambitions was as veiled in shadow as his midnight revels had been. The baseness of his ingratitude, though, was beyond doubt. His suicide echoed the end of his father. Julia's fate was, if anything, even more cruel. Branded an adulteress, she paid the price laid down by her own father's law: exile to an island. Pandateria, the remote and windswept destination chosen to serve as her prison, was furnished with an agreeable enough villa, yet this hardly served to make up for its downside: that it was dull beyond words. Only Scribonia, her aged mother, was permitted to accompany her there. Otherwise, all company was banned, and even slaves had to be thoroughly vetted before they were permitted to make the crossing to the island. Wine too was forbidden, and all but the plainest food. Julia, whose scorn for the bogus economies of her father's household had always so amused her admirers, found herself condemned to a living nightmare of austerity and tedium.

Meanwhile, back in Rome, the fast set of whom she had been the undoubted queen reeled in stunned horror. A wave of copycat prosecutions threatened a witch-hunt. Even though the Princeps dismissed many of the accusations, a mood of dread settled over the city's salons. 'Who can deceive the sun?'[50] Ovid, casting its golden blaze as an all-seeing spy, imagined its gaze as capable of penetrating even the darkest bedroom, of fathoming the secrets of even the most careful adulterers. Yet even as he confessed to his nervousness, he refused to surrender to it. 'My sexual tastes are deviant,' he cheerily admitted, 'nor is it the first time they have got me into trouble.'[51] Nor, perhaps, the last. Julia might have been banished to a grim existence redolent of antiquity at its most brutally primitive, all weaving at the loom and turnips, but Ovid was not intimidated. He refused to abandon those values of urbanity and sophistication that he saw as embodying the true spirit of the age. In the months after Julia's exile, when the mood in elite circles was all paranoia, Ovid busied himself with a project that could hardly have been more provocative: a guide to the arts of love. Naturally, he made sure to hedge it about with the odd caveat. 'I reiterate – there's nothing illegal about my fun and games. No woman is caught up in them who shouldn't be.'[52] He protested too much, of course. In the wake of Rome's most notorious sex scandal, it took a peculiar degree of courage – or insouciance – to enthuse as Ovid did about the thrills and pleasures of seduction. Even more to give tips to a woman on how best to slip a guard, write messages in secret ink, and conduct an affair behind the back of an over-protective father. Advice such as this, in the wake of Julia's downfall, was as close as anyone among her circle dared come to open dissidence.

Out in the streets, it was different. Julia, witty and blessed with the popular touch, was the people's princess. The great events staged that year by Augustus, and which the entire city had been invited to celebrate, had only fed the public fascination with her. She was loved not just as Caesar's daughter but as the mother of two dashing boys. Both had played a key role in the dedication of the temple of Mars, and preparations for Gaius's departure on his mission to the East could hardly help but stir thoughts in people's minds of the wretched Julia, bereft now of her young princes. Beyond the splendour of Augustus's new forum, in the shadow of its massive screening wall, narrow streets slippery with filth teemed with people who saw in Caesar's daughter, in her sufferings and her sorrows, a glamorous proxy for their own misery. In squalid, crowded courtyards, in teetering tenement blocks, in slums far and wide across the city, the poor mourned the downfall of their favourite. Only months after the people had joined as one with the Senate to hail Augustus as Father of his Country, the unity that he had laboured so hard to foster was fraying. Demonstrations and demands for Julia's return, chanted publicly in the streets, contributed to the sense of a darkening mood. The newly dedicated temple of Mars, seen from the warren of alleys that stretched beyond it, began to seem less a monument to the greatness of a united people, more an embattled island amid a hostile sea.

Children of the wolf: Romulus, the founder of Rome, and his twin brother, Remus, are suckled in the 'Lupercal', a cave on the side of the Palatine Hill. The River Tiber reclines on his elbow beside them. (Wikipedia)

The murderers of Julius Caesar flee the scene of his assassination, as imagined by Jean Léon Gérome in 1859. (© Walters Art Museum, Baltimore, USA / Bridgeman Images)

Livia Drusilla. Beautiful, clever and fabulously well-connected, she would end up garlanded with honours unprecedented for a Roman woman. (Photo: Tom Holland)

Caesar Son Of A God rests his foot on the globe. (© bpk / Münzkabinett, Staatliche Museen zu Berlin)

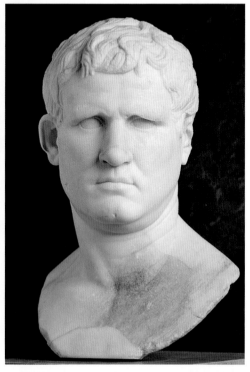

Marcus Vipsanius Agrippa: a supreme *consigliere*. (© Marie-Lan Nguyen / Wikimedia Commons)

Romulus carries armour stripped from an enemy king: the 'spoils of honour'. He was the first of a tiny number of Roman commanders to kill his opposite number in single combat. The painting is from the outside of a shop in Pompeii, but portrays a statue commissioned by Augustus, and placed in the Temple of Mars the Avenger.

Augustus as *Pontifex Maximus*, pious and austere in his service of the gods. (© Tarker / Bridgeman Images)

The Temple of Mars the Avenger, dedicated by Augustus on 12 May 3 BC, many decades after he had first vowed it to the god. (Illustration by Gareth Blayney)

Rome was a city in which the phallus was omnipresent. The penis of a Roman was expected to be as masterful as it was potent. (The Art Archive / Mondadori Portfolio/Electa)

The August Family as Augustus wished it to be seen. Agrippa, toga over his head, stands on the far left; the woman next to him (although it is just possible she might be Livia) is almost certainly Julia, his wife. The two boys are Gaius and Lucius: simultaneously the grandsons and the adopted sons of Augustus. (De Agostini Picture Library / G. Dagli Orti / Bridgeman Images)

Tiberius and his mother, Livia Drusilla. (Photo: Tom Holland)

Marsyas, a satyr thought by the Greeks to have been flayed alive, was believed by the Italians to have made a narrow escape, and fled to Italy. A statue of him in the Forum served the Roman people as a venerable symbol of liberty. (De Agostini Picture Library/Getty Images)

An altar raised at the crossroads of the Vicus Sandalarius. Gaius stands flanked by Augustus and Livia. (The Art Archive / Museo della Civilta Romana Rome / Gianni Dagli Orti)

Into the woods. The heights above the slaughter-ground which wiped out P. Quinctilius Varus, governor of Germany, and three entire legions. (Photo: Tom Holland)

A Roman cavalry mask, found on the site of the battle of the Teutoburg Pass. (Photo: Jamie Muir)

Augustus Caesar triumphant. A woman symbolising the civilised world crowns him with a wreath of oak leaves, while below him barbarians grovel as a victory trophy is raised. (© Ullsteinbild / Topfoto)

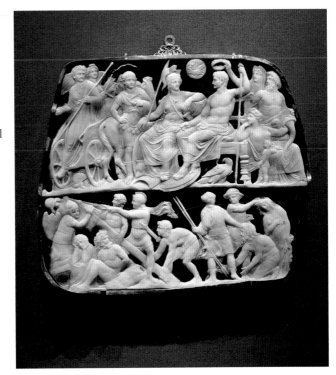

On his death bed, Augustus is said to have asked whether he had played his part well in the comedy of life. Even as an old man, he kept up his front. (Photo: Tom Holland)

Figs: reputedly, Augustus's favourite food. (Photo: Sophie Hay)

Pianosa, the small island off the west coast of Italy to which Agrippa Postumus was exiled. It was one of a number of islands used by Augustus and his successors as prisons for disgraced members of the dynasty. (Agefotostock TIP-MO232601)

Augustus himself, having just bared his teeth at the aristocracy, was hardly likely to yield to the mob. Nevertheless, as befitted a man endowed with the *tribunicia potestas*, he was sensitive to its hissing. He had long since learned to keep a beady eye on what happened in the slums. No regime could prosper that was content to leave them unregulated. This was not the least among the many insights that Augustus had brought to the art of government. 'The poor are like the paltry, obscure places into which shit and other refuse are dumped.'[53] While sufficiently a man of his class to take this commonplace for granted, Augustus had nevertheless come to appreciate how vital it was to plumb their depths. His agents, over the course of the decades, had duly fathomed the city's bowels. Registers of everything from prostitutes to snack bars had been assiduously compiled. Loose roof-tiles, dangerous paving-stones, leaking water-pipes: all had attracted the attention of ever more officious aediles. Plans of properties and lists of householders were drawn up in exacting detail. The image that haunted Ovid, of Augustus as the sun, his eye forever probing shadows, was one that the agents appointed to map the city, his many surveyors and officials, would doubtless have recognised. No matter that Rome's snarl, away from the gold and marble of the Princeps's *grands projets*, remained as much a warren as ever, the gaze of Caesar had come to penetrate even its darkest, most insalubrious corners. The great labyrinth of the vastest city on the planet, one that no one previously had ever before thought to trace, held few secrets from Augustus.

And knowledge, as so often, was power. It was a father's right, of course, to track what those under his authority were up to – not just to punish them when they did wrong, but to keep them secure from peril. In Rome, potential calamity was only ever a spark away. In 7 BC, arsonists had started a fire that at one point had threatened the Forum itself with immolation. Augustus, responding to this near-calamity in predictable fashion, had sponsored yet more lists. Officials were instructed to ensure that even the meanest attic in a high-rise be armed with a bucket. Health and safety regulations like these, by ensuring that neighbourhoods were less likely to go up in flames, reaped the Princeps massive reward. In a tinder-box such as Rome, there existed no surer path to popularity than the provision to nervous citizens of a reliable fire service. Augustus was not the first to have realised this. Back in 19 BC, with the Princeps absent in the East, a bold and ambitious nobleman named Egnatius Rufus had funded his own supply of firefighters, ending up so popular in consequence that it had completely turned his head. Seduced into aiming at the consulship against the explicit wishes of Augustus, he had sent the proxies appointed by the Princeps to administer Rome scrabbling to contain the damage. In the event, the coup had fizzled out ingloriously. Egnatius's attempt on the consulship had been suppressed, and Egnatius himself, flung into prison, had 'there met with the end that his life so richly merited'.[54] Augustus, though, had learnt his lesson. Only one man could be permitted to serve the city and its teeming masses as their guardian – and it was not Egnatius. Nothing to the benefit of the people but it was to proceed from the Princeps himself.

Which was why, despite their indignation at Julia's fate, Augustus could feel confident that their demands for her return were unlikely to degenerate into rioting, or worse. Seen from the summit of the Palatine, the city's smog-wreathed workshops and tower blocks might have appeared perfervid with menace: Rome's heart of darkness, from which Clodius, in the dying days of the Republic, had recruited his paramilitaries, and from which mobs, reduced to skin and bone by the various wars of the Triumvirate, had periodically erupted. Those days, though, seemed over. Augustus himself, armed with maps and detailed breakdowns of the city's population, had successfully brought order where before there had been only chaos. In 7 BC, prompted by his reform of the fire service, he had made a tour of Rome's various neighbourhoods. Rather than venture into the shapeless tangle of side-alleys, he had focused his attention on the crossroads, the *compita*, which stood at the heart of every district. These, like the knots of a giant net, spanned the city. Control the city and control the urban fabric. Augustus, like a master huntsman, knew what it took to make a catch.

The origins of the *compita*, so the Roman people believed, reached way back to the time when kings had ruled the city, and were the focus of intense local devotion and pride. Mysterious twin spirits, known as Lares, stood guard over them, and were celebrated every year in a wild festival named the Compitalia. Sacrifices were made before each crossroads shrine. Everyone, no matter how lowly, no matter how wretched, would be invited to join in the fun; even slaves would dress up for the occasion. All of which, not surprisingly, had long been regarded with deep suspicion by conservatives in the Senate. Their concern, though, was rooted in something more than simple snobbery. The Compitalia had often literally been a riot. This was why, in 64 BC, the Senate had voted to suppress it. Yet the ban had not lasted for long. Clodius, whose genius for street fighting had seen him refine it into a veritable political art, had made sure of that. Patronage of the festival had been a key factor in his ground-breaking brand of gangsterism. It had enabled him not only to recruit supporters, but to fashion them into a city-wide organisation. *Compita*, after all, were everywhere in Rome. 'The city has a thousand Lares.'[55]

What Clodius had achieved, by transforming their shrines into hubs for his own personal ambitions, was not forgotten. The poor, it seemed, could provide even the most blue-blooded nobleman with a political base. This, as Egnatius's abortive coup had demonstrated, was bound to serve power-hungry senators as a standing temptation. Clearly, then, the Princeps had been left with no choice but to put a stop to it for good. Rather than ban the Compitalia, though, as the Senate had always sought to do, he had made himself its patron. Augustus was never the man to suppress a venerable custom – not when he could twist it to his own ends. By touring the city's crossroads, by centring the provision of firefighting and other services on them, and by gracing them with marks of his favour, he had won hearts and minds across the entire immensity of Rome. Potential trouble spots had been transformed by his initiative into nerve centres of the regime.

Even in the darkest slums, then, even in the very roughest quarters, the authority of the Princeps blazed radiantly. Early in 1 BC, when Gaius set out, via the frontier on the Danube, on his mission to the East, he did so from the great temple of Mars, surrounded by the marmoreal splendour of its colonnades, in the presence of the standards won back from Parthia, before the awful gaze of the war-god. No dirtying of sandals in the filth of the side-alleys for Caesar's son. Yet there too, in the neighbourhoods beyond the new forum, his departure was much on people's minds. Head from the temple of Mars into the steaming agglomeration of workshops, fast-food stalls and brothels known as the Suburra, then skirt southwards, and a citizen would come to an ancient street, named after the cobblers who had once lined it the Vicus Sandalarius.* At the end of the street was a *compitum*; and here, newly chiselled, stood an altar. It had been placed beside the crossroads just a few months earlier by the officers responsible for the adjoining quarters: men of thoroughly humble origin, but no less conscious of their dignity for that. There had certainly been no protests at Julia's fate from these officials. Entrusted by Augustus with the key responsibilities of local government, permitted an escort of lictors on public holidays, men literally at the centre of all that went on in their neighbourhood, they could hardly have been more in the Princeps's debt. The new altar set up beside the crossroads was an expression of their gratitude. One side was carved with laurel, another with trophies of victory. Its front featured Augustus and Livia, who were portrayed standing on either side of Gaius, gazing at him approvingly. Julia was notable by her absence. The officials who had commissioned the relief, raising their gaze from the swirl and clamour of their own little patch of Rome, could feel themselves, however tangentially, embroiled in global affairs. Mars was not the only god

---

* In due course, after a century or so of gentrification, it would end up as the centre of the city's book trade.

summoned to keep watch over Gaius on his travels. So too were the Lares; and so too a novel and awesome power now increasingly honoured alongside them. Instituted by the Princeps on his tour of the *compita* in 7 BC, its cult had already taken root across the whole of Rome, wherever there was a crossroads to be found and a new altar raised: the animating spirit, the *Genius*, of Caesar Augustus himself.

With divine backing of this order, it seemed out of the question that anything could go wrong for Gaius. 'Grant him the popularity of Pompey, the boldness of Alexander, and my own good fortune.'[56] So Augustus prayed. Nor were gods the only guardians he made sure to provide his adoptive son. Marcus Lollius, a veteran of numerous provincial commands who also, perhaps tellingly, had long enjoyed a bitter feud with Tiberius, was assigned to the young prince as his mentor, and to serve Augustus as his eyes and ears. Watched over by the heavens and guided by a seasoned counsellor, Gaius was soon winning golden opinions. Cutting a dash wherever he went, he processed through the cities of the East to the furthermost limits of Roman power. Here, on an island in the Euphrates, he enjoyed a flamboyant and successful summit with the king of Parthia; shortly afterwards, and he was busying himself with the slaughter of various barbarians, 'for the better security of all mankind'.[57] Unsurprisingly, news of Gaius's progress was greeted with rapturous excitement back in Italy. The hopes invested by the Roman people in their favourite could hardly have been more promisingly fulfilled. 'Not only had he governed well, but he had defeated or received into alliance the fiercest and most powerful of peoples.'[58] The gods, it seemed, had been listening to his grandfather's prayers.

Abruptly, though, they withdrew their favour. First, in a spectacular bust-up, Lollius was accused of taking bribes from various local potentates, and pressured into drinking poison. Then, late in AD 2, the devastating news reached Gaius that his brother Lucius had fallen sick and died in Gaul. The following year, meeting the commander of an Armenian fortress for a parley, Gaius himself only just survived a treacherous attempt on his life. Even though he went on to secure a notable victory over the Armenians, the wound his would-be assassin had given him failed to heal, and Gaius, his health and self-confidence shot, fast became a shadow of his former self. When he wrote to Augustus with a request to lay down his command, the Princeps ordered him home, and Gaius duly embarked on the long journey back from the eastern front. It was too late. Gangrene had set in. By mid-February AD 4, after an agonising journey across icy mountains and then by merchant vessel along the southern coast of Asia Minor, Gaius was finally ready to take ship for Italy. He never boarded it. On the 21st, the adopted son and appointed heir of Imperator Caesar Augustus breathed his last.

Back in Rome, the news broke like a thunderclap. Ovid, who had woven into his guide to seduction the stirring announcement that Gaius was destined to conquer Parthia, opted not to remove it from his published poem, but instead to let it stand, a memorial to high hopes raised and dashed. 'Your twin fathers, Mars and Caesar – both have endowed you with their awesome power.'[59] Sentiments such as this, transmuted from flattery into mockery by Gaius's pathetic end, could hardly help but raise a sardonic smile in the circles where Ovid mixed. Out on the streets, it was different. There, grief at the fate of Julia's two sons was raw. Once again, agitators took to demanding the return of their princess from over the water. Once again, Augustus refused. 'Fire will sooner mix with water,' he vowed, 'than she will come back.'[60] When they heard this, protestors lined the Tiber and hurled flaming torches into its currents. Even Augustus was unsettled. The continuing violence of the agitation, despite the fact that years had passed since the exile of his daughter, perturbed him. After a decent interval, so that he did not seem to be buckling under pressure, he gave orders for Julia to be transferred from her bleak and treeless prison to confinement in Rhegium, a naval base in the toe of Italy. It was hardly Rome; but even the dreariness of a provincial port was an improvement on Pandateria.

Nor was Julia alone in being sprung from an island confinement. For her erstwhile husband too, the past years had been difficult ones.

Tiberius's retirement to Rhodes had inexorably become an exile. Divorce from his wife, the necessary consequence of her adultery, had been a divorce from Augustus as well. Then, the following year, his grant of *tribunicia potestas* had expired, an ominous development for a man who had so wilfully alienated the Princeps. His legal immunity from insult and prosecution was no more. Tiberius, it appeared, had grievously miscalculated. Although, as a Claudian, he could still command influence across the Roman world, his prestige was in eclipse. Cities began to throw down his statues; puppet kings to snub him. Then, with Gaius's arrival in the East, his plight had taken a further turn for the worse. One night, at a drunken dinner party, a companion of Tiberius's stepson had offered to take ship to Rhodes and bring back the head of the 'exile', as he was derisively known. Gaius had refused – but when Tiberius, alarmed by news of the episode, asked for permission to head back for Rome, that too had been refused. A year had passed. Tiberius had continued to beg for an end to his exile. Finally, in AD 2, permission had been granted – but on humiliating terms. Though head of the Claudians, and his people's greatest general, Tiberius was forbidden to take part in public life. When the news reached Rome of Gaius's death, he was living in a location that could not have spoken more loudly of his retirement from both the Senate and military service: the gardens of Maecenas.

But now, abruptly, everything was transformed. Augustus faced a shattering moment of crisis. The loss of Gaius, the golden youth who had been both his son and his grandson, his 'sweetest little donkey',[61] was more than a devastating personal blow. It had also ruined his dearest hopes for the succession. Of his five grandchildren, only three were now left him – and of these, two were girls. It was true that Agrippina, ambitious and self-assertive, 'had a masculine cast of mind, with no concern for feminine foibles'[62] – but the notion of a woman, no matter how able, ruling the world was clearly a nonsense. Julia, meanwhile, was quite another matter. Chic and flamboyant, she showed alarming signs of taking after her mother in more than name. To boast both the largest house in Rome and the smallest dwarf, as she did, was hardly the surest way to her grandfather's heart. That left Agrippa, the posthumous son and namesake of Augustus's great brother-in-arms; and sure enough, on 26 June AD 4, the Princeps duly adopted him as his son. The boy, though, was only fifteen – and Augustus, by now two decades nearer to the grave than he had been when adopting Gaius and Lucius, dreaded that time was running out. For all that he still looked youthful and serene in his statues, he was now sixty-six years old, by any reckoning an old man. Death might claim him at any moment. It was out of the question, after all his long labours, that he should put his achievements at risk by leaving the world in the hands of a child. That being so, there was really only one course open to him. Shortly after the news of Gaius's death had reached Rome, Augustus arranged for Tiberius to be awarded a fresh grant of the *tribunicia potestas*. Then, along with Agrippa Postumus, he adopted at the same time a second son. Tiberius Claudius Nero became a Caesar.

It was, for Augustus, a painful compromise. True, there could be found in his adoption of two heirs an echo of the consulship, that venerable institution which had ensured for so long that no one man should wield supreme power in Rome – but that echo was deceptive. Augustus understood, none better, the true nature of the regime that he had forged; and he knew Tiberius. Agrippa Postumus was likely to prove no match for the flinty head of the Claudians. The Princeps had made his decision – and it was one that had, to all intents and purposes, sidelined his own flesh and blood. Not, of course, that he was prepared to acknowledge this. His regime remained publicly as Julian as ever. Tiberius, by virtue of his adoption, had ceased to rank legally as a Claudian at all. Not only that, but Augustus went to great lengths to ensure that the twin lines of his household, his own and that of Livia, would end up so tightly intertwined as to be indistinguishable. The robustly competent Agrippina was duly given in marriage to Tiberius's nephew, the son of Drusus, that much mourned hero of the German front. Simultaneously, despite already having a son of his own, Tiberius was obliged by the Princeps to adopt Germanicus, as he was known in honour of his dead father. Julians and Claudians, their distinctiveness blurred by adoptions, their identities blended by marriage, were to share a common destiny. Proud and ancient though their two respective lines were, it was the glory of Augustus to offer both a resplendent new status. Neither Julian nor Claudian, the future was to belong instead to a single house: the August Family.

Such was the spin, at any rate. Plenty had their doubts. Agrippa himself, as the Julian most obviously blocking a Claudian monopoly on power, certainly had few illusions as to how exposed he was. Young and inexperienced, he made no attempt to hide his resentment from his grandfather. By the time that he came officially of age, a year after his adoption by Augustus, he had already developed a reputation for surliness and aggression. Out on the streets, though, the mood of violence was altogether more threatening to the Princeps's plans. Enduring affection for Julia and her children combined with distaste for Claudian ambitions to render Tiberius a profoundly unpopular choice of heir. The stiffness which Tiberius himself prized as an ancestral Roman value was widely viewed by the urban poor as an expression of coldness and hauteur. The grant of *tribunicia potestas* to a man so unapologetically blue-blooded could not help but seem to the plebs a provocation. It was to protect the rights of the people that the office of tribune had first been instituted; and the Princeps, for as long as he had been at the centre of Roman affairs, had shown himself their protector and friend. But now, as Augustus aged and the power of Tiberius waxed, the plebs were gripped by a new mood of unease. Troubles came not as single spies, but in battalions. News of revolts and barbarian raids arrived from distant frontiers. Sardinia was briefly lost to pirates. Money to fund the military budget began to run out, and Augustus, in a desperate attempt to plug the gap, was reduced to introducing the first direct tax on Rome's citizens for over a century and a half. Meanwhile, the great programme of urban regeneration, which had provided work for so many, was grinding to a halt. A plague broke out. Misery filled the crowded slums, and the pits of the *carnarium*, dumping grounds for carcasses and every kind of refuse, were kept open day and night. Then fires swept through the city, so devastating that they completely overwhelmed the ability of the local authorities to combat them, and the Princeps was left with no choice but to fund a new and centralised service. The *Vigiles*, crack squads of firefighters, were paramilitary in purpose as well as organisation, for they were mandated to police the streets as well as to put out conflagrations. That Rome was in an ominously combustible mood was all too clear to Augustus. Worse than plague, worse than fire, was the return to the city of a menace that had last gripped it back in the darkest days of the Triumvirate: famine. As a young man, Augustus had been cornered by a starving mob and almost torn to pieces. He knew what it was to look into the eyes of the hunger-stricken. Now, informed that the granaries were almost empty, he made sure to let everyone know that he was contemplating suicide.

There were plenty, it seemed, who wished he would act on his threat. Even though the grain shortage was ultimately mastered, the mood of crisis was not. Some were daring to think the unthinkable. The great fire, it was reported, had originated in different places across the city, 'but all on the same day',[63] a clear sign of arson. Then, at the height of the famine, fly-posters had appeared on buildings across Rome, openly calling for the Princeps to be toppled. Attempts by his agents to trace their source had failed. No single man, they concluded, 'could possibly have planned or initiated such a manifestation'.[64] To the Princeps himself, though, the protests appeared anything but spontaneous. He sniffed conspiracy. Already, in the same year that he adopted Tiberius, he had uncovered a plot against his life by Pompey's grandson. On that occasion, revealing through an imperious display of mercy the full force of his contempt, he had taken the conspirator to one side, given him a tongue-lashing, and then graciously permitted him to serve as consul. Such mercy could easily be afforded. A nobleman, even one with the blood of Pompey the Great flowing in his veins, presented no plausible threat. His peers, although brought to tolerate the supremacy of the August Family, would never permit one of their own to emerge as Princeps.

But what of conspiracy from within the August Family itself? That, Augustus knew, was where the surest menace lurked. Battered by fiscal crisis, struggling to combat the miseries that repeatedly swept Rome, grown neurotic and sour with age, he had no patience with family sentiment. When evidence was uncovered implicating Agrippa Postumus in sedition, the Princeps spared the nobleman involved in the plot but crushed his own grandson. Agrippa was formally disinherited, exiled from Rome, and then banished to a remote island off Corsica named Planasia. Here he was placed under a close military guard. His property was transferred to the military treasury. All mentions of him as a member of the August Family promptly ceased: he became a non-person.* Augustus himself never spoke of his youngest grandson again, except to refer to him and his mother Julia as two ulcers, two boils.

And soon a third would erupt. In AD 8, a decade after Julia's ruin, news broke of an eerily similar scandal. Her daughter and namesake, already notorious for the raciness of her lifestyle and her taste in dwarves, was found guilty of adultery. A third member of the August Family was exiled to a barren island. Yet as with the elder Julia, so with the younger. Amid the swirl of innuendo, the gossip of sexual misdemeanours, there were whispers of vastly more serious offences. Rumours, garbled and contradictory though they often were, hinted at an attempted coup. There had been a plot, it was said, to spring the elder Julia and Agrippa Postumus from exile. Whole armies had been primed to expect them. Augustus, meanwhile, was to have been assassinated in the Senate House. Quite how accurate the various details of this conspiracy were, let alone how they might have fitted together, was impossible to clarify. Nevertheless, as workmen moved in to demolish the palatial complex of the younger Julia's house, and

---

* Take, for instance, an arch built at Ticinum in northern Italy (modern Pavia) in AD 7 or 8, which celebrated the August Family with ten statues – including the dead Gaius and Lucius. Their younger brother was notable only by his absence.

guards waited to put to death the baby with which she was pregnant, it was clear that the charge of adultery veiled as much as it revealed. It was telling, for instance, that Julia's husband, supposedly the injured party, should have been put to death as a criminal.[65] Nor, perhaps, was it entirely a coincidence that another man too, someone long celebrated for his tweaking of the Princeps's tail, should have been dealt a blow almost as devastating. Julia was not alone, that fateful year of AD 8, in being delivered a sentence of exile.[66]

Calamity caught up with Ovid on the island of Elba. Planasia, where the wretched Agrippa Postumus languished under armed guard, could be seen from where the poet was staying as a blue smudge on the horizon; a grim reminder of Augustus's vengeful anger. Not that Ovid needed much reminding. He was already up to his neck in trouble. When a ship arrived from the mainland, the news it brought was so grim that it reduced him to tears. Havering initially between confession and denial, he finally broke down, and revealed all to the friend with whom he was staying. The wrath of the Princeps, which Ovid had long been courting, had finally caught up with him. His guide to seduction, in which he had advised women how to cheat behind the backs of their men, and paid ironic tribute to the dead Gaius as a favourite of the gods, was still being read by the trendsetters, still provoking smiles of amusement among the fast set: a feat of *lèse-majesté* for which the author, it appeared, was now at last to be made to answer. But there was worse. What exactly it was that Ovid had done, what the 'mistake'[67] that now threatened him with ruin, he would never publicly state; but he would go on to offer certain clues. His fault had been one that it was perilous to mention in public. He had seen something that he should not have done, 'a deadly outrage'.[68] Whatever it was that he had witnessed, it had served to bring down on his head 'the richly merited wrath of Caesar'.[69] In the tense and scandal-racked context of that fateful year, there was only one episode sufficient to explain such terrible fury. Whether by accident or as the result of his own imprudence, Ovid had clearly found himself sucked into the slipstream of Rome's most lethal rivalry: the struggle between Julians and Claudians for the rule of the world.[70]

When Ovid boarded ship from Elba and bade his host farewell, it was the last time the two friends would ever see each other. That December, 'shivering with the bitter cold', the poet took another ship, 'out into the waters of the Adriatic'.[71] Not for him, though, the short voyage to some island off the coast of Italy. Augustus, who had interviewed the desperate and repentant poet personally before settling his fate, had chosen for him a very different destination. For Ovid, that most urbane, most fashionable of men, the place nominated to serve as his prison could not have been more terrible.

He was bound for the ends of the earth.

Heart of Darkness

'Nothing lies beyond it except for cold, and hostile peoples, and the frozen waves of an ice-bound sea.'[72]

Ovid was appalled to find himself in Tomis. It was very much not his kind of town. Planted centuries earlier by Greek colonists on the bleak and gale-lashed coast of the Black Sea, it stood on the outermost limits of Roman power. Even though Ovid was exaggerating grotesquely when he complained that Tomis was one perpetual winter, the reality of its balmy summers did little to ease his mood of depression.* It was hard to imagine a town less like Rome. The water was brackish. The food was appalling. No one spoke Latin, and even the Greek spoken by the Tomitans struck Ovid as halfway to gibberish. Surrounded as he was by treeless desolation, the pleasures of the world's capital shimmered in his memory like hallucinations. 'Here,' he reflected mournfully, 'it is I who am the barbarian.'[73]

To Ovid, a man as fashionable as anyone in Rome, it came as a

---

* The city of Constanta, as Tomis is now known, is today one of Romania's most popular beach resorts.

shock to live among provincials who did not even realise that they were provincial. Within the low, crumbling fortifications of Tomis, there was no one to share with him his anguished homesickness for metropolitan chic. Beyond its walls, things were even more savage. The Danube, which lay some seventy miles to the north, featured on the maps of Caesar and his strategists as an immense natural frontier, a wide-flowing impediment to the brutes who lurked beyond it; but on the ground things were alarmingly different. During winter, when even the sea beyond the delta might turn to ice, the river would freeze solid; and then, mounted on swift ponies, their beards white with frost, barbarians from the savage wastes beyond the Danube would appear, predacious and unsparing. Plumes of smoke wisping above the sunless horizon would mark villages put to the torch, bodies left twisted by poisoned arrows, the survivors tethered and driven off with their belongings. In his nightmares, Ovid would imagine himself dodging missiles or else shackled in a coffle, and wake to find the rooftops bristling with a stubble of arrows. Looking out at the war-bands as they circled the walls of Tomis, he would feel himself penned inside a sheepfold. Rome seemed not merely distant, but impotent. 'For all her beauties, the vast majority of mankind barely registers her existence.' It was, for a man as devoted to the metropolis as Ovid, a devastating discovery to make. 'They do not fear the armed might of the Romans.'[74]

But there was even greater cause for anxiety. When Ovid looked at the Tomitans, he saw a people barely distinguishable from the barbarians at their gates. The men wore sheepskin trousers and were unspeakably hairy; the women carried water-pots on their heads. No one in Rome had lived like this for centuries. Back amid the gilded sophistication of his former life, Ovid had laughed at the nostalgia of the Princeps for the days of Romulus, and dismissed the first Romans as murderers, rapists, brutes. Now, transplanted to the ends of the earth, it was as though he had been exiled to the distant past as well. On the frontier between civilisation and barbarism, Ovid found himself in a realm where men seemed halfway to beasts – or worse. They were, he complained, 'more savage than wolves'.[75] Stranded on the margins of Roman power, he could gaze into the darkness that stretched far beyond it and feel its immensity, its potency, its colossal disdain for everything that he was. No wonder, marking the degenerate Greek spoken by his fellow townsmen, he began to fret that he might be losing his Latin. A potential for barbarism lurked within Romans too. The founder of their city, after all, had sucked on the teat of a wolf. Once, where now fountains burbled and porticoes offered shade to men of fashion, people had 'lived like beasts'.[76] Rome too, Ovid knew, had been one of the dark places of the world.

Perhaps, though, it was only out on the margins of civilisation, far from the fleshpots of the capital, that a man could properly appreciate just how far the Roman people had come since those distant days – and what the qualities were that had made possible their rise to greatness. Ovid, exiled to 'a frontier zone just recently and precariously brought under the rule of law',[77] was having his metrosexual nose rubbed by the Princeps in a brutal fact. There could be no arts of peace without a mastery of war. It was not, in the final reckoning, good drains or gleaming temples, let alone a taste for poetry, that distinguished a civilised man from a savage, but steel: the steel it took to stand shield to shield in a line of battle, and then advance. Wolf-bred though a Roman was, his proficiency at inflicting slaughter was not that of a wild beast. Training, rigid and relentless, had forged him into a single link in a mighty chain. A soldier was not permitted to marry: his comrades were all he had. A legion was less a pack of animals than it was a killing machine. Soldiers worshipped Mars as *Gradivus* – the god who gave them the courage to advance, step by measured step, obedient to the blasts of the war-trumpet, no matter what the danger. Against their relentless, heavy tread, there was little prospect of victory. Even the wildest, most bloodthirsty warband, when it charged a legion, was liable to break in the end. Unlike the savages from across the Danube, 'always descending like birds when least expected',[78] a Roman army was schooled in endurance. Its soldiers had been trained, no matter what, to eviscerate a foe, advance, and then, covered in blood, to eviscerate again. Had they not been, then their aptitude for inflicting slaughter on those who dared to oppose them would never have become so potent. 'It is discipline, strict military discipline, that is the surest guardian of Roman power.'[79]

Everything followed from this: the refusal to buckle in the face of setbacks; the dogged pursuit of victory, no matter how seemingly insuperable the odds; the patience to persevere in the face of repeated reversals and revolts. The Balkans, rather than the desolation of untamed menace that Ovid imagined them to be, were in fact, by the time of his arrival in Tomis, almost tamed for good. The process had been long and gruelling. Many years had passed since the future Augustus, eager for martial glory, had proclaimed the pacification of Illyria, and Crassus, a decade later, routed the Bastarnians. The greatest feats of all had been achieved by Tiberius, who in the years before his retirement to Rhodes had subdued what is now Hungary, a savage region infested by wild boars and even wilder tribesmen. The Pannonians, as they were called, were to prove themselves inveterately rebellious. Sporadic bushfires of revolt had combined, in AD 6, into a single terrifying conflagration. Merchants had been slaughtered, isolated detachments wiped out, Macedonia invaded. In the face of this devastating insurgency, even the Princeps had panicked. Unless urgent steps were taken, he had warned the Senate in hysterical tones, the Pannonians would be at the gates of the city in ten days. Fortunately, back from Rhodes, Rome's best general had once again been his to command. Tiberius, patient and relentless, was ideally suited to the crushing of guerillas. As attentive to the welfare of his own men as he was to the risks of ambush, he had blocked his ears to the shrill demands from the capital for immediate results. Slow and steady did it. 'The safest course, in the opinion of Tiberius, was the best.'[80] Week by week, month by month, he had broken the Pannonians. Their surrender had finally come in AD 8, a mass prostration before the victorious general on a river bank. The following year, even as Ovid was gawping in alarm at his first sight of barbarians, fire and slaughter were being visited upon the final, mountainous strongholds of rebellion in the Balkans. After the young Germanicus, entrusted with his first command, had proved himself as ineffectual as he was dashing, Tiberius moved in to deliver the *coup de grâce*. The pacification was complete at last. A vast block of territory, stretching from the Black Sea to the Adriatic and from Macedonia to the Danube, had been secured for good. Tiberius richly merited the gratitude of the Princeps and the approbation of his fellow citizens. 'Victory, her wings beating as ever above Rome's great general, had wreathed his bright hair with laurel.'[81]

But there remained work to be done. Ovid was not alone in marking how barbarians beyond the Danube were perfectly capable of negotiating the immense flow of its waters. Even the most formidable of natural boundaries could be crossed. The implications, for those tasked with securing the frontier, were tantalising as well as troubling. It remained the proud boast of the Roman people that their conquests were never made for conquest's sake. Their wars were fought, not out of avarice or blood lust, but rather to safeguard their city's honour and the interests of their allies. They had subdued the world, in effect, in self-defence. This was why, in the opinion of Roman statesmen, 'our global dominion may more properly be termed a protectorate'.[82] Would the heavens otherwise have permitted it to come about? Merely to ask the question was to answer it, of course. Clearly, then, it was for the world's own good that it be placed, to its outermost limits, under the tutelage of Rome. The long and glorious age of peace presided over by Augustus rested, in his own proud words, on 'the subjection of the entire globe to the rule of the Roman people'.[83] In practice, of course, as all those peering across the Danube were well aware, the subjection of the globe still had a way to run. Yet that it would come, and to the benefit of those conquered as well as of the conquerors themselves, was a conviction the Roman elite increasingly took for granted. The promptings of ambition and responsibility alike, not to mention obedience to the self-evident will of the gods, urged continued expansion. At stake was the ultimate in prizes: 'empire without limit'.[84]

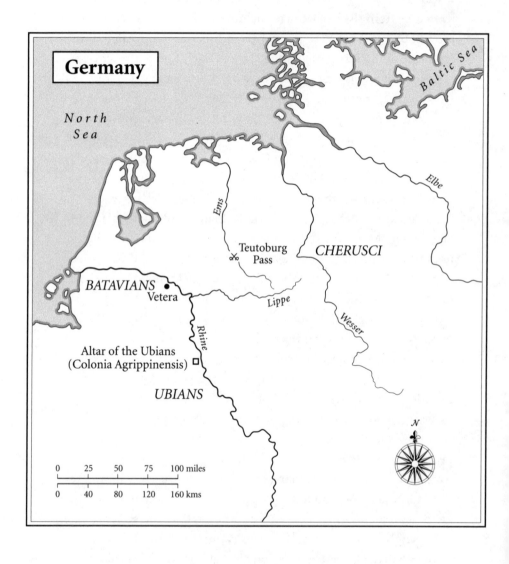

Germany

North
Sea

Baltic Sea

Elbe

Ems

Teutoburg
Pass

CHERUSCI

BATAVIANS
Vetera

Lippe

Wesser

Rhine

Altar of the Ubians
(Colonia Agrippinensis)

UBIANS

N

| 0 | 25 | 50 | 75 | 100 miles |
| 0 | 40 | 80 | 120 | 160 kms |

What this meant in practical terms could best be seen beyond the currents of a river almost as broad and formidable as the Danube itself: the Rhine. When Augustus, looking to win the favour of the war god, had planted a temple of Mars on its western bank, he had dedicated to the shrine, in a formidable statement of intent, the sword of Julius Caesar. The conquest of Gaul, which had successfully drained for good a great sump of pestiferous barbarism, was the obvious model to follow. Caesar himself, in pacifying the western reaches of the Rhine, had recognised that he could not afford to leave the eastern bank to its own devices. Twice he had bridged the river; twice he had delivered to the Germans who lurked beyond it a punitive demonstration of Roman might.* Decades on, it remained as pressing a task as ever to whip the various tribes beyond the border into line. Gaul could not be policed adequately, still less fattened up into the cash-cow it otherwise promised to become, with savages forever breaking in from across the Rhine. This had been embarrassingly brought home in 17 BC, when Marcus Lollius, the future guardian of Gaius, had accidentally run into a German warband, suffering the loss of an eagle. Depending on who reported it, this defeat had ranked as either a fleeting discomfiture, speedily rectified by Lollius himself, or else a crippling blow to Roman prestige, almost on a par with the defeat of Crassus. Whatever the truth of the incident, it had decided the Princeps, ever cautious, ever decisive, to adopt an altogether more proactive response to the problem of the Germans. Travelling north of the Alps, he had personally set in train a momentous series of policies. The better to tax it, Gaul had been subjected to an intrusive census. A mint, guarded by an elite squad of a thousand paramilitaries, had been set up in the recently founded colony of Lugdunum – the future Lyon. Gold and silver, coined in prodigious quantities, loaded into wagons and transported northwards along an ever-expanding

---

* There is no evidence that the 'Germans' had any notion of themselves as a distinct group of tribes, or thought of the lands east of the Rhine as a place called 'Germania'.

network of roads, had given a prodigiously muscular heft to the Roman presence in the West. Spasms of resentment in Gaul had been brutally stilled; a chain of six legionary fortresses built along the line of the Rhine; licence given by Augustus to cross the river and embark on the pacification of Germany itself. A feat as great and terrible as any in the history of Roman arms now beckoned: the winning for civilisation of the outermost limits of the world.

'It takes courage to advance into a forbidden realm of shadow.'[85] When Drusus, on his final campaign, had found himself hundreds of miles east of the Rhine, on the banks of a second mighty natural barrier, a river named the Elbe, a spectre in the form of a colossal woman had materialised before him and forbidden him to cross it. That the lands of the north were the haunt of phantoms and hideous monsters came as no surprise. In the gloomy forests which covered vast reaches of Germany, giant bull-like creatures roamed, and mysterious entities named elks, without ankles or knees; in the icy waters of the Ocean, which would retreat and then advance twice a day, tearing loose oak trees and engulfing entire plains beneath their flood-tides, there shimmered 'the outline of enigmatic beings – half-men, half-beast'.[86] Just as Ovid, peering askance at the Tomitans, had fingered them as lycanthropes, so in the savage reaches of Germany were the borders between animal and human even more unsettlingly blurred. Chieftains who wished for a policy briefing, it was reported by Roman scholars who had made a close study of German customs, were likeliest to consult a horse. Conversely, 'the towering stature of the Germans, their fierce blue eyes and reddish hair',[87] spoke of a nature barely less bestial than that of some steel-clawed bear, padding over mountain slopes. Geography could not be bucked. Their bogs and trees shrouded in a perpetual drizzle, Germans were the spawn of their environment. The gods, who had considerately endowed Rome with a climate ideally suited to the growth of a mighty city, had doomed the inhabitants of the chilly North to a backwardness that was at once torpid and ferocious, dull and intemperate. Landscape, weather, people: Germany was unredeemably savage.

Or was it? Much the same, after all, could once have been said of the Gauls. Bad memories of them in Rome ran very deep. Back in 390 BC, a Gallic horde had erupted into Italy, annihilated six whole legions and sacked the city itself. Only with the conquests won by Augustus's deified father had Gaul finally ceased to be a place of dread. Now, fifty years on, great changes were afoot beyond the Alps. Roman rule had brought to a people once notorious for their trousers and their gravy-soaked moustaches, their drunken brawling and their taste for collecting heads, a very different way of life. The grandsons of chieftains who had hurled themselves half-naked against the invading legions now draped themselves in the toga and rejoiced in the name of 'Julius'. Rather than guzzle wines indiscriminately, they were coming to develop a nose for the classiest Italian and Eastern *grands crus* – and even, remarkably, to plant the odd vineyard themselves. Most promisingly of all, dotted across a landscape that had previously boasted only villages and rough stockades perched on hills, cities were starting to appear: islands of civilisation complete with flashy monuments and street-grids. Augustus, who had brought the fruits of peace to his fellow citizens, had brought them to the Gauls as well. Foundation after foundation duly proclaimed its gratitude: Augustodurum and Augustomagus, Augustobona and – just to vary things – Caesarobona. The most spectacular of all the Gallic monuments to the Princeps had been raised by Drusus in Lugdunum, where an altar to Rome and Augustus, complete with a double ramp and two giant winged statues of Victory, had been inaugurated in 12 BC.[88] It provided, on neutral ground, and in a city that served as the hub of the provincial road system, a focus of loyalty for the whole of Gaul. Noblemen from more than sixty different tribes had flocked to its opening. As its first high priest, a man had been elected whose name, Gaius Julius Vercondaridubnus, perfectly expressed in its fusion of the native with the Roman the emerging mestizo order. Something startling had begun to glimmer: a future in which the Gauls, perhaps, would no longer rank as barbarians at all. 'Enslaved as they have been, and living as their captors instruct them to live, they are all of them now at peace.'[89]

And if the Gauls, why not the Germans? Admittedly, it was taken for granted by the Roman high command that the further from civilisation they advanced, the wilder and more obdurate their opponents were bound to become; but the two and a half decades of their campaigning beyond the Rhine gave them good grounds for hope. The priority, of course, had been the same as it ever was with barbarians: to demonstrate that resistance was futile. Season after season, columns of legionaries had duly tramped eastwards out of their winter quarters. Most of the German tribes, confronted by the steel-lined scale and sophistication of Roman military operations, had ended up offering churlish submission. One of them, the most ferocious of all, had even donated to Augustus as a token of their friendship the most precious object in their possession, a great bronze cauldron consecrated by the blood spilled into it from the slit throats of their prisoners. Any opposition, it went without saying, had been dealt with in brisk and imperial fashion. Tiberius, confronted by one of the tribes who had presumed to steal Lollius's eagle, had coolly rounded up all 40,000 of its members and dumped them on the far side of the Rhine. Deportations, though, had been the least of it. Massacres and mass enslavement had repeatedly served to rub German noses in the brute fact of Roman power. The very landscape had come to bear the invaders' stamp. Canals had been scored across the watery flatlands; roads cleared through the forests; pontoons laid out over bogs. Even the mighty Elbe, for all that it had stood proof against the ambitions of Drusus, had been vanquished in the end. No phantom women had appeared when, almost a decade on, another Roman army had arrived on its banks. At its head there had ridden a nobleman by the name of Lucius Domitius Ahenobarbus, or 'Bronze Beard': a legate who more than compensated for the notorious quality of his cruelty and arrogance by being married to Antonia, the elder of the Princeps's two nieces. He had crossed over the Elbe — a momentous achievement. The river, according to the most up-to-date calculations of the best cartographers, was believed to be almost as close to China as it was to the Atlantic. By compelling the tribes on its far bank to acknowledge Roman authority, Ahenobarbus had brought the giddy dream of global rule that much closer to fulfilment. With the Germans pacified for good, who would there be to stop Rome's onward march to the eastern Ocean?

It had taken the Princeps's deified father ten years to bring Gaul to heel; and his own armies, by AD 9, had been operating in Germany for more than double that time. Ahenobarbus, before departing the Elbe for the security of his winter quarters, had erected on its far bank an altar to Augustus. It was the second such monument he had established during his term of office. The first, planted at the opposite end of Germany, stood on the western bank of the Rhine, in the lands of a tribe, the Ubians, who had been firm allies of Rome since the time of Julius Caesar. The twin altars, framing as they did the vast expanses in between, served as potent symbols of Augustus's gathering confidence that what had for so long been a war zone was ready at last to be settled as a province. The prize was a rich one – potentially much richer than had first been thought. Germany, it turned out, offered more than merely swamps and forests. There were rich agricultural lands as well, and supplies of iron, and fine-quality goose-down, and a curious concoction fashioned out of goat lard and ashes named 'soap'. Already, since its introduction to Rome, high society had come to swear by it. In a city that had always valued blondes, this was perhaps only to be expected. Used in the right proportions, the miraculous product could give a hint of gold to even the dullest locks. Fashion victims, it was true, had to be careful not to go overboard: excessive application had been known, on a few calamitous occasions, to result in women going bald. Here too, though, it was a German export that provided the remedy. Ovid, in the happy days before his exile, had exulted in the boost given by the conquest of Germany to the potential sex appeal of his girlfriends. 'Send for the tresses of German prisoners,' the poet had advised one lover after an unfortunate accident with hair dye. 'You'll look splendid, adorned in the tribute shorn off all those victims of our triumphs.'[90]

Nevertheless, prized though auburn wigs were, the real wealth of

Germany was to be found, not in the hair of its women, but in the sword-arms of its men. Like a wild beast tamed to human purposes, a barbarian brought to acknowledge Roman superiority could, with careful handling, be trained in the requirements of military discipline. Combine these with his own native muscle and ferocity, and the result could hardly fail to be impressive. Just how impressive, indeed, was evident from the patronage of Augustus himself. The Princeps, who could have recruited warriors from any corner of the world to serve him as his bodyguards, had opted for Germans. Nostalgia for the simple days of Romulus had doubtless predisposed him to recognise in these hairy primitives certain welcome virtues. Savages they might be – but they were noble savages. Lacking the benefits of civilisation, they also lacked its degeneracies. 'No one in Germany finds vice a laughing matter.'[91] There, it was reliably reported, adultery in a woman was punished by shaving her bald, stripping her naked and whipping her the length of her village. Instincts as robust as these, if they could only be put to the service of Rome, promised much benefit.

The Ubians, with their long track-record of loyalty, had been serving alongside the legions since the time of Julius Caesar; but the widening of operations eastwards had required the enrolment of auxiliaries from tribes across Germany. One of these, a people named the Batavians, warriors of exceptional prowess who inhabited the watery flatlands where the Rhine met with the Ocean, had been signed up wholesale. Other tribes, less amenable to Roman blandishments, were subject to more targeted recruitment. When Tiberius, shortly before his posting to Pannonia, had followed in his brother's footsteps by leading an amphibious expedition to the Elbe, he had made sure to woo the elites in his path with honours, grants of citizenship and glamorous commands. The results, amid the traumatic convulsions of the revolt in Pannonia, had stood Rome in good stead. In the Balkans, German contingents had served Tiberius loyally and well. Meanwhile, in Germany itself, the tribes had remained at peace. No attempt had been made to capitalise upon Rome's distraction. The

Princeps's instincts appeared proven correct. Germany had been won for civilisation. It was ready to be given laws, a census, taxes: to become a province.

In AD 9, even as Tiberius was visiting fire and death upon the Balkans, travellers to the northern frontier would have found a very different scene. The Rhine was less a frontier than a highway. The markers of Rome's military presence were, of course, everywhere to be seen: sprawling legionary bases, supply depots, ships loaded with battle-engines churning up the river. Not all the traffic, though, was military. Boats carried grain as well as troops, barrels of wine as well as horses. Though most of this produce was destined for the mess-halls of the some 60,000 soldiers who constituted the occupation force, by no means all of it was. As in Gaul, so in Germany: the provincial authorities were eager to give the natives a taste of Roman living. In the territory of the Ubians, the altar to Augustus erected by Ahenobarbus was already coming to provide an equivalent to Lugdunum, a cult centre and capital rolled into one. Patches of concrete were starting to dot the river bank. Even beyond the Rhine, in the dreary expanses where men thought nothing of sporting top-knots and tight trousers, and women draped themselves in low-cut animal skins, it was no longer all wattle-and-daub. The odd refuge from barbarism was being painstakingly developed. Fifty miles and more east of the Rhine, it was now possible for travellers to enjoy a taste of the urban: raw, half-built settlements, it was true, but endowed with water pipes, and apartment blocks, and statues of Augustus.* Clearly, if a stone forum could be built amid the wilds of Germany, then it could be built anywhere. The future looked bright indeed. 'With cities being founded, and the barbarians adapting to a whole new way of living, they were on their way to becoming Roman.'[92]

---

* The key find which has served to demonstrate the scale and ambition of Roman urbanism east of the Rhine was made in the late 1990s, at Waldgirmes, some sixty miles beyond the river, in the state of Hesse.

Naturally, some regions remained more secure than others. For twenty years now, ever since the time of Drusus, the surest road taken by the legions into the heart of Germany had been along the course of a river named the Lippe. Flowing westwards as it did into the Rhine, its waters provided Roman shipping with ready access to the vitals of barbarian territory. The same bristling array of camps and supply depots that marked the frontier with Gaul now lined the Lippe. No longer, though, for the occupying forces, was the advance along its banks necessarily a march into a heart of darkness. The provincial authorities could now rely on sympathisers within the tribes them-selves to assist in the ongoing project of pacification. North of the Lippe, for instance, strategically placed midway between the Rhine and the Elbe, were the lands of a people named the Cherusci. Fractious though they had proven in the early years of Roman engagement in Germany, Tiberius had since brought them decisively to heel. Their chiefs, like many others, had been wooed and recruited as auxiliaries. Service alongside the legions had provided them with an immersive crash-course in Roman military culture. Typical was a young chieftain named Arminius, who had returned home to his tribal homeland fluent in Latin and garlanded with honours. Not merely a Roman citizen, he now ranked as an equestrian. 'Battle-hardened, quick-witted, and with an intelligence well in advance of the normal barbarian',[93] he was ideally qualified to serve the provin-cial authorities as their eyes and ears in the tribal heartlands. Arminius had been schooled in the modus operandi of the legions. He knew how their commanders thought. He understood their ambition to tighten Rome's grip on those zones where her writ as yet ran only feebly. Accordingly, when he brought news to the provincial author-ities that a revolt was brewing in the northern reaches of Germany, where the legions had only sporadically penetrated, he received a ready hearing. Rebellions were best nipped in the bud. Though summer was already fading, it did not take long for three of the five legions stationed in Germany to be commissioned with crushing the insurgency. Off the legionaries duly set. Heading out along trackways long since cleared by military engineers, there was nothing at first to obstruct the task force, no one to block its passage. Viewed from a distance, it would have seemed less a column of men, horses and wagons than some monstrous and predatory beast. Like a serpent it snaked and glittered, but the very earth shook with its passage.

In command rode the man who had issued the legions with their marching orders. Publius Quinctilius Varus, Augustus's legate in the region, was a man experienced in stamping out bushfires. A decade earlier, when faced, as governor of Syria, with a series of Jewish uprisings, he had proved more than equal to the challenge. It was not his capabilities as a general, though, that had principally recommended him to the Princeps. Augustus, ever careful to whom he gave the command of five legions, trusted Varus as his own creature: a man who had been married to one of Agrippa's daughters, and then to his own great-niece. Such a consideration would have counted for nothing, though, had Varus not also demonstrated throughout his career impressive competence in the various duties expected of a provincial governor: the provision of internal security; the administration of justice; the screwing of the natives for taxes. These, in Augustus's opinion, were precisely the talents that the semi-formed province beyond the Rhine now urgently demanded. After decades in which Roman leaders had only ever shown themselves to the Germans at the head of an army, Varus had begun to offer them a glimpse of something else. Peace, after all, had its own awesome aspects. The toga, the lictors, the *fasces*: these too, when it came to persuading barbarians to pay Roman taxes and to obey Roman laws, had their roles to play. Yes, Varus would not hesitate to apply devastating military force when necessary; but it was his intention, now that Germany was conquered, to win the peace as well as the war.

Passing through the lands of the Cherusci, the governor could feel reassured that his strategy was the correct one. As a general at the head of some 18,000 troops, he presented his hosts with the same show of martial invincibility that Germans everywhere had learned to dread; but as the legate of Augustus, he was simultaneously the face of Roman peace and order. Ties of mutual advantage had come to bind both provincial administrators and German warlords; if Varus had any cause to doubt this, he had only to look at his own retinue. There, riding with his auxiliaries, ever ready with advice, giving it in fluent Latin, was Arminius, prince of the Cherusci and Roman equestrian. As Varus and his legions headed further north, into regions where Rome's military engineers had rarely ventured, the guidance of a man familiar with such uncertain paths as did exist through the forests and marshes was invaluable. When Arminius offered to scout ahead of the column's vanguard, to check for ambushes and to clear the way, Varus naturally accepted. Who better than one of their compatriots, after all, to catch the insurgents napping?

Arminius, though, did not come back. Nor did any of the other detachments that Varus had sent out. The seeming explanation was not long in coming. Labouring through thick forest, preoccupied with felling trees and bridging ravines, the long and straggling Roman column was surprised by a sudden rattling of spears. From the deepest shadows they came; and as rain began to fall, turning the mountainside to mud and thickening the gloom, so the pattering of iron javelin-heads turned to a hail. The legionaries, prevented by the terrain from taking up their customary battle formations, had no choice but to toil on through the darkness of the forest, stumbling over the grasping roots and the corpses of their fallen comrades, until at last they reached a spot sufficiently open to serve them as a camp. Here, as the soldiers hurried to raise earthen palisades, and rain steamed and hissed into their watchfires, Varus was able to take stock. His situation was less than perfect, but hardly critical. Ambushes had always been an occupational hazard of campaigning beyond the Rhine. Even Drusus had suffered a few. The key, when pinned down in a hostile landscape, was to travel light and play things safe. Accordingly, Varus gave orders for the wagons in his train to be burned, the better to expedite an about-turn to the security of Rome's militarised zone. With awkward terrain both to the north and south of him, the route that he settled on was the obvious, indeed the only one. Skirting dense forest and mountains, it would take him and his legions through what was marked on Roman charts as '*Teutoburgiensis Saltus*' – the Teutoburg Pass.*

Accordingly, the next day, the long column of soldiers wound like a waking serpent out of its night camp, and headed into open country. To the left of the Romans rose oak-covered hills; to their right, a lush expanse of meadows and marshland, dotted with abandoned farmsteads and bright with the wildflowers of late summer. Nervous muleteers, ripping up handfuls of grass, began stuffing them into the bells slung around the necks of pack-animals, anxious to muffle the clappers. A wise precaution. Attacks were still coming whenever the woods along the path thickened. Varus, though, scorned to pursue his assailants. The barbarians, spectral troops emerging from out of the trees to hurl their weapons before receding and vanishing again, could hinder but not halt the column's advance. After three days of running battles, the legionaries had only been confirmed in their deep contempt for the German way of war. Weary and grimed with blood though they were, and despite the trail of corpses in their wake, they knew that in all the qualities required of a soldier, whether training, equipment or discipline, they still ranked as infinitely the superior. No wonder that the insurgents, lacking as they did even rudimentary armour, and armed only with weapons of crudely forged iron, refused to stand and fight. Instead, like insects bred of some undrained bog, they swarmed, and buzzed, and bit.

The third day of marching, and the marshes to the right of the legions, as though in mockery of the pestilential quality of their adversaries, were starting to darken and spread. Meanwhile, to their left, the forests on the hills were getting thicker. The wilds of Germany

---

* *Saltus* in Latin can mean both 'pass' and 'forest'. Tacitus's use of the word to describe the site of the battle has traditionally been translated as 'forest'; but the definitive identification of the battle-site with the foot of the Kalkriese Berg in southern Saxony, first made in the 1990s, now enables the correct translation to be made.

had never seemed so savage – nor the security of the militarised zone, with its camps, its hot baths, and its paved roads leading to the outside world, more enticing. On the legions tramped.

It began to rain. Ahead, grey and dim through the drizzle, loomed a forested spur jutting out from the line of the hills. Rather than attempt to clamber directly across it, the legionaries swung northwards, following its curve. As they did so, they found the bogs closing in on them. Streams scored the pathway, and the mud began to deepen into mire. Splashing and slipping, the legionaries stumbled on. Only at the very edge of the marshes was there anything like firm footing to be found – but it was impossible even for the most professional of soldiers to keep to the trackway, narrow and irregular as it was, and retain their coherence as a column. As a result, the further the legions advanced along the base of the hill, the more they began to lose order. Still worse, though, was to come. The column, even as it began to disintegrate, was being funnelled along its left flank, not by the natural contours of the hill, but by walls built of strips of turf, and topped with a palisade. Had any of the legionaries paused amid the driving rain and the chaos of the advance to study these impediments, then they would have recognised something startling about their design: that it bore the unmistakable stamp of their own construction methods. What were the walls doing there – and why would anyone trained in Roman warcraft have wanted to build them along the margins of a barbarian swamp? Perhaps, the obvious, the only answer had begun to dawn on some even before the harsh, reverberating war-cry for which the Germans were notorious abruptly sounded above the drumming of the rain; before spears in a deadly hail began to shred the length of Varus's line; before the slaughter became general. But by then, of course, it was too late.

The ambush was total. To the legionaries, it was as though monsters bred of the forest's own stock and stone were emerging from behind their ramparts to attack them, howling in barbarous tongues, thousands upon thousands, a horde vast beyond anything that a single tribe could possibly have mustered. No time, though, to take stock. The chaos in the Roman column was complete. Already, bodies punctured with spears lay awash in the shallows of the bog; now came an even deadlier harvesting. Swords slashing and hacking at the legionaries fashioned bloody havoc. Disoriented, rain-blinded, panicking, the soldiers had no prospect of taking up battle stations. Within minutes their column was irrevocably broken. Piles of the dead lay strewn along the reddening foreshore. The wounded, their entrails spilling into the mud or their bones broken, screamed for mercy, but there was none to be had, and their assailants moved among them, spearing or bludgeoning the dying wherever they lay. Soon, all along the reeking strand, the barbarians were fanning out, hunting what survivors remained. Some had sought to flee into the marshes, but there was no escape to be had there, only the sucking of mud among the reeds as their assailants waded after them. One of the standard-bearers, wrenching his eagle from its post, had wrapped it in his cloak and plunged with it beneath the bloody swamp-waters – but to no avail. Both he and his eagle, along with the two other standards, were taken. Meanwhile, those in the rear of the column had been frantically turning tail; but they too were hunted down. Only a very few, by hiding among the trees like beasts, managed to evade the pursuit. Otherwise, of the army led by Varus into the Teutoburg Pass, three whole divisions of the most formidable fighting force on the planet, there was no one left. The massacre was absolute.

Varus himself, desperate not to be taken prisoner, had fallen on his sword. Other officers were not so lucky. Rather than dispatch them along with the other Roman wounded, the victors had rounded them up alive. The captives had a dark foreboding of the horrors now in store. Everyone who served in Germany had heard tales of the deadly rituals practised by the natives in their swamps and groves. Their gods were greedy for human blood. Variety was the spice of death. And so it proved. Some prisoners found themselves being herded stumbling through the shallows of the marsh, then bound securely, and drowned where the mud was deepest; others were led into the forest. Here, where huge numbers of the barbarians had assembled, those officers with a particular grasp of German affairs had their best and last opportunity to work out just what might have happened to their army. No one tribe could possibly have summoned the numbers that had erupted from the woods above the pass. Someone, somehow, had forged a confederation out of the notoriously disputatious barbarians. No chance, though, to enquire directly. 'At last, you viper, you have ceased to hiss.'[94] So cried one German in triumph to a prisoner whose mouth he had sewn up after first hacking out the tongue. It was possible, though, for those whose eyes had not been gouged out, to look around them as they were being dragged to their deaths, and to mark one barbarian in particular who was presiding supreme over the rituals. His identity, to the officers who had long thought of him as a comrade, would have come, on a day of horrors, as one final, deadly shock. As their throats were slashed open, or they choked at the end of ropes slung over a tree, or waited kneeling for their heads to be severed with the blow of a sword, they would have known that the man who had destroyed both them and the dearest ambitions of Imperator Caesar Augustus was that princely equestrian of the Roman people, Arminius.

Cherchez la Femme

Tiberius was badly prone to spots. Tall, muscular and well proportioned, with piercing eyes that could supposedly see in the dark, and sporting the mullet that had long marked the Claudians as tonsorial trendsetters, he was by any reckoning handsome — except for the pimples. They would suddenly erupt all over his cheeks in a violent rash. Good-looking though he was, he never could stop the acne.

The blaze of a great feat too might end up spotted. Tiberius's record of service to Rome was on a par with that of the greatest generals in the city's history, and yet repeatedly he had found his victories tarnished by sudden disasters. In 9 BC, his victories in the Balkans had been overshadowed by the death of his brother in Germany; in AD 6, his string of successes in Germany by rebellion in the Balkans. Now, in the hour of his supreme achievement, the news arrived in Rome of a calamity beyond the city's worst nightmares. The numerous celebrations scheduled to mark the final defeat of the Pannonian insurgents were abruptly cancelled. A triumph was out of the question while the slaughtered remains of three legions lay as food for German wolves and ravens. The Roman people gave themselves over to mourning – but also to panic. A primordial dread, which the vastness and sweep of their conquests had served only to pacify, not eliminate, flared back into life: of barbarians descending on them from the depths of the gloomy north, erupting into Italy, crashing over their defences, making their city flow with blood. Reports that three great columns of fire had been seen rising above the Alps did nothing to calm nerves; nor a sudden plague of locusts in the capital itself. The presumption of Roman invincibility, which the Roman people themselves had come almost to believe, gave way among many citizens to its opposite: a despairing conviction that their empire was doomed.

Alarm was hardly eased by the evident twitchiness of the Princeps himself. To a man who had entrusted his own security to German troops, the revelation of Arminius's treachery came as a bitter personal blow. His guards were hurriedly reassigned to a variety of inaccessible islands. Other Germans in the capital, no matter their business, were expelled, while a state of emergency was declared on the city's streets. Meanwhile, in a house now safely denuded of barbarians, Augustus roamed around refusing to have his hair cut, and banging his head against doors. All his life, he had known with a supreme genius how to make play with the shadow-zone that lurked between appearance and reality: not just to veil his own power before his fellow citizens, but also, beyond the limits of Rome, to intimidate all who presumed to doubt Roman might. The agitation that he had betrayed in the Senate when brought news of the Pannonian revolt had shown how alert he was to the element of bluff in this; but now,

163

in the wake of the disaster in Germany, he found himself staring it full in the face. How was his great innovation of a standing army to cope with such a shock? The military foundations on which Roman supremacy depended, tested already to their limits in Pannonia, now stood revealed as alarmingly slight. Twenty-eight legions had been serving as the empire's garrison – a total reduced, after a single day's slaughter, by a ninth. The shock to Augustus's confidence was hardly surprising. Never at his best in a military crisis, the howl with which he repeatedly rent the Palatine mingled impotence with fury. 'Quinctilius Varus, give back my legions!'[95]

A vain prayer, of course. Instead, some other way had to be found to plug the gap. Already, the insurgency in the Balkans had stretched Rome's reserves of manpower almost to breaking point. Now, with the whole northern frontier in flames, the Princeps was left with no alternative but to impose measures that his lengthy stewardship of the Republic was supposed to have done away with: the summoning of veterans out of retirement, forced conscription, the execution of malingerers. At the head of this makeshift army of the north, barely rested though he was from the rigours of the Balkans, rode the only conceivable candidate for the job, Rome's man for a crisis, as tireless as he was able. Five years earlier, arriving in Germany, Tiberius had been greeted by those who had previously served under him with effusive displays of emotion. Veterans familiar with his painstaking style of generalship had mobbed him with tears in their eyes, yelling out their battle honours and hailing his return. Now, with the screams of Varus's legions echoing in every soldier's imagination, the arrival on the Rhine of a general famed for refusing to risk the lives of his men with pointless displays of machismo was all the more welcome. Showboating was absolutely not what the crisis required.

Instead, the desperate need was for retrenchment. So grievous had been the blow dealt by Arminius to Rome's prestige and manpower that everywhere north of the Alps now seemed at risk. Steadily, remorselessly, as was ever his way, Tiberius set about the task of shoring up Roman authority. First Gaul, then the defences along the

Rhine were stabilised. Girt around as they were by formidable palisades, and protected by the natural moat of the river, the huge camps on the western bank that for decades had provided the legions in Germany with their winter bases remained secure. East of the Rhine, it was a different story. There, a devastating firestorm kindled in the wake of Arminius's victory had overwhelmed the forward bases of Rome's push towards the Elbe. Half-finished towns stood abandoned. Statues of Augustus lay smashed amid rubble and weeds. Skeletons littered charred fortresses. Only a single base had been successfully evacuated – but that too, the moment the hurried withdrawal from it had been completed, had gone up in flames. It was as though the entire infrastructure of occupation had never been.

Familiar as he was with the perils of guerilla warfare, Tiberius knew better than to plunge into an untamed wilderness before first making sure of his rear. Lacking in drama though this task might be, it was no less critical for that. For a year and more, Tiberius duly confined himself to firming up the Rhine defences. Military bases were upgraded; units transferred from other provinces; the conscripts from Italy integrated into the overall command. By AD 11, eight legions stood camped out along the Rhine where before there had been only five, while in Gaul barely a horse was left. Only now did Tiberius finally venture to the far side of the river. The sorties were predictably punitive. Crops and villages were burned. Military roads were cleared of nettles. A zone along the entire eastern bank of the Rhine was secured. From here, were it to prove the wish of the Princeps, the reconquest of Germany could certainly be attempted – but Tiberius was under no illusions as to what a challenge it would represent. Beyond the Rhine, peril now lurked everywhere. A single error, a single failure to catch the flitting of a shadow on the slope of a hill or in the depths of a forest, and disaster might be total. No one, from the lowest to the highest, could afford to drop his guard. When a senior officer sent a band of soldiers over the Rhine to escort one of his former slaves on a hunting expedition, Tiberius was so irate that he immediately stripped the man of his command. The situation was far too tense for any hint of frivolity. Tiberius himself, practising what he preached, kept his baggage train to a minimum, made himself available day or night to his officers, and invariably slept without a tent.

This close, almost neurotic attention to detail, although reaping him no decisive victories, was sufficient to secure him a more limited aim. The Germans had been left in no doubt as to the capacity of the Roman war machine to regenerate itself. Three years on from the ambush at the Teutoburg Pass, legions were once again marching through Germany. Tiberius, who had avoided every ambush set for him and even survived an assassination attempt, could be well pleased with his efforts. Gaul and the Rhine stood secure. Barbarian hordes would not be descending on Italy after all.

The 'sole defence of the Roman people'[96] had achieved all that he possibly could have done. 'The vigilance of one man, and one alone,' as Augustus put it, 'has redeemed our affairs from ruin.'[97] In AD 12, with the end of the campaigning season and the return of his legions to their bases on the Rhine, Tiberius laid down his command at last, and headed back to Rome. There, the weather had been terrible all autumn, with black skies and endless rain. Abruptly, though, on the morning of 23 October, the clouds lifted, and bright sunshine began to dry the streets where crowds had massed to cheer Tiberius's triumph. The only showers that day would be of rose petals. Bright blazed the parade of captured weapons and armour, the collars hammered around the necks of fettered prisoners, the standards borne in stately-moving procession. Golden trophies, lit by the sun, gilded the marble of the Forum's buildings with their reflections, while finely decorated effigies, fashioned out of silver and carried aloft in front of Tiberius's chariot, portrayed for the Roman people the many victories won by him on their behalf. 'Barbarian towns, walls breached, inhabitants vanquished. Rivers, and mountains, and battles in deep forests.'[98]

Yet for all the clamour and spectacle, there was something lacking. A faint pall of dissatisfaction, of the kind that Tiberius had so often laboured under, loured over his great moment. The crowds were celebrating, not his stabilisation of the region beyond the Rhine, but his pacification of the Balkans. His mighty achievement in securing the Roman people from barbarian incursions, unglamorous as it was, went unsaluted. His fellow citizens, most of whom had never in their lives smelt the raw timber of a newly built palisade, still less the stench of a German bog, found little to interest them in the wearisome details of frontier duty. What they wanted was evidence of dash and daring – qualities which Tiberius had never had much interest in flaunting. The virtues he prized were altogether more antique ones, the attributes of the Roman people at their most heroic and upstanding: duty, determination, self-discipline. Riding in his chariot through the streets of Rome, stern-faced and stiff-necked, he scorned to play up to the cheering. Spectators who wanted a crowd-pleaser had to look elsewhere – and the perfect idol, as it happened, was ready to hand.

Among the battle honours paraded in Tiberius's triumph, some were listed as belonging to a second and altogether more swash-buckling commander: Germanicus. That the young man's escapades had often flirted with disaster, and on more than one occasion required his uncle to bail him out, was of no concern to most. What mattered were his affability, his style, his fresh-faced, dynamic good looks. Indeed, so keen was Germanicus to appear to best effect that he had gone to inordinate efforts to bulk up his naturally weedy calves. Vanity of such an order was a part of his inheritance. His father's son, Germanicus bore the stamp as well of a grandfather even more illustrious and charismatic than Drusus: for his mother was Antonia the Younger, the daughter of Marc Antony by Octavia. 'Whether in war or peace, you are the flower of our younger generation.'[99] Tiberius, flinty man of tradition that he was, had no time for such shameless gushing – but the Roman people, in the wake of their brief but intense infatuation with Gaius, remained in thrall to the cult of youth. Now, in the debonair Germanicus, they had a fresh heart-throb. Tiberius, by comparison, could hardly help but seem a man out of fashion.

Yet he was doubly caught in a bind. Despite his age and his many years of service to Rome, he remained legally a dependant, subject to the *patria potestas* of Augustus. The authority of a father, to a man so wedded to the values of his class as Tiberius, was not readily bucked. The same ideals that had inspired in him his lifelong republican contempt for monarchy also made him painfully aware of the duty that he owed the Princeps as a son. In another age, Tiberius's lineage and his many battle honours would have combined to win for him what the Claudians had always most craved: primacy among their peers. Not now. Primacy would come to him only by right of succession. Tiberius could not change this. His loyalty to Augustus was not just to a father, but to the saviour of Rome. Mortifying though it was that his own record of service should carry less weight in the affairs of the city than the favour of an ageing autocrat, too much was owed the Princeps to permit him to surrender to resentment. The same gratitude that fostered in Tiberius emotions of deep humiliation served to trump them as well. Trapped in a role that he despised, his very principles served only to confirm him as its captive.

The debt of duty, though, was not only to Augustus. 'I obeyed my parents. I gave way to their authority. Just or unjust and harsh, they always found me obedient and compliant.'[100] A mother was no less the guardian of the stern traditions of the Roman elite than a father; and Livia, for half a century her husband's constant and trusted companion, was nothing if not a model of matriarchal severity. In all the years of her marriage, she had never once let Augustus down. Obliged to serve him simultaneously as a paragon of domestic virtue and as *Romana princeps*,[101] the 'first lady of Rome', she had displayed a talent for squaring circles that 'was a match for the subtlety of her husband'.[102] When Livia attended a sacrifice, it was with her homespun *stola* pulled modestly over her head; when she kept to her loom, it was with her hair worn in a style of such ostentatious simplicity that ladies' maids across the empire breathed thanks to her for making it *à la mode*. No one, now that Livia was seventy years old, would have cause to doubt her forbidding chastity, nor upbraid her for behaving in a manner inappropriate to her station. Augustus was not the only one to be blessed in his relationship to such a paragon. A war hero of the venerable kind that Tiberius aspired to be was almost required to have a virtuous mother. Livia's brand of rectitude was no less true to the ideals of her family than was that of her son. 'Her behaviour' – as even those suspicious of her were obliged to acknowledge – 'was decidedly old school.'[103]

Which only made those who mistrusted her more suspicious still. It was, of course, taken for granted by all right-thinking citizens that women should keep their noses out of affairs of state: 'What an appalling business it would be were they to seize what are properly exclusive to men: the Senate, the army, magistracies!'[104] Augustus, conservative in everything except his own appetite for supremacy, naturally concurred – and Livia knew it. Yet the exercise of authority, in a state where the supremacy of its first citizen had long since ceased to depend upon formal position, was shadowed by ambivalence. Power, as it evaded its ancient limits, had begun to evolve and mutate. Although Livia held no formal rank, her privileges were of an order to put many a senator in the shade. Legal immunity from insult, that traditional prerogative of a tribune, had been hers since the distant days of the Triumvirate. She also enjoyed, by virtue of a series of decrees enacted by her husband, a quite exceptional degree of financial independence. Most conveniently of all, in a city from which carriages had traditionally been forbidden, she had the right to zip about in a *carpentum*, a lavishly decorated two-wheeler that traditionally only the most senior of priests had been permitted to use. The Roman people, alert as they were to the subtle markers of status that signalled a patron worth having, did not need anyone to join up the dots. They knew what they had in Livia. A woman graced by miraculous white chickens and laurel sprigs, whose name appeared above the entrance to many a renovated shrine, 'who alone had been found worthy to share Caesar's celestial bed'[105] – here was potency of a rare and awesome order. The authority that clung to her was like a perfume: rich, expensive, rare. Across the Roman world, her name had begun to be paired with that supernatural manifestation of her husband's greatness, his *Genius* – joined together as names on altars, as silver statues, as carvings of snakes. To keep a woman in her place was one thing – but a goddess quite another. Nevertheless, those who approached Livia for a favour tended to do so in hope as well as fear. 'Only when she helps people out of danger, or else endows them with some honour, does she manifest her power.'[106]

A reassurance which – as Livia herself, close and canny, perfectly understood – was as liable to raise hackles as to dampen gossip. She knew her city, and how the currents of rumour and slander eddied ceaselessly through its streets. Even praise might be a source of trouble. When Ovid, out of touch and despairing, publicly urged his wife to beg 'the First Lady'[107] for his release, the silence from the Palatine was deafening. To allude openly to Livia's influence over her husband, to imply that decisions might be taken on the say-so of a woman, to cast corridors or bedrooms as cockpits of power, were insults to the Princeps as well as his wife. The Senate House, as it had ever been, was the only proper stage for the discussion of affairs of state. So sensitive was Augustus to the charge that a woman's whisperings might sway him more effectively than the oration of a consul that he had ordered a daily record to be kept of all his household's activities. 'Say nothing and do nothing that you would not wish to see recorded in it openly'[108] – so Augustus had advised Julia and her daughters. Two of them had ignored the warning and paid a terrible price. To Livia, though, the Princeps had issued no such warning. There had been no need. Augustus had enough experience of his wife's discretion to know that it could be relied upon. Nevertheless, for everyone in Rome obsessed by the doings of the August Family, this begged an intriguing question. Had the taint of open scandal failed to attach itself to Livia because she was genuinely above suspicion – or was it rather because she was so deep in all her schemings?

Mother to Tiberius, she had become a stepmother as well. Not for her, certainly, the public thunderbolts unleashed by her outraged husband at Julia. It was Livia, when her disgraced stepdaughter was transferred from the prison island of Pandateria to Rhegium, who had obligingly seconded her some slaves;[109] Livia too, when Julia's own daughter was exiled in turn, who had stepped in with financial support. Not everyone, though, was convinced by these displays of philanthropy. 'For all the pity that Livia made sure to show her step-relatives in their ruin, she had worked hard, while everything was going well for them, to stab them in the back.'[110] Such, at any rate, was the allegation. The evidence for it, although circumstantial, struck many as convincing. Stepmothers in Rome were widely presumed to be malignant. In a city that had long viewed marriage as a manoeuvre in the battle for dynastic advantage, this was perhaps only to be expected. That Livia, with the world's most powerful man in her bed, should have sought to boost her son's expectations hardly came as a revelation. Doubly a Claudian, she had never forgotten the debt that she owed her peerless ancestry. Although reserved and careful in most things, the pride that she took in her line of descent was one emotion that she scorned to veil. Just outside Rome, overlooking one of the city's arterial roads, an ancient temple restored by Livia proclaimed it to the world. There, chiselled onto an immense frieze, her name appeared, resplendent above the traffic.[111] 'Wife of Caesar Augustus' – so she described herself. Strikingly, though, the epithet came second to another: 'Daughter of Drusus'. Pushy parenting, to a woman such as Livia, was not a crime but a solemn duty.

Yet just how far was she willing to go? Many, when they reflected upon how ravaged the August Family had been by disaster, suspected her of having played most foully. The downfall of Julia and her daughter were not the only calamities to have afflicted Augustus's plans for the future, after all. Since 29 BC, when Tiberius, riding in his stepfather's triumphal chariot, had stood on the left side of Metellus, the Princeps had suffered repeated bereavements. Again and again, his heirs had died in mysterious circumstances. Almost every Julian blocking Livia's son from the succession had fallen by the wayside. Marcellus, Lucius, Gaius: all were gone. No evidence existed sufficient to pin the blame for their deaths upon Livia – but that, to those who suspected her of responsibility, was precisely her fiendish cunning. A murder that left no traces was, notoriously, *muliebris fraus*,[112] 'a woman's machination'. The killers of Julius Caesar had struck their victim down in the open, stabbing and slashing at his body with their blades, leaving his corpse fretted all over with gashes; but when a man was given poison, he might not even realise that he was being murdered. No brute strength was required to slip a tincture into a goblet of wine. Subtly and silently, the venom would work its lethal magic. Little risk, given a practised hypocrisy on the part of the perpetrator, of her ever being fingered. Only by sucking on a citron, an exotic fruit from the forests of the distant East, might the victim hope to save himself – for no surer antidote existed than its bitter juice. 'It will help, when drinks have been poisoned by a pitiless stepmother, to drive the dark venom from the limbs.'[113] Perhaps, then, had Gaius and Lucius only been kept better supplied with Median citrus, the prospects for Tiberius's succession would have been very different.

Or perhaps not. Paranoia itself was a kind of poisoning, after all. Gossip and slander were the venoms of the mind. If Livia were truly what she seemed to be when she appeared arrayed in her *stola* before the Roman people – pious, loyal to her husband, the embodiment of Justice and Peace – then the blackening of her name was a crime as monstrous as those of which her critics accused her. If the sober virtues of Livia herself were to be cast as hypocrisy, then so too were those of the August Family as a whole. Far from serving as a model of traditional Roman values, the outward gleam of its sanctity would stand revealed as a sham, rotted from within by murderous and despotic passions. Clearly, with Augustus an increasingly enfeebled septuagenarian, and global peace dependent upon a secure and peaceful succession, such a prospect was beyond the pale.

'Do not be unduly indignant, should anyone speak ill of me':[114] so the Princeps had once counselled Tiberius. Now, in his old age, he was growing impatient with his own advice. No matter how venerable the city's traditions of invective, no matter how devastatingly he had himself exploited them back in his youth, how could he responsibly permit them to endanger the stability of the state? The security of the Roman people, so Augustus had come to feel in his old age, was more important than any right to freedom of speech. Already, Ovid had been dispatched into exile. Then, 'imposing an unprecedented punishment on literature',[115] the Princeps had condemned to the bonfire copies of a subversive history of the civil wars by a lawyer named Titus Labienus – a sentence so devastating to the author that he had committed suicide in protest. Finally, in a salutary demonstration of the new limits that were coming to be set upon the licence of libel, a second lawyer, a witty and waspish orator by the name of Cassius Severus, was banished to Crete for the crime of diminishing the *maiestas*, the 'majesty', of the Roman people. Here, for those concerned to uphold their city's traditional liberties, was a chilling and ominous precedent. The charge of *maiestas*, as it was familiarly known, had long been applied to treasonable actions – but never before to words. That, though, in effect, was the offence for which Severus had been condemned: 'defaming with vituperative writings eminent men and women'.[116] What punishment might be imposed for defaming the most eminent of them all – the men and women of the August Family – was left hanging in the air.

Ever since the gods, taking pity on the Roman people, had graced them with the peace brought by Augustus, the *pax Augusta*,[117] the world had dwelt in the shadow of what might happen when the Princeps died. By AD 13, when Tiberius was formally endowed by the Senate with powers equivalent to those of his adoptive father, it seemed that the answer had been definitively provided. Whatever Tiberius's private reservations, there could be no shirking now that the weight of responsibilities had been laid upon his shoulders both by Fate and by Augustus. Still, though, the ambivalences of his position continued to flicker and cast their shadows. Even as the Princeps's officially appointed colleague, Tiberius could not be declared his successor – for Rome, of course, was not a monarchy, nor her First Citizen a king. The regime fashioned by Augustus had been shaped to his own contours, and to his alone. That Tiberius could boast the most blue-blooded lineage in Rome; that he was his city's greatest general; that he had begun to manoeuvre his friends and associates into key provincial commands: these advantages, on their own, remained insufficient to secure him ultimate primacy. Only by squeezing and cramping himself into the mould of rule forged by the Princeps could he hope to obtain that, and to assure Rome and the world of peace. His own identity was insufficient. He had no choice but to subsume it into that of Augustus. His authority would never cease to derive from his relationship to the Princeps – and to his mother. Just as malign gossip about the August Family would corrode the foundations on which it rested, so would an assurance that no secrets were being kept, no unspoken rivalries festering, serve to buttress them. Caesar's household had to be above suspicion.

It was not enough, though, in a city such as Rome, merely to lean on a lawyer or two and imagine that gossip could thereby be silenced. No matter how secure Tiberius's position might appear, the partisans of Augustus's daughter had not forgotten that the Princeps had a second male heir: his grandson. Although condemned to penal custody, Agrippa Postumus remained very much alive. For all the ruthlessness shown by Augustus in dispatching him to a remote and barren island, his execution had clearly been a step too far. Those loyal to Julia and her children inevitably kept him in their hearts, while suspecting the worst of Livia. Agrippa, it was officially reported, had something not quite right with him: he was violent, savage, obsessed by fishing. Yet peculiarities of this kind, even if accurately reported, need not have resulted in exile. There was a second member of the August Family, of the same generation as Agrippa, whose infirmities were, if anything, even more of an embarrassment. Back in 10 BC, on the same day that Drusus was dedicating the altar of Augustus at Lyon, his wife Antonia had gone into labour and delivered him a second son. Tiberius Claudius Drusus, as the boy was named, had proven a mortifying contrast to the dashing Germanicus: 'a work of nature only half-completed',[118] as Antonia bitterly put it. He twitched and shook; he dragged his right leg; when he spoke, he barked in a barely intelligible manner, like some sea animal, and when he grew angry, he slobbered and blew spumes of snot. That these disabilities did not prevent Claudius from displaying a notably intellectual turn of mind hardly mattered. Since there was clearly no prospect of his ever attaining the magistracies and commands appropriate to his birth, Augustus and Livia had settled that he should be excluded from public life for good. What they had not done was to send him away from Rome under armed guard. Even when, following in the footsteps of Titus Labienus, Claudius embarked on a history of Augustus's rise to power, Livia's reaction to this lethally subversive choice of research topic was merely to hush it up. 'To give a frank and true account,' she told her grandson bluntly, 'is not an option'[119] — and left it at that. Agrippa would have been so lucky.

A year on from the granting to Tiberius of powers equivalent to Augustus's own, the rumours continued to swirl. It was reported that Agrippa, during his violent fits, would curse Livia by describing her insultingly as a 'stepmother';[120] it was reported too that Augustus, waking up at last to the wiles of his wife, had travelled in secret to Planasia, where he had embraced his grandson and burst into tears. 'Such marks of affection had they shown one another,' so the gossip ran, 'that the young man seemed likely to be restored to his grandfather's house.'[121] Yet the viral nature of these claims only emphasised what no one had any real interest in acknowledging: the degree to which, after forty years and more of Augustus's supremacy, decisions vital to the future of the Roman people were now veiled from their view.

Certainly, when the Princeps did cross with Livia and his retinue from the mainland, in the summer of AD 14, it was not to Planasia, but to Capri. Set like a jewel in the Bay of Naples, conveniently close to the glittering array of amenities that lined the arc of the Italian shore, but removed enough to offer him genuine privacy, it was a favourite residence of the Princeps. Here, despite a bad bout of diarrhoea, he distracted himself by giving banquets and handing out presents to assorted teenagers; and then, after four days, he returned to the mainland. With him went Tiberius, who was travelling onwards to the Balkans, there 'to consolidate in peace what he had conquered in war';[122] and the pair of them, once they had landed at Naples, rejoined the Appian Way and continued into Samnium. Only at Beneventum, the capital of the region, did they finally part. Augustus, with Livia still beside him, turned and headed back for Rome. His stomach, though, was still giving him trouble, and after leaving Samnium, he felt so ill that he was forced to halt his journey and take to his sickbed. By an eerie coincidence, the old family property where he found himself was the one in which, seventy-two years earlier, his father had died: a sign sufficiently ominous to prompt Tiberius's urgent summoning to his bedside. Opinion differed as to what happened next. Some said that Tiberius arrived too late; others that he came just in time for the dying Augustus to embrace him 'and commend to him the continuation of their joint work'.[123] But one thing was certain. As Augustus breathed his last, it was his wife to whom he turned. A kiss – and then his final words. 'Remember our union, Livia, for as long as you live – and so farewell.'[124]

The fateful moment, long dreaded, long anticipated, had come at last. Livia, at any rate, was well prepared for it. Already, both the villa and the neighbouring streets had been sealed off by her guards. Only when everything was ready for the transport of the corpse to Rome was the news of her husband's death finally broken to the world. Escorted by his bodyguard of lictors, all of them dressed in sombre black, and travelling by night to avoid the heat of the summer sun, Imperator Caesar Augustus then set out on his final journey. Knights and councillors from towns along the Appian Way accompanied him by torchlight; so did Tiberius, and so did Livia. It took them a fortnight to reach Rome; and at some point during those two weeks, between the departure of the cortège from the villa in which Augustus had died and its final arrival at his house on the Palatine, a centurion came galloping furiously towards the procession. Reining in his horse and swinging down from his saddle, he demanded to be brought before Caesar. Led into the presence of Tiberius, the travel-stained officer saluted him. 'What you ordered is done,' declared the centurion briskly. 'Agrippa Postumus is dead.' Tiberius, frowning, gave every impression of astonishment. 'But I gave no such order!' Then a pause. 'This will have to be accounted for in the Senate House.'[125]

He spoke as what he was: an aristocrat wedded to the traditions of his class. Naturally, when confronted by a crime as grievous and unforeseen as the murder of Augustus's grandson, he took for granted his duty to inform the Senate. That, after all, was what Rome was about. Among his confidants, however, there was consternation. One of them, learning of Tiberius's intentions, immediately alerted Livia. 'Domestic secrets,' he warned her, 'and friends' advice, and assistance provided by the security services – all must be kept hushed up.'[126] Tips that she hardly needed, of course. She knew better than anyone what was at stake. A command to execute the grandson of Caesar could only have come from the top: from Augustus, from Tiberius – or from herself. Since Augustus had never had any of his relations put to death, and Tiberius's surprise at the news from Planasia was self-evident, Livia had every reason to keep the crime from investigation by the Senate. A word in her son's ear, and the whole business was dropped. On the arrival of the funeral cortège in Rome, no mention was made of the execution of Agrippa Postumus. 'A cover-up ensured silence on the matter.'[127]

When the will of Augustus was formally opened and read out to the Senate, it confirmed in awful terms the disinheritance of his bloodline. 'Since cruel fate has snatched from me my sons, Gaius and Lucius, let Tiberius be my heir.'[128] Livia had triumphed. The dues of obligation owed to her Claudian forebears had been paid in full. The moment, appropriately for a woman of such infinite ambivalence, was marked by paradox. It was decreed by her husband's will that she be graced with the title Augusta and adopted posthumously as his daughter. Livia had become a Julian.

On the day of her husband's funeral, Julia Augusta – as she was now formally known – accompanied his corpse from the Palatine down to the Forum, where Tiberius and her grandson Drusus both delivered eulogies; then, travelling a short distance to where the pyre had been built, she watched in dignified silence as senators lifted the body up onto the brushwood. The fire caught; the flames began to lick; an eagle was released and soared up into the sky. Later, to a senator who claimed to have witnessed the spirit of Augustus similarly rising from the pyre and ascending into the heavens, Livia granted a massive donative. It was money well spent. When the Senate met for the first time a week after the funeral, on 17 September, it was to confirm that the dead Princeps was indeed to be worshipped as a god. His wife was appointed his priest. This, in a city where all the priesthoods except for those of Vesta were monopolised by men, was unprecedented. Astonishingly, Livia was even given a lictor.

After the burning of Augustus's body, the pall of ashes had soon cleared, and even though the remains of the pyre had continued to glow for four days, the pious and dutiful Augusta had been able on the fifth day of her vigil to gather up his bones and place them in a nearby mausoleum, readied for the purpose more than forty years before. A second pall, though, was not so easily dispelled. That Rome, with the execution of Agrippa Postumus, was now once again a city in which murder might be deployed as a manoeuvre in the great game of dynastic advancement was a fact no less true for being too dangerous to acknowledge. Already, as Tiberius prepared to shoulder the burden of rule bequeathed him by his deified predecessor, his reign had fallen into shadow. 'The execution of Agrippa Postumus was the first crime committed under the new Princeps.'[129] Which naturally begged a menacing question: how many more would there be?

II

COSA NOSTRA

4

THE LAST ROMAN

Taking the Wolf by its Ears

Until Augustus built him one, Mars had never had a temple within the sacred limits of Rome. The *pomerium*, ploughed by Romulus and consecrated by the blood of Remus, had always served to mark the border between the twin worlds of war and peace. Only when celebrating a triumph were a general and his army permitted to enter Rome; otherwise, it was sternly forbidden soldiers to trespass on land consecrated to Jupiter. The realm of Mars lay instead in an expanse of flat land that stretched between the western course of the *pomerium* and the curving of the Tiber. It was here, in ancient times, that the Roman people had convened in times of war; here too that they had gathered every year, in an assembly known as the *comitia centuriata*, modelled on the primordial army of the kings, to vote for their senior magistrates. A fitting place, then, to consign to the heavens a man who had secured more conquests for the Roman people than any citizen in history, and served them a record thirteen times as consul. Ascending from the flames of his pyre, the divine Augustus would have gazed down upon a plain long sanctified by the primordial rhythms of the campaigning season and the electioneering of statesmen: the *Campus Martius*.

Much had changed, though, over the course of his long supremacy, on the field of Mars. Even before his first appearance on the political scene, the ambitions of rival warlords had seen the ancient parade ground of the Roman people starting to vanish beneath marble and parkland. It was on the Campus that Pompey had planted his vast stone theatre; it was on the Campus that Antony had boasted a notoriously luxurious garden.[1] Both, inevitably, had ended up under the wing of Augustus – who had then, as was his habit, trumped them with spectacular developments of his own. Presented with a greenfield site right on the doorstep of Rome, he had naturally seized the opportunity to set his stamp on it once and for all. Mourners, as they gathered on the Campus to witness the final journey of the Princeps to his funeral pyre, had been able to admire an assemblage of his *grands projets*. Altars, temples, obelisks: all redounded to his glory. Particularly imposing was the mausoleum in which Livia had reverently deposited his ashes. Though it was common for tombs to line the approaches of Rome, none could possibly compare for sheer scale with that of Augustus. Built in the early years of his supremacy, it provided him in death with the kind of ostentatious residence that he had always been chary of in life. Certainly, no other citizen had thought to commission for himself a vast tumulus, complete with a marble base, a ring of poplars, and a gilded self-portrait on the top. A worthy resting place for the mortal remains of a god.

All of which, from the perspective of his adopted son, only made it the more intimidating to follow in his footsteps. Already, reading out Augustus's will to the Senate, Tiberius had choked, begun to sob, then handed over the document to Drusus to complete on his behalf. A revealing moment. Flinty as Tiberius was, and contemptuous of histrionics, he was hardly the man to fake a breakdown. A veil had briefly been lifted on the ferocious stresses that came with being the heir of Augustus. A fortnight later, on 17 September, the pressure had been ratcheted up even more. The Senate's decision to confirm the divinity of the dead Princeps meant that Tiberius, just like Augustus, had become *divi filius*, 'the son of a god'. A glamorous-seeming promotion, to be sure – but not one that necessarily worked to his advantage. Even though Ovid, desperate enough by now to try anything, would soon be lauding Tiberius from the distant shores of the Black Sea as 'equal in *virtus* to his father',[2] such praise was off-key, sycophantic, embarrassing. No one could equal Augustus. He had saved the Republic, redeemed the Roman people. Tiberius, no less than anyone else, had grown up in his shadow – and everybody knew it. The mould of what it meant to be an *imperator*, an 'emperor', had been irreducibly set. Even dead, Augustus continued to set the standard. Lying on his deathbed, he had demanded applause for his performance in 'the comedy of life';[3] but his heir, never a good actor, was now being obliged to take on the role of Augustus himself. Trapped on a stage-set not of his own making, the new Princeps had no choice but to act out a part already scripted for him by a god. The more that Tiberius Julius Caesar laid claim to the inheritance of his adoptive father, the less he could be himself.

'Only the deified Augustus had the strength of mind to cope with the burden of his responsibilities.'[4] Addressing the Senate in the wake of its confirmation that the dead Princeps had indeed ascended to the heavens, Tiberius spoke plainly. He was in his fifties. His eyesight was going. It was out of the question that he do as invited, and adopt the title of 'Augustus'. If anything, Tiberius informed his fellow senators, he would like to retire and live as a private citizen. Let the Senate rule. Patently, this was an attempt to play the same game that Augustus, veiling his dominance behind a show of false modesty, had always exploited to such brilliant effect – but it was also something else. Oppressed by the obligation to dissolve his identity into that of someone who had just been declared a god, Tiberius was making one last, despairing attempt to be his own man.

In his heart, after all, he remained what he had always been: an aristocrat among aristocrats, and proud of it. The dying Augustus, after his last conversation with Tiberius, was said to have expressed pity for the masses, fated 'to be ground between such remorseless jaws'.[5] The ideals with which the new Princeps identified were those of his ancestors from the upright, primeval days of the Republic: Claudians who, in the conflict between aristocracy and plebs, had stood resolute for the interests of their class. It was Tiberius's intention, in his first policy statement to the Senate, to present a measure that not even the most reactionary of them would have contemplated. A few decades earlier, out on the Campus, the old wooden voting-pens where the Roman people still gathered to elect their consuls had been given a comprehensive makeover. What had originally been nicknamed the 'sheepfold' was now, thanks to the sponsorship of Agrippa, an array of marble porticoes and colonnades: the Saepta. So beautifully did it gleam, indeed, that elections seemed rather wasted on it. With the voters of the *comitia centuriata* only meeting on an irregular basis, the complex had come to serve as one of Rome's premier venues for extravaganzas and luxury shopping. Now, in his address to the Senate, Tiberius took the final, logical step. Elections in the Saepta, he announced, were terminated. No longer would the *comitia centuriata* be assembling to vote for magistrates. Competition for the consulship was henceforward to be confined to the Senate House. Why should the plebs, raucous and vulgar as they were, be trusted with a responsibility that properly belonged to their betters? Only senators, those repositories of all that was best and noblest about the Republic, could be permitted to exercise it. The age-old dream of Roman conservatives down the ages seemed fulfilled at last. 'The lower orders, while not cringing before their betters, were to respect them; the mighty, while not despising their inferiors, were to keep them under their thumb.'[6]

A manifesto calculated to enthuse the Senate, it might have been thought. Tiberius was banking, though, upon two mutually exclusive fantasies: that senators would prove worthy of the great charge laid upon them; and that they would willingly and without compulsion do so by acknowledging him as Princeps. Three-quarters of a century before, returning home in triumph from his pacification of the East, Pompey had nurtured a similarly fond hope: that the Senate would recognise its duty to the Republic by freely doing as he said. The

The Julians and Claudians under Tiberius

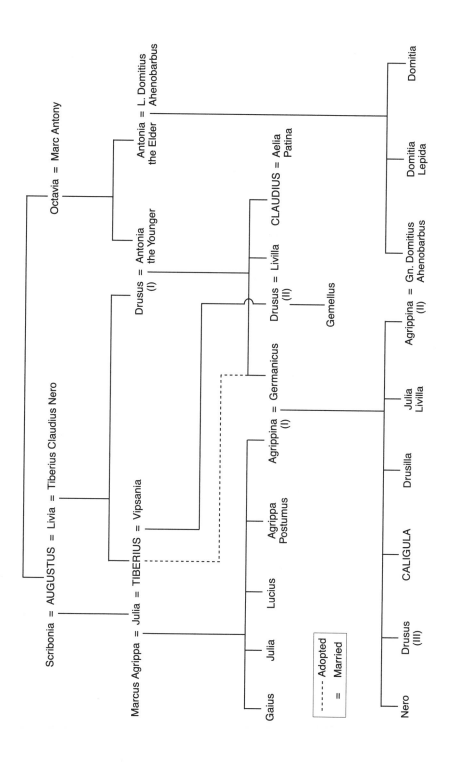

challenge of squaring that particular circle had helped to precipitate civil war and the ultimate dominance of Augustus; now, as senators listened to Tiberius in bemused silence, it resulted only in awkward squirming. The subtlety of what he wanted was far too knotted for them to unpick. That they should cast off the habit of obedience to an autocrat and reclaim their ancestral liberties, only then to demonstrate their principles by hailing him as Princeps: here was a paradox that few of them could fathom. The more that Tiberius insisted upon the pre-eminence of the Senate, the more the Senate insisted upon his. They understood – or rather, they thought they understood – the rules of the game. 'How long, O Caesar, will you suffer the Republic to lack a head?'[7]

Sure enough, by the evening of the 17th, a long, exhausting and fractious session had arrived at its foregone conclusion. Tiberius, frustrated in his attempt to emerge from Augustus's shadow, had reluctantly accepted, if not the supremacy pressed on him by the Senate, then at least that he would no longer refuse it. Yet the senators too, bemused by their dawning realisation that his hesitancy had been more than just a show, were left unsettled. The genius of Augustus had been for veiling the compromises, the contradictions, the hypocrisies of his regime. But Tiberius, racked by self-contempt, lacked a ready facility for putting his fellow senators at ease. He had been too long away from Rome – in Rhodes, the Balkans and Germany – to have anything like an instinctive command of their various factions and cliques. Augustus, sensitive to the problem, had attempted to ease it shortly before his death by formally 'entrusting the Senate to Tiberius'[8] – just as an anxious parent might make provision for his sons. This, though, when the new Princeps was reminded of it, and urged to accept the title of 'Father of his Country', only compounded his embarrassment. How was the founding claim of the new order, that the supremacy of Rome's first citizen was not equivalent to that of a monarch, to survive such a blatant transfer of title? Unsurprisingly, Tiberius turned it down. After all, had the new Princeps simply done as the Senate urged, and accepted that 'he had succeeded to the station of his father',[9] then the façade of a free republic would have sustained catastrophic damage – perhaps beyond repair.

All the same, the price paid by Tiberius was crippling. Rigid of principle, awkward of manner, hypocrisy did not come nearly as naturally to him as it had done to Augustus. The result, paradoxically, was to make him seem all the more a hypocrite. 'In his speeches, he never articulated what he really wanted, and when he did express a desire for something, invariably he did not mean it. His words only ever conveyed the opposite of his true purpose.'[10] A damning, but not unjustified, verdict. The bewilderment that senators felt in trying to fathom Tiberius's enigmatic silences, his muscle-bound circumlocutions, was due reflection of the Princeps's own tortured conscience. No matter how genuine the respect he felt for the Senate's venerable heritage of free speech, no matter how unvaryingly he showed his respect for the consuls by rising to his feet at their approach, there was one tradition that he would not, could not, honour. Tiberius, who had been leading his fellow citizens into battle since his early twenties, had spent many decades watching them bare their teeth and extend their claws. He knew what milk had been imbibed by the infant Romulus. To lead the Roman people, so he declared, was 'to hold a wolf by its ears'.[11] That being so, he was not prepared to take any chances. Even before he could move to deprive the *comitia centuriata* of their votes, he had already trampled upon another cherished tradition. Arriving in Rome with the corpse of Augustus, he had done so accompanied by a large retinue of troops. In the Senate House, in the Forum, in all the various places consecrated to the ancestral right of the Roman people to express themselves as they pleased, there had sounded the clattering of *caligae*, hobnailed military boots. *Pomerium* or not, spears and swords were everywhere in evidence.

True, there was something of a costume drama about many of these weapons, the parade-ground touch of a vanished era. The guards who attended the Emperor, when they walked the streets of Rome, sported arms reminiscent of the days of Pompey and Julius

Caesar. They also made sure to wear civilian dress. Innovation fused with heritage, and menace with reassurance: here, unmistakably, was the touch of Augustus. Almost half a century before, during his heroic defence of the Roman people against Cleopatra, he had been guarded, as was the right of any magistrate on campaign, by a *cohors praetoria*, a 'commander's unit'. Rather than disband this on his return from Egypt, as custom would have dictated, he had discreetly maintained it. Although he had stationed some of the Praetorians outside Rome, others had been billeted in various unobtrusive locations within the city itself. By 2 BC, the Roman people had become sufficiently habituated to these guards that Augustus had felt able to formalise their existence. Prompted, perhaps, by the shock of his daughter's downfall, he had instituted an official command.[12] Clearly, it was out of the question for a senator to be entrusted with such a sensitive responsibility; and so Augustus had appointed two equestrians. Neither he nor Tiberius would ever openly have admitted it, of course, but both men, in their preparations for the transfer of power, had realised that ensuring the loyalty of the Praetorians was now the key to securing Rome.

Sure enough, a few months before his death, Augustus had given his guards a massive pay rise; and in due course, when the oath of loyalty to Tiberius came to be sworn, only the consuls had taken precedence over their commander. Seius Strabo, the Praetorian prefect, was an Etrurian from the determinedly provincial town of Volsinii, famous for the invention of the hand-mill and not a great deal else; but he was competent, cultured and, crucially, an equestrian. He also had a son, Aelius Sejanus, who, despite an early posting on Gaius's ill-fated expedition to the East, had since become a much-valued partisan of Tiberius. The new Princeps did not take long to demonstrate his appreciation. One of his first appointments was to promote Sejanus to the joint command of the Praetorians alongside his father. Those alert to the substance of power, rather than to its show, had no doubt as to the implications. Tiberius's agonising in the Senate House was, to all intents and purposes, an irrelevance. 'In the military sphere, there had been no prevarication; instead, he had immediately adopted and begun exercising the powers of a Princeps.'[13]

Except that the military, of course, were not confined to Rome. Out on the frontiers, the perks and donatives lavished on the Praetorians had not gone unnoticed. In Pannonia and Germany, where the desperate efforts of the previous decade had required conscripts to be force-marched to the front and reservists chivvied out of their retirement, resentments ran particularly deep. 'Floggings and injuries, harsh winters and summers on manoeuvre, grim war and peace without profit – all relentless!'[14] No sooner had tidings of Augustus's death reached the northern front than mutterings like these were flaring up into direct insubordination. With startling speed, the flames of mutiny began to spread along the Danube and the Rhine.

Brought the news, Tiberius was appalled. He knew, none better, the vital importance of keeping the frontiers secure. It was the measure of his dismay that he sent as his emissary to Pannonia both his only natural son, Drusus, and his most trusted lieutenant, Sejanus. The mission was to prove perilous. Riding into the very heart of the camp, Drusus found his attempts at negotiation confronting a firestorm of rage. When his withdrawal was blocked, it seemed, as dusk fell, that he and his whole escort might be lynched. Drusus, though, was not his father's son for nothing: obdurate and untiring in equal measure, he spent the night working on the mutineers, summoning them, by the pale light of a full moon, to a sense of their duty. Gradually he worked them round. When, by lucky chance, a lunar eclipse cast the camp into sudden darkness, the soldiers took it for an omen, wailing that the gods were sickened by their crimes. By daybreak, the mutiny was effectively over. Two of the ringleaders were put to death that same morning, and others hunted down. Steady rain then extinguished the final embers of revolt. Drusus, who had never before been inside a legionary camp, let alone been given responsibility for three legions, had risen to a mortal challenge with courage and skill. He could be well satisfied with his efforts. So too, back in Rome, could Tiberius.

Nevertheless, the jolt given to his confidence was a jarring one. As a general, he had always set a premium on obligation and commitment. The oath of duty spoken by a legionary, the *sacramentum*, was of a peculiarly fearsome order, and to break it a terrible thing. The men who swore it, although granted by its terms a licence denied civilians to fight and kill, were simultaneously deprived of rights that were the essence of citizenship. There was nothing of Rome's chaotic snarl of streets in the measured grid of a legionary base. No matter where it might be planted, whether beneath the grey clouds of the North or the broiling African sun, its plan would be identical to that of every other camp across the empire. Within its ditches and palisades, discipline was absolute. Everyone, from general to lowest recruit, knew his place. The self-description of one particular centurion might well have applied to all. 'For I am a man set under authority, with soldiers under me: and I say to one, "Go," and he goes; and to another, "Come," and he comes.'[15] It was the pledge of the citizen who swore the *sacramentum* that he would readily commit himself to obedience. The sanctions against insubordination were correspondingly ferocious. Not for nothing was the emblem of the centurion a vine-stick. So notorious was one particular martinet for breaking his on the backs of his men that he was nicknamed 'Bring Me Another'.[16] Cornered by the mutineers in Pannonia, he had been torn to pieces. In Germany too, it was the centurions who bore the brunt of the soldiers' hatred. In Vetera, a huge legionary base standing guard over the confluence of the Rhine with the Lippe, many of the officers were pinned to the ground and given sixty strokes with their own rods, before being flung into the river. Then, drunk on their own violence, the mutineers began to contemplate savageries better suited to the barbarians they were supposed to be standing guard against: the abandonment of their positions, the sacking of the Altar of the Ubians, a bare sixty miles to the south, the despoliation of Gaul. Such, it seemed, was the menace of a wolf that had tossed off its rider.

In the event, although the mutiny in Germany was on a much graver scale than that in Pannonia, it too was suppressed – and by a son of Tiberius to boot. Germanicus, adopted by his uncle a decade earlier, had followed his first consulship in AD 12 by travelling north of the Alps, there to serve as governor of Gaul and commander-in-chief of the German front. News of the mutiny reached him hot on the heels of the announcement of Augustus's death; and so naturally he headed directly to the Rhine. There, lacking the helpful inter-vention of an eclipse, and desperate not to risk the frontier firmed up with such effort by Tiberius, he adopted a number of expedients. Concessions were combined with executions, histrionic appeals with threats. Sure enough, by mid-autumn, order had been restored. The legionaries of Vetera, in a violent spasm of repentance, first massacred the more mutinous among their own comrades, then demanded of Germanicus – who with his customary showiness had affected to be appalled by the slaughter he found in their camp – that he lead them against the barbarians. A quick strike across the Rhine, the incinera-tion of fifty square miles' worth of villages, and the soldiers were left much cheered up. 'Returning to camp for winter, it was with their confidence boosted, and recent events quite forgotten.'[17]

But Tiberius did not forget them. There had been a sinister dimen-sion to the mutiny in Germany lacking in Pannonia. The concentration of troops along the Rhine, as Tiberius himself knew better than anyone, was easily the most formidable in the entire empire – and Germanicus, on his first arrival in Vetera, had been pressed by the mutineers to ride at their head on Rome. That Germanicus himself had reacted with horror to the suggestion, dis-playing throughout an unimpeachable loyalty to his uncle, had not set Tiberius at rest. Reports of the events in Vetera provided an uncomfortable parody of his own coming to power. The stilted expressions of support that he had received from the Senate seemed mocked by the violent enthusiasm of the legionaries for his nephew; his own agonised prevarications, when set against the flamboyant shock displayed by Germanicus at the soldiers' urgings, could not help but seem the more insincere. Most unsettling of all, to a man appalled by any hint of mob rule, were the reports of the mutineers' ultimate ambitions. 'They wished to have a new leader, a new order, a new system of government; they presumed to threaten the Senate, even the Princeps, with new laws – laws which were to be dictated by themselves.'[18] Nothing, to the man who had just terminated centuries of voting on the Campus, could possibly have appeared more monstrous.

It did not, though, come as a total shock. Tiberius had painful memories of the irresponsibility of the masses: of their scorn for the discipline and self-control that were properly the virtues of the Roman people; of their shiftless enthusiasm for the young, the glamorous, the wilful; of their identification with his former wife and her children. All the more alarming, then, that the canker of insubordination should have infected soldiers he had personally trained, in camps he had buttressed himself. Indeed, it had seemed, during the worst moments of the mutiny, that very little was sacred. Visiting senators had been manhandled, a former consul almost lynched. Even Germanicus himself, defying the mutineers' demands, had at one point been jeered and menaced: for when he had declared, with a typical flourish, that he would rather stab himself than betray Tiberius, a soldier had drawn a sword and offered him the loan of it. Popular though he was among the legions in Germany, there were others more popular yet. Germanicus had a woman of radiant glamour present with him on the frontier. Not all Julia's children were dead or exiled. Agrippina, the last of Augustus's grandchildren still at liberty, had been married to Germanicus a decade earlier – and during the mutiny had accompanied her husband to the Rhine. A bold step for a pregnant woman, but Agrippina was of a fiery and martial disposition, and had known what she was doing.

For many decades now, the legions had been encouraged 'to display a particular fidelity and devotion to the August Family'.[19] Who were senators, then, to command their loyalty, compared to a woman whose grandfather had for so long been their paymaster, and whose mother was still hedged about with tragic glamour? The two emotions of self-interest and sentimentality had combined to ensure a warm welcome for Agrippina on the Rhine. It helped too that she had brought with her the youngest of her three sons, a precocious infant by the name of Gaius. Kitted out in a miniature soldier's uniform, the toddler had fast become the idol of the camp. *Caligula*, the legionaries nicknamed him, 'Military Bootikins'. As the mutiny reached its climax, Germanicus had capitalised upon the affection in which the boy and his mother were held by ostentatiously sending the pair of them to a local tribe of Gauls for safekeeping. So upset had the soldiers been by this reproach to their honour, and so ashamed, that they had promptly submitted. The suppression of the mutiny had been Agrippina's as well as her husband's.

The news, lapped up by an adoring public back in Rome, endowed the city's golden couple with a more aureate glow than ever. Just a hint of the cutting-edge as well. Wives did not normally accompany magistrates of the Roman people abroad. 'Not only are women frail and and ill suited to hardship, but when they slip the leash they become vicious, scheming and hungry for power.'[20] Such had long been the considered wisdom of moralists. But there were other traditions as well. In the stirring tales of heroism that the Roman people never tired of relating, even in an age when most of them had never been in a war, women too had their roles to play. The presence on the Rhine of Augustus's granddaughter had something of a scene conjured up from a nobler, remoter age. In the earliest days of Rome, after all, when the tides of war had often reached the city's gates, women had been no less on the front line than Agrippina was now. They too had heard the blast of trumpets; they too, standing on battlements, had watched the glinting of iron as their husbands marched off on campaign. It was not wholly unknown, in the stories told of Rome's early days, 'for a girl to serve as a beacon of courage to men'.[21] Past and future; duty and dash; fortitude and flamboyance: Germanicus and Agrippina seemed to offer the Roman people a taste of everything they most admired.

The next two years of campaigning would set the seal on this mystique. Whereas the measure of Tiberius's success as General of the North had been that he gave people back in Rome nothing to talk about, his nephew's ventures across the Rhine provided them with a constant adrenaline rush. There were ghosts stalking the untamed forests and bogs of Germany – and Germanicus, with his taste for the grand gesture, his relish for taking chances, his inimitable capacity for avoiding disaster by the skin of his teeth, was set on staring the spectres in the face. For two years, he committed himself to a cause that Tiberius had scorned to make his priority: vengeance. Arminius, the treacherous schemer who had brought three legions to their ruin, was relentlessly harried. His wife and unborn son were captured; his allies suborned; his forces cornered, after two long summers of campaigning, and put to the sword. A monument fashioned out of captured arms was raised to Tiberius on the battlefield, while archers busied themselves shooting down the numerous fugitives who had attempted to hide in trees. Germanicus, it seemed, had proven himself worthy of his admirers' most heated expectations.

Except that there remained much to be done. The victory was incomplete. Arminius, elusive as ever, had managed to hack his way to freedom after disguising himself by smearing his face with gore. Such a camouflage was fitting. Everywhere beyond the Rhine, it had sometimes seemed, was streaked with his bloody fingerprints. During his first summer of campaigning, Germanicus had made a point of visiting the Teutoburg Pass, where there were still great piles of whitening bones to be seen, and rusting spear-tips, and skulls nailed to trees – and then, after touring the scene of horror, had laid the first turf of the funeral mound with his own hand. The dead, though, were not easily confined to their graves. Shortly after the burial of the slaughtered legionaries, Severus Caecina, Germanicus's deputy in northern Germany, had found himself trapped by Arminius between forest and bog; and that night, as the darkness thickened and Caecina tried to snatch some sleep amid the howling and chanting of the expectant barbarians, he had dreamed that the blood-boltered Varus rose from the marshes, summoning him and trying to take him by the hand. Frantically, Caecina had thrust the spectre back into the swamps; but although the next day he had succeeded in extricating his men from the trap and breaking free for safety, rumours of his annihilation had already reached the Rhine. Panic had duly swept the camp on the western bank. Cries had gone up to demolish the bridge. Only Agrippina had stood firm. When Caecina and his exhausted men finally reached the river, it had been to find Augustus's granddaughter waiting at the bridgehead, ready with food, bandages and congratulations. Such was the measure of Germanicus's charisma that even a near-disaster could add to his legend.

By the autumn of AD 16, two of the three eagles lost by Varus had been redeemed. 'One more summer of campaigning, and the war will be over!'[22] So Germanicus promised. One last stiffening of the sinews; one final push. The Roman people, seduced as they were by the record of their hero's exploits on the eastern front, and by their city's birthright of victory, were more than happy to rally behind such slogans. Not Tiberius, though. Yes, honour had demanded that fire and slaughter be visited upon the contumacious Germans, and that Germanicus, as the man destined to rule the Roman world, be given experience of what it meant to lead legions in war – but enough was enough. The lure of ultimate victory was as insubstantial as a mist over a German bog. Not only that – it was cripplingly expensive. Braving a return along the North Sea coast after his victory over Arminius, Germanicus and his fleet had been caught up in an autumn storm and suffered devastating losses. Every brush with disaster, no matter how thrilling it might be to follow from a distance, could not help but remind Tiberius of the fate of Varus. Accordingly, despite Germanicus's frantic insistence that one final season of campaigning would ensure that Roman rule was extended once and for all to the Elbe, the hero of the hour was summoned home.

There, signal honours awaited him: a second consulship, a triumph. Tiberius, determined to banish any whisperings of a breach between him and his prospective heir, lavished gold on the cheering crowds. His nephew's youth and magnetism were actively trumpeted. An arch built in the Forum hailed the recapture of the eagles lost by Varus. No matter the Emperor's private conviction that the campaigning had in reality been a waste of effort and expense, he made sure to welcome home Germanicus as 'the conqueror of Germany'.[23]

Not everyone was convinced by this display of family affection. Some, puzzled as to why the General of the North should have been recalled just as victory seemed within his grasp, freely attributed it to his uncle's jealousy. The charge was venomously unfair – and yet, for all that, not lacking an element of truth. Though Tiberius had been obediently following the wishes of Augustus in grooming Germanicus for greatness, it would have been hard for him to track his nephew's progress and not feel a stirring of envy. He remained what he had been since his first awkward speeches to the Senate as Princeps: a man profoundly uncomfortable in his own skin. The task of taking on the semblance of Augustus had not grown any easier with time. Oppressed by its demands, Tiberius had begun to live in shadow. The comet-blaze of his nephew's celebrity increasingly gave to his own reticent and withdrawn nature the quality of enigma. 'What a contrast there was between the young man's easy manner, and his exceptional good humour, and the haughty and opaque reserve which characterised how Tiberius spoke and appeared.'[24] While Germanicus roamed the wilds of Germany and sailed the northern Ocean, Tiberius skulked in Rome, never once in two years setting foot outside the city. The austere aristocrat who had been testing himself since the age of sixteen in combat against Rome's foes, who had once turned his back on Augustus rather than compromise his dignity, who had always scorned the smooth and practised hypocrisies of the fashionable elite, now found himself obliged to negotiate a swamp more treacherous than any he had faced beyond the Rhine. Such a world was better suited to the talents of his mother than to his own; and when his enemies, sneering at him behind his back, jeered that it was the Augusta who had secured him his rule of the world, rather than his own record of *virtus*, the mockery stung. Not surprisingly, then, when senators proposed with practised malice that the title 'Son of Livia' be included on his inscriptions, Tiberius responded with fury. Rather than risk substantiating the charge that he had profited from her influence, let alone that he remained under her thumb, he made a point of avoiding his mother's company whenever he could. Repeatedly he warned the Augusta: 'do not meddle with affairs of importance inappropriate to a woman.'[25]

He still needed her, though. Reports from the Rhine of Agrippina's performance in the mutiny had served as a salutary reminder to Tiberius that the bloodline of Augustus, charged as it was with a mystique that he could never hope to share, retained its hold upon the affections of the Roman people. Agrippina herself, though a rogue and unwelcome presence in the house of which he was now the head, was married to the hero of the hour, and therefore in effect beyond his control. Not so her mother. Julia's final ruin had been sealed by her father's death. By the terms of Augustus's will, everything permitted her in her exile – her allowance, her household, her possessions – had become Livia's. The Augusta, although by now formally a Julian, had shown the woman who was simultaneously her stepdaughter and adoptive sister not a shred of family feeling. Instead, chill and implacable, she had ordered all supplies to the wretched exile cut off. Julia, deprived of all hope, had starved herself to death. No one doubted that Livia, in the exercise of this cruelty, had been serving her son's interests. Clearly, people presumed, 'he had calculated that the sheer length of her exile would prevent her death from being noted.'[26]

In the clandestine and increasingly murderous battle between the bloodline of Augustus and that of his wife, it was Livia who had triumphed. Her son ruled as emperor; her grandson had no conceivable rival as his heir. In the great mausoleum of Augustus, whose priest and daughter Livia had become after the reading of his will, no space was given to the ashes of the disinherited Julia. Claudians had become Julians, and Julians, purged amid conditions of squalor and secrecy, had vanished altogether from the roster of the August Family. The blaze of the deified Augustus's glory illumined only the single daughter: Julia Augusta, the woman who had previously been his wife. It shed its lustre upon only the single son: Tiberius Caesar Augustus. To those who gazed full upon the brilliance and did not think to shade their eyes, there seemed no shadows, no hint of darkness, only gold. Tiberius, as Augustus had been, was 'the very best a Princeps can be'. The son of a god, he served as a model fit to be copied by all mankind. 'Great though he is as the ruler of the Roman world, he is greater still as an example to it.'[27]

Praise that would have brought a bitter smile, perhaps, to Julia's pinched lips as she lay starving, or to Agrippa Postumus, as he rotted on Planasia, dreaming of freedom, fated never to leave. Except that the obscurity of their deaths, veiled as they were from the gaze of the world, encouraged people to wonder. Two years after Agrippa's supposed execution, a remarkable rumour began to sweep Rome. 'The news was only whispered at first – as forbidden stories always are.'[28] Augustus's grandson, so it was reported, had cheated death. 'Preserved by the heavens',[29] he had slipped his guards, procured a boat, reached the mainland. The Roman people, their love for Julia's children undimmed, began to speak of it in ever more breathless tones. Senators and equestrians, too, so it was said, were rallying to Agrippa's cause – even members of the imperial household itself. They were sending the young man funds; they were sending him inside information. The whole of Italy seemed to be yearning for the story to be true.

Few, though, ever saw the man who claimed to be Agrippa. He was constantly on the move, avoiding public spaces, keeping to the night. When at last he was captured, it was by subterfuge. Tiberius's agents themselves had been operating in murk and shadow; and when they tricked their elusive quarry into believing them to be his supporters, and met him in conditions of strictest secrecy, there was no one to witness his abduction to the Palatine. There, in the house of Caesar, the truth soon came out. The man whose claims had set all Italy seething was an imposter, a former slave of Agrippa's by the name of

Clemens. Obdurate in the face of torture, he refused to betray his associates; and so Tiberius, who had no wish to give the affair any further publicity, decided to let sleeping dogs lie. He instructed that no further inquiries were to be held. The whole business was to be covered up. As for Clemens himself, he was naturally to be executed, and his body covertly dispatched.

First, though, so it was reported, Tiberius himself made sure to study the imposter; and then, marking the slave's close resemblance to his dead master, even down to the styling of his hair and beard, addressed him directly. 'How did you manage it? How did you make yourself into Agrippa?'

Back came the mocking answer, as though from the depths of the Emperor's most private fears. 'Why – in the same way that you transformed yourself into Caesar.'[30]

The People's Prince

When Tiberius persuaded Germanicus to return from the German front, it was partly by appealing to his sense of fraternal affection. 'Leave your brother, Drusus, the chance to win some glory of his own'[31] – so the Emperor had urged. It was an effective tactic. The bond between the two young men was a close one. Cousins as well as adoptive brothers, both were capable of taking pleasure in the achievements of the other. While it had been essential that Germanicus, as the elder and the chosen heir of Augustus, be trusted first with the command of legions in war, now that he had been successfully blooded, and had burnished his name to a dazzling sheen, it was Drusus's turn. Tiberius was worried that his son was altogether too fond of his pleasures. He needed toughening up. Accordingly, with the Germans too busy licking their wounds to be any further trouble, Drusus was given an immense command spanning the whole of the Balkans. Here, he proved as deft and effective an operator as he had done on his previous trip to the region. Tribes beyond the frontier were successfully destabilised, various warlords brought to sue for asylum, Roman power further entrenched. Tiberius, surveying the achievements of Germanicus and Drusus along the vast sweep of the northern frontier, could justly feel that the future was bright.

Romulus and Remus were not the only models of brotherhood to be found in the annals of the Roman people. More positive exemplars were also to hand. Tiberius himself, who had braved peril and exhaustion to be at his brother's side as he expired, served as stirring proof of that. 'Affections later in life ought never to diminish such a primal love.'[32] Indeed, the bonds of fraternity could link even those who did not share the same blood. Ferocious though competition among the Roman elite was, it did not always have to result in enmity. Shared experiences could on occasion serve to foster a sense of mutual loyalty. For the ambitious, after all, there was only ever one ladder to climb; and a high achiever, as he mounted rung after rung, might repeatedly find himself on campaign or in office with the same colleague. Memories of comradeship might well reach all the way back to adolescence. Tiberius's own experience was typical. His colleague during his second consulship in 7 BC had been a man he had first served alongside when he was sixteen, during the war fought by Augustus in the wilds of northern Spain.[33] Forty years on, the two seasoned servants of the Roman people had many memories in common. Gnaeus Calpurnius Piso was someone whom Tiberius was proud to call a friend.

It took a special kind of breeding for a man to be treated by a Claudian as a peer. Piso's ancestry blended descent from the second of Rome's seven kings with a record of achievement that even Tiberius could rate. The commitment of his family to the traditional values of the Republic was of a famously obdurate order. His father, unlike Tiberius's own, had consistently opposed the ambitions of the House of Caesar – and as a result, had found himself again and again on the losing side. Only in 23 BC, when Augustus persuaded him to serve as consul, had he finally been reconciled to the new regime. That same

June, with the Princeps so ill that he had summoned Agrippa to his side, and handed over his ring in the belief that he was dying, he had also given Piso's father a book carefully detailing his stewardship of Rome's military and financial resources. A telling gesture. It had mattered profoundly to Augustus that men of pedigree and principle be suborned to his cause – and Piso's father had been as prized a catch as any.

Piso himself was very much his father's son. 'A man of few vices, he had only this flaw: that he mistook inflexibility for constancy.'[34] Whether this did qualify as a flaw was, of course, a matter of opinion. What might appear rigidity and arrogance to those outside the ranks of the ancient nobility was prized by men such as Tiberius and Piso as essential bulwarks of their city's greatness. 'Just as following the customs of our ancestors produced outstanding figures, so did these same excellent men make sure to preserve our traditional way of life, and the institutions of their forefathers.'[35] Now, more than ever, amid all the bewildering sea-changes of the new age, it was the duty of those who led ancient houses to maintain the moorings that anchored their city to the bedrock of the past.

This was why, during his joint consulship with Piso, Tiberius had funded the restoration of a monument in the Forum that for a century and more had served as its most notorious shrine to reaction. There was no building in Rome more ironically named than the Temple of Concord. Originally built in 121 BC, it commemorated the bloodiest outbreak of class warfare in the city's history. Conservatives in the Senate – an ancestor of Piso's prominent among them – had waged an ultimately murderous campaign against those two doughty tribunes of the plebs, the Gracchi. It was not only the two brothers themselves who had been murdered; thousands of their followers had ended up as corpses in the Tiber. Tiberius, by ostentatiously repairing the monument built to this repression, had been laying down a marker. To be sure, that his gesture had infuriated the great mass of the Roman people was regrettable – but it could not be helped. The existence below the Capitol of the beautifully refurbished Temple of

Concord, complete with his own name over the doorway and a lavish complement of artworks, made a statement that no one could mistake. Endowed though he had been with a tribune's powers since AD 4, Tiberius continued to identify himself with the oldest, sternest, stiffest values of his class. 'Worthy of my forebears, careful of the Senate's interests, steadfast in danger, and fearless of such resentment as I may incur serving the public good':[36] his was a manifesto worthy of Appius Claudius the Blind. That his first dealings with his fellow senators as Princeps had been awkward in the extreme had done nothing to shake his resolve. Concord between the Senate and the People of Rome, yes – but on the Senate's terms. There was to be no pandering to the masses on Tiberius's watch.

The backing of men like Piso, however, was crucial. The failure of most senators to meet his high expectations of them continued to nag at the Princeps. As on the Rhine, so in the Senate House, he trod a slow but determined step. Although senators down on their luck might well be given a helping hand if he judged them deserving, those who sat silent and nervous in debate, waiting for him to take a lead, were rarely so blessed. Though Tiberius was a masterly orator, endowed with tremendous qualities of sarcasm and dignity, of irony and power, the effect of his presence on those intimidated by his greatness was only to make them shrink all the more. Sometimes he would keep silent; at other times intervene abruptly; at other times yet lose his temper altogether and erupt. Many senators, unsure what rules they were meant to be playing by, found themselves lost and bewildered; and there were occasions when Piso, habituated as he was to his friend's way of thinking, would publicly alert him that he had placed them all in an invidious situation. Such interventions, far from provoking the Princeps, invariably struck home. Independence of mind was precisely what Tiberius wished to foster – provided, of course, that it conformed to the ideal which men like Piso, of proven pedigree and record, so notably embodied. Genuine debate, under such circumstances, was not out of the question. Sometimes, it was almost possible to believe that the Princeps did indeed take his place

202

in the Senate merely as one among many. Once, Piso even won backing for a motion that Tiberius and Drusus had both publicly opposed. No matter that it was then promptly vetoed, all the senators could briefly feel good about themselves. It was, everyone in the House had been able to agree, 'a particularly good illustration of the democratic form of government'.[37]

Not that anyone outside its walls greatly cared. After all, the vast mass of the Roman people, denied by Tiberius their right to a meaningful vote, no longer had a stake in the election of their magistrates. Instead, they had other favourites. They had not forgotten their devotion to the glamorous and tragic family of Julia. The same star quality that had seduced mutinous legionaries on the Rhine now had the crowds swooning in Rome. On Germanicus's return from the front, the whole city had streamed out to welcome him, Agrippina and their children. Little Gaius, not yet five years old, and whose nickname of 'Caligula' appealed to everything that was most sentimental about the Roman people, was their particular darling. During Germanicus's triumph, he had ridden proudly beside his father. Also present in the chariot had been his two elder brothers, Nero and Drusus, and their baby sisters, Agrippina and Drusilla. Everything about the spectacle might have been calculated to delight the cheering masses – and appal Tiberius. Germanicus, it seemed, could not help but cut a dash.

All of which placed the Princeps in a quandary. Clearly, with the wishes of Augustus still sacrosanct, Tiberius remained committed to grooming his nephew for the succession – and Germanicus's apprenticeship was far from over. Now that he had completed his term of office north of the Alps, it was time to broaden his horizons and send him east. There, trouble was brewing again. The flashpoint was one that had long been a cause of tension between Rome and Parthia. The kingdom of Armenia, a land of icy mountains, thick forests and notoriously effective poisons, lay sandwiched uncomfortably between the rival empires: too indigestible to be swallowed, too tasty to be left alone. Tiberius himself, almost forty years before, had been sent there by Augustus on his first independent mission – and a great success it had turned out to be. A puppet king had been imposed at the point of a sword; the right of Rome to meddle in Armenian affairs triumphantly affirmed. Where there was opportunity, though, there inevitably lurked peril. It was in Armenia, after all, that Gaius Caesar, Augustus's precious grandson, had received his fatal wound. Tiberius, whose own rise to greatness would never have happened without Gaius's untimely death, had good reason to appreciate the disaster that might overtake a headstrong prince. Nor was it only Germanicus's personal safety at stake. The annihilation of Crassus and his legions at Carrhae still cast a long shadow. Embark on too madcap an adventure, and the entire Roman order in the East might be put in peril. Tiberius knew, as he weighed up his options, that whatever he did would be a risk.

In AD 17, shortly after celebrating his triumph, Germanicus was formally appointed by the Senate to the command of the eastern provinces, with an authority over the region's various governors equivalent to Tiberius's own. 'There can be no prospect of a settlement there,' the Princeps informed the House with a perfectly straight face, 'unless his wisdom be brought to bear on it.'[38] Shortly afterwards, Germanicus set out on his mission. With him went the seemingly ever-pregnant Agrippina and the young Caligula. First stop was a courtesy call on Drusus's headquarters in the Balkans; second, the bay of Actium. Almost fifty years had passed since Germanicus's two grandfathers, the one natural and the other adoptive, had met on its waters to decide the fate of the world; and the young man's imagination, as well it might have done, 'conjured up for him vivid scenes of tragedy and triumph'.[39] Then, like so many pilgrims before him, he headed on eagerly to the Greek world's most celebrated tourist attraction. Crowned by the Parthenon, garlanded and perfume-hung with memories of past achievement, Athens had always shimmered in the yearnings of Roman romantics. Horace had studied in its schools; so too Ovid, who on his journey into exile had found himself haunted by memories of his happiness there as a young

The East

man. History and philosophy, art and *savoir faire*: the city had it all. 'Athens, once mistress over waves and land, has now made Greece a slave to beauty.'[40] The highly cultured Germanicus, whose idea of relaxation was to pen a Greek comedy or two, was duly smitten. So too were the Athenians. They may have fallen from their past greatness, but they had no rivals when it came to buttering up dignitaries. To a man such as Germanicus, who liked nothing better than being liked, it was heaven. Sailing on from Athens, his spirits were much buoyed. When Agrippina, just before landing in Asia Minor, paused on the island of Lesbos to give birth to a third daughter, Julia Livilla, it seemed that the gods were smiling on him and his mission.

Trouble was already brewing, though. Not far behind, blunt and unaccommodating where Germanicus himself had been emollient and affable, travelled a legate with a very different take. Piso, who regarded rudeness to foreigners as one of the primordial virtues which distinguished a Roman aristocrat from lesser men, had no time for diplomatic niceties. Arriving in Athens, he delivered a speech that was pointedly rude. The Athenians were unworthy of their heritage; they were scum, the dregs of the earth. Chauvinism such as this, a bristling contempt for the Greeks as a conquered and decadent people, was the reverse of the cultural cringe so recently displayed by Germanicus – a cringe, Piso informed his hosts, that was incompatible with Roman dignity. His point made, he continued on his way – only to be caught in a storm off Rhodes. Saved in the nick of time by a warship doubling as a lifeboat, Piso's mood was hardly improved by discovering that the man to whom he owed his life was Germanicus. The meeting between him and his rescuer was as stiff as it was brief. Only a day after he had narrowly avoided shipwreck, Piso was on his way again. His destination: the province which more than any other served as the key to Roman security in the East, a land of famous and teeming cities, fabulous wealth, and a frontier directly abutting the Parthians. Piso was heading east as the new governor of Syria.

That Tiberius, like Augustus, thought long and hard before appointing anyone to a military command went without saying.

Syria, which had a garrison of four full legions and lay many weeks distant from Rome, was a more sensitive command than most. Delegation did not come easily to the Princeps. As a general in the field, his attention to detail had been remorseless – but as emperor, with the whole world his responsibility, he had reluctantly accepted that he could no longer afford to micromanage. True, he often seemed on the verge of surrendering to temptation, of setting off on a grand tour of the provinces, of attempting to monitor every last aspect of Rome's dominions; but again and again he would cancel his travel plans. 'Callippides', men began to call him, after a famous mime whose party trick had been to imitate the sprinting of an athlete while staying rooted to the spot.

The dispatch of Piso to Syria was Tiberius's most Callippidean manoeuvre yet. Chopping and changing governors was not his normal style. His preference was for keeping them in place. 'Even corrupt legates?' he was once asked. 'Better blood-glutted flies on a wound than thirsty ones,' came the mordant reply.[41] The circumstances now, though, were exceptional. Despite having brought himself to trust Germanicus with the administration of the East, Tiberius could not bear, in the final reckoning, to leave his nephew unsupervised. He needed someone in Syria he could trust. The loyalties of the incumbent governor, whose daughter was due to marry Nero, Germanicus's eldest son, were far too split for comfort. Only a man in whom the Princeps had absolute confidence, who shared his values, his instincts and his background, would do. So it was, as Germanicus made his way to Armenia, there to follow in Tiberius's own footsteps and impose Rome's choice of a king, that Piso, after landing in Syria and travelling some fifteen miles upriver, arrived in the great metropolis which served the whole of Roman Asia as its cockpit: Antioch.

Like Alexandria, the city had originally been a capital of kings. Founded in 300 BC by a general of Alexander the Great, the sway of its rulers had once reached as far afield as India. Although it was a parvenu among the ancient foundations of Syria, Antioch had long since outgrown them all. Laid out by its founder on a grid pattern between the river Orontes and the towering peaks of an adjacent mountain, peopled by transplanted Athenians, and endowed with every appurtenance of a Greek city, from theatres to gymnasia, it had firmly stamped the Levant with the brand of Macedonian ownership. For two and a half centuries, fatted on the riches of Asia, it had served as a showcase for royal excess. Ivory tusks and huge silver dishes, jewel-encrusted diadems and immense public banquets, golden jars filled to overbrimming with cinnamon, and marjoram, and nard: 'to gaze at all the wealth on display was to be struck with wonder and stupefaction.'[42] With avarice as well, of course, in the case of a man like Pompey; and sure enough, in 63 BC, the vain and venal conqueror had no sooner appeared with his legions in Syria than he was swallowing it up. Almost eight decades on, the new governor, as he arrived to take up his post, would have seen reassuring marks of Rome's dominance everywhere in the erstwhile seat of empire. To enter Antioch was to be left in no doubt that it lay now beneath the claws of the wolf. Above a gleaming new gateway in the eastern wall was set a statue of Romulus and Remus, complete with lupine wet-nurse; midway along its central thoroughfare, gazing serenely out across the city from atop a column, stood a statue of Tiberius. Meanwhile, in the governor's headquarters, where soldiers were garrisoned, tax records stored and law courts established for the brisk and ready sentencing of criminals, Roman supremacy had its intimidating apparatus. Nowhere else in the city, nor in the province beyond, was there any conceivable rival to Rome's monopolisation of force. A governor had the right to crucify, or burn, or throw to beasts anyone he pleased. Piso, as the man who commanded such terrifying powers, was aptly a figure of dread and awe.

Which said, the presence on the scene of Germanicus naturally complicated matters. Piso's authority was not as absolute as it would otherwise have been. Confident that Tiberius intended him to serve as a counterbalance to the young prince, he duly set about shoring up his support among the province's garrison. Although, on previous tours of duty, he had shown himself a ferocious martinet, he now relaxed the leash restraining the legions under his command, and granted his men licence to throw their weight around even more brutally than they were normally permitted to do. Provincials, of course, already knew to tread carefully with their occupiers. A legionary might well force a civilian to serve him as a porter or provide him with a billet — and no woman, certainly, ever met a Roman soldier without a certain measure of dread. Now, though, with the slackening of their discipline, the military were given the run of both towns and countryside. The new governor was hailed appreciatively by his men as 'the Father of the Legions'.[43] Meanwhile, his wife, an intimate of Livia's by the name of Plancina, aped the role played by Agrippina in Germany. Attending manoeuvres, she paraded her own interest in the welfare of the troops. Piso began to grow in confidence. When orders arrived from Armenia for reinforcements, he felt sufficiently sure of himself to ignore them. Germanicus, embroiled as he was in settling the frontier to the north, had no choice but to swallow this insubordination; and in the event, displaying an acumen and a diplomatic finesse that made a mockery of his uncle's forebodings, he was able to achieve with his own resources all that he had been sent to do. Unsurprisingly, though, when he and Piso met again in the winter quarters of one of the four Syrian legions, relations between the two men were frostier than ever. 'When they parted, it was in open enmity.'[44]

Yet there was more to this clash of egos than the awkward circumstances of their mutual appointments. Deep issues of principle, reaching to the heart of Rome's new order, were at stake. Twenty-five years previously, Tiberius had retired to Rhodes rather than endure the presumptions of a jumped-up princeling; but then, when Gaius had come to the East armed with powers equivalent to those wielded by Germanicus now, the older man had been left with no choice but to bite his tongue and swallow repeated snubs. Piso, a man of Tiberius's own generation and background, was determined not to suffer a matching humiliation. Like his friend, he scorned the notion of monarchy; like his friend, he cleaved to the virtues and principles defined for him by his ancestors. Tiberius himself – who twice, first in Pannonia and then in Germany, had saved the Republic – Piso was willing to acknowledge as Princeps; but not Germanicus. It was as a Roman aristocrat that he intended to govern his province.

Matters came to a head at a banquet hosted by the king of Nabataea, a land ruled from the rose-red city of Petra, and which had long been subordinated by treaty to Rome. When the king, as a gesture of hospitality, presented his guests with golden crowns, a heavy one for Caesar's son and a lighter one for everyone else, Piso snorted in derision. Who did Germanicus think he was – a Parthian? Ever since the time of Scipio Africanus, it had been a point of principle among the Roman elite that they were the superiors of even the showiest Oriental. The dignity of the Republic, Piso believed, obliged him to maintain a principled contempt for everyone and everything in his province. Degenerate though Athens might have been, it was as nothing compared to the degeneracy of Antioch. The city's Greek façade did not prevent its Roman masters from rating its inhabitants as, at best, mere imitations of Greeks. The crowds thronging its streets had long since come to possess a mestizo quality. Descendants of the Athenians settled there by its founder mingled with natives from across the entire Near East. In Rome, where unguents from Syria were highly prized, the oil with which dandies would perfume and anoint their hair struck moralists as repugnantly suggestive of the country as a whole. To men such as Piso, everything about the Syrians was unsettling. Their merchants were too smooth-tongued; their priests too effeminate; their dancing girls altogether too depilated. From the tops of mountains, where ecstatic worshippers would offer up sacrifice to eerily formless gods, to the depths of Antioch's bars, where bodies moving to the sound of tambourines would writhe in the deviant fashion for which Syrians were notorious, the province seemed to fester with slavishness and immoderation. Confronted by such a country, what was a Roman to do but cling all the more tightly to the standards of his own?

Except that Germanicus, whose courtesy and grace towards a

whole assortment of foreigners had so provoked the ire of Piso, could legitimately point out that xenophobia was not the only tradition inherited from the great men of their past. The same Scipio Africanus who had always sternly upheld the majesty of the Republic in the face of Oriental monarchy had also, while touring the Greek cities of Sicily, done the locals the courtesy of copying their fashions. Now, as Germanicus continued his tour of duty by travelling from Syria to Egypt, he repeated the trick. Arriving in Alexandria, he dismissed his guards, put on sandals and dressed up as a Greek. This, to the inhabitants of a city founded by Alexander the Great, whose incomparable library boasted more volumes of Athenian literature than Athens herself, and who bitterly resented that a palace once occupied by their own monarchs should have ended up the headquarters of a foreign governor, was a wildly popular gesture. As in the capital, so in the Roman world's second city: Germanicus's easy charm proved adept at winning hearts and minds.

This was a considerable feat. No Roman had matched it since the time of Antony. The Alexandrians were notoriously hard to please. Perverse and flighty, they were so prone to street brawling that even a woman might think nothing of 'grabbing a man's genitals in a fight'.[45] Now, though, when the Alexandrians rioted, it was out of enthusiasm for their guest. He and Agrippina, the crowds began to chant, were both of them '*Augustus*'. Germanicus, appalled, promptly ordered the demonstrations broken up. It would not do, as he was all too painfully aware, to be hailed by a title that 'only his father and grandmother were entitled to wear'.[46]

But too late. News that Germanicus was playing to the gallery in Alexandria could hardly help but reach Tiberius – and it did not go down well. However sensitive a posting Syria might be, Egypt was even more so. Such was its wealth, after all, that it had effectively bankrolled Antony's bid for world domination – a detail that no Caesar was ever likely to forget. Augustus, for all his boast that he had 'added Egypt to the empire of the Roman people',[47] had kept such a vice-like grip upon the new province that it had ranked, in practice, as his own personal fiefdom – a display of neurosis that Tiberius had naturally made sure to emulate. No members of the Roman elite were permitted to enter Egypt without his express permission; only equestrians were ever appointed to govern it; even a hint of uppitiness, and a governor would ruthlessly be removed from office. Indeed, it was the measure of Tiberius's anxiety to secure the province that within months of succeeding Augustus he had appointed as his legate in Alexandria none other than Seius Strabo, erstwhile prefect of the Praetorians, and father of his most trusted partisan. Meanwhile, beyond the purlieus of the great harbour-city, along the banks of the Nile, where ancient, animal-headed gods were still worshipped by Egyptians who might not speak a word of Greek, nor ever have seen a Roman, the distant Princeps was being honoured in primordial fashion. Just as once, back in the fabulous mists of time, Egyptian scribes had chiselled into temple walls the names of their own native kings, carefully set within regular ovals, so now, whenever fresh ovals came to be engraved, they would contain within them the name of Tiberius. In Egypt it was less as the first citizen of the Roman people that he ruled than as a pharaoh.

Nothing, then, could have done more to set the Princeps twitching than to have the grandson of Antony and the granddaughter of Augustus hailed as gods in Alexandria. When Germanicus returned to the city from a Nile cruise, it was to find a furious missive waiting for him from Rome. Had the terms of Tiberius's criticisms not chimed so readily with those of Piso, then the contretemps would doubtless soon have been forgotten – for Germanicus, after all, had never intended to step on his uncle's toes. As it was, he returned to Syria to find its governor newly emboldened. The campaign of insubordination waged by Piso had hit fresh heights of insolence during his absence – and Germanicus, when he discovered that his every last order had been countermanded, decided that enough was enough. Silver-haired Piso may have been, of an ancient family, and seasoned in the service of the Republic – but Germanicus tore a strip off him nevertheless.

The governor, his dignity fatally injured, resolved to depart Antioch. Before he could leave, though, news came that his adversary had fallen ill. Piso's spirits duly soared – only to be dashed by an update, which reported a recovery, and that the whole of Antioch was offering up sacrifices in relief. Piso, whose judgement was by now fatally clouded by the sheer intensity of his loathing for Germanicus, sponsored his lictors to break up the celebrations, and then retreated down the Orontes to await further developments. These, as it turned out, were already spiralling out of control. Antioch was rife with talk of poison and sorcery. Not only, it seemed, had Germanicus suffered a relapse, but his servants, pulling apart his bedroom, had discovered marks of witchcraft secreted in the walls and under the floorboards: bones, dried blood, smears of ash. Germanicus himself, as he lay dying, had specifically fingered Piso as the man responsible.

So it was, for the second time, that the journey of a young Caesar to the East ended in calamity. Yet though the loss of Gaius had certainly been a grievous blow to Augustus, and though Livia's hand in it would subsequently be darkly suspected, it had not set off such reverberations as the death of Germanicus now threatened. His last words, delivered with his customary heightened emotion from the capital of Roman Asia, could hardly have been less helpful to Tiberius. First, he had openly accused the Princeps's legate and friend of plotting his murder. Then, even while urging Agrippina to rein in her instinctive tendency to grandstand, he had simultaneously instructed everyone else gathered around his deathbed to take full advantage of it. 'Display before the Roman people the granddaughter of the deified Augustus, and recite to them the names of my children!'[48]

Such an appeal embodied everything that the Princeps had always most mistrusted in his nephew; yet even as Germanicus was delivering it, the man sent to Asia to serve as a check upon his instincts, and to embody the stern and flinty instincts of Tiberius himself, was only stoking the flames. Piso remained too blinded by the insult done his honour to let it lie. At the news of his rival's death he flung open temples in his joy, raising sacrifices to the gods and lavishing fresh donatives on his men. Then, when the senators in Germanicus's train appointed one of their own number, a former consul by the name of Sentius, to serve as governor in his place, Piso resorted to force in defence of what remained, after all, legally his office. Citizen faced citizen: 'Pisonian' took up arms against 'Caesarian'.[49] Fifty years after the battle of Actium, it seemed that the evils of civil war, 'long since laid to rest by the divine will of the deified Augustus, and by the virtues of Tiberius Caesar Augustus',[50] were returning to plague the world.

The human face of the crisis, as the dying Germanicus had known it would be, was provided by Agrippina. Rather than wait for spring, she embarked for home the moment that the ashes of her husband's pyre had cooled. Pausing only to swap insults with Piso after an inadvertent brush with his flotilla, she set sail across the wintry seas for home. When she finally docked at Brundisium, it was as though the whole of Italy had massed to greet her. As the pale-faced widow appeared on the gangplank, the urn containing her husband's ashes in her hands, and Caligula and little Julia Livilla by her side, the sobs and wails of the crowd blended into a single animal howl of pain. Ever since the definitive confirmation of Germanicus's death, Rome had been sodden with grief. 'Not an honour that love or wit could devise but it had been bestowed upon him.'[51] Now, in the slow and stately journey of his ashes towards the city, there was the flavour of one final tribute: not merely a funerary procession but a triumph. Praetorians provided the fallen hero with his escort; lictors reversed their *fasces* and standards were stripped of their adornments; incense burned by mourning bystanders wreathed with its bitter perfumes the entire length of the Appian Way. Forty miles south of the capital, the ashes were met by Germanicus's brother, the shambling and decidedly unheroic figure of Claudius, by his adoptive brother, Drusus, and by the four children that he and Agrippina had left behind them in Italy. Then, on reaching Rome, the procession was joined by the two consuls and an array of senators. Through packed streets muffled save for the wailing of mourners it continued along its

way. Only out on the Campus did it finally come to a halt. Illumined
by the blaze of a multitude of torches, and watched by the black-
mantled silhouette of Agrippina, Germanicus's mortal remains were
reverently consigned to their final resting place: the great Mausoleum
of Augustus.

Meanwhile, of his uncle, the First Citizen of the Republic, there
was not a sign. As ever, Tiberius regarded the parading of grief as
beneath his dignity. Neither he, nor Livia, nor Germanicus's mother
were glimpsed in public. Who were any of them, as they mourned
their loss, to be dictated to by the lachrymose self-indulgence of a
mob? The mood of the city, though, was turning ugly. The absence of
the Princeps from the very public displays of mourning was read as an
insult. Worse – as a confession of guilt. Germanicus's dying charge,
that Piso had poisoned him, was on everybody's lips. Such an accu-
sation was not easily rebutted. For Tiberius to have pointed out, as he
might well have done, that the climate of the Levant was notoriously
unhealthy, that many there had succumbed to disease, that the supposed marks of witchcraft found under Germanicus's floorboards
might just as plausibly have been animal remains, would have been
insufferably demeaning; and yet his silence hung heavy in the air. The
Roman people, in their grief and their anger, did not find it hard to
adduce a motive. Gazing on their hero's widow, they hailed her as the
last grandchild of Augustus left standing. Raising their hands to the
heavens, they prayed that her children 'would outlive their foes'.[52]

Tiberius was bitterly stung. Although he had always been contemptuous both of the plebs and of those who sought to woo them,
it did not stop him from flinching on occasion at the consciousness of
his unpopularity. To be scorned as a cuckoo in the nest, streaked with
the blood of innocent fledglings, threatened damage to more than his
reputation. The Princeps was not alone in being menaced by the crisis.
The Senate, whose authority and values Tiberius had always aspired
so dearly to uphold, had begun to feel threatened too. There was an
acrid flavour to the city's mourning for its favourite. It was widely
believed out on the streets that Germanicus had been murdered

because of his friendship for the masses. He had favoured equal rights for all, so it was rumoured, and aimed to restore to the Roman people their lost liberties. The crowds, when they gathered with their torches on the Campus to greet the funeral procession, had done so ranged as though in assembly, ready to vote. Clinging as he was to the ears of the wolf, Tiberius could feel the rising of its hackles, sense the baring of its teeth, smell the hunger on its breath. He knew that it wanted meat.

Nothing for it, then, but to toss it prey. The sacrificial victim, as Tiberius was painfully aware, selected himself. Piso's attempt to clutch onto his province had not gone well. Routed in battle and flushed out from his bolt-hole by Sentius, he had been left with no alternative but to sue for terms. The best he could obtain was a safe-conduct back to Rome. Sailing up the Tiber into the eye of the storm, he and his wife settled for a calculated display of *sangfroid*. Rather than cringe before the fury of the Roman people, he opted to dock, at the busiest time of day, directly opposite the Mausoleum of Augustus, where Germanicus's ashes had only recently been laid; and then, that same evening, to host a slap-up dinner party. Down in the Forum, where the garlands adorning Piso's villa could clearly be seen, the crowds seethed in disbelief. Next day, to no one's surprise, an official indictment was registered with the consuls.

Still Piso's peers shrank from applying the *coup de grâce*. The consuls referred the investigation to the Princeps; the Princeps to the Senate. Piso, indomitable as ever, refused point-blank to confess the crime of which everyone outside the courtroom had already convicted him: he had not, he insisted over and again, poisoned Germanicus. True, this did nothing to exonerate him from the other accusations; for it could hardly have been more self-evident that he was guilty of rank insubordination, and of fomenting civil war. Yet even in pressing these charges, the prosecution had cause to hesitate. Not a senator but he was uncomfortably aware that Piso had been the legate of Caesar. Correspondence between the two men, despite requests, remained strictly embargoed. As for Tiberius himself, he was the most uncomfortable of all. The Princeps remained on the horns of a truly agonising dilemma. Spare Piso, and the darkest suspicions of the Roman people would be confirmed; wash his hands of an old friend, throw a trusted ally to the wolves, permit a man of ancient and distinguished family to be lynched by a mob, and the betrayal would be devastating. So Tiberius havered; and out on the streets the fury and indignation grew.

The climactic eruption, when it finally came, forced everybody's hand. Demonstrators toppled Piso's statues, hauled them to the base of the Capitol, then dragged them halfway up the flight of steps that led to the summit of the hill. Here, in full view of the Forum, they set about smashing them to pieces. The symbolism could hardly have been more pointed. On one side of the Gemonian Steps, as they were known, loomed the city's only prison, where criminals were held before execution; on the other, the Temple of Concord, recently and controversially renovated by Tiberius. The Princeps, recognising the direct challenge to his authority, sent in the Praetorians to save and restore the statues, then to escort Piso himself in a litter back to his house. The next morning, in a gesture of continued defiance, the accused returned to the Senate House; but he knew, the moment he walked in, that the game was up at last. Not a sympathetic look; not a voice that wasn't raised in anger. Most chilling of all was the expression of Tiberius: 'pitiless, passionless, closed to all emotion'.[53] That evening, when Piso returned home, he readied himself for bed as he had always done; and then, while his wife was out of the room, ordered the doors to be closed, and cut his throat.

In death as in life, the vengeance of the bereaved plebs pursued him. The Senate, obedient to their hatred, declared it a crime for any to mourn Piso, ordered all portraits of him destroyed, confiscated half his property, and commanded his son to change his name. Copies of their decree were dispatched to cities and camps across the known world. Simultaneously, with unctuous formality, senators expressed their gratitude to the Princeps for avenging Germanicus. The Roman people, though, remained contemptuous and unconvinced. They knew that Tiberius, rather than permit the total ruin of Piso's family, had expressed pity for it in its disgrace, and for the terrible end of Piso himself. Their suspicions of the Princeps still festered. An opponent of their interests, yes – but a murderer of their champions too. To be branded with such a reputation was grim enough. But there was worse. The Senate, the body in whose interests Tiberius had been willing to sacrifice his popularity with the plebs, had been left badly bruised by the crisis. The fate of Piso, who had first been recruited by the Princeps as an ally and then abandoned, struck many senators as salutary. Far from serving them as a model of antique rectitude, Tiberius appeared to many in the wake of events in Syria a veritable monster of hypocrisy. The scorn with which he had always regarded those who did not adhere to his own stern codes of morality was now met in the Senate House by a matching suspicion of him. Inexorably, even those allies whom Tiberius most needed were starting to worry whether he could be trusted at all.

And perhaps, among their number, in the wake of so toxic a crisis, was Tiberius himself.

Consigliere

Rome was a city crowded by the dead. Even though ascension into the heavens, whether on a comet-blaze or the beating of an eagle's wings, was an apotheosis granted only a Caesar, there were other ways of becoming a god. The blood of pigs, spilt over the earth of freshly dug graves, could serve to consecrate the spirits of even the humblest. Raise prayers to the departed, scatter violets on their tombs, make them offerings of meal, and salt, and wine-soaked bread, and they in exchange would stand guard over the living. *Manes*, these shades were called: spirits who could be summoned from the underworld to extend the lives of those who mourned them, to offer advice in dreams, to protect the harvest in the fields. Back in the days of Rome's rise to greatness, during the terrible war that had finally witnessed the annihilation of Carthage, they had even fought by the side of the Roman siege force, after its commander had dedicated the city to them as a blood-offering.[54] The living were keen, therefore, to honour the *Manes* with appropriate festivals. In February, for ten whole days, temples would be closed, fires extinguished on altars, and magistrates appear only in the plainest of clothes. It was perilous to deny the dead their due. One year, it was said, feeling neglected, they had risen from their tombs. As funeral pyres blazed eerily across Rome, a phantom throng of the departed had filled the city with their howling.

'Actually, I find this quite hard to believe.'[55] Ovid was not alone in his scepticism. Anyone with intellectual tastes, and the money to afford their cultivation, was liable to dismiss the *Manes* as superstition. Some philosophers, fashionable and bold, went so far as to teach that nothing of the spirit survived the grave. Nevertheless, even among the smartest of the smart set, the yearning for immortality abided. Ovid himself, whose exile to the Black Sea had offered him a grim taste of what it might be to descend into the underworld, had grown far too familiar with the threat of oblivion not to fight it to the end. Back in AD 17, amid the various excitements of Germanicus's triumph and his departure for the East, news of the poet's death had created barely a ripple in Rome. His voice, though, had not been wholly silenced. One last collection of poems, one final testament, had remained to be published. 'Time erodes both steel and stone.' So Ovid had written in the months before his death. Nevertheless, from beyond the grave, he continued to defy its corrosive power. So long as he had readers, he was not, perhaps, wholly dead. Time, to that degree, had been cheated. 'The written word defies the years.'[56]

Poets were not alone in appreciating this. The great knew it too. Their names were inscribed everywhere in Rome: on the pedestals of statues, on monuments in the Forum, on publicly displayed lists of consuls and priests, and generals awarded a triumph, reaching way back to the origins of the city. The surest punishment was not death but to be consigned to oblivion. In Spain, the awareness of this had prompted the widespread vandalising of Piso's monuments, while on the Greek island of Samos, in a burst of misapplied enthusiasm, the locals had chiselled out the name of his brother by mistake. In Rome too, the people had clamoured for Piso's name to be erased from every inscription in which it appeared; but this Tiberius had refused. Content though he was to license its removal from a statue of Germanicus, he would go no further. Something more than pity for his old friend had stayed his hand. Rome would no longer be Rome without the record of all that its great families had achieved. The Princeps knew himself the guardian, not just of his city's future, but of its past.

Tiberius had no illusions as to what this might mean in practice. Bleak, sardonic and much schooled in ambivalence, he was the opposite of naïve. Once, when an acquaintance of his youth attempted to remind him of times gone by, he cut the man off in mid-flow: 'I do not remember what I was.'[57] Much the same might have been said of the vanished Republic. The virtues and ideals to which Tiberius remained emotionally committed were no longer what they were – and Tiberius knew it. The last generation that remembered them as more than quaint anachronisms was inexorably passing away. In AD 22, sixty-three years after the slaughter at Philippi, a particularly venerable mooring to the past was snapped when Junia, the aged sister of Brutus, died. Her brother, who had assassinated one Caesar and perished fighting another, had continued to rank under Tiberius as what he had been ever since his death: a non-person. 'The best cure for a civil war is to forget that it ever happened.'[58] Silence, though, could sometimes be deafening. At Junia's funeral, the effigies of her ancestors, fashioned out of 'shining stone and ingenious wax',[59] had accompanied her to her tomb – but of her brother, the most celebrated of all her relatives, there was no portrait to be seen. Neither was there one of her long-dead husband, a second conspirator against the Dictator by the name of Cassius – and who also, like Brutus, had perished by his own hand on the battlefield of Philippi. Two conspicuous absentees. Watching the procession, no one could fail to be aware of the twin assassins, risen from the land of the dead to greet Junia, prominent among the *Manes*. The old lady's will, when it was read, turned out to contain a second, even more pointed omission. All the leading citizens of Rome were saluted – all save one. Of the Princeps there was not a mention.

Tiberius disdained to show resentment. Women, in his bitter experience of them, were most trouble when closest to home. Rich and well-connected though Junia had been, she was neither the richest nor the best-connected woman of her generation. That honour, as Tiberius knew none better, rested with a very different widow. In AD 22, the same year that saw Junia make her departure for the underworld, the equally venerable Augusta had herself fallen ill – only to stage a full and sprightly recovery. No one was much surprised. Livia Drusilla, as she had once been called, was well known for her mastery of drugs. There was more, though, to her aura of indestructibility than a well-stocked medicine box. The Augusta, who had cloaked herself in the privileges bequeathed her by her deified husband much as she had always draped herself in her *stola*, was a woman like none in her city's history. Everything about her was exceptional. Priest, tribune, even princeps: never before had male rank worn such disorienting female form. All that, and a mother too. 'How excellently the Augusta served the Republic by giving birth to its Princeps':[60] so the Senate had formally pronounced. A story told of the tree sprung from the laurel sprig dropped decades before into Livia's lap repeated the compliment in eerier form. It was said that its leaves had begun to wither just before Augustus breathed his last – even as one of its branches, carried by Tiberius in his triumph and then planted next to the original tree, had begun to flourish. It was as though the line of the Caesars itself had become the Augusta's to nurture, tend and own. *Genetrix orbis*, people had begun to call her – 'procreatrix of the world'.[61]

Not, of course, that this did much to improve her son's mood. There was more at stake for Tiberius than personal resentment. He could not help but view the abiding influence of the Augusta on affairs of state, despite his best efforts to rein her in, as a standing menace to his own authority. Her meddling in the trial of Piso had been particularly toxic. Plancina, the condemned man's wife, had been a favourite of the Augusta's – and the Augusta made sure to look after her favourites. Even as Tiberius was washing his hands of Piso, he had been obliged to come to the Senate and appeal to them for Plancina's life. A mortifying experience. The crimes of which Plancina had stood accused, from poisoning to witchcraft, could not have been more sordidly feminine – nor could the spider's web of the Augusta's intrigues, long kept hidden from public view, have been more embarrassingly laid bare. Tiberius, whose distaste for the company of women was matched only by his disapproval of their involvement in affairs of state, had been left doubly besmirched. The dark insinuations of Agrippina that the Princeps was a schemer of murderous hypocrisy, implacably hostile to her and to her children, appeared, to her many admirers, substantiated. Agrippina herself, cheated of her vengeance on Plancina, was left all the more embittered. Relations between her and the Augusta went from bad to worse.

Tiberius, trapped as he was between his mother and his stepdaughter, found himself hopelessly entangled in the meshes of court gossip. On a previous occasion, rather than tolerate the various compromises and humiliations of dynastic manoeuvring, he had walked out on Rome altogether. As Princeps, of course, he could hardly retire to Rhodes – but with Drusus, his son, now seasoned in the demands of leadership, a man with both a triumph and two consulships to his name, Tiberius could at least contemplate a measure of retirement. Anything to get away from the two importunate widows in his life.

Except that soon there would be three. Livilla, the sister of Germanicus and Claudius, was a woman whose husbands had always been characterised by their great expectations. The first had been Augustus's grandson, Gaius; the second her own cousin, Drusus. An ugly duckling as a child, she had grown up a famous beauty, commended to the Senate by her husband as his 'best beloved'.[62] Tiberius too had reason to value her: in the grim weeks that followed Germanicus's death, she had provided her uncle with a brief respite from the crisis by giving birth to twin boys. Livilla, though, was decidedly not a woman to bring harmony where there was discord. As a child, she had been notably spiteful, mocking her younger brother Claudius for his disabilities – and as an adult, she would prove no less malevolent. Fractious, flighty, and bitterly resentful of anyone who threatened her children's prospects, she combined a roving eye with a deep capacity for hatred. By AD 23, only a couple of years after her husband had publicly praised her to his fellow senators, their marriage was in crisis. Drusus himself, whose taste for fast living had never left him, and whose brutality was so pointed that sharp swords were called 'Drusian' in his honour, appeared to be entering into a sharp decline. Hot-tempered and violent, he was increasingly the worse for drink. At one point, at a party with Sejanus, his erstwhile partner in the suppression of the Pannonian mutiny, he had lost his temper and punched the Praetorian prefect in the face. His father, alarmed, began to worry for his health. Then, in September, Drusus fell seriously ill. By the 14th, he was dead.

Twice, first with the loss of Agrippa, then with that of Gaius, Augustus had been poleaxed by such a blow. Tiberius, frozen-faced as ever, scorned to betray his grief. Arriving in the Senate House, he calmed the ostentatious displays of mourning. 'I look for a sterner solace. I keep the Republic in my heart.' Even so, there could be no disguising the scale of the calamity that had befallen him and his plans. Bluntly, the Princeps spelt out the implications to his fellow senators. He had been banking upon Drusus, he explained, to mould and train Germanicus's sons, who bore in their veins, thanks to their mother, the blood of the deified Augustus. Ushering in Caligula's two elder brothers, Nero and Drusus, Tiberius commended them to the House. 'Adopt and guide these young men – these offspring of an incomparable bloodline.'[63] It was a raw and painful moment. Tiberius's increasing sense of exhaustion; his longing for a partnership that might help to alleviate it; his yearning to believe that loyalty to Augustus might yet be squared with the traditions of the Republic: all were laid bare. When the Princeps ended his address by promising, in a tone of high emotion, to restore to the consuls the reins of power, he may even have believed what he was saying.

If so, however, it was only for a moment. Tiberius's words were met in the Senate House with sullen scepticism. His listeners had heard it all before. Tiberius too, after a decade of struggling to educate senators in what he expected from them, had begun to despair of their partnership. 'Men readied for slavery,'[64] he had taken to muttering under his breath as he left the House. Hardly surprising, then, with Drusus dead and the Senate a broken reed, that Tiberius should have begun to cast around elsewhere for support. Heir of the Claudians though he might be, he did not scorn the ambitions of the upwardly mobile – provided only that they were able. Men of the meanest origins imaginable, even men rumoured to have been fathered by slaves, had been known to get Tiberius's backing. 'His achievements,' so the Princeps observed of one such parvenu, a gladiator's son who would eventually rise to become governor of Africa, 'are paternity enough.'[65] The more isolated and weary Tiberius came to feel, the more cause he had to value such servants. This was why, in the desolating aftermath of Drusus's death, he did not turn to one of his own bloodline for succour, nor to one of the companions of his youth, nor to anyone in the Senate House, but to a mere equestrian, an Etrurian from a drab and provincial background: Lucius Aelius Sejanus.

Even while Drusus was alive, Tiberius had been honouring the Praetorian prefect with marks of favour. Other people brought him problems; Sejanus brought him solutions. When Pompey's great theatre caught fire, it was the Praetorians who rushed to fight the flames and prevent them spreading; in recognition of this, and in obedience to Tiberius's evident wishes, the Senate voted to honour the Prefect with a bronze statue in the rebuilt complex. Naturally, the majority of senators did so through gritted teeth, but there were sufficient of them alert to the shifting tides of influence, or who had been admitted to the Senate by Sejanus's influence, to provide the Prefect with a potent faction. By AD 23, the year of Drusus's death, he had begun to establish himself even more decisively as the coming man. In the north-easternmost corner of Rome, on one of the highest vantage points in the city, workmen had been labouring for two years on a massive construction project. Walls of brick-faced concrete and gateways bristling with towers sheltered within them a massive grid of barracks: the unmistakable stamp, branded onto the very fabric of Rome, of a legionary camp. No longer, under Sejanus's prefecture, were the Praetorians to be scattered across the city. The days of veiling their existence were over. Instead, concentrated within a single fortress, and commanded by officers appointed by the Prefect himself, they were now directly in the capital's face. Equestrian Sejanus may have been, but what magistracy was there open to a senator that could compare for sheer intimidating menace with command of the Praetorian camp?

Sejanus himself, though, was painfully aware that his power as yet rested on shifting sands. He held no magistracy, was not even a senator. His authority was no more legally grounded than that of Maecenas had been. Without Tiberius he would be nothing – and Tiberius was sixty-five. The death of Drusus, though, had enabled Sejanus to glimpse a dazzling opportunity: the chance to establish himself, not as a Maecenas, but as an Agrippa. The August Family, now that Tiberius had lost his son, consisted principally of untested boys. Were the Princeps himself now to die in turn, there would be an urgent need for someone to serve as regent to his heir. After all, as Tiberius himself had openly acknowledged to the Senate, Germanicus's sons would never prove worthy of their descent from Augustus without attentive grooming. Sejanus, skilled as he was in the near impossible task of reading his master's thoughts and fathoming the many ambivalences that characterised them, had long since recognised the paradox that lay buried in their depths. Between Tiberius's devotion to the Senate as he imagined it should be, and his contempt for it as it actually was, existed an irreconcilable tension. To an operator as penetrating and subtle as Sejanus, there lurked here a tantalising opportunity. The faith that Tiberius had so publicly expressed in the Senate as the guardian of young Nero and Drusus was a precarious thing. Confidence and suspicion, in the Emperor's mind, were merely different sides of the same coin. Admiration for the codes of his class, for the traditions of the Senate, for the legacy of the Republic: all might easily be corrupted. The task of perverting Tiberius's instincts, and playing upon all that was most paranoid in his complex and mistrustful mind, was one for which Sejanus, in the event, would prove lethally fitted.

The key to the Prefect's strategy was Agrippina. Haughty, combustible, and impatient to see her sons elevated to the rank that she believed appropriate to their lineage, everything about her served to rub Tiberius up the wrong way. When Sejanus whispered in his master's ear that her ambitions were breeding factionalism in the Senate, just as those of her mother had once done, the Princeps was inclined to believe it. The first open flashpoint between the two came early in January 24. It was the turning point of the Roman year, and Janus, the god after whom the month was named, served as its gatekeeper. Two faces he had: one gazing backwards, at time past, and one looking fixedly into the future. An appropriate moment, then, for priests to offer up prayers for the safety of the Princeps. That particular year, though, there was a change to the formula. The names of Agrippina's two eldest sons, Nero and Drusus, were mentioned alongside that of the Emperor. Tiberius exploded. When he demanded to know of the priests whether the boys had been included at their mother's request, they flatly denied it; but the Princeps was barely mollified. The sinister precedent of the teenage Gaius and Lucius, shamefully over-promoted decades previously, still weighed on his mind. In a speech to the Senate, Tiberius sternly warned against spoiling the young princes. Agrippina, meanwhile, was only confirmed in her resentment of him. Relations between the two turned icier still.

Sensing his opportunity, Sejanus made sure not to waste it. His priority, if he were to isolate Agrippina and weaken her hold over her sons, was to destroy her allies in the Senate. Naturally, under a Princeps as respectful of legal proprieties as Tiberius, there could be no question of resorting to open violence in pursuit of this goal – but

Sejanus had no need to do so. It was the law itself which constituted his weapon of choice. Over the course of the year, a number of prominent men who had seen service with Germanicus were brought to trial by the Prefect's allies in the Senate. The charges ranged from extortion to *maiestas*. One committed suicide before a verdict could be reached; others were dispatched into exile. Nothing about the process ranked remotely as unconstitutional. The law courts had always been an arena in which the great manoeuvred for advantage. The ability to sway judges was a talent that had been the making of many an ambitious senator. Although to defend a man from the hounding of his enemies was traditionally regarded as the more honourable course for an orator to take, no disgrace attached itself to prosecution. Tiberius, who had himself secured the conviction of a would-be assassin of Augustus when only twenty, certainly saw nothing untoward about it. 'It is perfectly acceptable to bring prosecutions, just so long as it is done as a service to the Republic, in the cause of bringing down its enemies.'[66] How, then, could the Princeps fail to approve what was hallowed by both tradition and his own example?

Sejanus, though, with his pathologist's eye, had penetrated more deeply into the changed circumstances of the age than his master. The law, long cherished by senators as the bulwark of their liberty, now promised the man ruthless enough to exploit it the perfect opportunity to terrorise even the boldest among the elite into abject submission. The irony of this was peculiarly bitter. What had delivered the Senate into Sejanus's hands was an innovation originally designed to enhance its dignity. Once, back in the rumbustious days of the Republic, trials of the great had been a public entertainment, staged before the full gaze of the Roman people – but no longer. Instead, under Augustus, senators had been granted leave to sit in judgement on their own, in the privacy of the Senate House. At the time, they had greeted this as a novel and welcome burnishing of their status. Now, too late, they found that it had been a trap. The senator sitting in judgement on a peer accused of treason against the Princeps could not help but feel exposed. His vote was bound to be monitored. So too

227

the enthusiasm with which he pushed for conviction. The more sple- netically he demanded punishment, the more would his loyalty be noted. Sejanus had no need to bully his enemies into silence. He could leave senators themselves to do that. Paranoia and ambition would combine to keep them all at one another's throats.

Nevertheless, keen to rub his message home, the Prefect made sure to demonstrate what the penalty for any outspokenness would be. First, the inveterately abrasive Cassius Severus, who had been exiled to Crete in the dying days of Augustus's reign, was retried and sen- tenced to an altogether bleaker prison: a tiny rock in the Aegean. Then, the following year, came an even more ominous development. Back in 22, when the Senate had voted to place a statue of Sejanus in Pompey's theatre, only one senator, a noted historian by the name of Cremutius Cordus, had dared to protest. Now, three years on, the Prefect unleashed his attack dogs. The charge against Cremutius was a novel and chilling one: that in his history he had praised Brutus and Cassius, and named them 'the last of the Romans'.[67] When the wretched historian, rising to his feet, protested to his fellow senators that the liberty to praise the dead, no matter who they were, was an ancient birthright of their city, and one that Augustus himself had personally sanctioned, Sejanus's agents howled him down. 'And as they barked at him, he knew himself cornered.'[68] Leaving the Senate, Cremutius headed directly home. There, he starved himself to death. An application by the prosecution that he be force-fed, the better to inflict on him an edifying punishment, was registered too late with the consuls to be put into effect. His books, by official decree of the Senate, were burned.

The fate of Cremutius, destroyed because of what he had written about the past, offered to senators the glimpse of a terrifying future. It was one in which every bond of citizenship, every link of friendship, every web of favour and obligation, threatened a snare. A shared con- fidence at a dinner party, a snatch of conversation in the Forum: risk suddenly lurked everywhere. 'To comment on anything was to risk prosecution.'[69] Familiarity, in such a world, was a kind of infection.

The gods clearly agreed. As though in mockery of the new spirit of dread abroad in the Senate, they now sent to Italy a disease that spared the masses, and women of every class as well, but struck devastatingly at men of the elite. Manifesting itself first as an inflammation of the chin, before going on to cover the entire face and upper body 'with a hideous scale',[70] it was spread by their habit of kissing. *Mentagra*, Tiberius termed it, grimly humorous as ever – 'gout of the chin'.[71] By an official edict, he forbade citizens to give one another even the most innocuous peck upon the cheek. Gestures that once had served to celebrate a shared union now spelt only danger. The more intimate a relationship, the more it threatened calamity. The Roman upper classes knew themselves disfigured, blighted, sick.

So too, looking in the mirror, did the Princeps himself. Bald and bent with age, his face had grown ulcerous with sores. Whether it was *mentagra* itself that had come to afflict him, or some other ailment, Tiberius needed no reminder of how treacherous close contacts might be. Within his own household, attempts to patch over the various rivalries and hatreds festering within the August Family were barely more effectual than the plasters that speckled his face. No moment so sacred, no moment so intimate, that it might not start to suppurate.

Even a sacrifice raised to Augustus was capable of being ruined. It was Agrippina, bursting in on her uncle as he was seeking the favour of his deified predecessor, who desecrated one such ritual. Distraught that yet another of her intimates was being brought to trial, she laid the blame, not on Sejanus, but on Tiberius himself. The sight of her uncle standing before a statue of her grandfather, his head piously covered by his toga as befitted a priest, drove Agrippina into a paroxysm of fury. 'A man who offers up victims to the god Augustus,' she spat, 'ought not to be persecuting his descendants! You think that his divine spirit has been interfused into mute stone? No, if you want his true semblance, then look for it in me – a woman with his heavenly blood in her veins!' Tiberius only fixed Agrippina with a baleful gaze, then reached out and held her with his skinny hand. 'So,' he hissed, 'you think that your not being in power means you suffer persecution?'[72]

It still needed one final confrontation, one climactic insult, before the breakdown in relations between the two could be rendered terminal; and it was engineered, inevitably, by Sejanus. The Prefect, who had his agents everywhere, even among the circle of Agrippina's friends, employed them to deliver a fatal warning: that Tiberius was planning to poison her. The charge could not have been more grotesque – but Agrippina believed it. Invited to dine with her uncle, she ostentatiously refused to touch her plate. When Tiberius, scarcely able to believe his eyes, directly offered her an apple, she passed it to an attendant uneaten. That a man who had first drawn his sword in defence of Rome while he was in his teens, who had twice saved his city's dominions from implosion, who over the course of his long and incomparably distinguished career had fought many a battle, staring into the whites of his adversaries' eyes, meeting their steel with his own, and washing himself in the gouts of their blood, should now be charged with so underhand, so offensively feminine a crime: here was a mortal slight.

And not only to the Princeps. To the Augusta as well. The rumours reported of her activities had, if anything, grown only darker since her elevation to near-divine status. It was whispered, and widely believed, that Augustus himself had been the victim of her lethal facility with poison. On the last day of his life, it was reported, Livia had gone out into the garden of the villa where they were staying, and smeared the fruit of the fig tree that was growing there with venom – which Augustus, whose love of figs was well known, had promptly devoured. Now, by spurning Tiberius's offer of fruit so blatantly, Agrippina was raking up the embers of this slander, insulting the mother as well as the son. The Princeps, scorning to dignify his step-niece's gesture with a direct acknowledgement, turned instead to the Augusta. 'Who can blame me,' he demanded, 'that I should contemplate stern measures against a woman capable of alleging that I would poison her?'[73]

He had already put in place one particular measure. He flatly refused to grant Agrippina permission to remarry. So badly had this gone down with her that she had ended up sobbing into her sickbed. Surely, she had pleaded, there were men in Rome who would reckon it no dishonour to shelter the wife of Germanicus and his children? Indeed there were – which was precisely why, of course, Tiberius refused to countenance it. A widowed member of the August Family was dynastic gold. It did not help that rumour linked Agrippina to a man the Princeps particularly detested: an able and ambitious ex-consul by the name of Asinius Gallus, whose contributions to debates in the Senate had always been reliably snide.[74] Worse, Gallus had been married to Vipsania, the woman divorced by Tiberius many years previously on the orders of Augustus, and who had always remained the one true love of his life. The prospect of welcoming such a man into the August Family was too monstrous to be borne. Gallus's personal failings, though, were not the principal stumbling block. Had he never been a trouble-maker, had he instead been a loyal and supportive ally, the Princeps would still have refused permission. Agrippina, and Livilla as well, were far too valuable to be sprung from their widowhood.

Even Tiberius's most trusted deputy had been unable to shake him from this resolution. Agrippina was not the only person in his immediate circle with marriage on the mind. Back in 23, the year of Drusus's death, Sejanus had divorced his wife, Apicata. Despite giving him three children, her rank had failed to keep pace with the Prefect's ambitions – and so, naturally, she had had to go. For two years, Sejanus had bided his time. When he finally made his move, in 25, his aim could hardly have been set higher. Writing to Tiberius, it was to make a formal request for the hand of Livilla. A rare false step. Taken by surprise, the Princeps prevaricated. Reluctant though he was to deliver Sejanus a direct snub, he made clear his reservations. Allowing Livilla to marry, he explained, would inevitably intensify the rivalry between her and Agrippina. The two women already detested each other. To worsen their mutual hatred was a risk not worth the

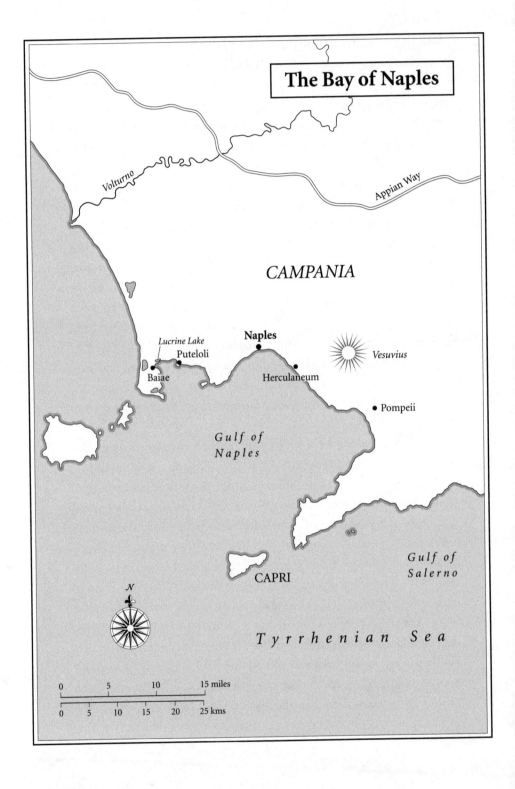

The Bay of Naples

Volturno

Appian Way

CAMPANIA

Lucrine Lake
Puteloli
Naples
Baiae
Herculaneum

Vesuvius

• Pompeii

Gulf of Naples

N

CAPRI

Gulf of Salerno

T y r r h e n i a n   S e a

0	5	10	15 miles
0	5	10 15	20 25 kms

payback. 'It would effectively split the House of Caesar in two.'[75] Sejanus, taking the hint, had beaten a retreat.

The episode, though, had not been without value to the Prefect. Tiberius, normally so close and secretive, had revealed depths normally kept well concealed. Sejanus appreciated better than anyone else in Rome the full degree of his master's exhaustion: with the women in his household, with the various factions in the Senate, with the capital itself. 'So it was that Sejanus began to cast the drudgeries of the city, its jostling crowds and all the people endlessly pestering Tiberius, in the worst light possible; and to speak in praise of calm and solitude.'[76] These sentiments were nothing radical. Retirement was not an alien principle to the Roman elite. The citizen who had served his fellows well was rarely begrudged his withdrawal from the political rough-and-tumble. Just as Horace had revelled in the charms of his Sabine farm, so would distinguished senators retreat from Rome to enjoy the out-of-town leisure activities appropriate to their rank: chatting with philosophers, showing off priceless works of art, adding extensions to their already massive villas. Swanky estates were to be found dotted across the Italian countryside; but the largest concentration lay along the coast south of Rome. In the Bay of Naples, which boasted real estate more expensive than anywhere save the most exclusive quarters of the capital itself, so numerous were the villas lining the coast 'that they gave the impression of forming a single city'.[77] Some might hug the shoreline, others perch on cliffs – but all bore dazzling witness to the premium set by eminent Romans on a sea view. A high-end property overlooking the Bay of Naples had long been an accepted mark of greatness. The villa left by Julius Caesar to Augustus, perched as it was on a rocky promontory, was renowned as a particular beauty spot. Augustus himself, by dying after a pleasant few days on Capri, had enjoyed what many Romans would have regarded as the perfect send-off.

Loyalty to him in Campania, the region which boasted the Bay of Naples, had been particularly strong. Back in the dark days of the civil wars, when Italy had been menaced by pirate fleets, Agrippa had moored his ships directly among the bay's most famous oyster beds, in a sheltered stretch of water named the Lucrine Lake, not caring what damage they did. The civil wars, though, had ended, and the fleet had been moved to a new base on a nearby promontory, where any damage to shellfish could be kept to a minimum. The Bay of Naples, beautiful and deliciously expensive, had come to serve as the principal ornament of the peace presided over by Augustus. Even the beasts of the deep had arisen to applaud it: a dolphin, as though sent by the gods to proclaim the new era, had befriended a boy who lived beside the Lucrine Lake and carried him every day to school. The story, which seemed conjured from a vanished world of myth, exemplified the distinctive appeal of the Bay of Naples, combining as it did the height of fashion with a distinctively antique feel. Certainly, to a man of Tiberius's sophisticated cultural tastes, the region offered more than just baths and oysters. If not quite as Greek as Rhodes, the island to which he had retired many years previously, it preserved a flavour of something inestimably precious: a touch of the settlers from Greece who, many centuries before, had come sailing into the bay and founded Naples. Nowhere, in short, promised the grim and weary Princeps a more tempting refuge. Naturally, it was out of the question for him to relinquish the charge entrusted him by the gods and the deified Augustus – but this did not have to be an insuperable problem. Campania was only a single day's ride away from Rome. A Princeps of sufficient acumen could certainly look to rule the world from there. It would need only one thing: a deputy back in the capital able and loyal enough to merit his trust.

Already, in AD 21, Tiberius had tested the waters by spending much of the year in Campania. Now, five years on, he planned an even lengthier stay. Setting out from Rome, he travelled relatively light. Only a single senator accompanied him. Also in his train were an assortment of literary scholars, men who shared Tiberius's fascination with abstruse details of mythology, and who could cope with the fiendishly difficult quizzes that the Princeps was in the habit of springing on his guests. Sejanus too, ever the devoted deputy, rode with the party. Although, as his master's proxy in the capital, he could hardly be spared for long, he and the rest of the party made a leisurely speed. Sixty-five miles south of Rome, Tiberius turned off the Appian Way and headed along a side-road for the coast. Here, waiting for him on the seafront, stretched an enormous estate: the villa of Spelunca. Sheer scale, though, was not the only aspect of the complex appropriate to his greatness. Beyond the residential quarters, up hills and past promontories, amid arbours and pavilions, in gardens, by walkways and on cliffs, works of art had been placed with masterly precision, so as to seem almost alive when illumined by torches and framed by the twilight. Some were antiquities, some freshly sculpted – but all bore witness to their owner's distinctive interests. Holding up a mirror to his fascination with the dimensions of myth, Spelunca served the Princeps as a landscape of fantasy – peopled by gods, and heroes of epic, and fabulous beasts. An emperor in such a theme park of wonders might well feel, even if only for an evening, that he had left the pressures of the capital far behind.

Once, back in the time of Aeneas, a second hero – a Greek – had come sailing past Spelunca. Although called Odysseus by his own people, in Latin he was known as Ulysses. Famously crafty and famously long-suffering, he had spent ten long years struggling to get home from the sack of Troy – fighting off monsters and negotiating with witches as he did so. Tiberius, who knew for himself what it was to struggle against debacles and domineering women, clearly felt an affinity with the hero.[78] Down by the sea, where a natural cave looked out onto the waters once plied by Ulysses, Tiberius had fashioned the most remarkable dining space in the world. *Haute cuisine* was one of the few extravagances on which the notoriously stingy Princeps delighted in lavishing his wealth. A noted wine snob, with a taste for vintages that had been treated with smoke, he also took a particular interest in vegetarian cooking – whether it was discovering a new variety of asparagus, sourcing exotic root vegetables from Germany, or insisting over the heads of rival gourmands that cabbage was far too delicious to rank as vulgar.

Nowhere, though, had his fascination with the arts of the table expressed itself more innovatively than at Spelunca. Pools washed with sea water enabled fish to be cooked fresh on site; pontoons over the shallows permitted guests to enjoy their banquet directly in the mouth of the cave, to the lapping of the sea all around them; flickering torches lit the inner depths of the grotto. 'There, nature had ingeniously imitated art'[79] – but not so ingeniously as art had then embellished nature. Immense statues illustrating various exploits of Ulysses provided diners with an incomparable tableau. A monster rose out of a pool inside the cave; a one-eyed giant sprawling on his back filled its innermost recess. Fine food, spectacular sculpture and a setting pregnant with myth: even Tiberius could feel happy at Spelunca.

Perhaps, though, it was possible to be too close to the world of epic. The giant eerily illuminated by torches in the rear of the cave had been the son of Neptune, god of the seas, who was known, thanks to his habit of lashing out periodically with his trident, as 'Earth-Shaker'. The tremor, when it came that evening, hit Spelunca without warning. Boulders began to fall, crashing down onto the mouth of the grotto. Numerous attendants bringing food were crushed in the avalanche, while the guests, rising in panic, fled for safety across the shallows. The elderly Tiberius, struggling to his feet, was unable to make his escape from the cliff-face – and the Praetorians, when they came hurrying to the scene of disaster and saw only rubble where the Princeps had been lying, inevitably feared the worst. Clambering over the debris, they heard the voice of their prefect calling out to them; and when they pulled away the boulders, it was to find Sejanus crouching over his master on hands and knees, the embodiment of a human shield.

A miracle – and pregnant with meaning, clearly. Tiberius himself took away two lessons from the episode. First, that he had in Sejanus an incomparably trustworthy servant, a man who could be trusted with anything. Second, that the gods had delivered him a warning never again to set foot in Rome.

Caprice

AD 28. The first of January. A propitious and joyous time. It was a day when the perfume of burning saffron hung heady over the Forum; when temples were unbolted and altars reconsecrated to the gods; when fat bullocks were led up to the summit of the Capitol and their necks bent to the axe. Meanwhile, in the Senate House, a letter was being read out from the Princeps, offering the traditional season's greetings. Few senators were expecting any surprises. It was a holiday, after all.

This time, though, there was to be a twist. A year and more Tiberius had been absent in Campania – but he still had his eyes and ears in Rome. The man he had taken to calling 'the sharer of his cares'[80] was tireless in his cause. Sejanus had his spies everywhere – sniffing out subversion, keeping track of sedition. Now, Tiberius informed the Senate, a particularly shocking instance of *maiestas* had been uncovered. An equestrian by the name of Titius Sabinus had spoken blatant treason to one of Sejanus's undercover agents. Three more of them, squeezed into Sabinus's attic, had overheard every last word. Since all four of the Prefect's agents were prominent senators, there could be no disputing their evidence. Sabinus had slandered the Princeps, suborned his servants, plotted against his life. Clearly, then, his fellow senators knew what they had to do. And do it they duly did.

When the Praetorians came for Sabinus, they jerked a hood down over his head, then slung a noose around his neck. His despairing protest, bleak and punning, was worthy of Tiberius at his most sardonic: a muffled lamentation that sacrifice was being offered up, not to Janus, but to Sejanus.[81] Then he was hauled away, his destination the city's prison. Unbolted that same day as Rome's temples had already been, it swallowed up Sabinus into its bowels. Soon afterwards, a limp bundle was slung out onto the Gemonian Steps. There, where Piso's statues had been vandalised eight years earlier, the corpse of the executed man was exposed to the gaze of the Forum. As crowds gathered, drawn by the spectacle, his dog stood guard over the body and howled inconsolably. When people tossed it scraps of food, it would carry them back to its master and lay them beside the corpse's mouth; and when, in due course, men came with hooks to drag Sabinus to the Tiber, the dog followed the body all the way to the river, then jumped in after it, 'trying to keep it from sinking'.[82]

Ever given to sentimentality, the Roman people could recognise in the misery of this faithful hound a mirror of their own grief for the family of Germanicus. Sabinus had been a close associate of their dead favourite, and in his fatal discussions with Sejanus's *agent provocateur* had aggressively expressed his pity for Agrippina. Tiberius's departure from Rome had done nothing to ease the pressure on the unhappy widow. Just the opposite. Operating on the presumption that the Princeps had washed his hands of Agrippina once and for all, Sejanus had felt licensed to work ever more openly for the downfall of her family. His particular target was her oldest son, Nero – who, as the heir apparent, represented the most immediate threat to the Prefect's own prospects. It helped that Nero himself was brash and headstrong; helpful too that Drusus, the next in line, was so consumed by envy of his elder brother that he preferred to side with Sejanus.

Only Caligula, the youngest of Agrippina's three sons, was too clear-sighted to play the Prefect's game. Still in his mid-teens, the travails of his family had already bred in him a pitiless appreciation of how capricious and cruel the workings of power could be. Certainly, he felt no obligation to share in the doom closing in on his family – not if he could possibly help it. Accordingly, when Agrippina was obliged by Sejanus to leave Rome, and found herself placed under effective house arrest in Campania, Caligula turned for sanctuary to the one person with sufficient authority still to defy the Prefect. 'Ulysses in a *stola*',[83] he nicknamed the Augusta – high praise indeed, coming from an operator of his already seasoned aptitude for cunning. She in her turn delighted in her great-grandson as a chip off the old block. Caligula – for the moment, at any rate – could reckon himself safe.

Which was just as well. The noose was tightening all the time. With

Sabinus dead, Tiberius wrote again to the Senate, praising it for its prompt action in keeping the Republic from danger, and hinting darkly at further plots. Even though he mentioned no names, everyone knew whom he meant. When Sejanus, in his regular briefings, warned his master of the iniquities of Agrippina or the thuggishness of Nero, there was no one now to contradict him. So determined had Tiberius been to leave behind the gossip and importunities of court life that even Campania had proven inadequate to his purposes. Within a few months of his arrival there, he had abandoned its various pleasure resorts, evacuating himself and his retinue to Capri, the private island bequeathed him by Augustus. There, where no one could approach its two jetties, let alone land on them, without his express permission, he could feel far from the madding crowd at last. From his family too. Decades previously, campaigning in Pannonia or Germany, Tiberius had always been a general to put a premium on security. The man who on his campaigns had invariably slept without a tent, the better to avoid the risk of assassination, now lived in dread of his own relatives: a frightened and unhappy woman, a gauche and inexperienced boy. What had once been a healthy instinct for self-preservation was darkening, in old age, into paranoia.

Tiberius's retreat to his cliff-girt island, though, was no abdication. He remained too much a man of duty to turn his back entirely on the charge bequeathed him by Augustus. The Princeps held true to his responsibilities both to the August Family and to the Roman people. So it was, even as Agrippina found herself placed under ever stricter supervision, that he arranged to provide her daughter and namesake with a match worthy of her status: Gnaeus Domitius Ahenobarbus, impeccably aristocratic son of the first Roman commander to cross the Elbe. So it was too, whether by inviting privileged guests over to join him on Capri, or by going on the odd foray to the mainland, that the Princeps set limits on his isolation. He would still, every once in a while, make himself available to the privileged few. Those who wished to see him, though, had no alternative but to do so fully on his terms. Tiberius had not the slightest intention, as yet, of heading back to Rome. Even the grandest senators were obliged to beat a path to Campania – where they might well find their access to the Princeps held up or even barred by Sejanus. Many, to their indignation, were reduced to camping out on the Bay of Naples, among the various other suitors. The shame of it was deeply felt. To be reduced to crawling before a mere equestrian; to begging him for favours; to serving his interests in exchange for his patronage, like the humblest, most cringing of spongers: these, for the elite of Rome, were unconscionable humiliations. Yet what was the alternative? Senators found themselves stumbling through a strange and terrifying world – one in which everything seemed turned on its head. Honours, once the badges of glory and achievement, now served to brand those who gained them as crawlers. Pedigree and independence of mind, the qualities most admired by Tiberius in his fellow senators, seemed ever more likely to spell their ruin. 'As for a famous name – that threatened death.'[84]

And, of course, it threatened no one more than Augustus's descendants. A year on from the execution of Sabinus, and two deaths served to herald the endgame. The first was that of Agrippina's wretched sister Julia, exiled more than twenty years by her deified grandfather, and breathing her last on the tiny island where she had been languishing ever since. She had been a prisoner so long that it came as news to many people in Rome that she had not died years before – but the same could hardly be said of the second loss suffered by the August Family in 29. The death of the Augusta, whose father had perished at Philippi, who had shared the bed of a god, and who had been awarded more titles, honours and tokens of rank than any other woman in her city's history, was experienced by the Roman people as a fateful moment, one last farewell to a past already becoming legend. So moved were senators that they even voted to raise an arch in her honour. Tiberius, whose grief at the loss of his mother appeared decidedly muted, did not approve. The proposal was quietly buried. So too, with the stern admonition that the Augusta herself would never have been so vain as to lay claim to divine honours, was a senatorial vote to declare her a goddess. The funeral itself was a modest affair. Tiberius, who had been vacillating for days about whether to leave Capri for the ceremony, did not in the event appear. The Augusta's body had already begun to stink by the time it was finally consigned to the flames. The funeral address was delivered, to universal praise, by the seventeen-year-old Caligula.

Who was painfully aware, of course, even as he gave his speech, that the future had just turned a little more uncertain. Others too had good cause to be nervous. Over the next few years, many of the Augusta's protégés would be brought to ruin. These ranged from consuls to women such as Piso's widow, Plancina. Most prominent of all, though, was Agrippina. No matter that she and her grandmother had never got along, the Augusta had always been a woman to hold Tiberius to his obligations. For as long as he had been Princeps, she had served him as a living reminder of his duty to Augustus – who had never left anyone in any doubt that the sons of Germanicus were his appointed heirs. Certainly, in the minds of their devoted admirers, it was no coincidence that a letter from the Princeps denouncing both Agrippina and her eldest son, Nero, should have arrived in the Senate House almost the moment that the Augusta's funeral was done. As crowds massed in the Forum, brandishing likenesses of Agrippina and Nero and chanting that the letter was a fake, the senators squirmed. Unclear what it was exactly that the Princeps intended them to do, they did nothing. Menaces from Sejanus, and a second letter from Tiberius, left them no room for doubt. Obediently, the Senate then did as prompted. Agrippina and Nero were both condemned as conspirators against the Princeps, and Nero, for good measure, declared a public enemy. But were these measures really sufficient to the horror of their crimes? If only, the Senate added unctuously, they could be sentenced to death! Tiberius, though, had other plans. As ever, he was guided both by what was strictly legal, and by the example of Augustus. Nero and his mother, shackled and under heavy guard, were transported to separate prison islands off Italy. Agrippina, in a twist typical of Tiberius's baleful humour, was sent to Pandateria, where Julia, her mother, had long before been sent by Augustus.

For the Princeps, ever one to savour a grudge, the official condemnation of his ex-wife's daughter was a delicious vindication of his darkest suspicions. For Sejanus too it was a mighty triumph. He knew, however, to a degree unsuspected by Tiberius, how foully he had played in framing Agrippina; and he knew as well, high though he had mounted the ladder, how parlous were the rungs he still had left to climb. Two goals remained to be met: the final elimination of Germanicus's heirs; and the establishment of a right of guardianship over Drusus's. Of the two sons that Livilla had delivered her husband back in 20, only one now remained to her, a nine-year-old nicknamed in memory of his dead sibling 'Gemellus' – 'the Twin'. Were Germanicus's two remaining sons to be declared public enemies, as Nero had already been, then Gemellus, as Tiberius's grandson, would be the only heir left standing.

Not that Sejanus was alone in appreciating this. Livilla, who had enjoyed Agrippina's downfall as much as anyone, was fully alert to the ally she had in the Prefect. The prospect of seeing her son as Princeps, over the heads of Nero, Drusus and Caligula, was one calculated to delight her envious and ambitious spirit. Already she had played an enthusiastic part in Sejanus's schemes. Her daughter, Gemellus's elder sister, had been married to Nero, and on Livilla's instructions had served the Prefect as his eyes and ears. Just as Sabinus had been doomed by spies in his attic, so Nero had been betrayed in his bed. There was nowhere, it seemed, beyond the Prefect's reach.

Yet even as his fellow citizens, cringing before his fame and power, began to pay him honours so extravagant that they seemed to cast him, not as the servant of the Princeps, but as his partner, Sejanus never forgot how precarious the foundations of his greatness remained. That his statues were paired with those of Tiberius; that formal delegations had taken to meeting him at the city gates whenever he returned to Rome; that some had even begun to offer sacrifices to his image, almost as though he were the Deified Augustus himself: none of this deceived the Prefect. His fortunes still hung by a thread. Without the favour of Tiberius, he would be nothing. A year on from the downfall of Agrippina, a fresh triumph over her sons served, by a frustrating irony, only to emphasise this all the more. The same dirty tricks that had done for Nero now secured the condemnation of Drusus as well. The suborning of the young man's wife, the briefings against him by security agents, the slanders whispered in his grand-uncle's ear by Sejanus himself, proved more than sufficient to doom him. Proclaimed by the Senate a public enemy, as his elder brother had been, Drusus was immured in a dungeon on the Palatine. Now, with only Caligula standing between Gemellus and the succession, Sejanus had ultimate victory almost in his grasp. Almost – but not quite. Caligula, who had been staying with his grandmother, Antonia, after the death of the Augusta, was summoned by Tiberius to Capri. There, of course, he was effectively beyond the Prefect's reach. That Caligula himself was as much the hostage as the guest of his great-uncle helped Sejanus not at all. To frame a young man directly under Tiberius's nose was an almost impossible challenge – even for a practitioner in the arts of disinformation as seasoned as the Prefect.

What, though, if he could end his dependence on the patronage of his master? In Rome, a shift in the balance of power between the two men was increasingly bruited. Tiberius, absent from the capital for four years, had begun to seem to many a shrunken and faded figure – 'the lord of an island, nothing more'.[85] The Prefect himself knew better; but he also knew that his patron, weary of Rome and weary of life, would not be around for ever. Time was running out. Having come so far, Sejanus could no longer depend for his future prospects upon the favour of a sick and aged man. To win he would have to dare.

When news reached Rome that Nero, transported to a penal island the year before, was dead, few failed to detect the hand of the Prefect in his miserable and squalid end. A guard, it was rumoured, had appeared before the prisoner, brandishing a noose and a butcher's hook; and Nero, rather than suffer himself to be murdered, had committed suicide. Whether true or not, it added to the aura of menace that clung to Sejanus: the man who commanded access to the Princeps, who had built a legionary camp directly overlooking Rome, who had deployed terror more blatantly in the city than anyone since the darkest days of the Triumvirate. Yet even as he intimidated the Roman people, he made sure to woo them as well. When Tiberius, in a telling mark of favour, arranged for him to become consul and agreed to serve as his partner, Sejanus naturally revelled in his official status as the colleague of the Princeps. Now at last he was a senator; now at last he wielded power that was legally sanctioned. Simultaneously, though, as a man who had risen from provincial obscurity to dizzying heights, his election provided him with the perfect opportunity to pose as something more: as a man of the people. After the formal vote in the Senate House, the new consul-elect staged a flamboyant parade around the Aventine, the hill of the plebs. Here, in a pointed echo of the elections on the Campus banned by Tiberius, he hosted an assembly. The potential insult to his master was massive — but Sejanus was content to take the risk. Princeps, Praetorians, people: he needed them all.

By 31, the year in which he entered his consulship, the Prefect could feel confident that all his schemes, all his manoeuvrings, all his ambitions were close to fruition. Although Caligula, infuriatingly, remained at liberty, the sense that Tiberius was finally ready to take the decisive step and reveal his long-term plans for his 'partner in toil'[86] began to build with the heat of summer. That spring, bidding his deputy farewell after a consultation with him on Capri, the Princeps had freely expressed his devotion, hugging his deputy tightly and declaring that he could as easily spare his own body and soul as Sejanus. Still, though, even as rumour and counter-rumour swept Rome, no definitive statement arrived in the sweltering city.

Summer turned to autumn. The Prefect continued to sweat. Finally, on 18 October, the long-awaited moment arrived. It was dawn. As Sejanus, standing on the steps of the great temple of Apollo, where the Senate was due to meet that day, gazed out from the Palatine at the waking city, he was joined by a fellow prefect. One-time commander of the city's firefighters, the *Vigiles*, Sutorius Macro had just come from Capri – and he bore with him a letter from the Princeps. It was addressed to the new consul, Memmius Regulus, a trusted henchman of Tiberius who had taken office only three weeks before, and was presiding over the Senate that same morning. In strictest confidence, Macro revealed the letter's contents to his commander. Sejanus was to be given the *tribunicia potestas*, the privileges of a tribune. Momentous news indeed. Back in the days of Augustus, first Agrippa and then Tiberius himself had been granted the identical bundle of powers – and on both occasions, it had served to mark the respective men as the partner of Augustus's labours. Unsurprisingly, then, Sejanus was as delighted as he was relieved. As he hurried inside the temple, the look on his face was one that everyone could read. Cheers greeted him, and bursts of applause. When he took his place, senators flocked to sit beside him, eager to bask in his glory. Macro, meanwhile, handed over the letter from Tiberius to Regulus. Then he turned and left. Sejanus, listening impatiently to the letter as the consul began to read it out, did not bother to wonder where he might be headed.

Tiberius, of course, had never been a man to cut to the chase. Nevertheless, as senators listened to Regulus read out his letter, they found themselves growing perplexed. Far from praising Sejanus, the Princeps seemed to have only criticisms of his colleague. The placemen who had bunched themselves around him began to inch nervously away. Sejanus himself, listening in consternation, could not move – for various magistrates had stepped forward to block his path. Only after Regulus had ordered him three times to stand did he finally rise to his feet – by which stage it was clear to everyone that Tiberius had cut his deputy loose. When the consul ordered Sejanus to be led from the chamber and incarcerated in the same prison that had once held Sabinus, no one attempted to defend him. As news of the Prefect's downfall swept across Rome, crowds began to mass in the Forum, booing and jeering the prisoner, and toppling his statues as he was dragged past them in chains. When Sejanus sought to cover his head with his toga, they yanked it off him and began punching and slapping him about the face. So much for his attempts to woo the Roman people. Worse than a failure, they had cost him the backing of his patron.

That afternoon, with Sejanus languishing in the city prison, senators reconvened amid the splendour of the building opposite, the Temple of Concord. There, in the supreme monument to the suppression of uppity commoners, they voted for him to be executed. He was garotted that same evening, and his corpse slung out, as Sabinus's had been, onto the Gemonian Steps. For three days, teeming crowds of those who had detested the Prefect for his arrogance, his cruelty and his ambition gleefully kicked and trampled it to a pulp. Only once it had been reduced to an unrecognisable mess was the body finally dragged away on a hook. Slung into the Tiber, the man who had aspired to govern the world ended up as food for fishes.

Meanwhile, flashed along a chain of bonfires, the news was being brought to Capri. As he waited on the island's highest cliff to receive it, Tiberius had been taking nothing for granted. A ship lay at anchor, ready to evacuate him to a legionary base in the event of his plans going wrong. Dread of Macro failing to seize command of the Praetorians, of Sejanus defying the attempts to topple him, of losing his hold on Rome: Tiberius, whose suspicions of Germanicus's family had induced in him such creeping paranoia, had suddenly realised the full, appalling scope of his error. Obsessed as he was by scotching Agrippina, he had failed to consider that he might all along have been nursing a viper at his breast.

It was Antonia, the grandmother of Caligula, who had opened his eyes to the danger. The old woman, having already watched two of her grandsons destroyed by the Prefect, had been frantic to stop him framing a third. Accordingly, in a letter sent to her brother-in-law by her most trusted slave, a Greek by the name of Pallas, she had spelt out her suspicions. To the naturally secretive and suspicious Tiberius, who for so long had cherished his deputy as the one man he could trust, the realisation that Sejanus might have been playing him for a fool was devastating. Even the possibility that the Prefect might pose a menace had been sufficient to doom him. Slowly, surely, inexorably, Tiberius had drawn up his plans. Consummately skilled though Sejanus was in the arts of guile and conspiracy, his master had outsmarted him. The Prefect, taken wholly by surprise, had found himself entangled in a web more lethal than any that he had spun. The spider had ended up a fly.

Nor was Sejanus the only one to perish. Many others were dragged down with him. Some – his eldest son, his uncle – were formally sentenced to death, others lynched by vengeful mobs. The Praetorians, who felt a particular need to demonstrate their loyalty to the Princeps, did so by rampaging through the city, burning and looting as they went. 'Not a person of Sejanus's faction, but he was trampled down by the Roman people.'[87] The deadliest vengeance of all, though, was taken by Apicata, his abandoned wife. Writing to the Princeps, she levelled allegations against Sejanus so monstrous, so unspeakable, that she killed herself the moment she had made them.[88] Tiberius, having unsealed the letter, read with mounting horror of just how far, and how terribly, he had been deceived. For a decade, Apicata claimed, his most trusted servant had been having an affair with Livilla. Together, the pair of them had poisoned Drusus. There had been no limit to the ambitions, the depravity and the treachery of the couple. Remembering how Sejanus had once requested the hand of his niece, Tiberius could feel the scales dropping from his eyes. A eunuch of Drusus's, a physician of Livilla's: both, when they were tortured, confirmed the truth of Apicata's claims. Tiberius was duly convinced. Handed over to her mother, Livilla was locked up in a room and starved to death. Her statues, her inscriptions, her very name: all were obliterated. Senators, frantic to demonstrate their loyalty to the vengeful Princeps, queued up to damn her memory. Meanwhile, with Sejanus's eldest son already put to death, orders were given for his two youngest children to be taken to the city prison. One, a boy, was old enough to understand what lay ahead; but his little sister, bewildered and not knowing what she had done wrong, kept asking why she could not be punished like any other child – with a beating? Since it would naturally have been an offence against the most sacred traditions of the Roman people to put a virgin to death, the executioner made sure to rape her first. The bodies of the two children, once they had been strangled, were dumped on the Gemonian Steps.

So many judicial murders, so many corpses left to the gaze of the Forum. When Agrippina perished on her penal island, two years to the day after the execution of her deadliest enemy, Tiberius made great play of his mercy in not having had her strangled or exposed on the Gemonian Steps. The downfall of Sejanus had done nothing to ease his mistrust of her. She and Nero had remained in captivity. So too had Asinius Gallus, the man suspected by Tiberius of plotting to marry Agrippina, and whose condemnation a cowed and compliant Senate had been nudged into pronouncing back in 30. For three years the wretched man had been kept in solitary confinement, given just enough to keep him alive, and forcibly fed whenever he attempted to go on hunger strike. To Tiberius, torn between a vengefulness grown more cruel and fearful with old age, and an abiding instinct to procrastinate, such a punishment – a living death – had represented the perfect compromise. Gallus, Agrippina, Drusus: all three, when they finally perished, did so of hunger. Drusus's end was particularly terrible. Like his mother, who had lost an eye during the course of one beating, he had been in the charge of brutal gaolers, soldiers and ex-slaves, who did not hesitate to use the whip on the son of Germanicus at the slightest hint of disobedience. In the final week of his life, he was reduced to gnawing on the contents of his mattress. When he died, it was with screams and imprecations. His final curse on Tiberius was a chilling one: as a monster who had drowned his own family in blood.

When these details were reported to senators, they listened in perplexity, puzzled that a man as secretive as the Princeps should ever have permitted the reporting of such horrors. Tiberius, though, felt no compunctions. The eyes of the Roman people had to be opened. Menace lurked everywhere. Even among his closest advisors, his own family, treason was a constant. It gave Tiberius no pleasure to acknowledge this. He had loved Sejanus, and he had loved his brother – two of whose grandsons had ended up starving to death in his prisons. The Senate too, that body in which the Princeps had always placed such trust, and in whose interests he had always laboured so hard, had shown itself rotten with ingratitude. To purge it of the taint of collaboration was a murderous task. On one particularly fell day, twenty senators, Sejanus loyalists all, were executed in a single dispatch. Guards ringed the corpses, forbidding relatives and friends to display any marks of grief; and when the bodies were finally hauled from the Gemonian Steps and dumped into the Tiber, they drifted away ponderously on the currents, a rotting tangle of carrion. Yet Tiberius, when he felt that his own security was not at stake, was still willing to grant mercy to a colleague – and to confess to the Senate his state of anguish. 'Every day, I feel myself succumbing to misery.'[89]

Most rife of all with treachery, though, and most seductive, was the capital itself. Every year, in the wake of Sejanus's downfall, the Princeps would set out for home; and every year, rather than enter the city, he would wander the countryside beyond it, or else make camp in the shade of its walls, before scuttling crab-like back down the coast to Capri. To be a permanent exile from Rome was more than he could bear; to return there, impossible. It was a torture that might have been designed by the gods. Certainly, there could be no doubting their hand in Tiberius's reluctance to pass the city gates. The earthquake at Spelunca had been only one of many portents sent to ward him from the city. On one occasion, as he approached Rome, he went to feed his pet snake and found it dead, devoured by ants. So transparent a warning of the menace presented to him by the mob was this that he had immediately turned round in his tracks. Tiberius was skilled in the reading of such signs. Right from the earliest days, they had accompanied his career. While he was a student, 'a donkey had given off large sparks as it was being groomed, thus predicting his future rule';[90] while a young officer, 'altars consecrated by victorious legions in times of old had blazed into sudden fire.' An adept of primordial wisdom, of veiled mysteries, of the science of the stars, Tiberius knew how to trace the patterns cast on mortal affairs by the shadow of the heavens.

Such learning, of course, could be dangerous in the wrong hands. Back in 12 BC, Augustus had confiscated and burned more than two thousand books which claimed to reveal the future; two years into Tiberius's reign, the Senate had ordered all astrologers out of Italy. Particularly prominent ones risked being thrown off a cliff. Knowledge of where the world was heading had become far too sensitive to be permitted the average citizen. A Princeps, by contrast, needed all the guidance he could get. Tiberius's own instructor in occult studies was an astrologer by the name of Thrasyllus, whose talents had first impressed him during his exile on Rhodes, and who had since become a bosom companion.* The presence by his side of such a seasoned observer of the constellations was a great reassurance to the Princeps. The pulse of things still needed to be kept. Quarantined as he was from the sordid mass of humanity, Tiberius aimed to fix his gaze instead on higher things, upon wonders untouched by equivocating senators, fractious mobs and ambitious widows.

Even Augustus had found Capri a fitting home for marvels. His villa had been liberally adorned with them: the bones of giants, the skeletons of sea monsters. Tiberius too had a fascination with such treasures – so much so that his curiosity about them was celebrated across the world. Brought the tooth of a colossal hero whose remains had been exposed by an earthquake in Asia Minor, he had reverently measured it, then commissioned a full-scale model of the dead man's

---

* Various stories are told of how this particular astrologer passed the audition. According to one account, he accurately foretold that Tiberius was planning to throw him off a cliff; according to another, he correctly identified a ship approaching Rhodes as the bearer of a summons back to Rome.

head.* Such attention to the details of the fantastical was typical of Tiberius. When a merman was spotted playing a conch shell in a Spanish cave, or a mysterious voice was heard crying out from a Greek island that Pan, a god with the legs and huge genitals of a goat, was dead, the Princeps demanded a full report. Witnesses were grilled, official inquiries set up. Nowhere, though, did the Princeps's obsession with squaring the rival dimensions of the earthly and the heavenly, the mortal and the supernatural, express itself to more spectacular effect than on his island retreat. Twelve separate villas, some converted by the Princeps and some built from scratch, dotted the island in transparent homage to Mount Olympus, home of the twelve most powerful gods of Greece. Some of these complexes stood perched on cliffs, louring over sea-lanes once navigated by Ulysses and Aeneas; others led down to caves, where, set amid the lapping of blue waters, statues of mermen and sea-nymphs adorned the flame-lit depths. Everywhere, grottoes, gardens and porticoes, graced by the Princeps with learned, teasing names and fashioned in obedience to his immaculate taste, provided the perfect setting for young actors to pose as Pans and nymphs. As at Spelunca, so on Capri: Tiberius dwelt amid a mythological theme park.

And by 37, eleven years after his departure for Campania, he was coming to seem almost a figure of myth himself. It was inevitable, in a city as addicted to scandal as Rome, that the Princeps's lengthy absence on a private island should have fuelled the rumours told of him. His brooding shadow still lay heavy over the capital. The plebs had neither forgotten nor forgiven his haughty contempt for them, nor the Senate his brutal purging of the supporters of Agrippina and Sejanus. The smears of blood on the Gemonian Steps were not easily washed away. Tiberius had come to seem, in his old age, a ghoulish figure of dread: embittered, paranoid and murderous. Of what hellish cruelties he might be capable away from the public gaze, amid the seclusion of Capri, was a question fit to send shivers up the spines of

* The 'hero' was almost certainly a mastodon or mammoth. See Mayor, p. 146.

eager Roman gossips. Many stories were bandied about. It was claimed, for instance, that a few days after the Princeps's first arrival on the island, while he was standing on a cliff, a fisherman had clambered up the rocks, bringing with him a huge mullet as a gift for Caesar; and that Tiberius, the man whose fearlessness in the service of Rome even his bitterest enemies acknowledged, had been terrified by the intruder. So terrified, in fact, that he had ordered his guards to seize the wretched trespasser and scrub his face with the mullet. The man, screaming, was said to have cried out in the midst of this torture, 'I only thank the stars I did not give him the huge crab I also caught!'[91] And so Tiberius ordered him scrubbed with the crab as well. Rome too, so many had come to believe, had been similarly treated by the Princeps. She had become, under his rule, a face shredded and bloodied to the bone.

That Tiberius was capable of being vengeful hardly came as news. More unsettling, perhaps, were the vices that he had previously kept concealed. To the Roman people, privacy was something inherently unnatural. It permitted aberrant and sinister instincts free rein. Only those with sexual tastes they wished to keep veiled from their fellow citizens could have any reason to crave it. Hostius Quadra had indulged his unspeakable perversities in the isolation of a mirrored bedroom – but Tiberius, for eleven years, had enjoyed the run of an entire island. People in Rome were not fooled by his high-flown pretensions to scholarship. They suspected that his claims to an interest in the arcane details of mythology were merely an excuse to indulge in pornographic floor-shows. Decades before, when the future Augustus had celebrated his marriage to Livia, crowds in the streets below had rioted when news broke that the wedding guests were dressed up as gods. Now, though, in the playground that Tiberius had made of Capri, there were no censorious mobs to keep the Princeps's fantasies in check. The nymphs and Pans with which he peopled his grottoes were not there merely to pose. Rapes and fantastical copulations were rife in the tales told of the gods. What greater pleasure, then, for an old man fascinated by their doings than to watch their couplings being graphically restaged?

The frisson derived not just from the performances but from the cast. All his life, Tiberius had been pledged to certain fundamentals: the dignity of the Senate, the ideals of the aristocracy, the virtues of his city's past. Yet as Ovid, left to die by the Princeps at the ends of the world, had always understood, 'desire is fuelled by prohibitions.'[92] Tiberius's choice of performers could hardly have been more transgressive. Young and attractive, many were not merely paragons of modesty but children of the Princeps's own class. 'Beauty and good bodies; uncorrupted innocence and distinguished ancestry: these were what turned him on.'[93] Obliged to pose as prostitutes, to hawk for business like the lowest class of sex worker, to perform sometimes three or four at a time, the offspring of the nobility summoned to Capri could hardly have been more humiliated. The spectacle of their degradation was a hideous desecration of everything that the man watching it had always held most dear. But that, of course, for the Princeps, was precisely what made it so exciting.

Naturally, he despised himself for it. Tiberius, heir to the Claudian name, the greatest general of his generation, a man who by virtue of his many services to the Republic would have deserved to rank as Princeps even had his divine father not adopted him, knew the standards by which he would be judged – for he shared them. But he was weary. Twenty long years he had been holding the Roman wolf by its ears. Almost into his ninth decade, he felt himself a man out of time. His best hopes for his city had turned to dust. The Senate had failed him. Indeed, it was the measure of his peers' depravity that so many had become complicit in his own. Men whose record of service to Rome reached back to the days of the kings, when gods had still walked the earth, now competed to pimp their children to him. Faced by the evidence of such degeneracy, Tiberius no longer felt any great concern to secure the future of his fellow citizens.

Which was just as well – for the ruin that had left the August Family maimed and bleeding spelt potential calamity for the Roman people as well. The House of Caesar would soon need someone new at its head – but who? No one seasoned in the arts of war and peace, as Tiberius himself had been when he succeeded Augustus, was ready to hand. Indeed, male heirs of any description were decidedly thin on the ground. There was Claudius, the twitching, stammering brother of Germanicus – but a man with such literally crippling disabilities was never going to make a Princeps. Then there was Gemellus – but he was still very young, and Tiberius himself, painfully conscious of Livilla's affair with Sejanus, could hardly help but wonder whether his grandson truly was his grandson. That left Caligula, the people's favourite. His popularity – owing as it did everything to his parents, and absolutely nothing to any actual record of service – was a perilous attribute to have, of course. There were plenty in Tiberius's train who thought it inconceivable that the grim old man would ever permit a son of Agrippina to succeed him. Caligula, so Thrasyllus prophesied, was as likely to become emperor as he was to ride a horse across the sea. No one, though, was more alert to the perils of his situation than Caligula himself. He knew better than to give his great-uncle the slightest cause for resentment. His face remained a mask. 'Not a peep was heard from him at the condemnation of his mother, the destruction of his brothers.'[94]

Such a display was sufficient for Tiberius. As a man who in his old age had surrendered to the pleasures of hypocrisy, it amused him to wonder what emotions his great-nephew might be veiling behind his inhuman show of composure. Caligula, if truth be told, did not seem a man much given to grief at the suffering of others. Quite the contrary – he gave every impression of enjoying it. Slavishly obedient to the Princeps in everything, it was the darker dimensions of Tiberius's whims and pleasures for which he showed the greatest enthusiasm. The horrifying fate of Agrippina and his brothers did not inhibit him from taking an intimate personal interest in the punishment of criminals. He was also more than happy to keep pace with his great-uncle's relish for mythological re-enactments. Ever since his childhood, when the soldiers of the Rhine had strapped him into the miniature pair of boots that gave him his nickname, Caligula had displayed a taste for dressing up. Capri, that wonderland of stage sets, enabled him to give it free rein. Wigs and costumes of every kind were his to try on, and opportunities to participate in pornographic floor-shows freely granted. Tiberius was happy to indulge his great-nephew. He knew what he was leaving the Roman people in the form of their favourite – and he had ceased to care. 'I am rearing them a viper.'[95]

Many, of course, in Rome, would have retorted that it took one to know one. Memories of the man the Princeps had once been were long since faded. As tales of the great war hero who had twice hauled the Republic back from ruin gathered dust, fresher stories told of Tiberius now had currency among his fellow citizens. No rumour of his perversities was so hideous that it could not be believed in Rome. That he had trained little boys to slip between his thighs as he went swimming and tease him with their licking; that he had put unweaned babies to the head of his penis, as though to a mother's breast; even, most repellently of all, that he enjoyed cunnilingus. Yet beyond the streets and taverns of Rome, where slanders of the mighty, and mockery of their pretensions, had always bred, there were others who saw Tiberius in a very different light. In the provinces, where the twenty-three years of stability that he had provided the world might win him praise even among the notoriously snippy intellectuals of Alexandria, he had ended up widely admired as a prince of peace. 'For wisdom and erudition,' one declared flatly, 'there is nobody of his generation to compare.'[96] Bloodstained pervert and philosopher-king: it took a man of rare paradox to end up being seen as both.

By March 37, though, it was clear that Tiberius's long and remarkable career was nearing its end. After one last abortive attempt to enter Rome, he had returned to Campania, where storms and a stabbing pain in his side prevented him from crossing back to Capri. Despite a customarily stern-willed attempt to pretend that nothing was wrong, he was eventually forced to retire to bed. Shortly afterwards a terrible earthquake shook the Bay of Naples. On Capri, which for so many years had provided Tiberius with his home and his refuge, a towering lighthouse built on the island's highest cliff was toppled into the sea, and its fires extinguished.[97] The old man, skilled in the art of reading the purposes of the gods, had no need of Thrasyllus to tell him what the sign portended. Sure enough, from his bed, he made dispositions for the transfer of power. In his will, both Caligula and Gemellus were named as his heirs, but the Princeps had no illusions as to what his grandson's fate promised to be. 'You will kill him – and then someone else will kill you.'[98] So Tiberius had once told Caligula. Unsurprisingly, then, as he felt death come upon him, he found it hard to let go of his signet ring. Even after removing it he could not bring himself to hand it over, but instead held it tight in his palm, and for a long while lay motionless. In time, many stories would be told of what happened next: that Caligula had assumed his great-uncle dead; that just as he was being hailed as the new emperor, news had been brought that the old man was still alive; that Macro, a seasoned operator who had long since attached himself to the rising, not the setting, sun, had ordered Tiberius suffocated beneath a pillow. The truth was less melodramatic. The Princeps, stirring at last, had called for his attendants. None had come. Tottering to his feet, he had called out again – then collapsed.

'Reckon yourself happy only when you can live in public.'[99] Such was the Roman conviction.

Tiberius Julius Caesar Augustus had died alone.

5

LET THEM HATE ME

Show Time

In Rome, news that the old man had died at last was greeted with predictable gallows humour. 'To the Tiber!' went up the cry.[1] Caligula, conscious that the dignity of the role bequeathed him by Tiberius would hardly be enhanced by handing over his predecessor's corpse to be dragged through the streets on a meat hook, refused. Arriving from Campania in the city he had last seen six years before, he was dressed soberly in mourning. The funeral he gave Tiberius was dignified and ornate. The speech over the body was delivered by Caligula himself. The ashes were laid to rest in the great Mausoleum of Augustus.

So far, though, and no further. Escorting the funeral cortège, the new Princeps had been mobbed the length of the Appian Way by joyous crowds, cheering him and hailing him as their chick, their little one, their darling. Caligula, who for so long as his great-uncle was alive had betrayed not a flicker of grief for his murdered mother and brothers, now played with relish to the gallery. The speech he gave over Tiberius's corpse was largely a paean to Germanicus. Then, a few days later, he set out for the prison islands on which Agrippina and Nero had perished. Ostentatiously braving stormy weather, so as to make his filial piety all the more evident,[2] he returned up the Tiber with their ashes, placed them in litters normally used for carrying the statues of gods, and had them interred amid much sombre and flamboyant pomp in the Mausoleum of Augustus. The Roman people, ecstatic that their favourite had at last come into his own, gave themselves over to wild celebration. For three months the smell of roasting meat hung pungent over the city, as hundreds of thousands of cattle were immolated in a grand gesture of gratitude to the gods. After the long winter of Tiberius's old age, spring, it seemed, had come at last.

Not that Caligula was naïve enough to take this mood of optimism for granted. Although he had long been isolated from the capital, his time on Capri had not been wasted. His presence at Tiberius's side had given him an instinctive and pitiless understanding of the workings of power. Unlike his grimly austere predecessor, who had scorned to lavish bribes on the people, Caligula was more than happy to buy popularity. The treasury was full – and the new Princeps took full advantage. Donatives were splashed out on the citizens of the capital, on the legions and – most generously of all – on the Praetorians. Nor was the Senate neglected. Caligula showed himself alert to its sensitivities. The serving consuls were permitted to serve out their term of office; and when the Princeps did finally lay claim to the consulship, three months into his reign, his choice of colleague signalled a pointed rejection of his predecessor. Claudius, Caligula's uncle, had hitherto been denied even the most junior magistracy; but now, at the age of forty-six, he was elevated simultaneously into the Senate and to the consulship. More was to follow. Giving his first address as consul, Caligula explicitly repudiated all the most detested features of Tiberius's reign: the informers, the treason trials, the executions. To the listening Senate, it sounded almost too good to be true.

Which perhaps it was. When senators, in the wake of Caligula's speech, rushed through a decree that it be read out every year, the measure reflected less their joy at a new beginning than dread that he might change his mind. There was no one in the Senate, after the traumas and tribulations of the previous reign, who could believe any longer in the silken hypocrisies that had once served to veil what

Rome had become. The true balance of power had been too nakedly exposed for that. The Senate itself, like a battered wife frantic to forestall a beating, had made sure, in the first days of Caligula's reign, to deny him nothing. An attempt by Tiberius in his will to secure a share of his inheritance for Gemellus had been speedily annulled; 'the absolute right to decide on everything'[3] bestowed with a solemn and awful formality upon Caligula. Few senators had been put at ease by their new master's smooth assurances. The man who as a toddler had posed as a soldier was now acting out a new role, that of Augustus. No matter how convincing his performance, everyone suspected that it was just that: a performance.

There was only one shred of reassurance. The new emperor was not, as Tiberius had been when he succeeded Augustus, a man battle-hardened in the service of Rome – and Caligula seemed to appreciate as much. Ever at his ear was the man who had done more than anyone to facilitate his accession, the Praetorian prefect Macro. This in itself, to senators who had learned to dread overreaching equestrians, was hardly a recommendation – except that Macro was no Sejanus. High-minded and bluntly spoken, he did not hesitate to lecture his young protégé on what was expected of a Princeps: 'for, like any good craftsman, he was keen that his own handiwork, as he saw it, not be damaged or destroyed'.[4] Granted, senators could hardly help but feel a little twitchy at the very public drills that Caligula insisted on having the Praetorians perform for their benefit; but Macro was not the only advisor by the emperor's side. There was also one of the Senate's own.

Four years before becoming emperor, Caligula had been married to the daughter of a man particularly prized by Tiberius, a one-time consular colleague of Drusus's by the name of Junius Silanus; and Silanus, even though his daughter had since died in childbirth, retained signal status as the emperor's father-in-law. Like Macro, he presumed a right to serve as Caligula's guide in the various arts of governance; unlike Macro, he did so as a representative of the antique virtues of the nobility. 'Well bred and eloquent, his rank was a commanding one.'[5] It was no shame for anyone, even a Princeps, to be swayed by such a man. Certainly, Caligula showed himself a quick learner. The prosperity and order that Rome's dominions had enjoyed under Tiberius continued unbroken. The frontiers held firm; the appointments to provincial commands were shrewdly chosen; peace was universal across the Roman world. In the capital itself, workmen who had long cursed Tiberius's refusal to invest in infrastructure projects were delighted when Caligula commissioned two new aqueducts and a thorough-going upgrade of the Palatine. Books that had been banned under his predecessors, including the speeches of Titus Labienus and Cassius Severus, and the histories of Cremutius Cordus, were restored to public circulation. 'With such moderation did Caligula behave, in short, and such graciousness, that he became ever more popular, both with the Roman people themselves, and with their subjects.'[6]

Nevertheless, in the Senate, they still held their breath. Popularity and youth, to conservatives, could hardly help but seem a sinister combination. Not since the darkest days of the Triumvirate had Rome been so dependent upon the whims of so young a man. Senators observed with alarm that their new emperor, even as he posed before them as a new Augustus, played a very different part when before the plebs. Caligula, it was evident, positively revelled in the applause of the masses. When he insisted that they greet him, not with pompous or stuffy formality, but as though he were a citizen just like themselves, they delighted in his common touch; when he restored to them the right abolished by Tiberius to vote for magistrates, they hailed him as the people's friend. What they adored most of all, however, was the sheer blaze of his glamour. He might be prematurely balding, and possessed of large feet and his father's spindly legs, yet Caligula knew how to thrill a crowd. The Roman people were bored of grim old men. Now at last they had an emperor who seemed to glory in living the dream. That summer, opening a new temple to Augustus, Caligula rode to the inauguration in a gilded triumphal chariot. Six horses pulled him. 'This,' so it was noted, 'was something wholly cutting edge.'[7]

Cheers and chariots went naturally together. In a triumph, the pace was stately, the rider arrayed in purple and gold; but there were other spectacles more dangerous, more thrilling, more visceral. Between the Palatine, home of Caesar, and the Aventine, that great smog-wreathed warren of slums, stretched a long, straight valley; and here, ever since the days of Romulus, perilously rickety chariots had been racing one another up and down its course. The Circus Maximus it was called – and fittingly so. No other city in the world could boast a vaster stadium. Even Augustus had found himself intimidated by the sheer heaving mass of spectators who would cram themselves into its stands on race days. Although, back in the year of Actium, he had commissioned a box in the Circus, the 'Pulvinar', for his own private use, and justified it, with a familiar sleight of hand, by sharing it with symbols of the gods, he had rarely used it. He had found himself altogether too conspicuous, too exposed, when sitting there. Instead, rather than endure hundreds of thousands of eyes fixed upon him, he had preferred to watch the races from the upper storeys of friends' houses. Augustus, incomparable as he had always been in his ability to distinguish between the reality and show of power, had known what he confronted in the Circus – and had respected it. To feel the blast of its noise hot against the face was to feel the breath of the wolf.

Which was why, when sitting in the Pulvinar, Augustus had always made sure to behave like a fan. It was important that the First Citizen be seen to share in the pleasures of the Roman people. Even so, there were limits. Augustus had not bestowed the gifts of peace and order upon the world only to tolerate a free-for-all at sports events. The long-standing presumption of most spectators that they should be allowed to sit wherever they pleased had struck the Princeps as deeply offensive. Entertainment was all very well – but not at the expense of proprieties. As in the bedroom, so on the bleachers – Augustus had sought to regulate his fellow citizens' appetites by means of legislation. With great punctiliousness, the banks of seating in public venues had been divided up between various categories of Roman. Senators,

The Julians and Claudians under Caligula

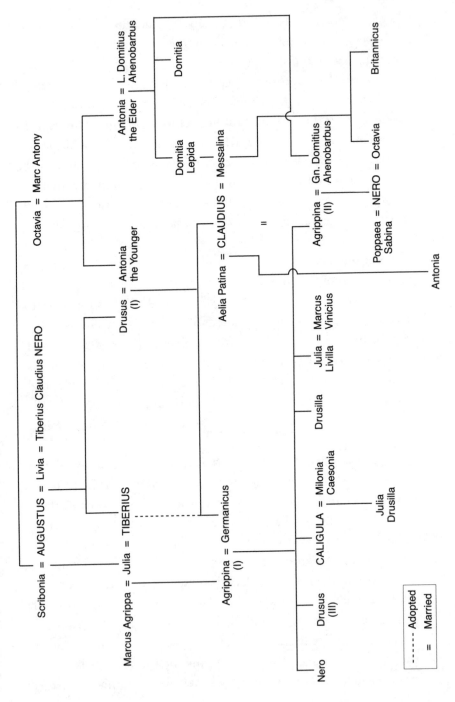

naturally, had been awarded the best vantage points; women the worst. Wear a blinding white toga, and a man could expect to sit near the front; wear a dark and grimy tunic, and he would have to take his luck at the back. Soldiers, foreign ambassadors, boys and their tutors: all had been allocated their respective blocs. The larger the venue, of course, the harder these rules were to police; and the Circus Maximus itself, as the largest venue of all, was correspondingly the most challenging to regulate.[8] Nevertheless, the principle established by Augustus was one that everyone who benefited from it could recognise as eminently sound. Rich or poor, male or female – all had to know their place. Entertainments were serious matters. They provided mirrors in which the entire Roman people, from First Citizen to the basest ex-slave, could see themselves reflected. Macro, speaking in his young master's ear, sought to spell out the implications. 'What matters when you watch the races in the Circus is not the sport itself, but rather to behave appropriately in the context of the sport.'[9]

There was, though, another perspective. Despite the many years that he had spent away from Rome, Caligula had not been wholly cut off from the capital's youth culture. The offspring of the nobility summoned by Tiberius to Capri, there to pose and perform as prostitutes, had brought with them to the island a distinct touch of metropolitan chic. One of these, a performer so adept at sex games that he was said to have ensured his father's promotion first to the consulship, and then to the governorship of Syria, had become a particular intimate of Caligula's. Aulus Vitellius was racy in every sense of the word. Not merely a fan, he was himself an accomplished charioteer. Naturally enough, he had made sure to share with Caligula his passion for the sport. The contrast with Tiberius, who had despised anything enjoyed by the mob, and scorned to squander money on keeping them entertained, could hardly have been greater. Now that he was out of the old man's shadow at last, Caligula had every intention of blazing an opposite course. Although, on becoming emperor, he had declared himself shocked by the antics on Capri, and ready to drown anyone who had participated in them, the joke was firmly on those who believed this show of outrage. Vitellius, whose youthful brush with prostitution would never be forgotten by his enemies, remained the Emperor's bosom companion. Even as Macro was sternly advising Caligula to maintain his distance from the pleasures of the Circus, his friend was busy stoking his obsession.

The Roman people, long starved of public extravaganzas, found their new emperor a most munificent sponsor. Races were held from dawn to dusk; glamorous entertainments, featuring wild beasts and cavalry manoeuvres, laid on in the intervals; the tracks made to sparkle with vivid reds and greens. Caligula himself, far from maintaining an aloof and neutral presence, rooted shamelessly for his favourite team. Its champion charioteer was lavished with gifts, and its champion horse, Incitatus or 'Hot Spur', supplied with a stable of ivory and marble built by Praetorians. Simultaneously, in a crowning gesture of fandom, Caligula commissioned his own private race-course, on the far side of the Tiber from central Rome, complete with an obelisk brought specially on a massive transport ship from Egypt. Restrained in his enthusiasm he was not.

But that, for Caligula himself, was precisely the point. Back in the days of Augustus, the relish of Rome's trendsetters for offending the stuffy and the uptight had ended up so dangerous as to risk criminal charges. Now, with Caligula installed on the Palatine, one of their own enjoyed the whip-hand. The proprieties that his great-grandfather had been so anxious to uphold were, to the youthful Princeps, things to be mocked, subverted, undermined. His apprenticeship on Capri, where he had watched the sons and daughters of senators hawk themselves like streetwalkers, had opened his eyes to the extremes of novelty and spectacle the power of an emperor might command. Far from veiling his own supremacy, he delighted in flaunting it. There was to be no watching chariot races from neighbouring buildings for Caligula. Instead, resplendently visible in the Pulvinar, the toast of a grateful and cheering people, a patron such as the Circus had never before enjoyed, he delighted in what it meant to rule as the master of Rome.

He presided over magnificence; but he presided as well over peril.

Races were potentially lethal events. Even a charioteer as skilled as Vitellius walked with a permanent limp, the result of an accident. He had been lucky. Crashes were often fatal. Many a citizen, in the dark days of the civil wars, had dreaded that Rome herself was doomed to end up a mess of splinters, shattered axles and tangled reins. Now, whenever a chariot careered out of control and left a twisted body crumpled on the side of the track, it served the Roman people as a very different reminder: of Caesar, who had graced them with spectaculars beyond their forefathers' wildest imaginings, and was the master of death as he was of life. And they loved him for it.

In the Circus, to manoeuvre for victory was invariably to risk life and limb. In the world beyond the race track it could sometimes be the same. That October, eight months after coming to power, Caligula fell dangerously ill. Alarmed by the potential threat to their own positions, Macro and Silanus immediately scouted around for a new protégé. There was only one possible candidate. Even as Caligula lay at death's door, his two most prominent henchmen began clearing the way for Tiberius's grandson, the eighteen-year-old Gemellus, to take over the reins. But they had moved too fast. In the Circus, the charioteer who clipped the hub of a rival's wheel while attempting to overtake would invariably end up broken and mangled in the dust. Macro and Silanus had committed a similarly fatal error. Caligula did not die. Instead, he made a full recovery. Rising from his sickbed, he moved with lethal dispatch and cunning.

First to perish was the hapless Gemellus. Charged with treason, he was paid a visit by two senior officers, who considerately instructed him in the best way to commit suicide, and then stood by as he demonstrated the efficacy of their lesson. Macro, as the man with the Praetorians at his command, presented Caligula with a potentially greater challenge – but one to which he showed himself no less equal. Like a sacrificial bull being adorned with garlands, the Prefect was first graced with the supreme honour of the governorship of Egypt, and then, before he could leave for his province, ordered to kill himself. The charge, a highly plausible one, was that he had referred to

Caligula as 'his work': self-evidently, a mortal insult to the Princeps's dignity. Macro's suicide left only Silanus standing; but he too, once it had been intimated to the Senate that he no longer retained his son-in-law's favour, took the hint, slitting his own throat with a razor. Caligula could be mightily pleased with the skill that he had brought to clearing the stage.

To Rome's elite, of course, the ease with which their young emperor had liquidated his two most formidable allies came as an altogether less pleasant revelation. If power-brokers of the stature of Macro and Silanus could be forced to kill themselves, then nobody was safe. 'Remember,' Caligula was said to have told his grandmother, 'I am allowed to do anything to anybody.'[10] Unlike Tiberius, he did not feel the slightest embarrassment at the awesome scope of his power – and the discovery of how readily he had been able to dispose of his unwanted mentors only encouraged him to test its limits further still. No paying lip-service to the ideals of the vanished Republic for Caligula. They bored him – and he had no patience with being bored. Nevertheless, in trampling them down, he was not going wholly against the grain of the past. The colour and clamour of the Circus, to which he had become so addicted, were traditions as venerable as any in Rome. The Senate House, to a man of Caligula's instinctive showmanship, could hardly help but seem dreary in comparison. Resolved as he was not merely to preside supreme over the cockpit of power, but to make a display of it, he looked elsewhere for his inspiration: to the Roman genius for putting on a show.

The pleasure that Caligula took in watching other people suffer was nothing new. For centuries, the Roman people had been assembling en masse to enjoy the spectacle of men contending in desperate struggle, and to exercise over them the powers of life and death. Traditionally, these shows had been mounted in the heart of Rome, in the Forum itself. There, across from the Senate House, the great men of the Republic had regularly commissioned the building of temporary wooden amphitheatres, staging in them, for the benefit of potential voters, contests between trained killers named 'gladiators'.

Fighters bound, if volunteers, by a fearsome oath to endure 'brand-ings, fetters, whippings, and death by sword',[11] these men ranked as the lowest among the low – and yet, for all that, the attitude of spectators was not merely one of contempt. The Roman people admired courage and martial proficiency. Julius Caesar, when he was still a man on the make, had sought to win the love of his fellow citizens by equipping gladiators, for the first time, with silver armour; but later, after his crossing of the Rubicon, he had trained his legions to fight as though they themselves were in the arena. Senators proscribed by the Triumvirate had been known to do as a defeated gladiator would, and bare their throats to the swords of their assassins. Former consuls had not been ashamed to look to the example of such slaves and find in them a model of their own ancestral *virtus*. Amid the horrors of civil war, the whole of Rome had become an amphitheatre.

Much, of course, had changed since then. Augustus had brought the blessings of peace to Rome. The days when ambitious noblemen could hope to win supremacy for themselves by staging dazzling shows in the Forum were long gone. There was effectively only one patron left: Caesar. A Princeps, it went without saying, could spend as lavishly he pleased. The result, over the course of Augustus's primacy, had been ever more spectacular games. Ten thousand gladiators had fought in eight alone. Rule by a Princeps, though, was not necessarily good news for the fans. Tiberius, whose contempt for public entertainments had been total, had naturally scorned to squander money on gladiators. Following the death of Drusus, who had loved watching them with a passion extreme even by Roman standards, and had been nicknamed after a particularly famous one as a result, the staging of blood sports had ground to a halt. Star gladiators themselves had mourned the lack of opportunity to demonstrate their skills. 'What a golden age we have lost!'[12] Indeed, so desperate had the Roman people become to feed their addiction that in AD 27, when an entrepreneur staged a gladiator show in the nearby town of Fidenae, 'huge crowds of men and women, of every age'[13] had flocked from the capital to watch it. The result had been the worst disaster in the history of Roman sport: the amphitheatre, unable to cope with the sheer volume of spectators, had collapsed under their weight, crushing thousands to death. The horror of this calamity would long be remembered – for it had struck a particular nerve. The crowds who went to watch other men die did not care to be reminded of their own mortality. 'Kill him! Lash him! Burn him!'[14] The excitement that spectators took in watching trained warriors fight for their lives was all the greater for knowing themselves to be the masters. Caligula, as passionate a fan of gladiatorial combat as Tiberius had been dismissive of it, understood this with icy clarity. More than that – it amused him to make play with the knowledge.

Only menace a man with violent death, and his struggle to evade it could provide rich entertainment – no matter the victim's rank. Who better to put this proposition to the test than Caligula, whose sense of humour was as malicious as his powers were absolute? His chosen victim, an equestrian by the name of Atanius Secundus, was guilty of little more than excessive flattery. Back when the Princeps was on his sickbed, Atanius had sworn an extravagant oath. Only restore Caligula to health, he had promised the gods, and he would fight as a gladiator. Naturally, he had not expected to be taken up on this vow. His aim had been merely to stand out from the other sycophants. Once back up on his feet, though, the Emperor took Atanius at his word. With a perfectly straight face, Caligula ordered the wretched equestrian into the arena, to fight there for the amusement of the crowds. Predictably enough, paired against a trained killer, Atanius did not last long. The spectacle of his body being dragged away across the sands of the arena on a hook provided Caligula's joke with more than just a cruelly emphatic punchline. It also delivered a threat. No equestrian could sit in an amphitheatre, in one of the seats reserved for him by law, and watch in equanimity as one of his own was made an object of public diversion. Senators too were bound to feel unsettled. The menace was implicit. No one so high-ranking, it seemed, but Caligula reserved for himself the right to make sport with his death.

It was, for the Roman nobility, all most disconcerting. The notion that a Princeps might regard them with derision was as novel as it was shocking. No matter how painful their subordination to the new order established by Augustus, neither Augustus himself nor Tiberius had ever sought deliberately to rub their noses in the dirt. Just the opposite. Both men had been firm believers in the values upheld by Rome's traditional elite. Caligula, though, was revealing himself to be a very different order of Princeps. Raised on the private island of an autocrat, seduced by the cheers of the Circus, backed by the swords of Praetorians, he felt not the slightest empathy with the presumptions of his own class. A year and more after his accession to the rule of the world, he still paid a certain mocking obeisance to his partnership with the aristocracy; but it was evident that he was starting to weary of smoothing their ruffled feathers. As a signal of this, he took a title in September 38 that earlier, out of respect for the grey hairs and craggy self-regard of the Senate, he had pointedly refused: 'Father of his Country'. The chance to humiliate his elders had simply become too good to miss.

Indeed, in so far as Caligula felt loyalty to anything, it was to his family – and to his sisters in particular. Julia Livilla, the baby girl born on Lesbos during Germanicus's fateful journey to the East, was now a young woman in her early twenties; her two elder sisters, Agrippina and Drusilla, were both already married. All three, while Tiberius was alive, had shared with their brother the perils of being their mother's children; all three, when Caligula finally came into his inheritance, had been graced with spectacular honours. Privileges were lavished on them that it had taken Livia a lifetime to acquire. Even consuls, when they took a vow of allegiance to Caligula, were obliged to include his three sisters in the oath. The most startling novelty of all, though, was their appearance on a coin minted during their brother's first year in power, and which portrayed them in the guise of winsome deities. Never before in Roman history had living individuals been represented on a coin as gods. Well might traditionalists have flared their nostrils.

Truth be told, the fondness of Claudians for their siblings had long been a cause of suspicion. Back in the dying days of the Republic, Clodius's intimacy with his three sisters had provoked dark and delighted accusations of incest. Now, almost a century on, the same rumours inevitably began to swirl around the children of Germanicus.* Given the prurient taste of the Roman people for scandal, they could hardly have done otherwise. What, though, was idle gossip to perturb the master of the world and his sisters? Agrippina, in particular, was hardly the kind of woman to care what her inferiors thought. In ambition and self-assurance no less than her name, she was every inch her mother's daughter. Married off by Tiberius to the thuggish but impeccably aristocratic Domitius Ahenobarbus, she was the only one among her siblings to have had a child – and a son, what was more. Unsurprisingly, her hopes for the boy were of the highest order. Like her mother, though, she had a tendency to push too hard. Eager to alert the world to the fact that Caligula had no children of his own, she asked him to name her son, confident that the choice would signal a glorious future for the boy – only to have her brother smirk, glance across at their twitching, dribbling uncle, and suggest 'Claudius'.

In the event, Agrippina had to be content with calling her son Lucius Domitius Ahenobarbus, after his father. She knew better than to force the issue. Fond though Caligula was of his eldest sister, he was unwilling to offer either her or Julia Livilla marks of favour at the expense of his favourite, Drusilla. No one was dearer to him. Even

---

* The earliest datable allusion to Caligula committing incest with his sisters is in *The Antiquities of the Jews*, written by Josephus more than half a century after his death (19.204). Josephus, though, was well informed about Caligula's reign, and drew on sources written much closer in time to it. As ever in a city as addicted to scurrilous gossip as Rome, the existence of a rumour did not mean that it was actually true. No contemporaries of Caligula mention it; and it was only with Suetonius that the rumours really took wing. 'Have you committed incest with your sister?' he described Caligula as asking his friend, the noted wit Passienus Crispus. 'Not yet,' Passienus is said to have replied, quick as a flash (quoted by the Scholiast on Juvenal: 4.81).

though she had already been married off by Tiberius before he came to power, this had not prevented her brother, once emperor himself, from supplying her with a new and altogether more glamorous husband in the form of his principal favourite, Marcus Aemilius Lepidus. The great-grandnephew of the most ineffectual of the Triumvirs, Lepidus was said to have had a youthful and passionate fling with Caligula – and whatever the truth of such scurrilous gossip, it was certainly the case that the two men were very close. The Emperor had not only fast-tracked his friend through assorted magistracies, but had then explicitly named him as 'successor to the throne'.[15] It was the wife, though, not the husband, whom Caligula truly adored. During his illness, he had made this clear in the most startling manner. Rather than explicitly name Lepidus as his successor, he had instead appointed Drusilla herself as 'heir to his worldly goods and power'.[16] Not even Livia at her most ambitious could have dreamed of such an honour.

Unsurprisingly, the devastation that Caligula felt in the summer of 38, when his beloved sister died, was so flamboyant as to prompt unprecedented displays of mourning. Too distraught to attend her funeral, he retreated to an estate outside Rome, where he sought to distract himself from his misery by playing board games and alternately growing and hacking at his hair; and then, when these measures proved inadequate, by drifting around Sicily and Campania. Meanwhile, back in Rome, a resourceful senator declared that he had seen Drusilla ascending to heaven – and Caligula, rather than mock the man for his sycophancy, as he might normally have done, gave him a massive reward. Drusilla was officially declared divine, the third member of the family, after Julius Caesar and Augustus, to become a god. Life-sized golden statues of her were placed in both the Senate House and the temple of Venus Genetrix; anything that smacked of fun was officially cancelled; a man who sold hot water for adding to wine was promptly put to death on a charge of *maiestas*. The Roman people, 'unsure whether Caligula wished them to mourn his sister or worship her',[17] cowered in the shadow of his terrifying grief.

By the early autumn, when Drusilla's elevation to the heavens was officially confirmed, the Emperor had recovered sufficiently to look to the future. Reminded by his sister's death of his own mortality, he briskly procured himself a new wife. That Lollia Paulina had already been married to Memmius Regulus, the consul who had presided over Sejanus's downfall, naturally bothered Caligula not a jot. Lollia was both beautiful and fabulously rich, with a taste for wearing pearls and emeralds wherever and whenever she could sport them. Although she was the granddaughter of the Lollius who had lost an eagle to the Germans and then committed suicide on the eastern front, no stain had been left on her eligibility by this disgrace. Any son she bore would be worthy to rank as a Caesar.

Naturally, Caligula's patent determination to father an heir did nothing for the prospects of either Agrippina or Lepidus, but the Princeps was in no mood to care about that. The more he adjusted to the seeming limitlessness of his own supremacy, the less inclined he was to tolerate anything that might obstruct it. Graced as he had been with an excellent education, and with years of literary chat at Tiberius's table, he had no problem in quoting from the classics to justify himself: "'Let there be one lord, one king.'"[18] In token of this, in the New Year, the Emperor entered his second consulship. Although he only held it for a month, his brief term of office served its purpose: to remind the Senate that he could take up and discard Rome's supreme magistracy as and when he pleased. Simultaneously, in the background, an ominous and familiar drumbeat was striking up again. Men who under Tiberius had languished in prison, and been released by Caligula in the joyous first flush of his coming to power, began to find themselves under arrest once more. The charge of *maiestas*, abolished with great fanfare in the first weeks of his supremacy, was quietly resurrected. Terror was blended with flashes of Caligula's customary malevolent humour. When a junior magistrate by the name of Junius Priscus was discovered, after he had been put to death, to be much poorer than he had always maintained, the Emperor laughed, and declared that he had died beyond his means. 'He fooled me. He might just as well have lived.'[19]

The joke, as so often with Caligula, derived from the scorching quality of his gaze: from his willingness to strip away the veil of dissimulation, to expose the sordid baseness of human instincts, to question whether anyone ever did anything save for motives of self-interest. The Roman people had long made much of their supposed virtues; but Caligula, so unsparing in the analysis of his own motivation, was no longer interested in pandering to their self-conceit. For two years, he had indulged senators in the pretence that they were partners with him in the rule of the world. Now he was bored of it. The record of their cant stank to the heavens. Almost seventy years before, on that fateful day when Augustus had been voted his new name, he and the Senate between them had woven a fabric of illusion so subtle that few since had been prepared so much as to acknowledge its existence. Now Caligula was ready to rip it down and trample it under foot.

His trap had long been set. In the first weeks of his supremacy, he had informed the Senate in a tone of gracious magnanimity that all the paperwork relating to the *maiestas* trials under Tiberius, all the transcripts of those who had brought accusations against their fellows, all the details of the various senators who had stabbed one another in the back, were burned. But he had lied. He had kept the records – and now he ordered them read out to the Senate. His listeners' mortification was almost beyond enduring. But there was worse to come. Painstakingly, with relish, Caligula detailed every opportunistic shimmy of which the Senate had been guilty. Its members had licked the feet of Sejanus and then spat on him when he was down; they had cringed and grovelled before Tiberius and then traduced him the moment he was dead. Tiberius, though, had seen through them to their malign and contemptible core – and had advised on how to handle them. 'Make your priorities your own pleasure and security. For they all detest you – they all long to see you dead. And if they can, they will murder you.'[20]

273

The naked brutality of the regime that had planted itself, over the course of the previous century, within the heart of Rome, and what had once been a free republic, now lay visible to all. Whatever else might be said about Caligula, he was at least being honest. It was an honesty, though, as pitiless as the African sun. Where were senators to hide now? Nothing of the hypocrisies with which they had been cloaking and adorning themselves was left to them. Their mingled servility and malignity had been brutally exposed to the world. It was not only the Senate, though, that Caligula was attacking. The lies told by his predecessors, the deified Augustus and Tiberius, also stood revealed. The pretence to which both men had clung, that Rome remained a republic, had become unsustainable. The power of the emperor was total — and Caligula no longer saw any point in disguising it. As token of this, he declared the charge of *maiestas* officially restored, and commanded that his words be inscribed upon a tablet of brass. Then, without waiting to hear what the Senate had to say, he turned on his heels and walked briskly out.

As it was, the Senate had nothing to say. So stunned and appalled were its members that they sat frozen in silence. It took them a whole day before they were finally able to present their response. By an official vote of the Senate, it was decreed that Caligula be thanked for his sincerity, praised for his piety and granted annual sacrifices in recognition of his clemency. It was agreed as well that he should be granted an 'ovation', a lesser form of triumph that entitled a general to ride in procession through Rome on horseback. He should celebrate it, the Senate declared, 'as though he had been victorious over his enemies'.[21]

Which in a sense he had been. Telling senators to their faces that they hated him and wished him dead, Caligula had taunted them that they would continue to honour him 'whether they wished to or not'.[22] Behind their pinched and frozen faces, though, there was anger as well as fear. Nor were these emotions confined to the Senate House. Even in Caligula's own innermost circle, even among those few people he genuinely loved, there was a growing anxiety about the future. Senators were not the only people whose self-esteem the

Emperor was happy to trample down. Certainly, he had no intention of letting his sister's ambitions stand in the way of his own. Less than a year after his marriage to Lollia Paulina, Caligula divorced her, on the grounds that she was unable to give him a child. Determined not to make the same mistake twice, he then promptly married his mistress, who had not only had three children already, but was heavily pregnant by him. Milonia Caesonia was neither young nor beautiful – but whatever it was that Caligula wanted in a woman, she had it. Like her husband, she enjoyed dressing up, and would often ride by his side in military procession, decked out in a cloak and helmet; while should Caligula, ever one for a titillating tableau, demand that she pose nude for his friends, she would readily oblige. Such was evidently the way to his heart – for he was to prove as constant in his devotion to her as he had been in his affection for Drusilla. Unsurprisingly, then, the birth to Caligula of a daughter, named Julia Drusilla by the delighted father, was greeted by both Lepidus and Agrippina with sullen and brooding resentment. Both, in their different ways, had felt themselves tantalisingly close to securing the succession; both, confronted by Caesonia's evident fertility, knew that their prospects had suffered a potentially fatal blow.

Late that summer of 39, on the last day of August, Caligula celebrated his birthday. He was twenty-seven. He had been emperor for two and a half years. He could be well pleased with all that he had achieved for himself in that time. A cowed Senate, a grateful people, a city endowed with plentiful shows and extravaganzas: Rome was well on its way to being moulded to his wishes. For now, though, it was time to look further afield. Brought up as he had been among the legions of the Rhine, Caligula knew perfectly well that Rome was not the world. The job that his father had begun remained to be completed: the barbarians of Germany, who had defied both Augustus and Tiberius so effectively, were Caligula's to conquer. All very well to stage fights in the city's arenas; but there were real battles, fought by real soldiers against real adversaries, to be staged as well.

Gaius Julius Caesar Augustus Germanicus was going to war.

275

A Joke Too Far

Even in a city as habituated to gossip as Rome, there was a special quality to rumours from a distant front. The news of a campaign would spread first as a murmuring; then, as the hum increased to a roar, people would start shouting and perhaps, if there were victories to celebrate, breaking into applause. Caligula's departure for the Rhine promised everyone in the capital rare excitement. Not since the days of Germanicus had there been such a marshalling of military capabilities – and Caligula, unlike his father, would be riding to war as emperor. Hopes were high. The Germans, their great victory over Varus by now a distant memory, had returned to their customary state of feuding. The Cherusci, Arminius's tribe, were particularly diminished. Arminius himself, whose fame had come to serve as a standing provocation to rival chieftains, was long since gone from the scene – murdered in the year that Germanicus, his great opponent, had also died. The Roman people, long starved of the thrills that tales of conquest had traditionally provided them, could look forward with relish to learning the details of Caesar's doings.

Nor were they to be disappointed. Even though, in the event, the stories reported of Caligula that autumn would touch only rarely on martial exploits, they were to prove no less sensational for that. Peril there certainly was – but the chief threat to the Emperor's life was not to be found beyond the Rhine. Instead, if the astonishing rumours that began to sweep Rome were true, it lay altogether closer to home. Even before Caligula's departure from the capital, hints of a crisis that reached right to the top were setting tongues to wag. In early September, both consuls had been summarily dismissed from office, their *fasces* snapped into pieces, and one of them forced into suicide.[23] Then, accompanied by Lepidus, his two sisters and a retinue of Praetorians, the Emperor had set off for the German front at break-neck pace. So fast had he travelled, it seemed, that his arrival on the banks of the Rhine had taken the legate there by complete surprise. Gnaeus Cornelius Lentulus Gaetulicus was a seasoned operator, a former intimate of Sejanus who had survived his patron's downfall by dropping discreetly menacing reminders of just how many legions he had under his command. Tiberius, too jaundiced greatly to care, had been content to let him be; but at damaging long-term cost. Much as Piso had done in Syria, Gaetulicus had cemented his authority over his men by cutting them plenty of slack – with the result that the frontier, rotted by a decade of his lax discipline, was no longer fit for purpose. Flabby and decrepit centurions lazed around in their tents, even as barbarians, slipping across the border in growing numbers, capitalised with glee on the renewed opportunities for raiding.

Caligula, whose earliest memories were of his father's frenetic efforts to repair the Rhine defences, was not impressed. Caught short by the Emperor's sudden arrival, Gaetulicus was arrested, interrogated and put to death. His replacement, a noted martinet by the name of Galba, bore witness yet again to Caligula's eye for talent. It was not long before the new general on the Rhine had toughened up his men sufficiently to start scouring Gaul clean of all intruders. Caligula himself, meanwhile, was busy proving himself his father's son. First he systematically weeded out all incompetent and unfit officers; then he embarked on a number of sallies against the Germans. Though it was late in the campaigning season, he was hailed by the troops under his command no fewer than seven times as '*imperator*'.*
Meanwhile, in preparation for the following year's campaigning

---

* It is Dio, even as he claims that Caligula 'had won no battle and slain no enemy', who lets slip this detail (59.22.2). Two contradictory traditions are to be found intertwined in the reports of historians such as Suetonius and Dio: in one, Caligula's military record is a laughable thing of whim and folly; but in the other, he is portrayed as a stern and effective disciplinarian in the best tradition of his father and Tiberius. Even though the fog that envelops this period of his reign is unusually dense, there are enough scattered details to make it probable that Caligula did make a tour of the Rhine in the autumn of 39, did stamp his authority upon the legions stationed there, and did win a few scattered engagements. Equally, it has to be acknowledged that Caligula may not have advanced to the Rhine until shortly after the New Year.

season, two new legions were in the process of being recruited: the first to be raised since the annihilation of Varus's army thirty years before.[24] Retiring for the winter to Lugdunum, Caligula could feel that he had made his mark.

Except that barbarians, all along, had been the least of his worries. Back in Rome, where reports of the Emperor's seven victories over the Germans were, of course, assiduously promoted, the tides of gossip surged with very different news. The execution of Gaetulicus, coming as it did so soon after the removal of two consuls, had not gone unnoticed. All three men, it was whispered, had been embroiled in the same conspiracy. It was this that explained why Caligula, determined to foil it, had left for the German front at such a furious pace. By late autumn, the news was official. Gaetulicus had indeed been executed for his 'nefarious schemes':[25] a plot to raise the armies of the Rhine against Caligula and install a new emperor in his place.[26] But who? The answer, when it came, constituted the most unexpected, most shocking revelation of all. The first token of it arrived with a delegation sent by the Emperor to the great temple of Mars the Avenger, with orders to present to the god three daggers; the second in the person of his sister, Agrippina. Just as her mother had done when bringing back the ashes of Germanicus from Syria, she arrived in Rome clasping a funerary urn. And in the urn were the remains of Lepidus.

Far from veiling the scandal, Caligula had chosen to make a full spectacle of the sordid details. Lepidus, the friend he had blessed with every conceivable favour, was reported to have grievously betrayed him. He had bedded both Agrippina and Julia Livilla; had conspired with the two sisters to seize supreme power; had spun a web of conspiracy that reached from the Senate House to the Rhine. Whether it was Gaetulicus, in a doomed attempt to secure a pardon, who had betrayed Lepidus's role in the plot, or some other informer, no one could quite be sure; but there was no doubting the molten quality of Caligula's hurt. Lepidus himself, ordered to bare his throat to an officer's sword, had been swiftly dispatched; Agrippina, once she had obeyed her brother's orders and borne her dead lover's remains all the way back to Rome, was sent with her sister into exile. Like their mother and grandmother before them, the pair were transported to barren islands off the Italian coast, while their household possessions – jewels, furniture, slaves and all – were flogged off in Lugdunum to status-hungry Gauls.

Worse for Agrippina was to come. Shortly after the revelation of her treachery, her husband, the brutish Domitius Ahenobarbus, succumbed to dropsy, and her son, for whom she had played so dirty and hard, came into the care of his aunt, Domitia. 'No less beautiful or wealthy than Agrippina, and of a similar age',[27] the two women were natural rivals; and Domitia, keen to win her nephew's heart, made sure to spoil him rotten. Agrippina, who had always been as strict with the boy as she was ambitious for him, was appalled. Rotting on her prison island, though, there was little that she could do. She had already lost her freedom; now it seemed as though she might lose her son. Even so, as Caligula made sure to remind both Agrippina and Julia Livilla, they had even more to lose. 'I have swords in addition to islands.'[28]

Consuls, army commanders, even members of the Emperor's own family – all had joined in the conspiracy against him, and still their plotting had failed. Nevertheless, the shock to Caligula's self-assurance had been seismic, and his bitterness towards his sisters unsurprising. Though he had moved swiftly and ruthlessly to crush rebellion along the Rhine and to stabilise Rome's most militarily significant frontier, he had been left with little choice but to spend the winter reining in his plans for the conquest of Germany. The risk of further treachery was simply too great. The scale of Caligula's suspicions was laid bare when the Senate, frantic to cover its own back, sent a delegation of grandees led by Claudius to congratulate him on his foiling of Lepidus's conspiracy. The Emperor treated the embassy with open contempt. Most of the senators were refused entry to Gaul as potential spies; Claudius, when he arrived in Lugdunum at the head of the few granted access to the city, was pushed fully clothed into the river. Or so the story went. True or not, the rumour rammed home the point that Caligula wished to make. Those who had betrayed him could no longer expect to receive any marks of courtesy or respect. Both the Senate and his own family had been marked down as a nest of vipers. The state of war between emperor and aristocracy was now official.

All of which made it essential for Caligula to return to Italy as soon as possible. Nevertheless, this presented him with a challenge. It was clearly out of the question to depart the North without some feat to his name that he could promote in Rome as a ringing victory. So it was, with the first approach of spring, that he returned to the German front, where he inspected troops, noted with approval the improvements made by Galba to standards of discipline, and ventured another sally across the Rhine.[29] In the event, though, it was not Germany which was to provide Caligula with the coup he so desperately needed, but Britain.

There, despite the fact that no legions had crossed the Channel in almost a century, Roman influence had been steadily growing. With the island carved up between an assortment of fractious and ambitious chieftains, it was only to be expected that Rome should provide them with the readiest model of power. The most effective way for a British warlord to throw his weight around was to ape the look of Caesar. The king who entertained his guests with delicacies imported from the Mediterranean, or portrayed himself on silver coins sporting a laurel wreath, was branding himself a man on the make. Such displays of self-promotion did not come cheap or easy – and it was no coincidence that the most powerful of the island's chieftains had always made a point of staying on the right side of Rome. Cunobelin was the king of a people named the Catuvellauni, whose sway extended over much of eastern and central Britain; but that had not prevented him from setting up offerings on the Capitol, and from being assiduous in returning any Roman seafarers shipwrecked off his kingdom. Unsurprisingly, then, when one of Cunobelin's sons was exiled after launching an abortive land-grab on Kent, the presence of

Caesar on the opposite side of the Channel ensured that there was only one place for him to head.

Caligula, naturally, was delighted by this unexpected windfall. The arrival of a genuine British prince could hardly have been more timely. It was a simple matter, receiving the surrender of such a man, to represent it as the surrender of the whole of Britain. Couriers were promptly dispatched to Rome. They were ordered, on their arrival in the city, to ride as ostentatiously through the streets as possible, to proceed to the temple of Mars, and there to hand over the Emperor's laurel-wreathed letter to the consuls. The Roman people had their tidings of victory.

And sure enough, borne on the surging of rumour, the news of it was duly repeated through the city: the dangers braved by Caesar, the captives he had taken, the conquest he had made of the Ocean. These were the kinds of detail that his fellow citizens had always loved to hear. Yet even as they were being repeated across Rome, from the Forum to taverns and washing-hung courtyards, other accounts of Caesar's doings in the North were also circulating: cross-tides of gossip altogether less flattering to Caligula. It was claimed that he had scarpered back across the Rhine at the merest mention of barbarians; that the spoils of his supposed conquest of the Ocean were nothing but chests filled with shells; that the captives he was bringing back with him to Rome were not Germans at all, but Gauls with dyed hair. Caesonia, ever her husband's partner in bombast and theatricality, was even claimed to be sourcing 'auburn wigs'[30] for them to wear. How was anyone in Rome, far removed from the front, to judge between two such different slipstreams of propaganda? Caligula himself, returning at high speed from the Channel for Italy, had no doubt what was at stake – nor whom to blame for the blackening of his war record. 'Yes, I am heading back – but only because the equestrians and the people want me back,' he informed a delegation of senators who had travelled north to meet him. 'Do not think me a fellow citizen of yours, though. As Princeps, I no longer acknowledge the Senate.'[31]

Chilling words – and rendered the more so by Caligula's habit of slamming his palm down hard onto his sword hilt as he spoke them. The envoys' cringing was understandable; yet, if they imagined that the Emperor intended to limit himself merely to executing his opponents, they had underestimated the full shocking scope of his ambitions. The experience of the previous autumn, when it had seemed that the entire Roman nobility was ranged against him, had decided Caligula for good. His aim now was to hack away at everything that sustained the prestige and self-regard of the Senate, and to demolish the very foundations of its hoary *auctoritas*. This was why, rather than accept its tremulous offer of a triumph, he had contemptuously swatted it aside; and it was why, dismissing the envoys from his presence, he forbade any senator from so much as coming out to greet him on his approach to Rome. 'For he did not wish it to be hinted even for a moment that senators had the authority to bestow upon him anything capable of redounding to his honour – since that, after all, would imply that they were of a higher rank than himself, and could grant him favours as though he were their inferior.'[32] A penetrating insight. For decades, secure within its chrysalis, protected by the cunningly crafted hypocrisies of Augustus and the superseded traditions so valued by Tiberius, a monarchy had been pupating; now, with the return of Caligula from war, it was ready to emerge at last, to unfurl its wings, to dazzle the world with its glory. No longer was there to be any place for the pretensions of the Senate – only for the bond between Princeps and people.

Which was why, when Caligula arrived outside Rome from his northern adventure in May 40, he did not enter the city, but headed on south, to the Bay of Naples.* Here, where for generations the super-rich had devoted themselves to upstaging one another with

---

* Dio, writing in the early third century AD, implies that Caligula travelled to the Bay of Naples in the spring of 39, in the wake of his devastating speech to the Senate; but Seneca, in his essay *On the Shortness of Life* (18.5), makes it clear that the journey took place the following year. If absolute certainty is impossible, the context weights the balance of probability massively towards 40 rather than 39.

extravagant displays of spending, he had prepared the ultimate in showstoppers. No coastal villa, no ornamental folly, no luxury yacht, could possibly compete. Cargo ships conscripted from across the Mediterranean had been lashed together to form an immense pontoon. Stretching three and a half miles, it linked Puteoli, Italy's largest and busiest harbour, with Baiae, its most notorious pleasure resort.[33] Piles of earth had been compacted along the bridge, and service stations complete with running water built along its course, so that it looked like nothing so much as the Appian Way. Arriving in Baiae, Caligula offered sacrifice first to Neptune, the lord of the seas, and then – for what he was about to do had been consciously designed to awe and stupefy the world – to Envy. Ahead of him, the pontoon bridge with its great road of earth stretched all the way to Puteoli; behind him, fully armed, there waited a glittering line of horsemen and soldiers. Caligula himself, crowned with oak leaves and arrayed in the breastplate of Alexander the Great, climbed up into his saddle. Back from conquering the Ocean, he now intended to demonstrate his mastery of the seas in the most jaw-droppingly literal manner. The signal to advance was given. Caligula, his golden cloak gleaming in the summer sun, clattered forwards onto the bridge. 'He has no more chance of becoming emperor than he does of making a tour of the Bay of Baiae on horseback.'[34] So the soothsayer Thrasyllus had once told Tiberius. But Emperor Caligula had become – and now, sure enough, he was riding across the sea.

Never before had the Roman people seen anything quite like it. Massed in rapt stupefaction on the shore, the watching crowds were witnessing both a parody and an upstaging of Rome's haughtiest traditions. The unmistakable echoes of a triumph in Caligula's extravaganza existed only to put in their place all those hidebound and plodding generals who had been content, in celebrating their victories, to retrace the same unvarying route through the streets of Rome. To submit to convention was to submit to the guardians of convention – and Caligula was having none of it. Primordial custom decreed that a general embarking on his triumph be received by the chief magistrates of the Republic, and by the Senate; but none of these was to be seen on the Bay of Naples. Instead, Caligula had made sure to surround himself, pointedly, with those whom he felt he could trust: the Praetorians, his soldiers, his closest friends. The bridge of boats was no place for old men. To be an intimate of the Emperor's was, almost by definition, to share his taste for putting on a show. Just as Caligula himself, the day after crossing the sea to Puteoli, posed for the return journey in a chariot drawn by the most famous racehorses in Rome, so his friends, as they followed him back across the bridge, rattled along in chariots from Britain.* A touch of the exotic was only to be expected in a triumph; but Caligula, fresh though he was from the Channel, was hardly the man to confine himself to parading his mastery of the barbarous North. From the setting of the sun to its rising, the whole world was his to command – for which reason, in token of his universal supremacy, he made sure to ride with a Parthian hostage, a princeling, by his side. Not a detail of the pageant, not a flourish, but it had been painstakingly planned. Even darkness failed to dim the show. As twilight fell, so bonfires in a great arc blazed from the heights above the bay, illuminating the men who had participated in the crossing where they lay feasting on boats anchored the length of the bridge. As for Caligula himself, he remained on the pontoon; and when he had eaten and drunk enough, he amused himself by treating some of his companions much as he had done his uncle, and pushing them into the sea. Finally, determined that the celebrations not end in anticlimax, he ordered that some of the vessels where his men lay feasting be rammed. And as he watched the action, 'so his mood was all elation'.[35]

Spectacle, mockery, violence: Caligula had long displayed a genius

---

* Suetonius does not specify the chariots' place of origin, but the word he uses to describe them, *esseda*, refers to war-chariots of the kind used in earlier centuries by the Gauls, and in Caligula's time exclusively by the Britons. Maecenas, ever at the forefront of innovation, was supposed to have owned 'a British *essedum*'. (Propertius: 2.1.76)

for combining them in the cause of his pleasure. From the bridge of boats, he could make out on the horizon the silhouette of Capri, where he had studied at his great-uncle's feet the various arts of fusing display with humiliation. Tiberius, disgusted by his own proclivities, had preferred to keep them veiled from the eyes of the Roman people – but not Caligula. The tastes that he had honed on his predecessor's private island, whether for role-play or for obliging the offspring of senators to hawk themselves like prostitutes, had at last come into their own. No longer did Caligula feel the slightest qualms about parading them. What were standards of behaviour inherited from a failed and toppled order to inhibit the 'Best and Greatest of the Caesars'?[36] He had ridden on water, after all. Resolved as Caligula was to rub the noses of the nobility in their own irrelevance and desuetude, there was nothing any longer to keep him from the greatest stage of all. He had been away on his travels a whole year. Now, at last, it was time to return to Rome.

Caligula entered the city on 31 August, his birthday. The Senate had marked the occasion by voting him renewed honours; but the Emperor, although content on this occasion to accept them, made sure as he did so to flaunt the true basis of his authority. Soldiers surrounded him as he paraded through the streets: Praetorians, legionaries, a private bodyguard of Germans. So too did the Roman people; and Caligula, pausing in the Forum, clambered up onto the roof of a basilica and began showering them with gold and silver coins. In the resulting stampede, huge numbers were crushed to death – including over two hundred women and a eunuch. Delighted, Caligula repeated the stunt several days running. 'And so the people loved him – because he had bought their goodwill with money.'[37]

Not the goodwill of the aristocracy, though. Among them, there was only renewed despair. They knew perfectly well what the Emperor was up to. The powers of patronage that had always been the surest basis of their *auctoritas* were being simultaneously parodied and undercut. Worse – when Caligula sent plebs scrabbling in the dirt after his munificence, he was reminding ambitious senators that they were no less dependent on his caprices. Even the noblest of magistracies, those hallowed by the many great men elected to them over the course of the centuries, were in his gift. Caligula, unlike his predecessors, did not hesitate to rub in the fact. Skilled as he was 'in discerning a man's secret wishes',[38] he brought a lethal and merciless precision to the art of mocking them. Aspirations that for centuries had steeled the nobility in the service of the Republic were made the object of corrosive jokes. When Caligula declared his intention of appointing Incitatus, his favourite horse, to the consulship, so cruel was the satire that it seemed to the aristocracy almost a form of madness.

Yet escape from it seemed impossible. Helpless as senators were to suborn either Praetorians or German bodyguards, what practical hope did they have of liberating themselves? When Caligula, reclining at a banquet with the two consuls, suddenly chuckled to himself, murmuring that with a nod he could have both their throats cut on the spot, he was playing mind games with the entire aristocracy. 'Let them hate me, so long as they fear me.'[39] This line, a quotation from an ancient poet, summed up what had become, in the wake of the great conspiracy against him, the Emperor's settled policy towards the Senate. Surveillance bred terror – and terror bred surveillance. When a second plot was exposed shortly after Caligula's return to Rome, it was a senator who betrayed it.[40] The guilty men, all of them of the highest rank, were hauled before the Emperor where he was staying in his mother's villa outside the city. First he had them lashed; then tortured; and then, when they had confessed everything, gagged. By now it was night, and torches lit the gardens where Caligula and his dinner guests were strolling beside the river. The prisoners, pushed to their knees on the terrace, were forced to bend their necks. The shredded clothes stuffed into their mouths ensured that no defiant final words could be uttered before their heads were hacked off.

'Whoever heard of capital punishment by night?' To many senators, the real scandal of the business was less the executions themselves than that they had been laid on as an after-dinner entertainment. 'The more that punishments are made a public spectacle,

so the more they are able to serve as an example and a warning.'⁴¹
Here was the authentic voice of the Roman moralist, convinced that
anything staged in private was bound to foster depravity and deviance.
The presumption was a venerable one: prominent citizens should
never, under any circumstances, be permitted private lives. Stories of
what Tiberius had got up to on Capri served as a particularly salutary
warning of what was bound to happen otherwise. Nevertheless, there
were other lessons as well to be drawn from the episode. It was on
Capri, after all, that Caligula, granted licence by his great-uncle, had
honed his various tastes for dressing up, for participating in mythological floor-shows, for witnessing the upper classes debase
themselves. In truth, those who imagined that the only purpose of
inflicting punishment was to educate the Roman people in the
responsibilities of citizenship were grievously behind the times.
Caligula made sport with senators so as to intimidate the entire elite –
but also because it amused him. If sometimes the vengeance he meted
out to his victims was necessarily as swift as it was discreet, then his
preference in general was for toying with them in public. 'Only strike
such blows as permit a man to know he's dying.'⁴² The maxim was one
that Caligula treasured.

What Capri had been to Tiberius, the whole of Rome was now to
his heir: a theatre of cruelty and excess. Few senators were skilled
enough to negotiate its disorienting terrors. One such was Lucius
Vitellius, the father of Caligula's great friend, and a former consul
with an impeccable record of achievement. Summoned back from
Syria, where his feats as governor had included compelling the king
of Parthia to bow before his legions' eagles, he feared – correctly –
that his very accomplishments had made him an object of suspicion.
Accordingly, for his interview, he dressed in the coarse clothing of a
plebeian, then veiled his head as though approaching the altar of a
god. Prostrating himself with a flamboyant flourish, Vitellius hailed
the Emperor as divine, raising prayers to him and vowing him sacrifice. Caligula, not merely mollified, was highly amused. Yes, it was
a game – of the kind that the younger Vitellius, familiar with the

workings of Caligula's mind from their time spent together on Capri, had doubtless tipped off his father about. It was not, though, entirely so. Many decades before, at the wedding feast of Caligula's great-grandfather, the guests had come dressed as gods, provoking indignant crowds to riot; but now Augustus himself had ascended to the heavens. How, then, when Caligula appeared in public dressed as Jupiter, complete with golden beard and thunderbolt, were people to react? A cobbler from Gaul, laughing at the spectacle and telling the Emperor to his face that he was 'utterly absurd',[43] was sent on his way with a smile; but when a famous actor, an intimate of Caligula's named Apelles, was asked who seemed the greater, Jupiter or Caligula himself, and could only swallow and stammer, the reprisal was swift. The Emperor appreciated quick thinking as well as respect, and Apelles had failed him on both counts. The whipping given the wretched actor was apt as well as cruel. Not only did Apelles in Latin mean 'skinless', but Caligula was able to inform the wretched man, as the hide was flogged off his back, that his screams were so exquisite as to do him perfect justice as a tragedian. Between reality and illusion, between the sordid and the fantastical, between the hilarious and the terrifying, lay the dimension where it most delighted Caligula to give his imagination free rein. It took a man of Vitellius's rare perspicacity to appreciate this, and follow the implications through. 'I am talking to the moon,' Caligula once casually informed him. 'Can you see her?' Vitellius, dropping his eyes to the ground, smoothly played along. 'Only you gods, O Master, are visible to one another.'[44]

Because Vitellius understood the rules of the game, and was skilled at it, he was admitted to the highly exclusive circle of senators whom the Emperor was still prepared to acknowledge as friends. Most, bewildered by the sheer ferocity of the assault upon their dignity, found themselves helpless to serve as anything save the butts of his malevolent humour. Nothing entertained Caligula more than to fashion situations in which the elite would be obliged to humiliate themselves. Like the connoisseur of suffering that he was, he relished the opportunity to subject his victims to careful study. When he abolished the reserved seating that Augustus had instituted in arenas, it amused him in the extreme to observe senators and equestrians scrabble after places along with everyone else, 'women next to men, slaves next to free'.[45] Equally, there were times when he might enjoy a more intimate perusal of the extremes of misery to which a man could be reduced. On the same day that he had executed on a trifling charge the son of an equestrian named Pastor, Caligula invited the father to a banquet. Guards were stationed with orders to watch the wretched man's every last facial tic. Caligula, toasting his health, gave him a goblet of wine to drink – and Pastor drained it, 'although he might as well have been drinking the blood of his son'. Whatever was sent Pastor's way – whether perfume, garlands or lavish dishes – he accepted with a show of gratitude. Onlookers, not knowing his son's fate, would never have guessed the depths of misery masked by his frozen expression. The Emperor knew, though – and he knew the reason why Pastor wore such a fixed smile on his face. 'He had another son.'[46]

Caligula, who had himself lived under the suspicious gaze of Tiberius for years, never once in all that time betraying so much as a hint of grief for his mother and brothers, had fathomed a menacing truth. The sacred bonds of duty and obligation which, back in the days of the Republic, had enabled prominent families to perpetuate their greatness down the generations could now, under a Caesar such as himself, be made to entangle them, to catch them in a net. Six months after Caligula's return to the capital, his residence on the Palatine was crowded with hostages: 'the wives of Rome's leading men, and those children possessed of the bluest blood'.[47] Tiberius had retreated to Capri before surrounding himself with the offspring of the nobility; but Caligula, 'when he installed them and subjected them to sexual outrage',[48] had no intention of veiling the scandal. Quite the contrary. Over half a century before, Augustus had declared adultery a crime, sentencing women who cheated on their husbands to dress as whores. Caligula, installed in the very house of Caesar, preferred to turn such legislation on its head. Building work had extended the warren of houses and alleyways that constituted the imperial residence all the way to the Forum; and now, with the wives and children put up there in lavishly furnished rooms, 'young and old alike' were invited to ascend the Palatine and peruse the wares.[49] The affront to the aristocracy, even after everything else that they had suffered, could hardly have been more devastating. To the values enshrined by Augustus too. A brothel in the house of the August Family was a development fit to have made even Ovid suck in his breath. It was Caligula's most shocking, most transgressive, most subversive joke of all.

'Manifold though his vices were, his truest bent was for abuse.'[50] By AD 41, four years after his accession to the rule of the world, Caligula's genius for insult had the entire Roman elite cowering in its shadow. It was enough for one of his agents to enter the Senate House, fix a senator with his glare and charge him with hating the Emperor for the colleagues of the accused man immediately to leap up and tear him to pieces. No one, and certainly not Caligula's intimates, could ever afford entirely to relax. The Emperor liked to keep them all on their toes. One close friend, a former consul named Valerius Asiaticus, was publicly reproached for his wife's inadequate performance in bed – a rebuke that Caligula found all the more droll for the fact that Valerius was 'a proud-spirited man, and notably thin-skinned'.[51] Even a Praetorian might not be spared mockery. A senior officer named Cassius Chaerea, a grizzled veteran who had seen distinguished service on the Rhine and fought under Germanicus, provoked the Emperor to particular hilarity. Bluff and tough though Chaerea was, in the sternest tradition of the Roman military, his voice was discordantly soft; and so Caligula would give him as a watchword, whenever he was on duty, some phrase appropriate to a woman. It was not only the Emperor himself who was reduced to hysterics by this; so too were the other Praetorians. Caligula, as ever, knew precisely how to wound.

And knew as well how to turn it to his own advantage. When he called Chaerea 'girl',[52] or made obscene gestures with his finger whenever the Praetorian had cause to kiss his hand, the pleasure that he took in probing his victim's sensitivities was not his only reason for doing so. Caligula had need of a heavy to do his dirty work for him – and he judged correctly that Chaerea would make all the more effective a torturer or enforcer for his desperation to avoid the slur of effeminacy.

Nevertheless, it was a finely balanced call. Terror bred terror, after all. Caligula's capacity to trust those in his entourage, grievously wounded as it had been by Lepidus and his two sisters, had, with the exposure of the second plot against him, received a near fatal blow. The man who delivered it, a senator named Betilienus Capito, had been the father of one of the conspirators. Obliged to watch his son's decapitation, he had declared himself complicit in the plot as well – and had then, in great detail, provided what he claimed to be a list of everyone else involved. Almost no one close to Caligula was absent from it: his most trusted friends; the Praetorian high command; even Caesonia. 'And so the list was treated with suspicion; and the man was put to death.'[53] Nevertheless, Capito had achieved his aim. The terror that Caligula inspired in those around him was more than reciprocated by the paranoia that they induced in him. Indeed, the New Year saw him so twitchy that he made plans to leave Rome once again. As before, he aimed to follow in his father's footsteps. With a tour of the Rhine already under his belt, Caligula now turned his gaze towards the East. In particular, he yearned to see Alexandria; he spoke openly of his love for the city, 'and of how he planned to head there with all imaginable haste – and then, on arrival, to stay a considerable time'.[54] The end of January was duly set as the date for his departure.

First, though, there were games to celebrate. Staged in honour of Augustus, they were held in a temporary theatre erected on the Palatine – and so much did Caligula enjoy them that he added three extra days to the scheduled programme. On 24 January, the final day of the festival, and with his departure for Alexandria imminent, the Emperor was in an unusually relaxed and affable mood. The spectacle of senators scrabbling after unreserved seats afforded him as much amusement as it had ever done; at the sacrifices to Augustus, the splashing of blood onto one of his companions, a senator named Asprenas, made him laugh.* Then, to liven things up still more, he ordered huge quantities of sweets to be tipped out over the stands, and rare birds. As the spectators scrabbled after these treats, elbowing and shoving each other frantically, so Caligula's mood was even more improved. Finally, to set the seal on a thoroughly enjoyable morning, he watched a performance by Rome's most famous star, an actor named Mnester, as beautiful as he was talented, and with whose charms Caligula was notoriously besotted. The tragedy featured both incest and murder; and accompanied as it was by a farce in which there was much vomiting up of guts, not to mention a crucifixion, it left the arena awash with artificial blood.

Lunchtime arrived, and Caligula decided to dine and refresh himself in his private quarters. He and his entourage accordingly rose and left the forecourt in which the temporary stands for the games had been raised. They entered the August House, and Claudius and Valerius Asiaticus, leading the way, continued towards the baths along a corridor lined with slaves; but Caligula, informed that some Greek boys of noble family were rehearsing a musical performance in his honour, turned aside to inspect them. As he walked down a side-alley, his litter-bearers behind him, he saw approaching him Cassius Chaerea, together with a second officer, Cornelius Sabinus, and a troupe of Praetorians. Approaching the Emperor, Chaerea asked for the day's password. The reply, inevitably, was a mocking one – whereupon Chaerea drew his sword and struck a blow at Caligula's neck.[55]

His aim was not all it could have been. The blade, slicing through the Emperor's shoulder, was obstructed by his collarbone. Groaning in agony, Caligula stumbled forwards in a desperate effort to escape.

* So, at any rate, reports Josephus, whose account is the most detailed and contemporary that we have. According to Suetonius (*Caligula*: 57.4), the blood was that of a flamingo – and it was Caligula himself who was splashed by it.

Sabinus, though, was already onto him. Seizing the Emperor by the arm, he bent him over his knee. Down rained the swords of the Praetorians. It was Chaerea, aiming a second blow better than his first, who succeeded in decapitating his tormentor.[56] Even then, the Praetorians' blades continued to flash and hack. Several thrust their swords through the dead man's genitals. Some, rumour would later have it, even ate the Emperor's flesh.[57] One thing was certain: Chaerea found the taste of vengeance sweet. Only when Caligula's body had been mangled almost beyond recognition did he and his accomplices finally slip away, running through a set of alleyways and concealing themselves in what had once been Germanicus's house.

By now Caligula's litter-bearers, who initially, and with great courage, had sought to stave off the assassins with their poles, had also fled. Even when the Emperor's German bodyguard, alerted to their master's murder, came hurrying to the scene and drove off the remaining Praetorians, they left his trunk and severed head alone. As they spilled out through the streets of the Palatine, hunting the assassins, the corpse of Caligula lay where his murderers had left it. There it was found by Caesonia and her young daughter: a child that Caligula, witnessing her viciousness, and the relish she brought to scratching the faces of her playmates, had laughingly acknowledged his own. And there in turn they were found, mother and daughter together, prostrated by misery and covered in Caligula's blood, by a Praetorian sent to hunt them down. Caesonia, looking up at the soldier, urged him through her tears to 'finish the last act of the drama'[58] – which he duly did. First he slit her throat; then he dashed out her daughter's brains against a wall.[59]

So perished the line of Caligula: dead of a joke taken too far.

6

IO SATURNALIA!

Master of the House

Chaos spelt opportunity. None knew this better than the House of Caesar itself. This was why, ever since Augustus had emerged to supremacy from the horrors of civil war, it had jealously denied to anyone outside its own exclusive circles the chance to capitalise upon its often murderous rivalries. Now, though, with the assassination of Caligula, the dice had been thrown up in the air. The Palatine, from where Augustus had upheld the peace of the world, was given over to riot and confusion. German swordsmen, combing its tangle of alleyways and corridors, searched for the killers in a blood lust of their own. When they ran into Asprenas, the unfortunate senator whose toga had been dirtied during the sacrifices, they cut off his head. Two other senators were dispatched with equal brutality.

Meanwhile, in the theatre, confused rumours were sweeping the stands. No one could be certain that Caligula was truly dead. Some reported that he had escaped his assassins and made it to the Forum, where he was whipping up the plebs – 'who in their folly had loved and honoured the emperor'.[1] Senators sat paralysed, torn between their longing to believe the reports of their tormentor's death and their dread that it was all a trick. Their nerves were hardly settled by the sudden arrival of a posse of Germans, who, after brandishing the heads of Asprenas and the two other murdered senators in their faces, dumped them on the altar. Only the timely arrival of an auctioneer famed for his booming voice, who confirmed for the benefit of everyone in the theatre the death of the Emperor, and successfully urged the Germans to put up their swords, prevented a massacre. Caligula would no doubt have been disappointed.

Meanwhile, down in the Forum, some of the more ambitious among the Senate were already calculating what his elimination might mean for them. When indignant crowds surrounded Valerius Asiaticus and demanded to know who had murdered their beloved emperor, he replied with cheery insouciance, 'I only wish that I had.'[2] Clearly, the insult to his wife had not been forgotten. More was at stake, though, than the satisfaction of personal pique. Without an obvious heir to Caligula on hand, a dizzying prospect had abruptly opened up before the nobility. That afternoon, as the Forum seethed with protestors, it was no emperor who appointed guards to keep order, but the two consuls. When senators convened to debate the future, they did so not in the Senate House rebuilt by the Caesars, but high up on the Capitol, in the great temple of Jupiter, on a site redolent of Rome's venerable past. 'For those schooled in virtue, it is enough to live even a single hour in a free country, answerable only to ourselves, governed by the laws that made us great.'[3] So declared one of the consuls in a tone of soaring self-satisfaction. When Cassius Chaerea, reporting to the Senate that evening, solemnly asked the consuls for the watchword, the answer proclaimed to the Roman people that their ancient constitution was restored: 'liberty'.

Except, of course, that it would take more than fine words to resuscitate the Republic. The regime founded by Augustus had put down roots so deep that only those at its heart could glimpse how far they reached. Senators, whose rank was fixed for them by law, and whose stage was a debating chamber in which everyone sat on open display, were ill-placed to trace them. Few now lived on the Palatine, that great labyrinth of alleyways, corridors and courtyards, into which even the murderers of an emperor had been able to vanish with impunity. One who still did was Caecina Largus, an Etrurian like Maecenas, and of the same family as Germanicus's deputy on the Rhine. In the garden of his mansion there stood some beautiful lotus trees, of which Caecina was inordinately proud – as well he might have been, for from beneath their shade he was better placed than any number of his colleagues to monitor the *arcana imperii*, 'the secrets of power'. Currents were flowing of which the senators on the Capitol were only dimly aware. However proudly Chaerea might strut, Caecina knew that most Praetorians had no stake in any return to the Republic. Roaming the Palatine in the wake of Caligula's murder, they had been hunting his killers, not siding with them. Unsurprisingly, then, rather than join his colleagues in their grandstanding on the Capitol, Caecina opted to play a different game. Other, more certain routes to influence lay open. Caecina was not alone in suspecting that Rome's future had already been decided for her.

Some months before his assassination, Caligula had summoned the two Praetorian prefects to a private interview. Their names had appeared alongside Caesonia's on the list of conspirators drawn up by Capito – and Caligula demanded reassurance, despite his reluctance to believe them guilty. The two prefects, frantically assuring him of their loyalty, had lived to tell the tale – but the suspicions aroused by the meeting had not been eased. Both men knew full well what their fates might be were they to lose Caligula's favour; but they appreciated too the stake that they, and all the Praetorians, had in the survival of the House of Caesar. Who, though, could they adopt as a plausible candidate for the rule of the world? Lucius Domitius Ahenobarbus, the son of the exiled Agrippina and the only living male descendant of Germanicus, was a tiny child. Someone else would have to do. Someone adult, obviously, and a member of the August Family – and yet so despised and discounted by his relatives that not even Caligula had got around to eliminating him. Seen from such a perspective, the solution to the prefects' dilemma was obvious. Indeed – there was only one.

News of what the Praetorians were up to reached the senators on the Capitol as they were still debating the future of the Republic. It was claimed that Claudius, in the wake of his nephew's assassination, had hidden himself behind a curtain. A Praetorian, hurrying past, had seen his feet sticking out and pulled the curtain aside. When Claudius, falling to his knees, had begged for mercy, the soldier, raising him back onto his feet, had hailed him as *imperator*. A man less qualified to receive such a salute than the sickly and decidedly civilian Claudius it would have been hard to imagine, of course; but that had not prevented the Praetorians from bundling him into a litter, abducting him to their camp, and there, en masse, 'endowing him with supreme power'.[4] So, at any rate, it was reported to the Senate – who greeted the news with predictable consternation. Urgently, the consuls sent a summons to Claudius. He replied, in a tone of theatrical regret, that he was being kept where he was 'by force and compulsion'.[5] Notable scholar that he was, he knew his history. He appreciated that the surest way to win legitimacy as a Princeps was to insist that he did not want to be one. Just as Augustus and Tiberius had done before him, Claudius kept lamenting that he had no taste for supreme power – even while taking every step he could to secure it. One day into the restoration of the Republic, and already it was effectively dead.

By the following morning, with Claudius still securely ensconced in the Praetorians' camp, and crowds down in the Forum chanting for an emperor, the Senate was left with little choice but to accept this. All that remained for it to do was to question whether a man who dribbled and twitched, who had never served with the legions, and who was a Caesar neither by blood nor by adoption, was really the best man for the job. Various senators, demonstrating a signal failure to understand the rules of the game, immediately set about pushing their own claims. One, a former consul and noted orator by the name of Marcus Vinicius, could at least boast a link to the August Family – for he had been married for almost a decade to Julia Livilla, Caligula's disgraced youngest sister. A second, a man who had conspiracy and ambition running in his veins, sat at the heart of numerous spiders' webs. Annius Vinicianus was, as his name suggested, a relative of Marcus Vinicius, but he had also been a close friend of the executed Lepidus and knew Chaerea well. Unsurprisingly, then, there were plenty who detected his fingerprints all over Caligula's assassination. Vinicianus himself, by putting his name forward, did nothing to scotch such rumours.

It was not the habit of the Roman people, though, to favour men who operated in the shadows; and this was why, when Valerius Asiaticus put himself forward as a third candidate for the rule of the world, he could do so as a man renowned for the splendour of his lifestyle. His property empire stretched from Italy to Egypt; his gardens, a wonderland of exotic blooms and no less extravagant architecture on the heights above the Campus Martius, were the most celebrated in Rome; his sense of dignity, which Caligula had so wilfully offended, was true to the haughtiest traditions of the Republic. To the cowed ranks of the aristocracy, Valerius Asiaticus provided a welcome dash of colour, a reminder of what they had once been, before the rise to power of the Caesars. Despite that, though, he had no more realistic prospect of succeeding to the rule of the world than any of the various other senators making their pitch that morning. Not all his glamour and swagger could compensate him for one besetting drawback: he was not from Rome, nor even from Italy, but a Gaul. How could such a man hope to displace the brother of Germanicus, the nephew of Tiberius, a Claudian? Sure enough, by the afternoon of 25 January, Valerius Asiaticus – and everyone else on the Capitol too – had bowed to the inevitable. Through gritted teeth, senators who only the previous day had been talking in elevated tones about the restoration of liberty voted to entrust a man most of them despised with the full bundle of powers lately wielded by Caligula. Additionally, they granted him a title that the Senate had never before needed to bestow upon a Princeps: 'Caesar'. That evening, when the fifty-year-old invalid whom his own mother had described as 'a freak of a man'[6] left the Praetorian camp and headed back into the centre of Rome, there to take possession of the Palatine, he did so as the bearer of an appropriately splendid new name: Tiberius Claudius Caesar Augustus Germanicus.

The new emperor had played dangerously, but he had played well. As a young man, denied the opportunities provided as a matter of course to other members of the August Family, he had developed such a passion for gambling that he had even written a treatise on the subject: an addiction that, naturally enough, had only confirmed in their scorn those who regarded him as weak-minded. Yet it was Claudius who had enjoyed the last laugh. Though the odds had always been stacked against him, he had demonstrated an unexpected ability to play them. In the supreme crisis of his life, he had placed a bet that had won him the world. Not since Julius Caesar's crossing of the Rubicon had there been quite so blatant a military coup.

Naturally, like the shrewd and calculating operator that he had revealed himself to be, Claudius chose to veil this as well as he could. He knew that his position remained precarious. He was certainly in no position to enforce a rule of terror. Although Chaerea was put to death – as he had to be for his crime of murdering an emperor – and Cornelius Sabinus, who had joined in Caligula's assassination, committed suicide, deaths were otherwise kept to a minimum. In the Senate, everyone breathed a huge sigh of relief – and particularly those who had publicly opposed Claudius becoming emperor. When they agreed to vote him the same wreath of oak leaves awarded many decades previously to Augustus, 'because he had preserved citizens' lives',[7] it was more than an empty gesture. Coming after the terrors and humiliations inflicted on them by Caligula, an emperor who made play of his clemency was hardly to be sniffed at, after all. Claudius, who had suffered mockery his whole life, was sensitive to the dignity of others. Despite his lameness, he always made a point of rising to his feet when addressed by his fellow senators; and sometimes, should a particularly elderly senator be struggling to hear what was being said, he would permit the old man to sit on a bench reserved for magistrates. Claudius, unlike his nephew, was not a man to cause deliberate offence.

Nevertheless, he had no illusions as to his popularity with the Senate. Anxiety about his own personal security shaded into paranoia. All those allowed into his presence were first subjected to a vigorous frisking; he never dined but there were soldiers beside him; and when, a month after coming to power, he finally entered the Senate House for the first time, he did so accompanied by guards. Claudius knew what he owed the Praetorians – and he was not afraid to acknowledge it. One of his coins was stamped with an image of their camp; another showed him shaking hands with their standard-bearer. The friendship between emperor and Praetorians had been expensively bought. Vast handouts, equivalent to five times their annual pay, were lavished on them, a bribe so blatant that its nature could not possibly be concealed.[8]

Nor was that all. Ever since the accession of Tiberius, the legions on the frontiers had regarded it as their right to receive enormous donatives from a new Caesar. This was hardly a tradition that Claudius was minded to buck. Yet it confronted him with a massive financial headache. Even at the best of times, the funding of Rome's armies swallowed up a huge proportion of the annual budget. 'No peace without arms – and no arms without pay.'[9] Yet money, by the standards of the August Family, was precisely what Claudius had always been short of. Caligula, as much for his own amusement as for any other reason, had systematically mulcted his uncle of such millions as he could. At one stage, in order to raise the sums necessary to qualify for continued membership of the Senate, Claudius had been reduced to selling off his properties. Now, as emperor, the need to secure military backing faced him with a bill equivalent almost to Rome's entire annual intake of revenue. How to pay it?

The best bets are those placed with privileged knowledge. Claudius, practised gambler that he was, understood this as well as anyone. To have accepted the support of the Praetorians without first securing the funds necessary to keep them on-side would have been a lethal misjudgement. Claudius needed the backing of accountants as well as soldiers. In this, luck had favoured him. The two prefects had not been alone in lending him their support. At their fateful meeting with Caligula, a third man had been summoned for a grilling. Gaius Julius Callistus was a functionary, not a soldier – but no less a linchpin of the regime for that. While others busied themselves with the show of power, he presided over its secret workings. Consummate insider that he was, he understood what the House of Caesar had become: no longer, as Augustus had pretended it to be, the residence of a private citizen, but the sprawling nerve centre from which the world was run. Each day, just as at the home of any great nobleman, suitors would cluster at its gates, visitors pay their respects and eminent guests be entertained; but within its labyrinthine complex, away from the reception halls and the sumptuous banqueting rooms, operations were of an order that very few could comprehend. Every senator needed an agent to keep track of his assets; but none had assets on the scale of Caesar. There were his estates to run, of course, and his mines, and his warehouses: his *patrimonium*, as they were collectively called. But there was more. It was from the Palatine that the finances of the entire Roman world were administered: the taxes; the funding of the legions; assorted mints. Augustus, although he had made a point of leaving his accounts to be read out by Tiberius to the Senate on his death, had been purposefully vague: 'Those who want the details can consult with the requisite officials.'[10] Two and a half decades on, it was Callistus who had the figures at his fingertips, and knew the secret location on the Palatine where the reserves of coin were stored. Accused by Caligula of treachery, after his name too had appeared on Capito's list, he had faced the same excruciating dilemma as the two prefects: whether to hope that his protestations of innocence would be believed, or to conspire in the promotion of a new Caesar. That Claudius had been able to fund his coup showed the choice that Callistus had made.

Other aides prominent in Caligula's service had been eliminated in the wake of the coup: from his personal minder to the official who kept tabs on the aristocracy, and was never seen without twin books, 'Sword' and 'Dagger'. Even the two Praetorian prefects were forcibly retired in due course. Not Callistus, though. He remained under Claudius where he had been under Caligula: at the heart of power. Like Caecina Largus, the senator who owned one of the few private residences left on the Palatine, he was too shrewd, too knowledgeable, too valuable an ally to be cast aside. Caecina claimed his reward a year after the coup, when, as the new emperor's colleague, he served as a consul of the Roman people. Callistus, by contrast, was granted no such honour. His role remained, to outward show, far humbler. As Caecina strode through the Forum to the Senate House, guarded by his lictors, Callistus was up on the Palatine, surrounded by scrolls, vetting petitions to the Emperor. Yet the rewards enjoyed by the secretary were, according to many measures, no less than those enjoyed by the consul. Just as Caecina could boast a garden famous for its lotus trees, so had Callistus commissioned thirty pillars fashioned out of an eye-wateringly expensive brand of marble for his dining room. Although not a consul himself, he thought nothing of vetting candidates for the office. 'Indeed, so great was his wealth and the dread which he inspired that his power verged on the despotic.'[11] Yet this man notorious for his 'arrogance and the extravagant uses to which he put his authority'[12] was neither a senator nor an equestrian – nor had he even been born a citizen. Callistus, the man who had helped to topple one emperor and who controlled access to another, had spent his early life as the lowest of the low: a slave.

The clue lay in his name. 'Callistus' meant 'Gorgeous' in Greek, and was the kind of thing that no self-respecting Roman would ever allow himself to be called. As a name given to a slave, though, it was the height of fashion – partly because it provided a hint of foreign sophistication, and partly because everyone knew that Greeks made the best slaves. The real giveaway, though, was that Callistus had also adopted Caligula's first two names, Gaius Julius. Wearing these marked him out as a man who had been set free by an emperor – as an *Augusti libertus*. Hardly a status to impress a senator, of course – except that even the grandest of noblemen knew, to their agonised regret, that lineage was no longer everything. Having the ear of

Caesar might count for at least as much. As in the Senate, so in the back rooms of the Palatine: climbing the rungs of the ladder promised splendid rewards to those who could make it to the top.

Most, of course, were never in a position to try. Caesar's household teemed with slaves, and if many of these were employed in the basest of menial tasks, then others specialised in duties that offered them little better prospect of promotion. To be stuck with responsibility for the polishing of the emperor's mirrors, or the care of his perfumed oils, or the making of his fancy dress was hardly to be on the high road to influence and wealth. Secure a post handling his finances, though, and opportunities were altogether more promising. Even out in the provinces, the slaves who handled Caesar's accounts or dispensed cash to the legions on his behalf often did very well for themselves. One accountant in Gaul was the owner of sixteen slaves, including a doctor, two cooks and a man charged with looking after his gold, while a steward in Spain was notorious for dining off silver plates, and ended up so fat that he was nicknamed 'Rotundus'. Unsurprisingly, though, it was in Rome that advancement could be quickest. On the Palatine, 'ever at Caesar's side, tending to his affairs, privy to the holy secrets of the gods',[13] a slave was as well qualified as anyone to fathom the *arcana imperii*. Play his hand wrong and he might end up like the secretary of Augustus who, caught red-handed selling the contents of a letter, had his legs broken. Play it skilfully and he might end up like Callistus: not only rich, powerful and feared, but a freedman.

That they were willing to make citizens of slaves had always been a sacred tradition of the Roman people. Even their penultimate king, a much admired warrior and administrator by the name of Servius Tullius, had allegedly once been of servile rank. It was true that Claudius himself – whose private interests included ancient history as well as gambling – disputed this tradition, and claimed that the king had originally been an Etruscan adventurer named Mastarna; but most Romans had no time for such scholarly pettifogging. That Servius had been born into servitude was evident both from his name and from his insistence, made in the teeth of aristocratic opposition, that the Roman people would be strengthened, not weakened, by welcoming into their ranks such slaves as they chose to liberate. 'For you would be fools,' he had told his fellow citizens, 'to begrudge them citizenship. If you think them unworthy of its rights, then do not set them free – but why, if you think them estimable, turn your backs on them solely because they are foreign?'[14] The logic of this had seemed unanswerable; and so it was, over the course of the centuries, that slavery had served many an able man as a staging post on a journey to becoming Roman. When a law was passed in 2 BC, limiting how many slaves could be set free in a citizen's will, it made explicit what had always been a guiding principle of slave-owners in the city: that only the talented were qualified to join their ranks.

To walk the Forum, then, and to see foreigners for sale at the foot of the Palatine, their limbs shackled and their feet chalked white to mark them as imports, was, just perhaps, to see the high achievers of tomorrow. 'No one knows what he can do till he tries.' Such had been the maxim of a celebrated wit named Publilius Syrus, who as his name implied had originally been brought in chains to Italy from Damascus, but had gone on, after winning his freedom, to become Rome's leading dramatist, and to be crowned as such by Julius Caesar himself. His cousin, similarly enslaved, had ended up the city's first astronomer. Another freedman, originally transported in the same slave ship as the two cousins, had founded the study of Latin grammar, teaching Brutus and Cassius, no less. Rome, over the years, had measurably benefited from the influx of foreign talent. 'It's no crime,' as Ovid had once put it, 'to have had chalked feet.'[15]

Even the right to run for office, although denied to freedmen themselves, was open to their sons. Many had taken advantage. Although the magistrate who could trace his lineage back to a slave would naturally do all he could to hush it up, everyone knew that 'numerous equestrians, and even some senators, were descended from freedmen'.[16] Augustus himself, so stern in his insistence upon the proprieties of status, had been perfectly content to count the sons of one-time slaves as his friends. Vedius Pollio, the financier with the notoriously extravagant home furnishings, had been one such. So too had been an altogether more estimable adornment of the Augustan regime, the man entrusted by the Princeps with the hymning of Rome's rebirth, a poet still admired and treasured decades after his death. 'I am the son of a man freed from slavery.'[17] Horace, certainly, had never thought to deny it.

Yet even while honouring the debt he had owed his father, whose devotion and financial backing had given him such a stellar start in life, he had never entirely been able to escape a certain queasiness. 'No amount of good fortune can change a man's breeding.'[18] Horace had been sufficiently a Roman to dread that slavery might leave an ineradicable taint. The surest measure of a freedman's achievement was to father a son who despised what he had been. Perhaps this was why, far from being a soft touch, the slave-owning sons of former slaves tended to be notorious for their cruelty. Vedius Pollio, excessive in all things, had enjoyed feeding clumsy pageboys to enormous flesh-eating eels. Even Augustus had been shocked. Yet, however novel a spectacle a fish tank flecked with human body parts might be, it only made manifest what it was about slavery that made freedmen so keen to demonstrate that they had escaped it for good. To be a slave was to exist in a condition of suspended death. Such was the law. Although, under normal circumstances, it was forbidden a master to kill his slaves, there was otherwise no form of violence so terrible that it could not legally be inflicted upon a human chattel. The maid who inadvertently yanked her mistress's hair might well expect to have a hairpin jabbed into her arm; the waiter who stole from a banquet to have his hands cut off and slung around his neck. Dream of dancing, and a slave was bound to be whipped. At its most brutal, the scarring from such an ordeal would leave a permanent fretwork upon the back. Thongs tipped with metal were designed to bite deep. Unsurprisingly, then, it was required by law of a slave-dealer to state whether any of his wares had ever sought to kill themselves. Barbarians who committed suicide rather than suffer to be enslaved, as did an entire tribe taken prisoner during Augustus's

Spanish campaign, were rather admired. Equally, by the same reckoning, those who submitted to servitude showed themselves fitted
to be slaves. The baseness of it could never entirely be escaped.
Freedom was like an unscarred back: once lost, it was lost for good.

The presence of a man such as Callistus at the heart of power was,
then, profoundly disturbing to many Romans. Everyone took for
granted that slaves, by nature, were prone to any number of contemptible habits. Rare was the owner who did not complain about
their tendency to lie and thieve. It was evident from his obscenely
well-appointed dining room that Callistus was no less inclined to
pilfer as a freedman than he had been as a slave. Indignation, though,
was not the only response to the spectacle of his wealth. There was
anxiety as well. The man who had sold Callistus to Caligula was often
to be seen standing outside his house, waiting in line for the chance
to beg a favour – and being turned away, to rub salt into the wound.
Such a sight served to remind slave-owners of a truth that few of
them cared to dwell upon: that fortune was fickle, and that just as a
slave might become a free man, so might a free man become a slave.
'Scorn, then, if you dare, those to whose level, even as you despise
them, you may yourself well descend.'[19] Many centuries before, while
lecturing the Roman aristocracy on the need to accept freedmen as
fellow citizens, Servius Tullius had made a similar point: that of 'how
many states had passed from servitude to liberty, and from liberty to
servitude'.[20] It was perhaps no coincidence that Servius should also
have prescribed that slaves, during the festival of the Compitalia, be
the ones who made sacrifice to the Lares – and that they be permitted, what was more, to dress and behave like free men for the
duration of the festivities. Other days of the year witnessed similar
scenes of misrule. Early in July, slavegirls would put on their mis-
tresses' best clothes and offer themselves up for wild sex to passers-by;
in December, the cry of 'Io Saturnalia!' would herald an even more
riotous celebration of role reversal, in which slaves were allowed to
put aside their work and be feasted by their masters. It was, most
people agreed, 'the best day of the year'[21] – and yet a world in which

every day was Saturnalia was hardly one in which even the most party-loving citizen would care to live. Proprieties had to be maintained – for if they were not, then who could say where things might not end?

Enough had happened in recent history to suggest the answer. Not the least horror of the civil war had been the dread that the distinction between slave and free, so fundamental to everything that made the Roman people who they were, had begun to blur and come under threat. Former slaves, in blatant disregard of the law, had dared to usurp the privileges of equestrians, 'strutting around, flashing their wealth';[22] simultaneously, amid the chaos of the times, many a citizen had vanished into the chain-gangs of unscrupulous slavers. The problem had become so serious that Tiberius, during his first term as a magistrate, had been charged with touring slave-barracks across Italy and setting free all kidnapped prisoners. The order brought to the world by Augustus had, of course, helped to restore the chasm of difference that properly separated citizen from slave; but to those sensitive about their status, the character of his regime had only served to open up fresh wounds. Caligula, with his unerring talent for inflicting maximum pain, had naturally made sure to jab at them hard. On one occasion, in the full view of the Senate, a venerable former consul had expressed his gratitude for being spared execution by sinking to his knees – and Caligula had extended his left foot to be kissed, as he would have done to a slave. It had amused him too, as he dined, to be waited on by eminent senators dressed in short linen tunics, and to have them stand subserviently at his head and feet. Most devastatingly of all, he had granted slaves the right to bring charges against their masters: a licence of which many had taken enthusiastic advantage. Here, for the elite, had been one final, culminating horror: to discover that Caligula had his eyes and ears even in their homes, even in their most intimate moments, even among their basest menials.

Claudius, who had himself had a capital charge brought against him by one of his slaves, and only narrowly escaped conviction, was sympathetic to the sensitivities of his fellow senators. In token of this, one of his first acts as emperor was to sentence a lippy slave to a public flogging in the Forum. Claudian that he was, and scholar of Roman tradition, he was no revolutionary. Nevertheless, he had good reason to keep Callistus in his post. Unlike other men of his rank, Claudius had been confined by his disabilities to the domestic sphere in which talented freedmen were liable to make the running – and was in consequence unusually alert to their capabilities. Inexperienced as he was in the arts of government, yet earnestly resolved to provide the world with efficient administration, he had no wish to deprive himself of able subordinates.

Accordingly, far from slapping Callistus down, Claudius looked around for other, similarly talented freedmen to serve alongside him. One candidate selected himself: Pallas, the slave who had been entrusted by Claudius's mother with the letter to Tiberius that had ultimately served to bring down Sejanus. Freed in token of his services shortly before Antonia's death, he combined formidable administrative ability with an absolute loyalty to the Claudian house. So too did a third freedman, a master of back-room dealing by the name of Narcissus, who owed his power partly to the fact that he had been owned by the Emperor himself and partly to his own consummate skills as a fixer. Naturally, to resentful outsiders, his influence over Claudius could hardly help but seem sinister in the extreme: definitive proof that the new emperor was as befuddled and gullible a fool as everyone had always said he was. In truth, though, it illustrated the opposite: that Claudius was vastly more interested in setting his administration on a firm footing than with what his critics might have to say. He knew that he had no legal right to the Palatine, and that his possession of it was entirely a result of his coup; he knew too that his best chance of keeping hold of it was to exploit its resources to the full. The world needed good governance – and Claudius, in his determination to provide it, was content to grant his ablest freedmen such authority as they needed to be effective. No longer was there to be any pretence that Caesar's household was anything but what it was: a court.

Inevitably, despite these changes, the essentials of the regime remained unaltered. Claudius's reliance on his triumvirate of talented freedmen, while it boosted the efficiency of his government, did nothing to calm the swirl of intrigue and the scrabbling after power that had long been such features of life on the Palatine. The endless contest for advancement and advantage went on as it had ever done – but now with the addition of a new raft of power-brokers. Some adapted well to this development; others did not. Lucius Vitellius, ever alert to changes in the wind, smoothly added statues of Pallas and Narcissus to his household shrine, managing to remain as high in favour under Claudius as he had been under Caligula; but another senator, an experienced general named Silanus, proved hopelessly unequal to the demands of faction-fighting on the Palatine. Outmanoeuvred by his enemies, he was put to death on the orders of the Emperor only a year after Claudius had come to power. The precise details were murky, as so often with such cases; but all were agreed that the *coup de grâce* had been applied when Narcissus, hurrying to his master at daybreak, had reported seeing him murdered by Silanus in a dream. The episode made Claudius look both vindictive and credulous – an impression not helped by the damage already done to his authority by another, infinitely more titillating incident. Sex, incest and exile: less than a year after his seizure of power, the new emperor had found himself embroiled in an all too familiar kind of scandal.

It had begun, as so often before, with an attempt to project an image of domestic harmony. Keen to assert his authority as the head of the August Family, Claudius had summoned back his two nieces from the exile to which Caligula had sentenced them; but Julia Livilla, unlike Agrippina, had failed to learn her lesson. It was reported that she had begun an affair with a senator widely hailed – not least by himself – as the most brilliant man of his generation: a dazzling orator and intellectual by the name of Seneca. Nor was that the most titillating detail. It was rumoured as well that Julia's uncle, smitten by her youthful charms, had been spending altogether more time with her than was decent for an old man. Whatever the truth of this, it was certain that the mere rumour of it had made her a mortal enemy. Claudius's young and beautiful wife, Valeria Messalina was as well connected as she was famously pearly toothed. Like Julia, she was a great-grandniece of Augustus and had not the slightest intention of ceding advantage to a rival. Nor did it help that she was the daughter of Domitia Lepida, whose sister had taken the young Domitius under her wing after his mother's exile by Caligula, and was cordially detested by Agrippina as a rival for her son's affections. Unsurprisingly, then, relations between Claudius's wife and his two nieces were toxic. When news of Julia's affair with Seneca became common currency, it was Messalina whom many suspected of the leak. It certainly spelt disaster for the couple. Seneca was exiled in disgrace to Corsica, and Julia — once again — to a prison island. There, shortly afterwards, she was starved to death. A year on from the coup that had brought Claudius to power, all his talk of a new beginning already seemed so much hot air.

The most grievous blow to his reputation, though, was yet to come. A year after his coup, Claudius remained twitchy and insecure. That his administration was decidedly less murderous than his predecessor's did not impress his critics. Senators who had expressed their resentment of him on the fateful day of Caligula's assassination continued to scorn him as a fool, while the execution of Silanus at the behest of a freedman seemed to offer a grim portent of where his regime might be heading. Particularly resentful was Annius Vinicianus, whose ambition to lead the Roman world had been so decisively trumped by the Praetorians' support for Claudius, but whose relish for spinning subtle webs of conspiracy remained undimmed. A year on, midway through 42, he was ready to attempt a coup of his own. In the Balkans, the commander of two legions had committed to backing the insurrection; in Rome, numerous senators and equestrians. Delivered an insulting letter demanding that he retire, Claudius was so flustered that he briefly despaired of his prospects; but it was not in vain, as it turned out, that he had paid such hefty bribes to the military. The soldiers in the Balkans refused to join the uprising; their commander committed suicide; so too did Vinicianus. Others implicated in the conspiracy, hesitating to follow their leaders' example, had to be shamed into doing so. Most notorious for his hesitation was a former consul named Paetus. Holding his sword in a shaking hand, but dreading to fall on it, he had it snatched from him by his wife, who then promptly dropped onto it herself. 'See, Paetus,' she declared with her dying breath, 'it does not hurt.'[23]

The stern quality of this admonishment, redolent as it was of Roman womanhood at its most antique and heroic, was much admired; for everything else about the abortive coup had been squalid in the extreme. Once again, as in the darkest days of Tiberius's reign, there were corpses being dumped on the Gemonian Steps and hauled away on meat-hooks. Indeed, to bruised and bewildered senators, their world seemed as upended as it had ever been. Some of the conspirators had saved their skins by bribing Narcissus to intervene on their behalf; others, even more shockingly, had been put to torture. Here was the true measure of the scare that Claudius had been given: for there was only one class of person who could legally be subjected to such an indignity during an investigation into treason, and that was a slave. Specialists skilled in the art of extracting information tended to be found among private firms of undertakers, who would offer their services as a supplement to their regular income. Such men were proficient in using the rack to separate limbs from limbs, in applying pitch or scalding metal to bare flesh, in wielding an iron-tipped whip.[24] That such horrors had been inflicted upon senators and equestrians left scars upon the entire Roman elite that could not easily be healed. What were all the fine-sounding claims by the new emperor to clemency but a grotesque joke, and what all his publicly stated ambitions to serve as a new Augustus but a monstrous charade? The Senate licked its wounds, and did not forget.

Nor, after the first shock of the conspiracy against him had subsided, and he had found time to gather his breath, did Claudius. His first year as emperor had been potentially crippling to his reputation, and therefore to his long-term prospects – and he knew it. He did not despair, though. He knew too the infinite resources available to him as Caesar, and that there was much that even a man such as himself, old, incapacitated and widely despised as a fool, could do. No matter what, he remained the most powerful man in the world.

The following year, Claudius was determined, would see him demonstrate it once and for all.

Bread and Britons

In AD 42, one year after Claudius had come to power, a Roman governor by the name of Suetonius Paulinus led an army to the limits of Mauretania, and then beyond. The Moors, a people who lived just across the straits from Spain, and were renowned for their ability to hurl javelins while riding bareback and their high standards of dental hygiene, had long been within Rome's orbit; but only recently had the decision been taken to absorb them formally into the empire. There was much in Mauretania to excite the interest of the Roman upper classes – including, not least, its manufacture of the purple dye used to colour their togas. The last king of the Moors – who, by virtue of his descent from Antony and Cleopatra, had been related to Caligula – had opted, when summoned by his cousin to Lugdunum, to sport a particularly flashy shade of cloak. A fatal act of one-upmanship. Back in Mauretania, the Moors had greeted news of their king's execution with outrage. Rebellion had flared.

Claudius, inheriting the crisis from Caligula and reluctant to see it get out of hand, had duly ordered the kingdom transformed into a province. A hard-headed decision, made for hard-headed reasons – but not exclusively so. Scholar that he was, Claudius had an interest in distant regions that touched on more than affairs of state. South of the cities that lay just inland from the sea, where merchants from Italy were regular visitors and the architecture aped the best of Rome and Alexandria, there stretched an altogether different world. Inhabited by tribes so unspeakably savage that they ate flesh raw and thought nothing of drinking milk, it had never before been penetrated by Roman arms. In turn, beyond them loomed an even more fantastical land, one long believed to be swathed in perpetual clouds, and where the inhabitants were reported never to have dreams. Suetonius Paulinus was leading his men up into the Atlas mountains, 'the pillar which supports the sky'.[25]

Reality, in the event, did not quite measure up to the fables told of the mountain range. There were deep snowdrifts, even in summer – but no perpetual clouds. The deserts beyond the Atlas mountains were scorching, and covered in black dust. The natives lived like dogs. Nevertheless, the expedition was not entirely a wasted effort. The forests that surrounded the mountain range, Paulinus reported back to Rome, were filled with wonders: towering trees with leaves that were covered with 'a thin downy floss'[26] much like silk; wild elephants; every conceivable kind of snake. Back in Rome, Claudius was delighted by the news. It played to all his passions. As a private citizen, denied by his disabilities the chance to travel, he had lovingly transcribed the details of exotic flora and fauna into a panoramic gazetteer: the aromatic leaves sprinkled by the Parthians on their drinks; a centaur born in northern Greece that had died the same day. Now, as emperor, he had a far broader stage on which to display his enthusiasms. Roman conquerors had long been in the habit of bringing back to their city plants and animals from remote lands. This was why, in gardens of the kind owned by Valerius Asiaticus, the smog-choked citizen might have a chance to breathe in the scents of distant forests, and to marvel at the blooms of strange flowers. It was also why beasts like those discovered by Paulinus were regular sources of entertainment in Rome. Pompey had exhibited the first rhinoceros to be seen in the city, Julius Caesar the first giraffe. Augustus, as a token of his victory over Egypt, had ridden through Rome with a hippopotamus waddling in his train, while Claudius himself, on formal occasions, might order elephants hitched to his chariot. It was no coincidence that all these creatures, and many more, had come from Africa – for the continent was famed as 'the wet-nurse of wild beasts'.[27] Naturally, though, merely to exhibit them gave the Roman people an inadequate sense of the animals' ferocity, and of the achievement that transporting them from the ends of the earth represented. More educational, and certainly more crowd-pleasing, was to pit them in battle against trained huntsmen, and have them fight to the death. Only then could spectators gain a due sense of what legates like Paulinus, when they tamed lands teeming with lions and crocodiles, were achieving on behalf of the Roman people. Only then could they begin to appreciate the task undertaken by Claudius Caesar in pacifying and ordering the world.

Not that the subduing of wild beasts was the only measure of Roman greatness. At the opposite end of the world, amid the surging and the heaving of the Northern Ocean, lay challenges even more formidable than those met by Paulinus. No one could know for sure what lay beyond the limits explored by Roman fleets, although travellers spoke of islands inhabited by freakishly barbarous people, some with horses' hooves, others with ears so huge that they covered up their otherwise naked bodies – and ultimately, far beyond them, the mysterious land of Thule, and a terrible sea of frozen ice. For Claudius, the wilds and wonders of the Northern Ocean had a particular resonance, for it was his father, back in 12 BC, who had been the first Roman commander to sail it. Twenty-eight years later, Germanicus had repeated the exploit; and even though, since then, no Roman general had led a fleet across the Ocean, Claudius now had the chance to emulate his father and brother. Yet his ambitions did not stop at exploration. Lame though he was, and fifty-four years a civilian, he aimed at an even more heroic feat: the completion of a conquest left undone by Julius Caesar. It was time, not merely to cross the Ocean, but to carve out from it a new province: to win for the Roman people the island of Britain.

There were good reasons for Claudius to command its invasion in the early summer of 43. Circumstances had rarely looked so promising. The island itself was convulsed by dynastic upheavals. Not only had Cunobelin, the veteran chieftain of the Catuvellauni, recently died, leaving his lands to two sons, but a neighbouring kingdom on the south coast had collapsed into such savage factionalism that its king had fled to the Romans. Simultaneously, on the opposite side of the Channel, preparations for an amphibious assault were well advanced. At Boulogne, where Caligula had ordered the construction of a towering lighthouse, some two hundred feet high, to light the way across the Ocean, a fleet sufficient to transport four legions awaited the command to set sail. The soldiers massing there bore witness to years of forward planning. Caligula's expedition to the North had not, as his critics charged, been a mere exercise in wild irresponsibility. It was thanks to the two legions recruited on his orders that a substantial invasion force could be readied without unduly weakening the Rhine defences. Meanwhile, on the Rhine itself, all was quiet. So well had Galba's campaign of pacification gone that Claudius, in his role of commander-in-chief, had been awarded triumphal honours. Two of the more contumacious German tribes had been decisively crushed. The glow of victory had been further burnished by the recapture of an eagle lost to Arminius. No better portent could possibly have been imagined.

Or could it? To the legionaries camped out on the Channel coast, anything that stirred up memories of the fate of Varus was liable to provoke deep unease. Bad enough as it was to be trapped on the wrong side of the Rhine, how much more terrifying was the prospect of being stranded on the wrong side of the Ocean. Few knew much about Britain – but what they did know was deeply off-putting. The natives were, if anything, even more barbarous than the Germans. They painted themselves blue; they held their wives in common; they wore hair on the upper lip, an affectation so grotesque that Latin did not even have a word for it. Nor were their women any better. They were reported to dye their bodies black, and even on occasion to go naked. Savages capable of such unspeakable customs were clearly capable of anything; and sure enough, just as it was part of the terror of the Germans that they practised murderous rites in the depths of their dripping forests, so did the Britons have priests who, in groves festooned with mistletoe, were reported to commit human sacrifice and cannibalism. These 'Druids', as the priests were called, had once infested Gaul as well, until their suppression on the orders of Tiberius; but across the Ocean, beyond the stern reach of Roman law, they still thrived. 'Magic, to this very day, holds Britain in its shadow.'[28] No wonder, then, ordered to embark for a land of such sorcery and menace, that many soldiers should have blanched. Soon enough, murmurings were turning to open insurrection. Legionaries began to lay down their arms and refuse point-blank to board the transport ships.

Up stepped Narcissus. Sent ahead of his master, who had no intention of venturing to Britain until he could be confident that the invasion was a success, the freedman boldly addressed the mutineers and began to lecture them on their duty. He was immediately drowned out by howls of derision. The mood was turning uglier by the minute. It seemed that discipline had been entirely lost. Then all at once, one of the legionaries yelled '*Io Saturnalia!*' — and his comrades started to laugh. The cry was echoed across the entire camp. Abruptly, a holiday spirit took hold of the soldiers. The threat of violence was dissolved and the army brought back to obedience. When the legions boarded the transport ships, it was as though for a festival. Nor, from that point on, did anything further happen to shake their discipline. Instead, all went as well as the planners of the invasion could possibly have hoped. The seas for the crossing were calm; three bridgeheads established unopposed; the Britons twice defeated, and one of the two Catuvellaunian chieftains left dead on the battlefield. True, resistance was far from crushed. The surviving son of Cunobelin, a wily and indefatigable warrior named Caratacus, remained on the loose, while to the north and west of the island, in lands where even clay pots were a novelty, let alone coinage or wine, there lurked tribes who had barely heard of Rome. Nevertheless, with a crossing secured across the Thames and an encampment planted on the river's northern bank, the time had clearly come to send for the commander-in-chief. The glory of securing the final defeat of the Catuvellauni, and receiving their formal submission, belonged to one man, and one alone.

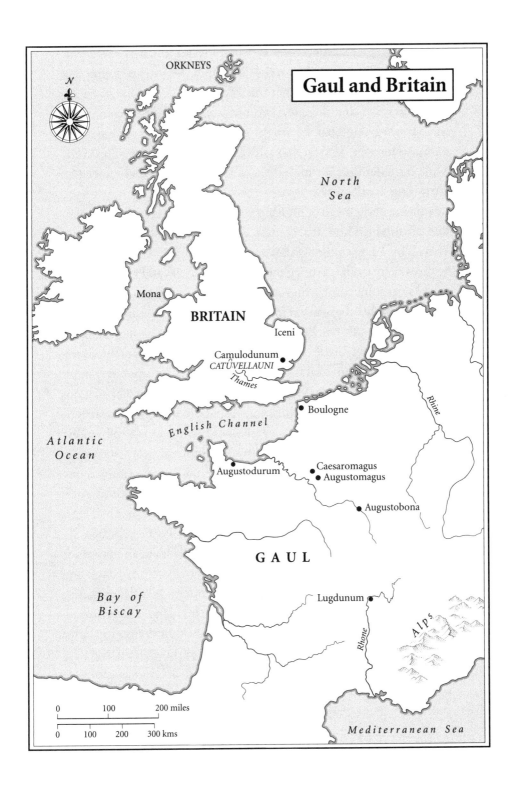

Hobble-gaited though he was, Claudius did not make a wholly improbable conqueror. Tall and solidly built, he had the white hair and distinguished features that the Roman people expected of their elder statesmen; and there was no difficulty, whenever he sat or stood still, in accepting that he might indeed rank as an *imperator*. For Claudius himself, who all his youth had been cooped up in his study while his elder brother played the war hero, the chance to lead an army into battle was a dream come true. He did not waste it. Advancing at the head of his legions, he did so as the embodiment of Roman might. The Catuvellauni, duly intimidated, began to melt away. The advance along the north coast of the Thames estuary towards their capital, a straggling complex of dykes and round-houses named Camulodunum, met with scant opposition. Camulodunum itself, with only rough-hewn fortifications and a demoralised garrison to defend it, rapidly fell. Entering the settlement in triumph, Claudius could legitimately exult that he had proven himself worthy of the noblest and most martial traditions of his family. The potency of his name now reached even further than that of Drusus or Germanicus had done. Shortly after the storming of Camulodunum, there arrived at Claudius's headquarters a slew of British chieftains – and among them was the king of a cluster of distant islands named the Orkneys, thirty in number, and so far to the north that their winter was one perpetual night.[29] Receiving the submission of such an exotic figure, Claudius could know his dearest ambitions for the invasion had been fulfilled. 'The Ocean had been crossed and – in effect – subdued.'[30]

Then, sixteen days after first setting foot in Britain, the Emperor was off again, back to Rome. He had no need to linger on a dank and amenity-free frontier. Let his subordinates pursue Caratacus, storm hill-forts and complete the pacification of the island. Claudius had accomplished what he had set out to do. The Britons themselves, after all, had never been the principal target of his exertions. He had always had other opponents more prominently in mind. The gravest threat to his security had never been Caratacus but his own peers. Seasoned gambler that he was, he had weighed the odds carefully before deciding to absent himself from the capital for six months. Even with Vinicianus and his fellow conspirators dead, the embers of insurrection were not completely stamped out. Shortly before Claudius's departure, an equestrian had been convicted of plotting against him and flung off the cliff of the Capitol; then, a portent that invariably foretold some calamitous upheaval to the state, an eagle-owl had flown into the sanctum of Jupiter's temple. Not surprisingly, before leaving on campaign, Claudius had made sure to take every precaution. The administration of the capital itself had been entrusted to that impeccably loyal courtier, Lucius Vitellius. Other, less tractable senators, meanwhile, had been graced with the supreme honour of accompanying Caesar to Britain. Prominent among them had been Valerius Asiaticus and Marcus Vinicius – both of whom, not coincidentally, had once asserted their own claims to supreme power. Now, with the conquest of Britain, there was no longer the remotest prospect of anyone wrenching it from Claudius's grasp. The glory of his successes filled the world. In Corsica, the exiled Seneca – desperate to be allowed home – hailed the triumphant *Imperator* as 'the universal consolation of mankind';[31] in the Greek city of Corinth, his victory was granted its own cult; on the far side of the Aegean, in the city of Aphrodisias, a vividly sculptured relief portrayed Britannia as a hapless and bare-breasted beauty, wrestled to the ground by an intimidatingly well-muscled Claudius. The man scorned all his life by his own family as a twitching, dribbling cripple stood, in the imaginings of distant provincials, transfigured into something infinitely more swaggering: a world-subduing sex god.

Naturally, though, it was in Rome that Claudius's victory made the biggest splash. The Senate, alert to what was expected of them, duly voted the returning hero a full complement of honours: a triumph, lots of statues, a particularly flashy arch. His family too basked in his glory. Messalina was granted the same right to zip around Rome in a *carpentum* that Livia had previously enjoyed, while their infant son was awarded the splendid name 'Britannicus'. Here, to a Caesar always painfully conscious that he lacked the blood of Augustus in his veins, were developments ripe with promise. Already, the previous year, he had secured for Livia the divine honours that both Tiberius and Caligula had neglected to award her – thereby ensuring himself a status as the grandson of a god. But it was not enough merely to draw on the past for legitimacy. Claudius knew that he had to look to the future as well. Now, with the gilding of his dependants, he had made a start. He had laid the foundations for a dynasty all of his own.

As a historian, and an attentive student of the past, the Emperor had a well-honed understanding of what it took to be regarded by the Roman people as a great man. His supreme role model, and the man whose name he swore his oaths by, was Augustus – as it was bound to be. Nevertheless, just as Tiberius had done, he thrilled to the tales inherited from Rome's distant past. The virtues and values of the Republic at its most heroic never ceased to move him. Both as an anti-quarian and as a Claudian, he felt profoundly bonded to traditions that had originated centuries before Augustus. To invade Britain, with its chariots, its mud huts and its phantom-haunted groves, had been, for a man like Claudius, to travel back in time to the very beginnings of his city, to that fabulous age when citizens had assembled on the Campus Martius before marching off to war against cities barely a few miles away. Claudius, in token of this, made sure to restage his storm-ing of Camulodunum directly on the Campus, so that for one day at least, amid the marble, the fountains and the softly ornamented arbours, the violent flash of weaponry might be witnessed there once again.

Then, in AD 51, came an even more glittering opportunity for him to pose like a hero from a history book. Caratacus, after a bold and increasingly desperate series of last stands, had finally been taken pris-oner by a rival chieftain, sold to the invaders and brought to Rome in chains. The nobility of his bearing as he was paraded through the streets excited much admiration; and Claudius, with the eyes of the Roman people fixed firmly on him, knew from his reading of history precisely what to do. Long ago, Scipio Africanus had captured an African king, and then, after leading him in his triumph, ordered him spared – a gesture of imperious magnanimity. Claudius, to wild approbation, now did the same. Upon his command, the shackles were struck off the British king. Caratacus, free to wander round Rome and to gaze at the people who had defeated him, played his part in the drama by wondering aloud that they should ever have aspired to conquer his own mean and backward land. The occasion, everyone could agree, had been like an episode from some collection of improving tales. In the Senate, Claudius was fêted with extravagant praise. 'His glory was equal to that of anyone who had ever exhibited a captured king to the Roman people.'[32]

Naturally, Claudius himself was far too shrewd to put much faith in this gushing. He knew that resentment of him in the Senate still ran deep. The Senate, though, was not Rome. Claudius, steeped as he was in the annals of his city, knew this better than anyone. Unlike Tiberius, whose own devotion to the inheritance of the past had only confirmed him in his instinctive disdain for the mob, his nephew looked more fondly on the plebs. He could appreciate, thanks to his years of study, that the many remarkable achievements of the Republic had owed quite as much to the people as to the Senate. This was why, a year before the capture of Caratacus, Claudius had capitalised upon his triumphs in Britain to make a potent gesture. Over the centuries, ever since Romulus had first ploughed the *pomerium*, various conquerors had extended the sacred boundary which marked the limits of Rome – for only those who had added to the possessions of the city were permitted by tradition to do so. This, at any rate, was the claim made by Claudius in a speech to the Senate – and who was there, knowing of his exhaustive antiquarian researches, to dispute his assertion?[33] For eight hundred years, ever since Romulus had bested Remus in their contest to found a city, the Aventine had lain beyond the limits of the *pomerium* – but no longer. On the orders of the Emperor, stone markers began to sprout, girding its slopes at regular intervals and proclaiming the hill no less a part of Rome than the Palatine. Back in the days of Tiberius, the attempt by Sejanus to woo the inhabitants of the Aventine had helped to precipitate his downfall; but now, seventeen years on, Tiberius's nephew held it no shame to court them. Claudius, it went without saying, had not forgotten his history. He knew full well what was commemorated by the shrine to Liber on the slopes of the Aventine: the class war won by the plebs in the first decades of the Republic, and the establishment of their political rights. Each marker stone, stamped as it was with the Emperor's prerogatives, served as a reminder that he held it a privilege to wield the powers of their tribunes. A conqueror, yes — but a friend of the people too.

Nor, in his own opinion, was there anything remotely un-Claudian about this. In contrast to his grim and haughty uncle, Claudius did not interpret the inheritance of his family's past as a licence to scorn the interests of the plebs. Just the opposite. Lavishing funds on structures that could serve the good of every citizen was a prized and venerable tradition among the Roman aristocracy. Why else would Appius Claudius, flush with the booty he had won in the service of the Republic, have spent it on a road? The thought of blowing it on some flashy but useless monument, in the manner of a pharaoh, could not have been more alien to the dictates of his city. Centuries on, it remained a proud boast of the Roman people that their most impressive structures, unlike those of foreign despots, were thoroughly practical in their purpose. 'Far better them than some pointless pyramid.'[34] Claudius, who could still remember what it was to count the coppers, agreed. Earnest as he was in his respect for the traditional values of his fellow citizens, he had no wish to squander money on projects that would fail to serve their long-term interests. Now that the bribes he had lavished on the armed forces in the first days of his supremacy were behind him, it was his aim to order his finances sensibly and spend the proceeds well. Plunder from Britain helped; so too the acumen of Pallas. Widely though the freedman might be detested as a vulgar upstart, there could be no faulting his head for figures. Evidence for this was twofold: that Claudius did not, like his predecessor, end up detested for his exactions; and that he was able, all the same, to invest spectacularly in infrastructure.

Germanicus: Tiberius's nephew and the darling of the Roman people. (Photo: Tom Holland)

Agrippina lands at Brundisium with the ashes of Germanicus, as portrayed by Benjamin West in 1768. (Philadelphia Museum of Art, Pennsylvania, PA, USA / Purchased with the George W. Elkins Fund, 1972 / Bridgeman Images)

Spelunca, where Tiberius
fashioned a mythological
theme park and narrowly
avoided being crushed to death
while dining outside this cave.
(Photo: Tom Holland)

The steep cliffs of Capri
helped to render the island
an impregnable retreat for
Tiberius in his final years, and
foster rumours of unspeakable
depravities. (Photo: Tom Holland)

Caligula addresses the Praetorian Guard. Mention of the Senate, standard on the coins issued by Augustus and Tiberius, is notable by its absence. (© bpk / Münzkabinett, Staatliche Museen zu Berlin)

'Nature produced him, in my opinion, to demonstrate just how far unlimited vice can go when combined with unlimited power.' Caligula, as anatomised by the philosopher Seneca. (Photo: Tom Holland)

A basement chamber on the Palatine which may, just conceivably, mark the very spot where Caligula was assassinated. (Photo: Sophie Hay)

In this 1871 painting by Sir Lawrence Alma-Tadema, Caligula lies dead at the base of a bust of Augustus, while Claudius is discovered cowering behind a curtain. (© Walters Art Museum, Baltimore, USA / Bridgeman Images)

Two captives led into slavery by a soldier. For many slaves, servitude constituted a living death; for a tiny minority, a gateway to power. (Wikimedia)

Claudius, flat-stomached conqueror of the fabulous lands beyond the Ocean, forces himself on a hapless and submissive Britannia. (© Dick Osseman)

The very model of a pious Roman matron: Messalina, with Britannicus on her arm. (De Agostini Picture Library / G. Dagli Orti / Bridgeman Images)

Gardens, in a city as crowded and polluted as Rome, were a supreme mark of status. Ownership, though, was known to spell peril as well as prestige. (Photo: Tom Holland)

The new harbour at Ostia. Begun and largely completed by Claudius, it was completed by Nero – who did not hesitate to take the credit. (© The Trustees of the British Museum)

It's complicated . . . Nero with his mother. (© Dick Osseman)

A ship sinks in the Bay of Naples, as portrayed in the bath-house beside the Marine Gate in Pompeii. (Photo: Tom Holland)

Gelding clamps: applied by slavers to handsome boys, and by devotees of the Syrian Goddess to themselves. (© The Trustees of the British Museum)

The Great Fire of Rome, as imagined by Hubert Robert in the early 1770s.
(Musée des Beaux-Arts Andre Malraux, Le Havre, France / Bridgeman Images)

The bronze colossus commissioned by Nero to stand guard over the entrance to the Golden House. Following his death, the statue would give its name to the great amphitheatre raised on the site of Nero's levelled architectural extravaganza: the Colosseum. (© bpk / Antikensammlung, Staatliche Museen zu Berlin / Johannes Laurentius)

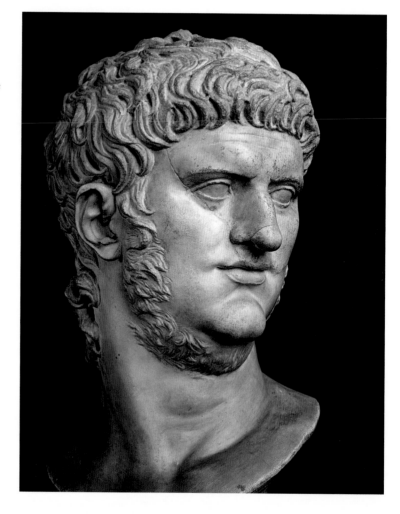

Nero Claudius Caesar Augustus Germanicus. (The Art Archive / Museo Capitolino Rome / Araldo De Luca)

The result, in a city where building sites had invariably been the surest source of employment, was a far more reliable source of income than promiscuous handouts of the kind favoured by Caligula. The prime focus of Claudius's engineering ambitions, though, lay well beyond the bounds of the capital itself. This was not because Rome, in the wake of its renovation by Augustus, had ended up so beautified that it had no need of further improvements. Quite the opposite. It was precisely because multitudes still festered in sprawling, smog-choked slums which seemed, to the rich in their airy villas, 'like the paltry, obscure places into which dung and other refuse are thrown',[35] that Claudius had resolved to sluice out the ordure. As a private scholar, he had been fascinated by hydraulics, writing knowledgeably about floodwaters in Mesopotamia; but naturally, historian that he was, he also looked to precedent to guide him in his actions. Others too in his family, from Caligula all the way back to the inevitable Appius Claudius, had commissioned aqueducts in their time. None, though, had brought to completion anything quite on the scale of the pair built by Claudius. Extending over many miles, crossing deep valleys and running through steep hills, they almost doubled the supply of water flowing into the heart of Rome. Everywhere in the city, even in the meanest quarters, where the snarl of back-alleys was matted with refuse and shit, lead pipes fed gushing fountains and provided a cooling touch of distant mountains. Although it was Caligula who had originally commissioned the two aqueducts, the achievement was very much Claudius's own. On their final approach towards the city, the towering grandeur of the arches as they strode across the fields, never betraying so much as a hint of a limp, was complemented by the distinctive character of their stonework: rugged and determinedly old-fashioned, as though hewn from the bedrock of Rome's past. 'Who can deny that they are wonders without rival in the world?'[36] Embittered senators, perhaps – but not the plebs. They knew they had in Claudius a leader who took seriously his duties to them as their champion.

Not, of course, that these duties were any longer what they had been in the distant age commemorated by the shrine to Liber on the Aventine. The days when the plebs had agitated for political rights were gone, and no one in Rome's slums greatly missed them. Why bother with elections, after all, when they never changed anything? This was why Caligula's restoration to the Roman people of their right to vote had been greeted with such yawns of indifference that it had soon discreetly been abandoned. Realities had changed – and everybody knew it. What mattered most to the poor, in a city so vast that many had never even seen a cornfield, still less harvested one, was to banish the spectre of famine – and only Caesar could guarantee that. In shouldering the responsibility for keeping his fellow citizens fed, Claudius was naturally concerned for his own survival – for he knew that even Augustus, in the dark days of the Triumvirate, had only narrowly avoided being torn to pieces by a starving mob. Yet as with the building of aqueducts, so with famine relief: the obligations laid upon an emperor had a venerable pedigree. The cause of keeping the Roman people fed had been championed by some of their most celebrated tribunes. It was Gaius Gracchus, in 123 BC, who had first legislated to subsidise the price of bread, and Clodius, sixty-five years later, who had introduced a free ration for every citizen. Augustus, although he privately disapproved of the dole, fretting that it would soften the moral fibre of the Roman people and keep them from honest toil, had known better than to abolish it – for of all the many bonds between plebs and First Citizen, there was none more popular with the plebs themselves. They valued it not simply because it kept them fed, but as an expression of their civic status. 'No matter a man's character, whether upstanding or not, he gets his dole by virtue of being a citizen. Good or bad, it makes no difference.'[37] Only in Rome, of all the cities in the world, did Caesar provide a corn dole; and only citizens, among the multitudes who inhabited the capital, were entitled to receive it. Any notion that the poor merited charity simply by virtue of being poor was, of course, too grotesque to contemplate. Everyone knew that people only ever suffered poverty because they deserved it. This was why, for instance, when Judaea was hit by shortages so terrible that it seemed to those suffering them that there must surely be 'a great famine over all the world',[38] Claudius took no steps to intervene – for what responsibility did he have to mere provincials? To fellow citizens, though, he did feel a duty of care – which was why, no sooner had he become emperor, than he was obsessing about the grain supply to Rome.

There had been troubles with it since the summer before his accession, the lingering after-effect of his nephew's most spectacular stunt. Without ships, of course, Caligula would never have been able to ride his horse across the sea; but without ships, there could be no transportation of grain from abroad. Rome, like an immense and insatiable belly, had long exhausted the ability of Italian farmers to keep her fed. This was why, from Egypt to Mauretania, the spreading fields of Africa were devoted to servicing the hunger of the capital. Every summer, massive freight ships would head for the Bay of Naples – for Puteoli, the city to which Caligula had crossed from Baiae, was the nearest port to Rome with docks sufficiently deep to harbour their bulk. Then would come the next stage of the journey: the reloading of the grain, half a million tons of it each year, onto smaller vessels, and the journey up the coast to the mouth of the Tiber.[39] There, surrounded by marshes and salt-flats, stood the port of Ostia; and beyond Ostia, lining the sixteen miles of quays that separated it from Rome, warehouse after giant warehouse, each one with windows so high and slit-like that they seemed a line of fortresses. There was much that could go wrong between Puteoli and the safe arrival of the grain in these depots; and Claudius, once the immediate threat of famine had been lifted, therefore resolved to attempt a solution appropriate to the greatness and ambition of the Roman people. As earnest as he was bold, as obsessed by the minutiae of detail as he was by the sweep of his global role, as ready to supervise plans beside a mudbank as he was to command the hollowing-out of the seabed, he aimed at an achievement no less heroic than the conquest of Britain. When engineers, informed of his intention to construct a deep-sea harbour at Ostia, threw up their hands in horror 'and told him on no account to contemplate it',[40] he ignored their warnings. He was Caesar, after all. If it served the good of the Roman people to refashion the land and sea, then Claudius would do it.

The project was set in train even as he was busy preparing for the invasion of Britain. Claudius himself was a regular visitor to the site. When it was reported one day in Rome that he had been ambushed there and killed, it was widely believed. The plebs, distraught, held the Senate to blame, and only a hurried announcement from the Rostra that the rumour was false and all was well, stopped them from rioting. Although Claudius seemed to many senators a ridiculous and sinister figure, the Roman people knew better; their devotion to him, bred of his palpable concern for their interests, demonstrated that an emperor might be lacking in glamour and still end up taken to their hearts. Caligula, building his private racecourse, had adorned it with an obelisk transported from Egypt; but Claudius, towing the ship that had brought it into the mouth of the Tiber, ordered it sunk, and used as the base for a lighthouse. Breakwaters too were built, and a mole extending the entire way out to the lighthouse, and all the appurtenances of an up-to-date, international port. The achievement, directly on the doorstep of the capital, brought home to the Roman people everything that made the scale and scope of their sway so astonishing: their absolute centrality in the scheme of things; their command of the world's resources; their dominion over the globe. Even the monsters of the deep, like the elephants and serpents stalked by Suetonius Paulinus, could be brought to acknowledge it. When a whale strayed into the half-completed harbour, Claudius summoned a squad of Praetorians to fight it from boats. Understandably, then, he found it hard to keep away from the site. Nowhere else provided him with a more fitting context in which to operate as the kind of ruler he aspired to be. Nowhere else enabled him to feel more exultantly what it was to be a Caesar.

Except that Ostia, by keeping him from Rome, was distracting him from his own household and its functioning. In AD 48, while he was on site at the mouth of the Tiber, Claudius received an unexpected request for an interview. The girl asking it, a concubine of the Emperor's named Calpurnia, was one of his favourite bed partners, and so naturally he granted it. Coming into his presence, so halting and stammering was Calpurnia that she sounded much like Claudius himself; but eventually, after a supreme effort, she managed to reveal what she had come to report.

And as he listened, Claudius Caesar realised to his horror that he had been made to look the fool that his enemies had always alleged him to be.

Deadlier than the Male

The art of attracting an emperor's attention was a fine one.

When Calpurnia came into Claudius's presence, she was accompanied, for good measure, by a second of his concubines. Those who wanted his ear often made sure to exploit his sexual tastes, for everyone knew that he only ever slept with women. Like his concern that people should feel free to break wind at table, or his insistence on adding three new letters to the Latin alphabet, the complete lack of interest he had always shown in forcing himself on male partners marked Claudius out as a true eccentric. Not that people particularly disapproved – for it was the way of the world that different men had different foibles, and just as some might prefer blondes and others brunettes, so were there a few who only ever fucked females, and a few who only ever fucked males.[41] That Galba, for instance, was the mirror image of Claudius – liking as he did 'mature, hard-muscled men'[42] – never did any harm to his standing as a model of martial rectitude. Seasoned soldier that he was, he well knew what it was to seize control, to thrust hard, to take possession.

Which was, it went without saying, the responsibility of every citizen who chose to have sex. Nothing was more shocking to Roman sensibilities than the man who, as Hostius Quadra had so notoriously done, submitted for his own pleasure to being fucked. The sword-stab of a penis was, of course, precisely what the female body had been shaped by the gods to receive; but the male body too was not lacking in orifices. Pay obeisance with the mouth or the anus to another man's cock, and a citizen was doubly shamed. It was not just that he was playing the part of a woman (although that was, of course, bad enough); it was also that he was playing the part of a slave. Just as it was the privilege of the free-born, male and female alike, to have any violation of their bodies condemned as a monstrous crime, so was it the duty of slaves to serve a master's every conceivable sexual need. For some, indeed, it might be their principal responsibility. Pretty boys, long-haired, smooth-shaven and glistening with oils, were must-have accessories at any fashionable *soirée* – and all the more so if twins. One senator, in the time of Augustus, had abandoned sub-tlety altogether, employing waitresses who served entirely in the nude. Every slave knew, as a matter of course, that the threat of rape, like that of corporal punishment, might be realised at any moment.

This did not mean that a master was necessarily incapable of ten-derness: Lucius Vitellius, for instance, ended up so besotted with one of his slavegirls that not only did he free her, but he took to mixing up her spit with honey and using it as a throat medicine. Such cases, though, were the exception that proved the rule. In general, the right of a master to glut his sexual appetites on a slave, rather as he might blow his nose or use a latrine, was taken for granted. It was a perk of ownership, plain and simple. 'No sense of shame is permitted a slave.'[43]

Except that freedom itself, in a city where even senators had been subjected to the rack and whip, was no longer all it had been. The implications, even for the grandest, were unsettling in the extreme. In AD 47, a year before Calpurnia came calling on Claudius at Ostia, one of the Senate's most flamboyant and charismatic figures had been destroyed. Valerius Asiaticus, charged with a variety of crimes, had been arrested in the pleasure resort of Baiae and hauled back to Rome in chains. His prosecutor had been an old associate of Germanicus's, a man as opportunistic as he was remorseless, by the name of Publius Suillius Rufus. His talent, given a victim, was for sinking his jaws in deep – and sure enough, at a private trial attended by both Claudius and Lucius Vitellius, Suillius had done just that. Rounding off the various charges, he had accused Asiaticus, for good measure, of the very ultimate in deviancy: of being 'soft and giving, like a woman'.[44] The prisoner, silent until then, had found this particular slander too much. 'Ask your sons, Suillius,' he had yelled. 'They will confirm that I am all man.' Desperate, aggressive banter – but also something more. The scorning of Suillius, a father to sons used by Asiaticus as women, had been the scorning too of an order so rotten that it had given power to such a man. Later, once Asiaticus had been sentenced to death, but permitted, on the recommendation of Lucius Vitellius, to choose how he died, he had made his contempt for Claudius's regime even more explicit. He would rather, he had declared, have perished at the hands of Tiberius or Caligula than on the say-so of the smooth-tongued Vitellius – whose mouth was rancid from his addiction to lapping at genitals. And then, having made sure that the flames of his pyre would do no damage to the trees of his beloved garden, Asiaticus had slit his wrists.

Defiant assertion of his own masculinity and suicide: no other means had been available to him, in the final reckoning, of maintaining his dignity as a citizen. That Claudius, paranoid and insecure, had feared to let him live was clear enough; but that was hardly the whole story. Senators, convinced as they were that the Emperor was mentally deficient, saw in Asiaticus's fate confirmation of all their darkest suspicions: that he was the gullible plaything of perverts, and even worse. 'He, more conspicuously than any of his peers, was ruled by slaves – and by women.'[45] Certainly, when it came to identifying the person ultimately responsible for the downfall of Asiaticus, the consensus was clear. Messalina had envied him his gardens and wanted them for herself. Worse: he had died to satisfy her passion for Mnester, former paramour of Caligula and Rome's most famous actor, who was rumoured to have been conducting affairs with both Messalina herself and an equally high-ranking beauty named Poppaea Sabina. The prosecution of Asiaticus had enabled two birds to be killed with one stone: for among the charges levelled against him had been one of adultery with Poppaea. Messalina, far from keeping discreetly to the sidelines, had been present at his secret trial; and she had deployed her agents, even as Asiaticus was being condemned, to bully her rival into suicide. Nothing, in short, could possibly have been more demeaning or grotesquely sordid. One of the most eminent senators in Rome, a man who had once aspired to rule the world, had been sacrificed upon the altar of a woman's jealousy.

'How shaming it is to be submissive to a girl.'[46] Ovid's maxim was one that Roman moralists had always taken for granted. Whether on the battlefield or in the bedroom, so clearly had men been intended by the gods to hold the whip-hand that very few of them ever thought to question it. 'An unhappy state indeed it would be which saw women usurp masculine prerogatives – be it the Senate, the army or the magistracies!'[47] The very prospect was incredible. Nevertheless, in a city where a feminine tiff over an actor appeared to have ended up destroying a two-times consul, it was clear that something had gone badly wrong. That women of wealth and breeding might exploit their influence on behalf of their menfolk was one thing; that they should openly flaunt it quite another. No matter the rumours whispered of Livia, she had always made a point, before ascending into the heavens and taking her place beside Augustus on his celestial throne, of operating from the shadows. Certainly, she had never thought to play her husband for a fool. That, though, it seemed – if the increasingly feverish swirlings of gossip were to be trusted – was precisely what Messalina was doing. A few days after the suicide of Poppaea Sabina, Claudius had invited her husband to supper and asked him where his wife was. Told that she was dead, he had simply looked bemused. Messalina, it seemed to those who despised the Emperor, had him wrapped around her finger. As gullible as he was besotted, he had delivered the great and the good into her hands. Consuls, a Praetorian prefect, the granddaughter of Tiberius: all had been eliminated as a result of her manoeuvrings. Those who prized their skins made sure to crawl to her. Lucius Vitellius, that veteran trimmer, had even begged permission to take off her shoes, 'and once he had removed her right slipper, he slipped it between his toga and tunic, carrying it round with him the whole time, and every so often kissing it'.[48] Not merely degrading, it was emasculating in the extreme.

And perhaps, for that very reason, truth be told, just a bit erotic. Ovid, had he lived to see the former governor of Syria raining kisses on a woman's slipper, would not have been unduly surprised. He had always enjoyed exploring the paradoxes that hedged propriety about.

> *Don't be ashamed (though shameful it is – which is why it's fun)*
> *To hold a mirror in your hand as though you were a slave.*[49]

As with adultery, so with role reversal: the greater the taboo, the more of a thrill it might be to break it. The pressure on a male always to take the lead, always to exact submission, served to close off whole dimensions of pleasure. That it was the responsibility of a respectable matron, while being fucked, to lie back passively and leave the action to her partner, was taken for granted by moralists; but that did not prevent some women, greatly daring, from spicing things up during sex by actually moving – almost as though they themselves were the males. Shocking, yes, and threatening to the masculinity of any self-respecting citizen, to be sure; but there were, for the man who found his partner bucking her thighs in time to his thrustings, or grinding her buttocks, or sucking and licking his cock, undeniable compensations. That a woman might be so sexually aggressive as to play the role of a man was certainly, for any self-respecting citizen, a most unsettling possibility; but there was rarely anything so deviant that some would not find it exciting. A woman such as Messalina was presumed to be, predatory in her ambitions and demonic in her taste for blood, was a figure fit to stalk fantasies as well as fears. Young, beautiful and dangerous, she was the very stuff of pornography.

There had always been something peculiarly delicious about the idea of the house of Caesar as a brothel. Tiberius, during his retirement on Capri, and Caligula, on the Palatine itself, had both made salacious play with it; but, as ever in a city as obsessed with rumour as Rome, it was gossip that gave it legs. Assiduous promotion of the August Family as the embodiment of traditional values had, as its dark side, the kind of stories told about Augustus's daughter: of how, 'wearying of adultery, she had turned to prostitution',[50] and ended up hawking her favours from the Rostra. Julia, though, had been loved by the Roman people; and so the stories told of her, scandalous though they were, had not been without a certain affection. Messalina, vindictive and murderous, seemed an altogether more terrifying figure. Her clitoris, it was darkly whispered, was of such monstrous size as to constitute 'a raging hard-on'.[51] With her hair concealed beneath a blonde wig and her nipples painted gold, she was said to work shifts in a low-rent brothel; to host parties on the Palatine at which the husbands of prominent women would watch on as they were cuckolded; to have challenged one of Rome's most experienced prostitutes to an all-day sexathon, and won. Such stories, though originally bred of Messalina's readiness to sniff out her opponents and destroy them, increasingly served to cast her as the opposite of calculating. A woman who, in terms of her talent for eliminating her enemies, ranked closer to a Sejanus than a Julia, she had come to be seen by the Roman people as a very different order of creature: carnivorous, irresponsible and heedless of every risk.

Which left her exposed. When Calpurnia and her fellow concubine arrived in Ostia and came into the presence of their master, their role was much like the one that Pallas, by taking Antonia's letter to Capri, had played in the ruin of Sejanus. Like Tiberius, Claudius had been more than happy to leave his dirty work to another, sanctioning his wife's manoeuvrings against men like Asiaticus while simultaneously playing up to his reputation for absent-mindedness. The comparison, though, did not end there. Just as Tiberius, reading Antonia's letter, had realised with an abrupt shock that he might be in mortal danger from a helpmate he had always trusted, so Claudius now suffered a similar moment of vertigo. Messalina, Calpurnia reported, was engaged in overt treachery. Astonishingly, she had taken as a lover the most handsome man in Rome, a consul-designate by the name of Gaius Silius – and actually married him. 'The people, the Senate, the Praetorians: all have witnessed the wedding!'[52] Claudius, whose first instinct when taken by surprise was invariably to panic, promptly went into a meltdown. It was bad enough that she had impugned his masculinity, his ability to maintain order in his own household, and, by extension, his competence as emperor; but there was worse. By marrying Silius, and permitting him to take possession of what was properly Caesar's, she appeared to be signalling a coup. 'Am I still in power,' Claudius kept wailing, 'or has Silius taken over?'[53]

Bundled into a carriage by his two most trusted senatorial aides, Vitellius and Caecina Largus, he remained in a state of shock as together they hurried back to Rome. When Messalina, riding out to meet him, vainly attempted to force an interview, he sat in silence; nor did the appearance on the roadside of their two children, seven-year-old Britannicus and his elder sister, Octavia, crack the frozen quality of his expression. Even when Claudius arrived in the Praetorian camp and addressed the assembled soldiers, he could barely bring himself to speak. 'No matter how justified his outrage, he was hobbled by shame.'[54]

Actions, though, spoke louder than words. Claudius's decision to take shelter in the Praetorian camp demonstrated both the scale of his alarm and his resolve to crush any hint of sedition. Silius and various of his high-born associates had already been rounded up. Hauled before the Praetorians, they were dispatched with brisk efficiency. Mnester too, despite histrionic appeals for mercy, was among those decapitated: for clearly, despite Claudius's initial instinct to spare him, it was out of the question to pardon a mere actor when so many senators and equestrians had already been put to death. Only the odd plea for mercy was granted. When a son of Suillius Rufus, demonstrating the truth of Valerius's accusations against him, declared that he could not possibly have committed adultery with Messalina because it was his habit, whenever having sex, 'to play the role of a woman',[55] he was dismissively sent on his way. Otherwise, though, the bloodbath was total. Claudius might be panicky, and reluctant under normal circumstances to indulge in repression; but he could always be relied upon to take no prisoners when faced by a crisis.

Meanwhile, only his wife remained on the loose. Frantic with misery, Messalina had taken shelter in the gardens purloined from Asiaticus just the previous year. There, sobbing among the flowerbeds, she was watched over by her mother, Domitia Lepida, who sought to comfort her daughter, in the noblest tradition of Roman parenthood, by urging her to prepare for an honourable death. In the event, though, terror won out over courage. When a squad of soldiers arrived in the gardens, Messalina could not bring herself to slit her own throat. Instead, it was left to a soldier to run her through. Her corpse was then dumped at her mother's feet. Her legacy was not only a name that would long serve the Roman people as a byword for nymphomania, but a sense of palpable bewilderment. Something about the episode struck many as not quite right. When people sought to explain what could possibly have persuaded Messalina, in a city as addicted to gossip as Rome, to imagine that she could get away with marriage to Silius, many shrugged their shoulders and confessed themselves bewildered. Had she really been swept to her doom by sheer lust? Or had Claudius been right to suspect a plot? But if a plot, then why had Messalina been willing to stake the prospects of her children on a conspiracy so self-evidently incompetent and half-baked? None of it quite made sense.

A familiar frustration, of course. The secrets of Caesar's household were invariably impenetrable to outsiders. The weakness of Claudius's position, which saw him as reliant upon freedmen as senators, had only made the situation worse. Conflicts on the Palatine, where rival factions fought in its subterranean depths for influence, only rarely disturbed the surface. Messalina herself, far from scorning to engage in the power struggles of her husband's freedmen, was rumoured to have slept with one of them, and then – once he had outlived his usefulness – to have had him put to death. True or not, it was certain that by the time of her downfall she had made enemies of Narcissus, Callistus and Pallas; and that the fingerprints of Narcissus, in particular, were all over her ruin. It was he who had sent the two concubines to their master in Ostia; who had assured Claudius of the truth of their story, when both Vitellius and Caecina had seemed reluctant to confirm it; who had shouted down Messalina when she sought an interview with her husband. Astonishingly, for the duration of the crisis, he had even managed to secure command of the Praetorians – thereby ensuring that those put to death were eliminated directly on his orders. By the time the carnage was done and all the blood mopped up, anyone in a position to contradict the story of Messalina's marriage to Silius had been silenced for good.

Whether it had truly happened, or whether Messalina had been the victim of a subtly crafted fiction, no one would ever know. Her statues were removed from their plinths, her name from every inscription. Narcissus, meanwhile, long obliged by his status as a freed-man to operate without official recognition, was now graced by his master with a fleeting but authentic taste of the limelight. By formal decree of the Senate, and as a mark of gratitude for his actions in pre-serving the Roman state, he was granted an honorary magistracy. It was, for a one-time slave, an unprecedented mark of favour. *Io Saturnalia* indeed.

Yet it was the nature of Caesar's household that its rivalries were like the hydra. Slice off one head and another would quickly sprout. The success of Narcissus in dispatching Messalina, and the predom-inance that it had brought him in the back-rooms of the Palatine, itself disturbed the balance of power that had long prevailed among Claudius's three most trusted freedmen. Callistus and Pallas remained as clear-sighted about the workings of their master's court as they had ever been. Indeed, when Callistus died soon after the great *dégringolade* of 48, it served perhaps as the ultimate measure of his influence: for he was one of the few men at the heart of power to enjoy a natural death. Pallas too, while having little choice in the short term but to swallow Narcissus's pre-eminence, had no intention of ceding it permanently. He knew his master well. More clearly than his rival, he could appreciate the scale of the humiliation that had been visited on Claudius, and the inevitable insecurities that it had served to reawaken. Messalina had been a mother as well as a wife; and her downfall had wreaked terrible damage on her children's prospects. How, after the scandal visited on his family, was Claudius to promote it as a model of Roman virtue now? As things stood, his task had been rendered impossible; and for as long as that remained the case, he was bound to feel that his legitimacy as ruler of the world stood in question. The old problem, that Claudius was no more descended from Augustus than any number of other ambitious senators, had abruptly come back into focus. There was, though, an obvious solution to hand. Pallas, clearer-sighted than Narcissus, knew that his master would have little alternative but to adopt it.[56]

During the years of Messalina's primacy, Agrippina had made sure to keep her head down. Her son had the blood of Germanicus as well as of Augustus flowing in his veins; and she herself, for good measure, was famously beautiful. The fate of her younger sister, exiled and eliminated after provoking Messalina's jealousy, had served Agrippina as a standing admonition; and so, rather than engage in court intrigue, she had devoted her energies to repairing her finances. Marriage to a fabulously wealthy senator had helped, as had his death a short while afterwards. Claudius, frantic for a way to burnish his own legitimacy after the calamity of Messalina's downfall, did not have far to look. That Agrippina was his own niece was indisputably a problem: so revolted by incest were the Roman people that it ranked alongside treason as one of only two charges that admitted the evidence of tortured slaves. Nevertheless, far from attempting to veil it, or having Agrippina adopted first into another family, as he might otherwise have done, Claudius was obliged to trumpet that he was marrying his own 'nursling'[57] – for it was precisely his niece's pedigree that rendered her so invaluable to him. Smooth as ever, it was Vitellius who served as fixer. Standing up before the Senate, he played it with his customary skill. After praising Claudius, with a perfectly straight face, as a model of sobriety, he urged a change to the law that forbade an uncle to marry his niece – for the good of Caesar himself, of Rome and of the world. 'For surely it was by the foresight of the gods themselves that our Princeps – who never sleeps with a wife who is not his own – has been provided with such a widow!'[58] Senators erupted in wild applause; out in the Forum, a carefully assembled crowd joined in with no less ecstatic cheering of their own. The Senate and the Roman people were united as one. Who, then, was Claudius to resist their demands?

Many, of course, away from the various stage-managed shows of enthusiasm, were shocked by what they regarded as a legal sleight of hand, and feared that no good could possibly come from such 'an illegal and deplorable union'.[59] Agrippina herself, though, was not among them. Marriage to the aged and dribblesome Claudius, no matter how physically unsatisfying it might be, marked as triumphant a return to the centre of power as her original fall from it had been precipitous. Naturally, a woman willing to prostitute herself to her own uncle could hardly expect to be spared the mockery of the Roman people; but their abuse, even so, was leavened with a certain grudging respect. Unlike the Emperor's previous wife, Agrippina was not diagnosed with nymphomania. 'In her private doings she was always most respectable – except when she had a sniff of power.'[60] Just as Augustus was said only ever to have committed adultery in order to spy on a woman's husband, so were Agrippina's supposed infidelities attributed to her implacable determination to reach the top. Such ambition, shocking and unnatural though it obviously was in a woman, marked her out as an indisputable heavyweight. 'Her style of dominance was not just abrasive – it was essentially masculine as well.'[61]

Forebodings that the world had been delivered up to the rule of a mistress as imperious as she was determined were only strengthened the following year. Few doubted the intensity of Agrippina's hopes for her son; and sure enough, it came as no great surprise when, in AD 50,

337

thirteen-year-old Domitius was formally adopted by his stepfather as a Claudian. No longer Lucius Domitius Ahenobarbus, the boy could now boast the altogether more impressive name of Nero Claudius Caesar Drusus Germanicus. Portraits of young Nero, round-faced and still with a hint of baby fat, immediately began to proliferate. It was his mother, though, whose radiance was truly coming to fill the world. Honours that not even Livia had enjoyed were lavished on her by her husband. For the first time, an emperor permitted his wife to be graced with the awesome title of 'Augusta' while he was still alive; to be shown in sculptures wearing the crescent-shaped diadem of a goddess; to appear with him on his coins. These, prior to the downfall of Messalina, had been minted on their reverse side with images designed to proclaim Claudius's many triumphs; but no longer. Now, where previously there had been soldiers, and triumphal arches, and self-aggrandising slogans, there gleamed only the heads of Agrippina and Nero. The sheer scale of the crisis required nothing less. The grievous wound inflicted on the August Family could not possibly be allowed to suppurate. Its future had to be presented, at all costs, as stable.

Naturally, those predisposed to see Claudius as a pliable dolt, the plaything of women and slaves, were only confirmed by this in their contempt for him. The Emperor himself, as he had done throughout his life, shrugged it all aside. At stake, so he believed, was not merely his own survival but the long-term security of the Roman people. Claudius had appreciated from an early age the terrible consequences of civil war. As a young man, embarking on a history of Augustus's rise to power, he had been roundly scolded by Livia and his mother, and persuaded to abandon it. 'No one,' they had told him, 'could ever give an accurate or frank account of what had really happened.'[62] Decades on, the menace of what might happen were he to slip, to squander the legacy of Augustus, to betray the inheritance of a peace that had lasted now for decades, still haunted Claudius. Schooled as he was in the history of the Republic at its flintiest and most austere, he understood that the ideal of citizenship might sometimes demand sacrifice. With Messalina consigned to oblivion and Britannicus still only nine years old, he could not rely on his own son to take the helm of the world. Claudius was old, and in declining health: it was too dangerous to leave Nero untutored in the demands of ruling Rome. Certainly, that winter, there were reminders everywhere of how narrow was the thread by which Caesar's fortunes might hang. Ominous-looking birds were seen flocking above the Capitol. Earthquakes shook the city. Meanwhile, in the warehouses along the Tiber, reserves of grain were running low. A hungry mob, cornering Claudius in the Forum, would have torn him to pieces had he not been rescued by a detachment of troops. It was a salutary lesson. The love of the people, the steel of the Praetorians: these were things that an emperor had to hug close to his chest.

As soon as he could, then, Claudius set about providing his prospective heir with both. The perfect opportunity was not long in coming. On Nero's fifteenth birthday, one year ahead of schedule, he was permitted to celebrate his coming-of-age. First, he lavished donatives on both the Roman people and the Praetorians; then he led the Praetorians on parade. Shortly afterwards, for good measure, he made his maiden speech in the Senate. Meanwhile, as Nero was busy cutting a dash in his gleaming new toga, or presiding over the Circus arrayed in best triumphal regalia, Britannicus was left to mope around wearing the distinctive striped toga of a child. When he briefly sought to fight back against his stepbrother's grandstanding by calling him 'Domitius', Agrippina went straight to Claudius and had the boy's teachers replaced with nominees of her own. Britannicus's principal tutor was put to death on a charge of plotting against Nero. The Augusta had form when it came to executing manoeuvres of this kind. She did not care to see anyone occupy a significant post unless he owed it to her. This was why, soon after her marriage to Claudius, she had persuaded him to appoint to the command of the Praetorians a man whose record of service to her family was as impeccable as his lack of pedigree was glaring. That Sextus Afranius Burrus was a distinguished officer, and even had a mutilated hand to prove it, did not alter the fact that he was irredeemably provincial – 'and as such could hardly help but be aware who was responsible for his promotion'.[63]

Below the surface waters of Caesar's household, where monsters of the deep fed on those weaker than themselves and yet were always hungry, Agrippina had shown herself as predacious as anyone. 'It is not arms which constitute the surest safeguard of power, but the ability to bestow favours.'[64] So Seneca, with the perspective provided by distance, had observed from his exile on Corsica. Agrippina, content to demonstrate the truth of his *aperçu*, had arranged, following her marriage to Claudius, for his recall to the capital. Her son needed a tutor – and who better than Rome's foremost intellectual? Seneca, naturally, had leapt at the chance. The chance to educate a future ruler of the world, as Aristotle had taught Alexander the Great, was every philosopher's dream. Not that Agrippina wanted her son taught anything as impractical as philosophy: rather, it was Seneca's talent for giving a speech that she had hired. Sure enough, when Nero stepped onto the floor of the Senate House, it was evident that his tutor had done his work. As senators grown lined and craggy in the service of Rome listened to the sixteen-year-old give them the benefit of his views on foreign affairs, they could detect no sign of nerves. Unlike Claudius himself, he appeared to the manner born. Fluent, strapping and intimidatingly bumptious, Nero could hardly help but present a contrast to the aged Emperor. His very youth, an inevitable cause of perturbation in a Senate House still scarred by its memories of Caligula, seemed transformed almost into a source of strength.

Nero was not the only one entering into manhood. In AD 53, in a seeming confirmation of his status as favoured heir, he married Octavia, Claudius's daughter by Messalina. There was, though, a second message broadcast by the marriage. Britannicus was only a year younger than his sister, and it served as a reminder to the Roman people that he too was on the verge of leaving childish things behind. Whether in the Senate, the Praetorian camp or the bars and street-markets of the city, he still had backers. In the household of Caesar too. Pallas, whose early support of Agrippina had seen him rewarded with public honours fit to put even those granted to Narcissus in the shade, was yet to establish total supremacy. Taking Britannicus by his hands, Narcissus would hug him and urge the boy to grow up fast. Claudius too, embracing his son, promised him, if he came of age, 'an account of all that he had done'.[65] By AD 54, when Britannicus turned fourteen, such a moment was plainly not far off. Nero had been arrayed in the toga of a man for the first time when he was only fifteen: why not the younger sibling too? Claudius began to talk openly of how much he was looking forward to the ceremony. Give it another year, and he would have double the number of candidates to succeed him – and then, of course, Nero's future might no longer look so assured.

It was certainly hard to doubt that some great perturbation was brewing. Blood rained from the sky; the Praetorian eagles were struck by lightning; a pig was born with the talons of a hawk. Meanwhile, in the law courts, Britannicus's grandmother, Domitia Lepida, was arraigned on a number of capital charges. Few doubted who lay behind the prosecution, for among the accusations was that she had deployed sorcery against the Emperor's wife. Nero – on his mother's instructions, it was said – appeared as a witness for the prosecution. Domitia Lepida, inevitably, was sentenced to death. Then, in October, the most formidable of Agrippina's adversaries departed Rome. Narcissus, as befitted the vastly wealthy man that he had become, suffered from gout; and for such an ailment there was no surer remedy than to take the waters in Campania. Naturally, he had no intention of risking a lengthy holiday. He could not afford to be away from the capital for long. But just a short break – what could possibly go wrong?

The answer came at dawn on 13 October – just three months before Britannicus was due to come of age. Claudius, it was reported, had been taken dangerously ill. The Senate was convened. Consuls and priests alike offered up prayers for Caesar's recovery. Meanwhile, on the Palatine, all the gates stood barred, while squads of soldiers blocked off the various approaches. Even so, there remained scope for optimism. Throughout the morning, reassuring bulletins were released, and various comic actors could be seen heading into Caesar's house – for Claudius, it was said, as he lay on his sickbed, had asked to be entertained. Then abruptly, at midday, the gates were flung wide open. Out came Nero, accompanied by Burrus, the new prefect of the Praetorians. A cheer was raised by the men standing guard; Nero was ushered into a litter; he and an escort of soldiers then headed straight for the Praetorian camp. Here, he announced to the listening men the news that Claudius was dead – before lavishing on them yet another eye-watering bonus. Then to the Senate House. Its members knew the role expected of them. All the various powers and honours possessed by his predecessor were bestowed with universal acclaim upon Nero. There was only one that the seventeen-year-old new Caesar, with becoming modesty, turned down: that of 'Father of his Country'. Plump, smooth-cheeked and with the rosebud lips of a girl, Nero knew better than to court needless ridicule. Then, by winning for his adoptive father divine honours, he secured for himself one final, clinching title: 'Son of a God'.

And Claudius? What had happened to him, that he had departed the Palatine so abruptly for the golden throne of an immortal? Rome had been stalked by fever all that year, and Claudius, sickly since birth, was sixty-three years old: it was hardly implausible that he might have died of natural causes. Inevitably, though, in a city ever alert to the faintest whisperings of criminality, the circumstances of his death raised eyebrows. When Nero, with a casual quip, declared 'mushrooms to be the food of the gods, since it was by means of a mushroom that Claudius has become a god',[66] it seemed to many that he was dropping a hint as to what had actually happened. Various accounts of the murder were given: that Agrippina had commissioned a notorious poisoner to lace a dish of mushrooms; that she had done the deed herself; that she had persuaded her husband's physician to stick a venom-drenched feather down his throat. No one could know for certain; everyone suspected the worst.

As for Nero, whether his mother had played foully on his behalf or not, he knew what he owed her. That evening, when asked for the first time as Caesar to give the Praetorians the watchword, he did not hesitate. The phrase he chose was an unstinting acknowledgement of his debt: 'Best of Mothers.'[67]

7

WHAT AN ARTIST

Mamma Mia

No member of the August Family had ever swung between such extremes of calamity and triumph as Agrippina. Alone among the numerous descendants of Augustus sentenced to exile, she had clawed her way back from ruin. She could never forget what it was to fail. For a year and more, the island to which she had been dispatched by her vengeful brother had mocked her with a barren parody of greatness. To the Roman elite, nothing screamed success quite like a sprawling estate with water features; and this, in her exile, Agrippina had been granted. Her prison had boasted much that would not have disgraced a villa on the Bay of Naples: artificial fishponds, fresh shell-fish and — of course — a sea view. All these various luxuries, though, had only emphasised the misery of exile. Isolation corroded every delight. It was ambience as well as setting that made for pleasure. Even Baiae, despite its exquisite beauties, would have counted for little without the strains of gossip and music that were forever drifting on its perfumed breezes.

Without its marinas too. The Bay of Naples, churned though its shipping lanes were by hulking freighters bound for Puteoli, and by the galleys of Caesar's fleet, was far from devoted to the demands of trade and defence. To drift past the various piers and grottoes that adorned the shoreline, escaping the heat of summer on the cool and crystalline waters of the bay, had long been a particular delight of the Roman elite. Caligula, predictably, had taken it to a new level of excess. Even as his sisters were rotting on their prison islands, he had cruised the coast of Campania in specially commissioned galleys, complete with baths, fluted pillars and vines. Nothing quite so exclusive as a palace that could float. Indeed, so close was the association in the minds of the Roman super-rich between pleasure and water, and between luxury and boats, that the bays of Campania were hardly sufficient to meet it. Any stretch of water was a potential source of enchantment. Caligula, when not in the mood to head for Baiae, had been alert to alternative options. Some twenty miles south of Rome, for instance, set among a ridge of hills above the Appian Way, stood the peaceful, grove-fringed lake of Nemi. Here, eager to sample its delights in style, Agrippina's brother had ordered the construction of a mammoth houseboat.* No expense had been spared – that, of course, went without saying. Mosaics, marble inlay, gilded roof tiles: Caligula's pleasure barge boasted them all. Even the lead pipes had been carefully stamped with his name. To Agrippina, long since redeemed from her exile, the boat served as a reminder of everything that had been denied her during her term of disgrace. That the same vessel commissioned by the brother who had incarcerated her was now the property of her son could hardly help but bring a certain smile to the Augusta's face.

Or perhaps not. Sumptuous though the boat was, and stunning its setting, on a lake so perfectly circular and glass-like that it was known

---

* Two ships were built on Caligula's orders at Lake Nemi: the first seems to have been a floating palace, the second a floating temple. They were still afloat in Nero's lifetime, but were then dispatched to the bed of the lake, where they remained for almost two thousand years. Recovered in 1929, they were destroyed in 1944 – though whether by American artillery fire, German arson or the cooking fires of Italian refugees has never been conclusively settled.

as the Mirror of the Moon, there was, for anyone as alert to the demands of power as Agrippina, a hint of the sinister about Nemi. This was not at first apparent. Like the Bay of Naples, the slopes of the lake appeared monuments to suburban chic. Julius Caesar himself had once built a villa there; Augustus's mother had come from the nearby town. Yet just as in Rome, amid the concrete and the marble of the Palatine, there remained memorials to the distant age of Romulus, so at Nemi, casting a chill over the scenes of luxury, there flickered the shadows of something very ancient indeed. Aeneas was not the only hero to have travelled to Italy in the wake of Troy's fall. In Greece, Agamemnon, the king who had served as commander-in-chief of the returning armies, had been murdered by his queen, Clytaemnestra; and she in turn, on the command of the gods, had been killed by their son, a young man named Orestes. Fearsome demons known as the Furies, armed with whips and torches of fire, had then pursued him for the monstrous crime of matricide. Orestes, in the course of his wanderings, had headed west, bringing with him a statue of Apollo's twin, the virgin huntress Diana; and at Nemi, in a grove above the lake, he had established a shrine to the goddess. From then on, in memory of the founder of the cult, its priest had always been a fugitive: an escaped slave who, after breaking into the sanctuary, had challenged the incumbent and succeeded in slaying him. A fatal victory – for every priest had to live with the knowledge that the time would come when he in turn would perish at the hands of his successor. For a thousand years and more, murder had followed murder in an endless cycle. Caligula, arriving at the shrine, and learning that the priest had been *in situ* for years, had amused himself by sponsoring a younger, fitter contender; but the last laugh had been on him. No less than the sanctuary at Nemi, the household of Caesar was a potential killing zone, where death might come at any minute to those who failed to watch their backs. Like the priest of Diana, Caligula had ended up sprawled in a puddle of blood – and Agrippina, whose own return from exile would never have happened without his elimination, had no intention of suffering his fate.

Certainly, she had good cause to keep the goddess of Nemi in mind. Already, on her marriage to Claudius, she had sought to expiate the offence of incest by sponsoring propitiatory rites with her husband in the sacred grove. Then, a few months later, Claudius had made a formal dedication to Diana: a request to the goddess that she keep both him and Agrippina safe, and Nero and Britannicus too. It had not been enough. The goddess had abandoned Claudius. Lamps still blazed in the shrine that he had commissioned at Nemi; but now he was dead, and it was widely rumoured that his wife had been responsible. True or not, Agrippina knew better than to rely for her own security on lighting candles to Diana. The lesson of the sanctuary at Nemi had not been lost on her. The goddess favoured those who made their own luck. So it was, with Claudius barely dead, that Agrippina had dispatched orders to her agents in Asia, instructing them to poison the province's governor – who, like her son, happened to be a great-great-grandson of Augustus. Such, at any rate, was the assumption in Rome, when the news arrived there of the wretched man's death. It was a perfectly reasonable one to make. The fate of Narcissus, arrested as he hurried back from Campania, had left no one in any doubt that Agrippina was clearing the decks. The suicide in custody of Claudius's favourite freedman had set the seal on her control of the Palatine. With Pallas now even more securely in charge of its finances than he had been before, Burrus in command of the Praetorians, and Seneca on hand to orchestrate dealings in the Senate, she could boast placemen everywhere. When senators voted her the Priesthood of the Deified Claudius, and double the number of lictors granted to Livia in her widowhood, it set the seal on an astonishing comeback. 'She dared to strive after the rule of the sacred world.'[1] Never before had the Roman people been able to say that of one of their women.

Yet the summit attained by Agrippina was a precarious one. Her very feat of scaling it could hardly help but inspire in most men bitter mistrust. Senators, summoned to meet on the Palatine, deeply resented what all of them knew was her brooding presence behind a

curtain, listening in on their every word. Seneca too, despite everything that he owed her, was profoundly unsettled by her pretensions.
Daughter of Germanicus that she was, Agrippina saw no reason why
she should not stamp her authority as firmly upon the frontiers as
upon domestic affairs. She certainly had form when it came to setting
her mark on military matters. Back when the chained Caratacus was
led before Claudius, there had been Agrippina as well, sitting directly
beside her husband, enthroned beneath the eagles – 'an unprecedented thing'.[2] Her abiding interest in Germany, where her father had
performed such heroic deeds and she herself had lived as a child, had
seen the capital of the Rhine renamed after her, so that the Altar of
the Ubians had become *Colonia Agrippinensis* – the future Cologne. Now,
though, in the first months of her son's reign, attention was focused
not on the northern frontier, but on Armenia, where the Parthians
were busy attempting to replace a Roman-backed king with a puppet
of their own – a crisis which Agrippina was resolved to take the lead
in handling. When an Armenian embassy arrived in Rome, she took
for granted that she should be seated beside her son to receive them.
Seneca, an inveterate civilian, but whose scholarly temperament and
lifelong respiratory problems had only heightened his respect for the
martial traditions of the Roman people, was appalled. Determined
that at least some bounds of propriety be respected, he instructed
Nero to rise from his seat, step down to meet his mother and take her
to one side. Scandal was duly averted.

'It was I who made you emperor.'[3] So Agrippina was forever
reminding her son. Nero, barely sixteen, and schooled as only a
Roman child could be in the habit of deference to his parent, had little
choice but to listen. Various innovations proclaimed as much to the
Roman people. On Nero's coins, his profile and Agrippina's, of matching size, were shown facing one another, as though in celebration of
their partnership; on his inscriptions, he made sure to include the line
of descent from his mother as well as his father. Nevertheless, there
had to be limits. He was ruler of the world, after all. He could not
afford to appear henpecked by his mother. Instead, shrewd enough

to recognise just what a *consigliere* he had in Seneca, Nero was content, even now that he was Caesar, to remain the student of his old tutor. Advised to meet the crisis in Armenia with iron-fisted determination, he boosted troop numbers along the eastern front and dispatched a veteran of the German frontier to take command of the situation – with the result that, soon enough, the Parthians were scrabbling to sue for terms. Meanwhile, back in Rome, Nero continued to pose with great aplomb as the model of a beneficent ruler. Graciously, he refused an offer from the Senate to erect statues of him fashioned out of gold and silver. He declared an end to the treason trials that had so stained the reputation of Claudius – and kept his word, what was more. On one occasion, brought a death warrant to sign, he sighed, then lamented with great theatricality that he had ever learned to write. 'No chance did he miss, in short, to parade his generosity, his mercy and his graciousness.'[4]

It was the nature of the factions lurking beneath the surface of Caesar's household always to seek out fresh battlefields. Now, in the struggle to market the young emperor, Agrippina and Seneca had found the perfect focus for their growing rivalry. Two potent but contradictory versions of Nero's image were being sold to the world: as the dutiful son of the Augusta, the daughter of Germanicus, without whom he would have been nothing; and as the father of his people, wise beyond his years, 'always forbearing in the care of his children'.[5] Nero himself, like a doll, found himself forever being draped in robes that others had chosen for him. Yet it was not easy to kick against this indignity. Agrippina had allies everywhere, and the burnishing that her incomparable ancestry gave to Nero's legitimacy was beyond price. Seneca, meanwhile, learned like no one else in the traditions prized by the Roman establishment, was invaluable for his ability to shape them to his master's needs. Neither could be jettisoned; and Nero, alert to the weakness of his own position, knew better – as yet – than to try.

Nevertheless, the more wearisome he found his mother and tutor, the more he yearned to flex his muscles. Opportunities were hardly lacking. When, chafing against the marriage to Claudius's daughter forced on him by Agrippina, he began to look around for a woman better suited to his tastes than the earnest and high-minded Octavia, he soon found one in the shape of a former slave named Acte. Agrippina was predictably appalled. 'A housemaid as my daughter-in-law?'[6] It was not to be borne. Rather than back down, though, Nero turned for assistance to his tutor – who promptly arranged for one of his associates to serve Acte and her lover as a go-between. Yet Seneca, even as he was assiduously promoting his youthful pupil as the model of responsibility, faced challenges of his own. Nero, bored of spending his time living up to his tutor's stern ideals, wanted to let off steam. He was strongly encouraged in this ambition by a young rake named Marcus Salvius Otho, whose flamboyant extravagance and taste for tossing unfortunates up and down in military cloaks made him very much a man after Nero's own heart. Otho, unlike Seneca, was not forever nagging him about his duty; Otho, unlike Seneca, was familiar with the seamiest, the most vice-ridden quarters of Rome. Whole new dimensions of experience and opportunity, barely hinted at in books of philosophy, were waiting to be discovered in the streets of the city: a thrilling prospect for any young man who, like Nero, 'had a love of the incredible'.[7] Increasingly, it was not Seneca who 'shared with him all his plans and secrets',[8] still less Agrippina, but companions like Otho.

Nevertheless, there remained at the heart of the young Caesar's regime the same throbbing, ominous tension between the show and the reality of power as had been present from the moment of his accession. Nero knew – because his mother was always reminding him of it – that he would never have ascended to the rule of the world without her manoeuvrings and manipulations; he knew too that he was not the only candidate to rule as Caesar. Always, hanging over his head, a reminder to him that he was not indispensable, lurked Britannicus. This had been brought unsettlingly home to Nero during the first Saturnalia of his reign, when his stepbrother, ordered as a forfeit to stand up and sing, had intoned a lament for his displacement. Agrippina, determined to keep her son in check, did not hesitate to menace him with the prospects of his rival. When Nero, greatly daring, dismissed Pallas from his post on the Palatine, his mother's fury at the sacking of her most valued agent was something terrible. 'I will take Britannicus to the Praetorian camp! The soldiers there will listen to the daughter of Germanicus!'[9] A mortal threat – and Nero knew it. Agrippina, as she had done all her life, played hard, and she played to win – even against her own son.

Bitter and humiliated, Nero vented his fury in the readiest way available: by repeatedly sodomising his stepbrother. Rape was, of course, the most physically brutal means a Roman had of asserting his dominance over a rival; but it was, in Nero's case, an expression of impotence as well. His mother, it seemed, had won. When, midway through 55, he invited Agrippina to a feast, making sure to host Britannicus and Octavia as well, there did not appear much doubt as to who held the whip-hand in the August Family. Then, in the course of the meal, Britannicus abruptly began to choke. His eyes bulged, he gasped for breath, his body went into spasm. All around him, his fellow guests rose in consternation – but Nero, lying back on his couch, watched on unconcerned. 'Epilepsy,' he murmured coolly – then glanced across at his mother. Agrippina, her face set, did her best not to betray her horror; Octavia too. The corpse of Britannicus, painted white to disguise its hideous discoloration, was bundled out of the Palatine that night.[10] As it was being borne across the Forum, so rain began to fall and washed the powder away. The storm, though, did not prevent a pyre from being lit on the Campus Martius and the body hurriedly cremated. The remains were buried in the Mausoleum of Augustus. With Britannicus dead, the line of the Claudians – that most formidable of all Roman families – was dead as well. Nothing was left but 'dusty ash and pale shadow'.[11]

Agrippina, who had fought so hard to disinherit Britannicus, now found herself mourning him with unforced abandon. Whether, as Nero solemnly persisted in claiming, he had succumbed to an epileptic fit, or else to something more sinister, the consequence was the same: there was no longer a ready heir on the Palatine. Any prospect of keeping Nero on a tight leash was now effectively gone – as Nero himself soon made clear. Politely but firmly, Agrippina was ushered from Caesar's house into her grandmother's old villa next door. She was stripped of her bodyguard; her face began to vanish from the coinage. No longer did suitors flock to her doors in the hope of patronage: an infallible symptom of trouble in a city such as Rome. Nostrils alert to the scent of blood duly began to flare. Agrippina had many enemies – and they were hungry to drag her down. Prominent among them, of course, was Domitia, her old rival for Nero's affections, and whose sister, Domitia Lepida, had been convicted on a capital charge just prior to Claudius's death. Agrippina's fingerprints had been all over that particular case; now, eager for vengeance, Domitia sought to pay her back in like coin. Her chosen agent was one of her freedmen, an actor much admired by Nero named Paris. Arriving on the Palatine under cover of darkness, and ushered into the Emperor's presence, he levelled a range of sensational accusations against Agrippina. That she was the lover of Nero's cousin, a great-grandson of Tiberius's by the name of Rubellius Plautus. That she intended to marry him. That she was plotting to replace her son with her new husband, and then to rule the world by his side. Nero, all the more paranoid for having drunk too much, was thrown into a full-scale panic. Summonses were immediately sent to Seneca and Burrus. Seneca arrived first, and Nero – according to one report – talked wildly of sacking the Prefect for being his mother's creature. The prospect of how the Praetorians might react to this move was a sobering one, though, even for someone as furiously inebriated as Nero; and sure enough, by the time of Burrus's arrival on the Palatine, he had repented of it. On one thing, though, he remained set. The time had come to solve the problem of his mother's mischief-making once and for all. The command he gave Burrus could not have been more explicit or shocking: to kill Agrippina.

But even Caesar could go too far. Burrus told Nero to his face that he was drunk, and would see things differently in the morning. Blunt by nature, the Prefect spoke with the self-assurance of a man alert to how loyal his men still remained to Germanicus's daughter. Sure enough, the attempt to eliminate Agrippina ended up spectacularly rebounding on its perpetrators, for it had shocked Seneca and Burrus into recognising just how exposed they would be without her. Ultimately, they had little choice but to sink or swim with the Augusta. A cursory investigation into the charges against their erstwhile patron, and their triumvirate was quietly patched up. Rather than challenge it, Nero opted to beat a tactical retreat. Not only was Agrippina fully exonerated of the charges against her, but she took the opportunity to seize back lost ground. Domitia was publicly humiliated by having her rights of patronage over Paris abolished, while others among Agrippina's accusers were banished, and her own partisans promoted. No one familiar with the constantly shifting balance of power on the Palatine could doubt what had happened. Nero had been forced into open concessions. The limits of his authority – Caesar though he was – stood glaringly exposed.

'Power comes in many forms.' So Seneca, after Nero's first turbulent year as emperor, reminded his master. 'A princeps has the sway of his fellow citizens, a father his children, a teacher his pupils, officers the soldiers appropriate to their rank.'[12] Yet Seneca, despite recognising that the very word 'princeps' had become something of a misnomer, and that Nero's powers were more properly those of a king, was betraying his blinkers. His understanding of how power should properly be exercised still drew on the primordial traditions of the Roman people: obedience to those placed in command; admiration for the iron disciplines of family and legion; respect for duty. These were the virtues of which Augustus had approved, and Tiberius, and Claudius. And yet all the while there lay over the teeming and brilliant capital, with its theatres and circuses, its games and plays, its processions and festivals and races, the heady perfume of a very different brand of power. Seneca, it was said, had dreamed the night after he had first been introduced to Nero that he was teaching Caligula; and perhaps the vision had been prophetic. To win the love of the people; to pander to their enthusiasms; to woo them with entertainments beyond their wildest imaginings: these were the policies by which Nero's uncle had lived and died.

Fifteen years on from his assassination, the hatred of the Roman elite for Caligula remained as venomous as ever. To Agrippina, in particular, the notion of presenting her brother to Nero as a role model could hardly have been more monstrous. To Seneca too: for Caligula had despised and mocked the philosopher as a pedlar of platitudes, and flirted with putting him to death. There were some in Nero's circle, though, who had fonder memories. Aulus Vitellius, that seasoned veteran of Caligula's revels, had made sure, with the practised smoothness that came naturally to his family, to slip into the new emperor's affections; and he, as a man who had raced chariots and bore the sports injury to prove it, could hardly have been more sympathetic to Nero's taste for glamour. Across the Tiber from the Palatine, marked by Rome's tallest obelisk, stood the private racecourse begun by Caligula but never finished: a dereliction which, encouraged by cronies such as Vitellius and Otho, Nero intended to correct. Like uncle, like nephew: compared to spectacle, and boldness, and the approbation of the Roman people, who cared what po-faced conservatives might think?

Except that, for the moment, Nero's dreams outpaced his nerve. When Seneca, appalled that his erstwhile pupil should be flaunting an interest in the Circus, let alone angling to ride chariots himself, sought to check his enthusiasm, the two men arrived at a compromise. Even though Nero's grandfather had been celebrated for his skill on the racecourse, and his father, scandalously, had run down a child while speeding on the Appian Way, Nero himself was content to practise in private. That the sport was unworthy of him, though, a distraction from worthier pursuits, he refused point-blank to accept. It was, he informed Seneca, the pastime of ancient kings, fêted in the songs of poets, favoured by the gods. For Caesar to drive a chariot was not, no matter what the fustier brand of senator might insist, an offence against the majesty of Rome – it was the opposite. Times had changed. To veil the blaze of charisma such as Nero's was pointless. One might as well hood the sun.

Even Augustus, after all, despite his posing as a magistrate of the Roman people, had dared to hint at what it meant to rule the world. It was why he had fostered the rumours that his mother had been impregnated by a snake; why, at his wedding feast, he had come as Apollo; and why, in the library on the Palatine, he had sanctioned a statue of himself dressed as his divine patron. Many were the attributes of the god. Climb from the Forum to Caesar's house, and there, above the road, surmounting the great arch built by Augustus, citizens could behold the famous sculpture of Apollo driving the chariot of the sun; if they continued to the summit of the hill and entered his temple, they would find waiting for them in the sanctum a very different portrayal of the god, garbed in the robes of a professional musician and holding a lyre, the seven-stringed *cithara*. What Augustus, nervous of how the Roman people might react, had been content merely to insinuate, Nero, youthful and golden, exulted in. Not content with completing the private circus begun by Caligula, he aimed to go one better by mastering the notoriously challenging *cithara* and singing his own compositions to it. Rare was the spare moment that he did not spend picking at its strings or fine-tuning his voice. Light and music, attributes of the most beautiful, the most terrible of the gods, were attributes worthy too of a youthful Caesar. Far from disgracing him, as Seneca charged, Nero's mastery of chariot and lyre, once honed to a superhuman pitch and made manifest to the Roman people, would serve to proclaim a golden age.

Such, at any rate, was the long-term ambition. For the moment, though, it remained a fantasy. Not yet out of his teens, Nero still struggled to dazzle the world as he knew himself capable of dazzling it. Too much stood in his way. The sour disapproval of withered and bony-fingered senators; the perpetual ebb and surge across the Palatine of the various tides of faction; the precarious loyalties of the Praetorians: all served as a block on the ambitions of the youthful Caesar. Nevertheless, the more habituated to power Nero became, the readier he was to explore what he might achieve with it. In 57, when he was nineteen years old, he inaugurated a new amphitheatre on the Campus Martius. Built in under a year, and incorporating beams fashioned out of 'the largest tree ever seen in Rome',[13] it was constructed on a scale commensurate with its sponsor's ambitions. Nevertheless, despite the vastness of the space, he had no interest in staging anything so vulgar as a simple bloodbath. Just as the amphitheatre itself, with its nets of gold wire suspended over the arena on elephant tusks, was decorated with an artist's attention to detail, so did the entertainments reflect Nero's fascination with dissolving the boundaries between the everyday and the fantastical. Those who crammed onto the bleachers were being invited to enter a world ancient and cruel, in which monsters were bred of unnatural lusts, and men with wings fashioned out of wax and feathers sought to fly. For the entertainment of the spectators, a woman imprisoned inside a heifer made of wood might be mounted by a bull, or a performer suspended high above the arena be let drop. Myth was rendered a thing of thrilling spectacle in which the screams, the scents of fear and the carnage were viscerally real. On one occasion, Nero himself was splattered by the blood of a man who had flown too close to the sun.

As Claudius had demonstrated, there were few limits to what a Caesar might commission, if he only had the vision and the cash. Nero prized ingenuity, and was certainly no less fascinated than his predecessor by great feats of engineering. In Ostia, the quays and breakwaters of the emerging port continued to swarm with workmen, and Nero, when it was formally completed, did not hesitate to take the credit.[14] Merely to bend the sea to his will, though, was inadequate to the scale of his ambitions. 'Never have there been spectacles to compare – for they put everything we have seen into the shade!'[15] The enthusiasm felt for Nero's shows, even among the most jaded of the Roman people, was as joyous as it was unforced: due reflection of the remarkable feats achieved by those responsible for their staging. Even as engineers at Ostia were turning the sea into dry land, so their colleagues in the heart of Rome, on the Campus Martius, were turning dry land into sea. The great naval battle of Salamis, re-enacted decades earlier by Augustus, was staged a second time in Nero's amphitheatre. Scenes were laid on to stupefied spectators that might have seemed conjured up from Puteoli or Baiae: the beating of oars; the gliding of war galleys; the surfacing of strange creatures of the deep. Indeed, so daring were some innovations that they would have startled onlookers even in the Bay of Naples. Particularly wondrous was a mechanical yacht that, as though it were being shipwrecked, 'seemed to disintegrate, releasing wild animals as it did so – and then, reassembling itself, to appear as good as new'.[16] Even Nero was impressed.

Agrippina, marking her son's taste for lavishing money on wonders and entertainments, was less so. As only a woman who had lost a fortune could do, she valued money. Incontinent spending struck her as both unwise and dangerous. When Nero bestowed a spectacular bonus on one of his freedmen, she ordered the money tipped out in a great pile in front of him, so that he could see for himself how much of a fortune he was squandering. Nero, with an insouciant shrug, immediately ordered it doubled. 'I hadn't realised that I was being so stingy.'[17] The older he became, the more tedious he found his mother's constant nagging. The demands of duty, of responsibility, of statecraft, increasingly oppressed and aggravated him. Infuriatingly, though, he found them impossible to dismiss. He was married to them, after all. His wife, the earnest and austere daughter of Claudius, was a living, breathing reminder of everything he owed his mother. That Agrippina was as close to Octavia as Nero found her uncongenial only intensified his irritation with the pair of them. Uxurious by nature, he deeply resented his loveless marriage. Acte, whose enduring hold on his affections had enabled her to grow sensationally rich, remained much cherished by Nero; but she, of course, as a one-time slavegirl, could not possibly become his wife. Then, in 58, he fell in love again – and this time the object of his passion was a very different class of woman. Poppaea Sabina, the daughter and namesake of the rival hounded to her death by Messalina, was beautiful, intelligent and stylish; but crucially, she was also the granddaughter of a man who had won a consulship. Her breeding, while hardly on a level with Octavia's, was far from contemptible. It was possible for Nero to look at her and imagine her his wife.

Naturally, there were various obstacles to be cleared first. The first of these, and the least insuperable, was Poppaea's husband – who happened to be Nero's close friend, Otho. Out on the streets of Rome, where the details of Caesar's love life were relentlessly picked over, the precise circumstances of Poppaea's bed-jumping were much debated: had Otho boasted of his wife's sex appeal once too often, or had he married her to facilitate his friend's cheating on Octavia? Whatever the precise truth, it is certain that by 58 Nero had decided that he wanted Poppaea exclusively for himself. Weighing up whether to have his friend put to death or merely banished to the limits of the world, he opted for the course of mercy, dispatching Otho to Lusitania, out on the Atlantic margins of Iberia, there to serve as its governor. Bosom companion or not, Poppaea's husband had outlived his usefulness. Keeping things under wraps had never been Nero's style. He preferred to flaunt his passions. There was to be no more veiling the affair.

Nero himself, of course, could afford to shrug aside the resulting scandal; and so, as it turned out, could Poppaea. The jealous hatred of those who traduced her as 'an arrogant whore'[18] was a price worth paying for Caesar's devotion. As ambitious as she was glamorous, the radiance of Poppaea's charisma exemplified everything that Nero most admired in a woman. Even the colour of her hair, neither blonde nor brunette, marked her out as eye-catching: praised by Nero as 'amber-coloured',[19] it was soon setting the trend for fashion victims across the city. Set against Poppaea's allure, the unhappy Octavia could hardly help but seem further diminished. The prospects of Agrippina too: indeed, it was the measure of just how challenging it had become for her to keep Nero in check that the rumours of her desperation alleged some shocking details. That she was aiming to wean her son from Poppaea by seducing him herself. That she had begun to make moves on him, painted and dressed like a prostitute, whenever he was drunk. That Seneca was so anxious about Agrippina's behaviour that he had sent Acte to warn Nero of the damage to his reputation. There were others, though, who alleged the opposite: that it was Nero himself, and not his mother, who had made the first move. The reality, of course, was lost to impenetrable murk. The delight that rumours of incest brought the Roman people was invariably exceeded only by the impossibility of knowing whether they were true.

Yet when it came to identifying the source of the gossip, the challenge was not insurmountable. Agrippina was a woman respected even by her enemies for her iron self-discipline – whereas Nero positively loved to shock. It was noted that he kept as one of his concubines a woman who looked exactly like Agrippina, 'and that whenever he fondled her, or showed off her charms to others, he would declare that he was sleeping with his mother'.[20] An outrageous boast – but almost designed, it might have been thought, to test the waters of public opinion. It was as though Nero, by deliberately scandalising the bounds set on the common run of humanity, wished to test just how far he dared to go. How did it feel, he seemed to be asking himself, to break a fatal taboo?

Long before, back when Nero was born, Agrippina had consulted an astrologer to discover what was written in the stars about her son. Two things, the astrologer had informed her: that he would rule the world – and kill his mother. 'Let him kill me,' Agrippina was said to have retorted, 'provided only that he rules.'[21] Was the story true? If so, then the fraying of relations with her son would doubtless have brought the prophecy often to mind. By early 59, though, the tensions between them appeared to be easing. Nero, in an ostentatious gesture of goodwill, invited his mother to share a holiday with him at Baiae. In mid-March, Agrippina arrived by ship from Antium, the town just south of Rome where her son had been born twenty-one years before. Nero greeted her in person, then escorted his mother to her villa, a sumptuous mansion once owned by Hortensius Hortalus. Here, leading her down to its jetty, he presented her with a splendidly outfitted gift: her very own yacht. That evening, Agrippina took a litter north along the coast to Baiae, where Nero was staying. Greatly affectionate, he gave her the place of honour next to himself, and talked with her until the early hours. By now, with night lying velvet over the Bay, it was too dark for her to take a litter back home; and so Nero, informing his mother that her new yacht was docked outside, escorted her down to the marina. There he embraced and kissed her. 'For you I live,' he whispered, 'and it is thanks to you that I rule.'[22] A long, last look into her eyes – and then he bade her farewell. The yacht slipped its moorings. It glided out into the night. Lights twinkled on the shore, illumining the curve of 'the loveliest bay in the world'[23] while stars blazed silver overhead. Oars beat, timbers creaked, voices murmured on the deck. Otherwise, all was calm.

Then abruptly the roof fell in. Agrippina herself was saved from being crushed to death only by the raised sides of her couch; but when the yacht, after drifting idly for a few minutes, began to rock and tilt, she was flung into the sea. A friend of hers, bobbing beside her, was so frantic to be rescued that she cried out, 'I am Agrippina'; but no sooner had she done so than she was being clubbed to death by oars and poles. Agrippina herself, keeping as silent as she could, swam away from what now stood revealed as a death-trap; and as she swam, she met with some fishermen, who pulled her from the waters and rowed her ashore.[24] From there, shivering and bleeding, she staggered back to her villa. All too aware of who most likely lay behind her attempted murder, but painfully conscious too, cornered as she was, that she had little choice save to play the innocent, she sent a message to Nero informing him of what had happened. Then she tended to her wounds.

Meanwhile, outside, crowds had gathered along the shore, a blaze of lanterns amid the dark of early morning. The bay echoed at first to their lamentations and prayers; but then, informed of Agrippina's survival, they gathered around her villa and made ready to rejoice. Suddenly, though, there sounded the beating of hooves. A column of armed men came galloping down the road. The crowds outside were roughly dispersed; soldiers surrounded the villa, then forced their way in. They found Caesar's mother in a dimly lit room, attended by a single slave. Agrippina confronted them boldly, but her insistence that Nero could not possibly have meant them to kill her was silenced when one of the men coshed her on the head. Dazed but still conscious, Agrippina looked up to see a centurion drawing his sword. At this, rather than protest any further, she determined to die as who she was: the daughter of Germanicus and the descendant of a long line of heroes. 'Strike my belly,'[25] she commanded, pointing to her womb. Then she fell beneath the hailstorm of her assassins' swords.

The shock of the crime echoed to the heavens. After the hurried disposal of Agrippina's body, her ashes were interred beside Julius Caesar's old villa, on a promontory overlooking the sea; and from this headland, it was reported, would repeatedly sound the blare of trumpets, to be echoed by other blasts from around the bay. Some said that Nero, retreating from the scene of the murder to Naples, was visited by his mother's ghost; and that he was haunted in his dreams, just as Orestes had been, by the whips and fiery torches of the Furies. His taste for bringing to life ancient myth had long been on show; but now, in the most shocking and audacious manner, he had himself taken centre stage as a hero of legend. All his devotion to theatricality, all his enthusiasm for stagecraft, all his relish for posing as someone infinitely beyond the run of common mortals, had contributed to an incomparable spectacular – and the news of it filled the world. The yacht that had capsized his mother was modelled, it was reliably reported, on the collapsing boat witnessed by Nero back in Rome; viewing Agrippina's corpse prior to its cremation, he was said to have stripped it naked, inspected it closely and then murmured, 'I did not know I had so beautiful a mother.'[26] Nero himself, far from punishing those who spread such rumours, seemed to revel in the melodrama of it all. When graffiti appeared in Rome, charging him with matricide, he made no effort to track down the culprits; and when a famously stern moralist by the name of Thraesa Paetus, rather

361

than concur with the formal condemnation of Agrippina as a traitor, opted to walk out of the Senate House in protest, Nero overlooked the offence. He knew the Roman people and he had judged their response correctly. He had gauged that his crime, precisely because so titanic, would end up only adding to his charisma. No mean or squalid matricide, he had successfully cast himself as a figure of tragic glamour, as a new Orestes. When he returned to Rome from Campania, the crowds lined up to meet him as though for a triumph.[27]

Nero's feelings of relief could not have been sweeter. He had played for perilously high stakes – and he had won. Right up to the end, Agrippina had maintained her hold on the affection of the Praetorians. When Nero, brought the news of her escape from the booby-trapped yacht, had ordered a detachment of them to her villa, there to finish her off, Burrus had told him flatly that they would never kill the daughter of Germanicus. Only with her execution by a specially commissioned hit-squad, and the coming of dawn, had Nero been able to relax: for Burrus, bowing to the brutal change of circumstances, had ordered his senior officers to present themselves to Caesar and congratulate him 'on foiling his mother's evil schemes'.[28] Nor had Seneca managed to keep his hands any cleaner. Obliged by Nero to ghost a letter of self-exculpation to the Senate, he too had found himself complicit in the murder. The only saving grace for him and Burrus was that at least they were not alone. Nero, on his return to Rome, proclaimed games that were to be 'the greatest ever',[29] a celebration of his victory over his mother. The entire Roman people were summoned. All were invited to dabble their fingers in the blood of Agrippina.

It was an offer which few refused. Staged in a range of venues across the city, the games were as spectacular as Nero had promised. An equestrian rode an elephant down a tightrope. Plays with the latest in special effects thrilled audiences with fiery spectacles of destruction. Lavish numbers of tokens were scattered among the crowds, entitling the lucky recipients to everything from jewels to wild animals, from blocks of flats to gold. Meanwhile, in the Forum, Nero himself was busy offering up sacrifice. That a lightning bolt had recently incinerated the table at which he was dining; that a woman had given birth to a snake; that there had been an eclipse: these, under normal circumstances, might have appeared menacing portents of doom. And perhaps they were; but if so, then they served only to enhance, not diminish, the glitter of Nero's stardust. By killing his mother, after all, he had saved Rome from her inveterate and ruinous lust for power; and he had done so at heroic cost. It was for the sake of his fellow citizens that he had taken upon himself the guilt of matricide; now, by celebrating their own salvation, the Roman people could share a role in the remarkable drama. When a comet, bright and ominous, appeared in the cloudless skies above Rome even as the festivities were in full swing, many feared the worst; but many more looked to Nero as what he claimed to be – their saviour. A century before, in the wake of the Ides of March, the blaze of a star across the heavens had heralded calamity for the entire world; but not now. Seneca, with no choice save to carry on playing the role of Nero's accomplice, duly hailed the role of his master: 'He has succeeded in redeeming comets from their evil reputation.'[30] A fitting tribute: for Nero, that summer of 59, had successfully transfigured murder into sacrifice, ambition into selflessness, and matricide into piety. Comet or not, there could be no doubting who was the star.

But it was not enough for Nero merely to play the impresario. That same summer of 59, he hosted another festival, a private celebration staged to mark the first shaving of his beard. The games were held on the far side of the Tiber, between the lake where Augustus had hosted his famous re-enactment of the battle of Salamis and the river itself. The entertainments lasted into the early hours. There were banquets held on barges, groves filled with grappling couples, and at midnight Nero himself, to exultant cheers, sailed out from the lake into the Tiber: touches of Baiae in the heart of Rome. The main focus, though, was on theatrical extravaganzas – and these, as the public games had done, featured performers from the cream of the elite. 'Neither breeding, nor age, nor public office served to inhibit them.'[31] One dancer, a former sister-in-law of Claudius's, was in her eighties.[32] The climax of the entertainments, though, was the stage debut of Nero himself. Plucking at the lyre, he sang to his audience of gruesome maimings and murders from ancient myth: of a boy castrating himself; of a mother killing her son. It was, for the twenty-one-year-old Caesar, a moment of the giddiest rapture. The spectators cheered and applauded. 'Our Apollo,' they cried, 'our Augustus!'[33] For some, though, the delight rang rather hollow. Burrus was there, with officers and soldiers of the Praetorians; so too Seneca, whose elder brother had introduced Nero onto the stage, and who himself had been obliged, in company with the Prefect, to serve as their master's cheerleaders, waving their arms and flapping their togas. 'The more instruments of torture the torturer has on display, the more he is liable to achieve – indeed, the very appearance of them is likelier to break a man than the patient endurance of pain.' So Seneca, without ever mentioning Nero, would later confide to a friend. 'In a similar manner, nothing is better able to brainwash and enslave us than the dazzle of spectacle.'[34]

And Nero, having now successfully tested the waters, had only just begun.

All the World's a Stage

In AD 60, almost two decades after crossing the Atlas mountains, Suetonius Paulinus was near to completing an expedition at the opposite end of the world.[35] As in Mauretania, so in Britain: his progress had been gruelling. The capture of Caratacus, far from signalling the end of British resistance, had provided only a brief respite from the task of pacification. Wales, where the Catuvellaunian chieftain had made his last stand, was the particular challenge. Mountainous and inhabited by notoriously untameable tribesmen, it had defied a succession of Roman governors. Suetonius, whose record in crossing mountains was second to none, had been the obvious man to finish the job. Sure enough, two years on from his appointment to Britain, he had succeeded in stamping the mark of Roman supremacy upon even the wildest reaches of the country. Only the island of Mona – modern-day Anglesey – still held out. And now, with his infantry massed in flat-bottomed boats and his cavalry instructed to breast the shallows, Suetonius was ready to cross the straits and finish off resistance for good.

But would his soldiers do as commanded? Mona was crammed with refugees; and these, crowding the shoreline, howled and chanted to such baleful effect that the legionaries found themselves briefly frozen with terror. There were women brandishing torches, who, with their black robes and tangled hair, looked like nothing so much as Furies; and there were Druids. But then, summoning up their courage, Suetonius's men began to make for the opposite shore. In the event, it proved a walkover. Soon the defenders were being set ablaze with the flames of their own torches. Charred corpses were left scattered across the beaches. Then it was the turn of the island's sacred groves to be felled: for Mona was dreaded by the invaders as the chief shrine of the Druids, and of the terrifying spirits appeased by their murderous rites. The defeat of barbarian savagery and the purging of shrines festooned with human entrails – Suetonius had achieved a double exorcism. The news of his feat, when it was reported back in Rome, served as a stirring reminder to the inhabitants of the capital that there still existed, in the remote corners of the world, thrilling dimensions of heroism and sorcery. Nowhere, it seemed, no matter how distant, lay beyond the reach of the Roman people.

A message that Nero, despite his own complete lack of military experience, was naturally keen to promote. Why should the blaze of his charisma not find reflection even in the darkest wastes of the North? A particular triumph was achieved when one of his event managers, sent to source amber directly from the Baltic, returned laden with spoils. The agent had made such a success of his mission that he brought back riches sufficient to adorn an entire arena. Nets;

weapons; even the stretchers used to remove dead gladiators: all were made to gleam the colour of Poppaea's hair. 'So globalised has everything become,' wrote Seneca in wonder, 'that nothing is left in its accustomed place.'[36] Whether in Nero's amphitheatre, with its glint of amber and its bears set to hunt seals, or amid the bustle of markets selling goods from as far afield as India, or on the hill above the Campus, where a great map illustrated for the benefit of passing citizens the full, dazzling extent of their sway, reminders of Rome's status as the ultimate in world cities were inescapable.* All roads led there, and all roads led from there. In the Forum, to mark the official spot where they began and ended, Augustus had erected a milestone sheathed in bronze: the centre of the world. Contemplating the immense spider's web that Roman greatness had succeeded in spinning across mountains, forests and seas, some still wondered just how far its threads might end up reaching. 'Perhaps, in time to come, an age will dawn when the Ocean loosens the bonds of things, when the full breadth of the earth will stand revealed, when new worlds will be disclosed, and when Thule itself serve merely as a way-stop to other lands.'[37]

Seneca, when he imagined Roman ships powering their way to as yet undiscovered continents, did not necessarily approve. As a philosopher, he saw nothing to celebrate in perpetual motion. The prosperity that was the mark of a great empire was, in his opinion, a treacherous and soul-destroying thing, characterised by perpetual restlessness, and destined only to torment itself. Yet even as he praised the delights of poverty, he could not help but be swept along by what he condemned. Nero's matricide, far from shocking Seneca into resignation, had only confirmed him in his determination to cling to power. The less inclined the youthful Caesar was to take his advice,

---

* There is an intriguing possibility that the bears which are described by the poet Calpurnius Siculus as savaging seals in Nero's wooden amphitheatre might be polar bears. Tellingly, though, there is no mention of their fur being white, and so the balance of probability must sadly be against it.

the more of a responsibility he felt to continue providing it. So Seneca remained at Nero's side; and by staying there found himself prey to the manifold temptations that power on a global scale presented. 'The wise man has no need to send legates overseas, to mark out camps on enemy shores, to decide where best to plant garrisons and forts.'[38] No doubt – and yet Seneca himself, as Nero's most trusted advisor, had little choice but to immerse himself in precisely such details. He was up to date on reports from the British front, and alert to conditions on the island. He had convinced himself that there existed, in the ambition of its chieftains to conform to the new order, a rare investment opportunity; and so he had lent them the funds they required to build, to dress and to live like Romans. But he had miscalculated. The Britons had little understanding of the workings of finance, nor were they in any position to pay back the hefty interest being charged on their borrowings. Adding to Seneca's discomfort was his growing awareness of how great a drain on Roman manpower the conquest of the island was proving to be. Access to British hoodies and hunting dogs hardly compensated for the huge expense of keeping four legions in the field. There had even been talk of cutting Rome's losses and withdrawing altogether.* Seneca, better placed than anyone to do a spot of insider dealing, duly ordered his agents in Britain to call in his loans.

The timing proved unfortunate. Debt collectors were already out in force across the new province. Officials with responsibility for its finances, determined to screw out such income as they could, had begun to exact demands of tribal leaders who ranked legally, not as subjects, but as allies of Rome. One such was Prasutagas, king of the Iceni, a tribe in the flat and rolling lands to the north of Camulodunum. Anxious to safeguard the interests of his daughters,

---

* It is Suetonius (*Nero*: 18) who tells us this. Although he does not specify a date, it is evident from Nero's determination to crush the insurrection in Britain that he would never have countenanced the province's abandonment in the wake of Boudicca's revolt.

he had named them as his heirs alongside Nero. On his death, though, the Roman authorities had moved to annex everything. The entire kingdom was stripped bare. Prasutagas's two daughters, far from being treated with the respect due their rank, were both raped, and his wife, a flame-haired warrior queen named Boudicca, bound to a whipping post and lashed. It was to prove a fatal error.

Seneca, had he been present, would not have been surprised, for he had no illusions as to the nature of human rapacity. 'Were a true representation of our lives to be flashed before your mind's eye, you would think yourself watching a city just taken by storm, in which all regard for modesty and right had been abandoned, and the only counsel was that of force.'[39] Yet Seneca himself was hardly innocent of what he condemned. Two years earlier, Suillius Rufus, the muck-raking prosecutor who had helped to bring down Valerius Asiaticus, had publicly charged him with draining the provinces dry; and even though Seneca, pulling strings, had arranged for his accuser to be convicted of embezzlement, and sent into exile, the allegation had stung. After all, seated as he was at the heart of the great web of Roman power, he had only to tug upon a single thread of it for villages at the far end of the world to be trampled down by soldiers, and women left bruised and bleeding. For all his scruples, and even if he had not intended it, Seneca too had played his part in the harrowing of the Icenian tribal lands. Doubtless this was why the gods, when they warned, in the wake of the whipping given to Boudicca, of imminent and terrible calamity, chose to send portents both to Britain and to Rome. Even as flood-tides in the Thames estuary turned to blood, leaving shapes like corpses on the beaches, so was barbarous laughter heard coming from the empty Senate House, and screams from Nero's amphitheatre. The world had shrunk for ill as well as good.

News that Boudicca, with the scars still fresh on her back, had summoned the Iceni to revolt and was sweeping all before her, reached Suetonius even as he was catching his breath after the capture of Mona. Mustering a squad of cavalry, he climbed back into his saddle at once. Then, instructing the two legions under his immediate

368

command to follow as fast as they could, he made directly for the eye of the storm. The nightmare that had never ceased to haunt the invaders since their first arrival in Britain, the dread that their occupation would end as Roman rule beyond the Rhine had ended, amid slaughter, fire and ruin, appeared on the verge of fulfilment. Camulodunum, rebuilt in the wake of its capture by Claudius as a showcase of what Roman town-planners could achieve, had been levelled to the ground. Littering the debris were the corpses of butchered prisoners and the bronze fragments of dismembered Caesars. Highborn women, their severed breasts sewn to their mouths, rotted on spikes. Meanwhile, of the two legions not serving in Wales, one had already been ambushed and almost completely wiped out, while the second, summoned by Suetonius to join him, was ordered by its own acting commander to stay in barracks. Many senior officials, rather than risk the fate of Varus's men, had already fled to Gaul. A single error by Suetonius, and Britain would be lost for good.

In the event, though, the province was saved. Suetonius, after taking the pulse of the insurrection in person, retreated, successfully made a rendezvous with his advancing legions and then waited to meet the firestorm. Two more Roman settlements were left as smoking rubble before the fateful moment came. The Britons, rather than adopt the tactics of Arminius and melt into the landscape the better to wage guerilla warfare, opted instead for a full-frontal assault. The result, secured in the teeth of satisfyingly massive odds, was a massacre. When the casualty figures were published, it was claimed that some eighty thousand Britons had perished for the loss of only four hundred Roman dead. Boudicca, whose gender and general savagery had made her seem to her adversaries an Amazon unleashed from the realms of myth, committed suicide. So too, brought the news of Suetonius's victory, did the legionary commander who had refused his summons to battle. It was all thoroughly stirring: 'a day of great glory, redolent of some victory won in ancient times'.[40] The Roman people, thrilling to the dispatches from the British front and revelling in how disaster had been averted, could enjoy the reassurance that they remained the same people they had ever been.

Not that martial virtue alone had ever been sufficient to explain their rise to greatness. The genius granted them by the gods was for peace as well as war. When the reprisals launched by Suetonius threatened to get out of hand, Nero was sufficiently perturbed to send one of his freedmen to report back to him on the situation; and sure enough, soon afterwards, Boudicca's conqueror was recalled. From the earliest days of their city, Rome's leaders had appreciated that generosity in victory was the surest way of securing their ends: 'for little is gained by conquest if it is followed by oppression'.[41] Romulus's abduction of the Sabine women, although inevitably it had led their outraged fathers and brothers to descend on Rome vowing vengeance, had culminated, not in slaughter, but in a peace treaty, and in the Sabines becoming Roman. Since then, many other Italian peoples had followed along the same path. The Marsians, the Samnites, the Etruscans: all had come to rank as the fellow citizens of their conquerors. No longer, though, were Rome's horizons confined to lands south of the Alps. If Italy could end up Roman, then why not the world? It was her mission, some had begun to claim, 'to unite previously distinct powers, to soften patterns of behaviour, to provide a common language to the numerous peoples hitherto divided by their savage tongues, to civilise mankind – in short, to unite all the peoples of the world, and to serve them as their fatherland'.[42]

Amid the charred fields of Britain, such a claim might have seemed grotesque; except that the official appointed by Nero to stabilise the shattered province's administration, and who had first called for Suetonius to be replaced, was not an Italian but a Gaul. Julius Classicianus served as a living reassurance to the Britons that Roman rule offered more than simple oppression. Citizen of Rome, yet married to the daughter of a Gallic chieftain, he was ideally placed to mediate between conquerors and conquered. Rather than tighten the screws on his subjects, he opted to build bridges. The Britons, having been brutally taught the price of resistance, were now graced by

Classicianus with the benefits of submission. The policy proved strikingly effective. Wounds began to heal, the embers of insurrection to fade. Soon, even with memories of Boudicca's revolt still raw, it was being decided in Nero's councils to reduce the garrison in Britain from four legions to three. The Ocean remained to Rome.

Naturally, there were limits to what could plausibly be achieved. No matter how successful the process of pacification, chieftains as barbarous as those of the Britons could never hope to share in the rule of the world. There were many in Rome who felt the same about Classicianus and his kind. Although the aristocrats of southern Gaul had been under Roman rule for almost two centuries, and had bred, in the flamboyant form of Valerius Asiaticus, a man who had briefly aspired to rule as Caesar, resentment at their presence in the Senate House had never entirely faded. In AD 48, in a debate on whether to admit chieftains from the central and northern reaches of Gaul, opposition to the prospect had been ferocious. Allow the descendants of men who had fought Julius Caesar, worn trousers and dripped gravy from their facial hair, into the Senate House? 'Why, it would be to import hordes of foreigners, in the manner of a slave-dealer.'[43] In truth, though, such complaints about Gallic savagery were disingenuous. It was not the backwardness of the Gauls that provoked the true resentment but the opposite: their growing wealth. Many a senator, denied the opportunity to boost his fortunes as his ancestors had once done, by looting barbarians, found himself impoverished by comparison with Gallic magnates.

Yet this, to those with an eye to the future, was precisely what made it so pressing to recruit them into the ranks of the Roman elite. Gaul, with its fertile soil and manpower, was already richer than many regions of Italy. Its aristocracy could not possibly be permitted to go their own way. Claudius, with the perspective that came from his deep reading in history, had made this argument with typical subtlety and erudition. 'Everything we now believe to be the essence of tradition,' he had reminded his fellow senators, 'was a novelty once.'[44] Why, Clausus, his own ancestor, the founder of the Claudian line, had been an immigrant. Senators had duly approved Claudius's speech.

371

Gauls had been admitted into their ranks. The Senate House had ended up just that little bit more multi-ethnic.

Meanwhile, beyond its walls, in the teeming streets of a city whose population now numbered well over a million, many had begun to wonder what precisely it meant to talk of the Roman people. Rome, as Claudius had reminded the Senate in his speech, had been founded on immigration. Exotic languages had been heard in the city for centuries. Street names still bore witness to the settlement of foreigners on them in ancient times: the Vicus Tuscus, where Etruscans had once congregated, and the Vicus Africus. Yet even as many Romans saw in their city's diversity the homage paid by the world to its greatness, and a potent source of renewal, so others were less convinced. All very well to host immigrants, so long as they ended up Roman; but what if they preserved their barbarous ways, infecting decent citizens with their superstitions? 'In the capital, appalling customs and disgraceful practices from across the world are forever cross-pollinating and becoming fashionable.'[45] A sobering reflection, to be sure: that to serve as the capital of the world might render Rome less Roman.

Such an anxiety was nothing new. Back in the first century of the Republic, a mania for outlandish cults had seen the Senate legislate to ensure that only the traditional gods be worshipped, and only with traditional rites. Since then, there had been numerous attempts to purge the city of alien ways. In 186 BC, the Senate had even launched a campaign of suppression against the worship of Liber, on the grounds that a Greek soothsayer had perverted its rituals and fostered unspeakable orgies. Egyptians and astrologers from Mesopotamia also tended to be regarded by most right-thinking citizens with profound suspicion. More alarming yet were the Syrians, with their devotion to a goddess, lion-flanked and jewel-adorned, whose cult, sinister as only a Syrian cult could be, had long been a thing of revulsion to every decent Roman. There was no value so fundamental, no propriety so settled, that her worshippers might not trample on them, and howl in exultant frenzy as they did so. Appearing to slaves in visions, the

Syrian Goddess had been known to encourage them to rebel; driving mad her most frenzied devotees, she would inspire them to make a sacrifice of their testicles. *Galli*, these self-castrated priests were called: wretches who, abandoning the privileges and responsibilities of manhood, had willingly chosen to become women. With their painted faces and their feminine robes, their depilated bodies and their braided hair dyed blonde, they could not possibly have been more offensive to Roman sensibilities. Unsurprisingly, then, the authorities had done all they could to prevent their fellow citizens from joining their ranks, banning the practice of self-castration outright at first, and then, from 101 BC, permitting it only under the tightest of regulations. Yet this had done nothing to diminish the popularity of the cult: disturbingly, it had turned out, some Romans quite fancied living as women. By the time that Claudius, surrendering to the inevitable, finally lifted all legal restrictions on citizens becoming *Galli*, processions in honour of the Syrian Goddess, complete with flutes, tambourines and spectacular displays of self-laceration, had become a common sight in Rome. Naturally, those who held fast to traditional values continued to find it all revolting. 'If a god desires worship of this kind,' Seneca declared flatly, 'then she does not deserve to be worshipped in the first place.'[46] For those on the cutting edge of fashion, however, a protestation of devotion to the Syrian Goddess had become an easy and entertaining way to shock. Rumour had it, for instance, that she was the only deity for whose cult Nero had any respect.

Yet when it came to sheer jaw-dropping weirdness, not even the beliefs of the Syrians could compare with those of their near neighbours, the Jews. Immigrants from Judaea had been settling in Rome for two centuries, mainly in the cheap housing on the far side of the Tiber, where the principal temple of the Syrian Goddess was also to be found; and in all that time, they had never lost their distinctiveness. No people in the world had customs more perverse or ludicrous. They abstained from pork; they took every seventh day off; they obstinately refused to worship any god save their own. Yet Jewish practices and beliefs, although self-evidently grotesque, were not without a certain glamour. Like the cults of the Egyptians or the star charts of the Mesopotamians, they were capable of seducing those with a taste for the exotic. This was why, from the moment that Jews had first settled in the city, the authorities had periodically sought to expel them. The policy, though, had never proven effective. Whether in 139 BC, when the Jews had been banned from Rome 'for trying to corrupt Roman values',[47] or in AD 19, when Tiberius had repeated the measure, or thirty years later, when Claudius had banished them yet again for making trouble at the instigation of a sinister-sounding agitator named Chrestus,* they had always crept back. A decade on from their expulsion by Claudius, they had once again returned to Rome. The fascination that they were capable of exerting, and the corresponding sense of alarm that they provoked in those contemptuous of foreign rituals, reached to the very top. 'They are the most wicked of peoples.'[48] Seneca's mistrust of the Jews would only have been confirmed for him by the reported interest of Poppaea in their teachings. The appeal of alien superstitions, it seemed, reached even into Caesar's bedroom. Many in Rome, when they contemplated the slave quarters of their own homes, or the shrines in the streets raised to mysterious gods, or the tenements crammed with immigrants from every corner of the world, dreaded what loathsome practices might be brewing in their city.

Nervousness about mass immigration and the peculiar cults that it had brought to Rome came to a head in 61, when the City Prefect, the man charged with the maintenance of order in the capital, was stabbed to death. His killer was one of his own slaves — and this, by the

---

* Suetonius. *Claudius*: 25.4. It is possible, indeed probable, that this is an allusion to arguments in Rome's Jewish community about the claims to messianic status of Jesus. Chrestus, it is true, was a common name, particularly for slaves; but against that, there is no recorded instance of a Jew in Rome ever being called it. A number of scholars have suggested that Suetonius might have derived his information from a police report, and that 'Chrestus' is a mistransliteration of 'Christus' — Christ. The truth, though, is ultimately unknowable.

terms of a stern law passed half a century before, required that every slave in the murdered man's household be executed. The savagery of the penalty generated widespread revulsion; and it seemed, in a debate on the matter in the Senate House, that clemency might prevail. In the event, what swung senators into backing the execution of the many hundreds of slaves owned by the murdered Prefect was a blood-curdling reminder of the numerous alien practices that had been imported into Rome. 'Nowadays, the slaves in our households come from across the world, and engage in every kind of weird cult – or none at all. Terror tactics alone can serve to keep this rabble in check.'[49] The law was duly upheld, the death sentence confirmed. Out on the streets, where many of the protestors were themselves freed-men, or else the descendants of slaves, furious demonstrations were held. Crowds armed with stones and torches sought to prevent the sentence from being carried out. Nero, rather than permit agitators to override the law, issued them with an official rebuke, and ordered soldiers to line the route along which the wretched slaves were led to their deaths. Yet there were limits to the vindictiveness that he was prepared to sanction. When it was proposed that the freedmen of the murdered Prefect be rounded up and deported, Nero vetoed the motion. 'What mercy has failed to moderate,' he declared, 'should not be aggravated by savagery.'[50]

Nero had a particular talent for judging the mood on the street. Unlike most senators, whose prejudices against the *plebs sordida* were rarely bred of personal experience, he was familiar with the seamiest reaches of the city. As a young man, he and Otho had often gone slumming together. Disguised as slaves, they had drunk, pilfered and brawled their way through the reddest of red-light districts. Respectable opinion, naturally enough, had been scandalised – particularly when a senator who had punched the man attempting to mug him, only to discover later that it was Caesar and make the mistake of apologising in public, had been obliged to commit suicide. Yet Nero, by plunging into the bowels of Rome, was educating himself as surely as he had done by listening to the lectures of his tutor. Virtue,

Seneca taught, was a thing of the city's heights, where the air was rar-
efied and regal; vice a thing of its murkiest depths. 'It tends to skulk
in the shadows, around the public baths and the saunas, in places
nervous of the authorities, soft, enervated and dripping with wine and
perfumes, either pallid or made up as one would paint a corpse.'[51]
Fulminations like this, far from warning Nero off the city's lowlife,
had naturally only encouraged him to sample its pleasures. When it
came to breaking the Roman people to his will, he was seasoned as
Seneca never would be. He knew when to feed them a carrot; and he
knew when to wield a stick.

A clear measure of this was provided by the man appointed as
Prefect of the *Vigiles*. Ofonius Tigellinus was a notorious chancer who
might easily have ended up being fingered by the Watch rather than
serving as their commander. As good-looking as he was impoverished, his initial career as a gigolo had seen him bed – or so it was
rumoured – both Livilla and Agrippina. Convicted of adultery and
exiled to Greece, he had been reduced to the humiliating extremity
of working in trade, before a pardon from Claudius had enabled him
to return to Italy and set up as a racehorse trainer. It was in that role
that Tigellinus had become an intimate of Nero – who made him
rich, and an equestrian to boot. Thuggish enough to keep order in
the streets, but steeped at the same time in their pleasures, he was ideally suited to his master's purposes. Tigellinus's elevation to the
prefecture of the *Vigiles* was to prove just a start. In 62, the most sensitive of all the posts open to an ambitious equestrian became vacant
when Burrus, after a long fight against throat cancer, finally died.
Honest and trustworthy, he had been a very different order of man
from Tigellinus; and Nero, in recognition of this, made sure to split
the command. Nevertheless, as one of the two Praetorian prefects,
Tigellinus was now ideally placed to do his master's dirty work – and
there was, as it happened, a particularly urgent job that needed
doing.

Three years had passed since the murder of Agrippina, and now
at last Nero was ready to cut the final thread that bound his regime

to that of his predecessor. Despite her husband's humiliatingly flamboyant affair with Poppaea, Octavia had been safe for as long as Burrus was alive. Beautiful, dignified and pathetic, she was precisely the kind of woman whom the Roman people loved. When Nero had once floated the possibility of divorcing her, Burrus had been openly dismissive. 'Sure,' he had scoffed, 'and be certain to return her dowry.'[52] Now, though, Burrus was gone; and his replacement had no loyalty to the family of Germanicus. When Nero instructed his new Prefect to dispose of Octavia, Tigellinus did not hesitate. The charge, as it invariably was whenever it became necessary to dispose of an inconvenient princess, was adultery. That the Prefect was a man as notorious for his promiscuity as his victim was celebrated for her modesty did not for a moment give him pause. 'Her private parts are cleaner than your mouth!'[53] So spat one of Octavia's attendants after being tortured by Tigellinus to make her testify against her mistress. He shrugged the insult aside. Most of Octavia's maids were all too ready to jump from a sinking ship. She was duly convicted of an affair with a slave. Yet just as Burrus had warned they would, the Roman people refused to tolerate the disgrace of Claudius's daughter. Rioting broke out. Poppaea's statues were toppled, Octavia's garlanded with flowers. Briefly, Nero wobbled. He proposed to remarry his unhappy wife. But then, with the fabrication of an altogether more detailed and watertight case against her, he rediscovered his courage. A second conviction was secured, and Octavia imprisoned on Pandateria. There, not long afterwards, she was put to death. Her head, dispatched to Nero, served as a trophy for his new wife: Poppaea Sabina.

A century before, when assassins in the employ of the Triumvirs had made a harvest of aristocratic heads, the winnowing had heralded global war. Not now, though. Poppaea's cradling of Octavia's head, no matter how indignantly the news of it might make crowds in the Roman streets seethe, did not threaten the order that Nero, for almost a decade, had provided the world. The provinces remained at peace; the frontiers held secure. In 63, a year after the decapitation of

Octavia, an enduring peace was negotiated between Rome and Parthia. It was agreed that Tiridates, a son of the Parthian king, should sit on the Armenian throne, but that at some point soon he should travel to Rome, there to receive his diadem in person from the hands of Caesar. A spectacle was thereby promised that could not have been more calculated to tickle Nero's fancy. For centuries, the Roman people had seen it as their birthright to grace kings with their favour; but never before had there been the prospect of seeing it staged for real in the heart of their city.

True, Nero himself had been nowhere near Armenia. When the Senate hailed him as *Imperator*, or when an arch was raised in honour of his victory on the summit of the Capitol, complete with a statue of him in full triumphal regalia, the fact that he had never seen a legion, still less led one into battle, was a minor detail. Nero understood that image, to a people far removed from the rigours of army life, was infinitely more vivid than garbled rumours of distant battles. What mattered to his fellow citizens was not whether flies had crawled over his wounds on some hellish and barbarous frontier, but the conviction with which he could embody their yearning for a prince of peace. 'There will be no more civil wars of the kind with which Rome once convulsed the globe; no more battles like Philippi to lament.'[54] Nero's task was to make the city, and the world, believe it.

The same responsibility, of course, had animated the career of Augustus and led to the establishment of the rule of the Caesars in the first place; but times were now far different, and the opportunities open to a talented and ambitious Princeps with them. Such, at any rate, was the conviction that Nero, after almost a decade in power, had come to hold. The old, uptight way of doing things, and the tedious inheritance from the past of obligations and taboos, were no longer to be borne. Restrictions on Nero's freedom of action had become intolerable to him. All were to be swept away. Octavia's head was not the only one to have been delivered to the Emperor in 62. His assassins had also been commissioned to eliminate two prominent senators linked by blood to the August Family. One was Rubellius

Plautus, the great-grandson of Tiberius rumoured to have been Agrippina's lover, and who had been living in placid exile on the Aegean coast; the other a descendant of Augustus's sister. Brought the news of these murders, senators shuddered. This was not least because, for the first time since Nero's coming to power, one of their own had just been condemned on a charge of *maiestas*. It was an agent of Tigellinus, informed that a magistrate had not only written a satire on the Emperor but actually read it out at a dinner party, who had brought the prosecution; and even though the death sentence, following an intervention by the indomitable Thraesa Paetus, had been commuted to one of exile, every senator could recognise the warning that had been served.

To Seneca, in particular, it had come as both a shock and a humiliation. Lashed as he was to the wheel of Nero's regime, he found himself powerless either to change what he saw as its increasingly disastrous course or to abandon ship. The best he could manage was to secure from his erstwhile pupil permission to retreat into semi-retirement. There, his mood continued to darken. Whether in his worsening health, in the person of a decrepit and toothless porter whom he had last seen as a handsome slaveboy, or in a clump of gnarled plane trees planted by his own hand in his youth, he found marks of decay everywhere. Even the world itself, it seemed to Seneca, was faced with ruin. His imaginings were haunted by the threat of a universal apocalypse. The end, when it arrived, would come from the sea: 'From the West the waves will roll in, and from the East. A single day will suffice to entomb the human race. All venerable things that have been preserved by fortune's favour and exalted by it, everything that is noble and beautiful, every great throne, every great people – all will be swallowed up.'[55]

Destruction, though, might be creative. This was what Nero had come to believe. No bad thing, in his opinion, for a world grown smoky and dull to be washed clean. Better a new beginning than a living death. The same crowds who had rioted in favour of the dull and sober Octavia would never, had they succeeded in their aims, have come to enjoy the spectacle of Poppaea as Caesar's wife. Proclaimed Augusta by a besotted Nero only a few months after their marriage, she blazed and glittered as neither Livia nor Agrippina had ever dared to do. Her mules were shod with gold; she bathed in ass's milk to preserve her perfect complexion; she gave her name to entire brands of beauty treatment. 'I hope I die before I get old'[56] – this prayer of Poppaea's, uttered after catching herself at an unfavourable angle in a mirror, summed up everything that her husband most adored about her. It spoke to one of his profoundest convictions: that it was only shallow people who did not judge by appearances. Spectacle, illusion, drama: these were the dimensions of rule that truly mattered. Attentive though Nero might be to the grind of business, his true obsession was with a project that he felt to be altogether worthier of his time and talents: to fashion reality anew.

In the summer of 64, he duly set himself to transforming his capital into a setting worthy of his hopes and ambitions for it. Rome's public places became the venue for a series of spectacular banquets. 'It was as though the entire city were now to serve as Nero's palace.'[57] Most extravagant of all was a party hosted by Tigellinus beside a lake on the Campus Martius. As he had done at the games held on the opposite side of the Tiber four years before, Nero gorged himself on a raft luxuriously outfitted with soft purple rugs and cushions. Boats adorned with ivory and gold towed him across waters filled with exotic sea beasts. The oarsmen, grouped according to age and specialisation, constituted the cream of Rome's male prostitutes. Meanwhile, on the banks of the lake, the Roman people flocked to a sensational array of entertainments. The clamour for these was hardly surprising. Food and drink were provided indiscriminately, while on the quays stood brothels staffed by the most remarkable array of whores in the history of Rome. There were slaves and free; professionals and virgins; the dregs of the slums and the wives of eminent senators – and none was permitted to refuse a client who wished to sleep with her. It was, for the crowds who flocked to use them, a dream come true: a magical fusion of the pleasures of the street with those of the palace.

Nero, familiar with both, had recognised a profound truth about the Roman people: that in their fascination with the shocking and illicit there lurked opportunity as well as menace. Scandal was corrosive to the authority of a natural showman only if there were an attempt to cover it up. Flaunt it, revel in it, rub the noses of the dull, the dreary and the unfashionable in it, and the authority natural to a Caesar would grow only the more brilliant. A few days after Tigellinus's great banquet, Nero was ready to put this thesis to an even more extravagant test. Like one of the *Galli*, he had himself painted and dressed as a woman, and then, amid a blaze of wedding torches, married to one of his freedmen. Far from veiling a ceremony that could not have been more perfectly calculated to outrage conservative opinion, he staged it in public – 'even the part that night hides when the bride is a woman'.[58] It was all a sham, of course. That Nero meant nothing serious by it was precisely the point. Even his veneration of the Syrian Goddess was not what it had been. Time would see him urinate on her statue. As a comet glowed eerily in the skies above Rome, and those appalled by their ruler's antics dreaded the worst, those with a keener understanding of fashion could not help but revel in the world of fantasy that Nero had conjured into being. It was one in which anything had come to seem possible.

And so it proved. On the evening of 18 July, two days after the comet had finally faded from sight, and as a full moon gleamed bright in the sky, fire broke out in Rome.[59] It began at the southern end of the Circus, in shops packed with flammable materials, and in next to no time was raging out of control along the entire length of the valley. Soon it was spreading at terrifying speed through the cramped wooden tenements of quarter after quarter, and racing up the slopes of Rome's hills. The *Vigiles* proved powerless to stop it. Panic swept the city. Many rallied to the support of their neighbours, helping those who were disabled to escape the onslaught of the flames; but others, roaming the streets in gangs, set to looting abandoned homes and to torching areas that were not yet on fire. Who these vandals were, no one could be certain, for rumour spread as wild through the city in its agony as the savage flames themselves. Crowds of refugees, smoke-blackened and homeless, took refuge where they could; and Nero, who had been away in Antium when the fire began, but had come hurrying back to take charge of the disaster, opened up both the public buildings on the Campus and his own private estates. Meanwhile, as shanty towns sprouted amid marble and flowerbeds, the silhouette of the city behind them was topped across its expanse by a towering tsunami of flame. Only after six days, and a frantic labour of demolition to create a firebreak, was it finally stopped. Even then, the nightmare was not over. Fire broke out a second time, raging for a further three days before once again being extinguished – this time, as it proved, for good.

The devastation had left anything between a quarter and a third of the world's capital as smoking rubble.[60] Nero, anxious to know the worst, and also to prevent the looting of such valuables as had survived, forbade anyone to return to the districts scorched by the fire until his own work-gangs had sifted the rubble. The reports brought back by the Emperor's surveyors could hardly have been more grim. Many of the city's most celebrated landmarks lay in ruins. From temples founded by Romulus and Servius Tullius to Nero's own great wooden amphitheatre, buildings from every era of Rome's history had been reduced to ashes. Irreplaceable trophies and treasures, priceless memorials to her past, were lost for ever. So too, more pressingly for the homeless, was an immense proportion of the city's housing stock. Hundreds of thousands of people had been left without either belongings or shelter. The mood, not surprisingly, was as angry as it was desperate. That a fire so calamitous and extensive could have been the result merely of accident seemed to defy all probability. People had not forgotten seeing gangs of mysterious hooded figures flitting amid the smoke and flames, brandishing torches. Who had they been? Feverishly, both in what survived of the city and in the immense expanse of tents and ramshackle hovels that now covered both the

Campus and Nero's private gardens, the question was asked and debated. Rome's suffering citizens were sure of only one thing: that the arsonists, once they were identified, deserved to suffer a fate as monstrous and terrible as their crime.

All of which played to Nero's strengths. Who better to devise a theatrical display of retribution than the man who had attempted to drown his own mother with a booby-trapped yacht? Sure enough, once the guilty had been successfully identified and arrested, they were subjected to deaths as grotesque as they were excruciating. Some, for the entertainment of spectators, were torn to pieces by hunting dogs; others were crucified in ways calculated to make them look ridiculous. The need to mock the arsonists as well as to punish them was a pressing one – for otherwise they would have risked haunting the imaginings of the Roman people. The culprits turned out to be the embodiment of everything that decent citizens had always most feared about immigration: the adherents of a sinister, not to say sociopathic, cult. 'Christians', they were called, after their founder, a criminal who had been executed in Judaea back in the days of Tiberius. Worse even than the Jews – whose teachings were at least ancient ones – they were motivated by 'a hatred for the norms of human society':[61] contempt for the gods, and scorn for all those not in their sect. Who could doubt, gazing at the smoking ruins of Rome, that they were the very embodiment of the enemy within? Now, though, thanks to Caesar's tireless efforts, they had been identified, and all was well. Nero, ever the showman, devised a particularly brilliant reassurance of this to his fellow citizens. Not all the Christians were hunted like wild beasts or nailed to crosses. Some, smeared with pitch and set alight, served as human torches: a punishment to fit their crime.* Erected in the Emperor's private gardens, they illumined the flowers and grottoes which Nero had invited the Roman people to come and explore. Nero himself,

---

* According to St Jerome, the total number of Christians martyred by Nero was 979.

dressed as a charioteer, wandered affably among them, mingling with the crowds: the very model of a responsible and popular Princeps. The message was clear. Fire had been tamed, and a menacing superstition with it. The future, thanks to Caesar's stewardship of it, was radiant. Where before there had been darkness, now all was light.

And already, barely the moment the rubble had cooled, this was becoming manifest across the blackened and traumatised capital. Nero had exciting plans for Rome. A city notorious for the cramped and twisting alleyways of its slums, in which teetering, wooden highrises had always cast entire neighbourhoods into permanent shadow, was to receive a comprehensive upgrade. As no one had been in a position to do for centuries, Nero aimed to redraw the map. There was to be no place for ugliness, cheapness and squalor in his capital. Boulevards that were broad and spacious; apartment blocks that did not reach for the sky, but were instead built on a human scale; streetfronts built of stone and adorned with colonnades: these were his prescriptions for a Rome renewed. Even as workmen grateful to be rescued from destitution laboured to clear up the rubble and dump it in the marshes beyond Ostia, Nero was busy with his architects, poring over plans. There was no time to lose. With incentives on offer to those who completed their projects of rebuilding fast, a city brought utterly low was soon being raised back to its feet. Seventeen years earlier, in the Saepta, Claudius had exhibited what was claimed to be a phoenix: a miraculous bird that, every 540 years, would incinerate itself in a mighty bonfire and then emerge from the flames reborn. The display had not been a success. 'No one doubted that it was a fake.'[62] What Nero was sponsoring, though, was far from a fraud. Rome had been consumed by fire; now, amid a mighty shimmering of golden plumage, she was coming back to life. A phoenix, beautiful and splendid, was emerging from the ashes.

Nowhere was this more dazzlingly evident than in the valley between the Palatine and a pair of hills to its east, the Caelian and the Oppian. Here, the damage had been particularly devastating. Fire had incinerated everything in its path, including a palatial development of Nero's and a half-built temple to Claudius. Even the Palatine had been swept by the inferno. Flames had lapped at the temple of Apollo itself. Buildings dating back to the time of the kings were gone, and all the venerable houses of the aristocracy that still, a century after the Republic's collapse, had lined the road that led from the Forum and served as a memorial to the power of Rome's ancient families. In disaster, though, lay opportunity. The fire had left free for development the primest real estate in the world. It was hardly in Nero's nature to let such an opportunity go to waste. Ambitious though his plans were for his fellow citizens, they were not as ambitious as his plans for himself. How could an artist of his vision possibly be expected to confine his living quarters to the Palatine? It was far too cramped, too stuffy. Extend his house to the bounds of the Caelian and the Oppian, though, and at last Nero would be able to live as a man properly should. Like Apollo, whose genius for poetry and music he was so touched by, and like the sun, whose proficiency at driving a chariot he had been emulating for many years, he merited a home appropriate to his infinite talents. He deserved a house that would induce gasps of wonder from the Roman people, and dazzle them with its blaze: a Golden House.

So that was what Nero commissioned. His two architects were justly celebrated, engineers famous for their ability to work with rough terrain and turn it to their advantage; his chief painter, a man so conscious of his dignity that he only ever did his decorations in full toga. Men like these, rising to the challenge set them by Caesar, proved fully equal to his hopes. The Golden House, as they sketched it out for Nero in their plans, was to offer the Roman people nothing less than a vision of what it meant to rule the world. Naturally, the complex would consist of exquisite living quarters, imposing façades and great works of art – that much went without saying. More than that, though, planted in the heart of the largest city ever known, they planned to build something utterly unexpected: a beautiful park. It was to feature a great lake, with buildings set around it to represent

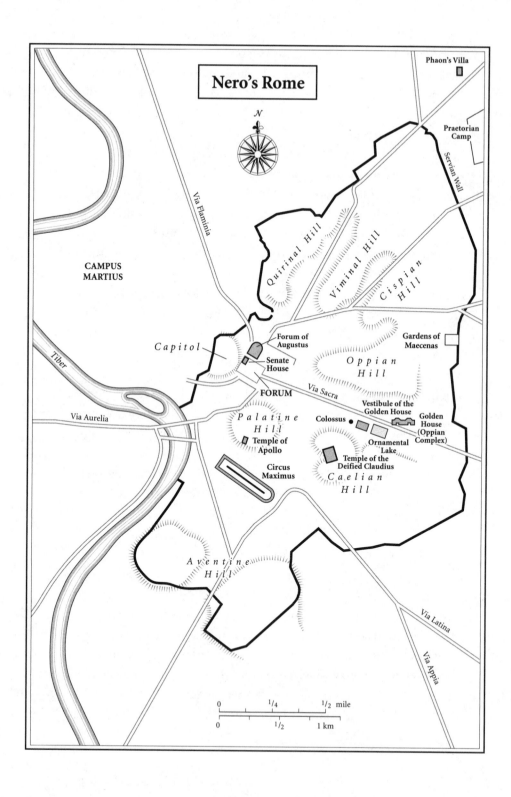

Nero's Rome

Phaon's Villa

Praetorian Camp

Servian Wall

N

CAMPUS MARTIUS

Via Flaminia

Quirinal Hill

Viminal Hill

Cispian Hill

Tiber

Capitol

Forum of Augustus

Senate House

FORUM

Via Sacra

Oppian Hill

Gardens of Maecenas

Via Aurelia

Palatine Hill

Colossus

Vestibule of the Golden House

Golden House (Oppian Complex)

Temple of Apollo

Ornamental Lake

Circus Maximus

Temple of the Deified Claudius

Caelian Hill

Aventine Hill

Via Latina

Via Appia

0   1/4   1/2 mile

0   1/2   1 km

cities; tilled fields and vineyards; woods and pastureland. Animals both wild and domesticated were to roam it. Not just a palace, it offered infinitely more. It was to be a portrayal of all the lands and seas that lay under the sway of Caesar.

The world ruled by Rome was to be brought to the very heart of Rome.

Gilding the Darkness

In May 64, three months before the firestorm that engulfed Rome, Nero travelled to Naples. Although he had never needed any excuse to visit the city, his purpose on this occasion was a specific one. Five years after the party held to mark the first shaving of his beard, Nero had decided to go public with his talent for the lyre. Where better to make his debut than in Italy's most celebrated Greek city? Sophisticated and cosmopolitan, Naples promised just the kind of audience that Nero wanted. He knew that traditionalists in Rome were bound to fume. Indeed, that was all part of the fun. The spectacle on offer was not merely innovative, after all, but positively *avant garde*: 'an emperor treading the boards'.[63]

Nothing was left to chance. Nero's preparations for the great event were meticulous. For months, he had been doing all the obvious things that a singer could do to strengthen his voice: giving himself regular enemas, lying on his back with a lead weight on his chest, eating nothing for days at a time but chives soaked in oil. He had even brought along a claque of five thousand cheerleaders, and ordered his guards to swell the audience so that there would be no chance of empty seats. He need not have worried. The shows were a sell-out. It was not only locals who flocked to the theatre, but fans from out of town as well. Among them were a posse of visiting Alexandrians, whose rhythmic style of applause so delighted Nero that he ordered his own personal cheerleaders to learn from them how it was done. Every inch the personable superstar, he would mingle with his audience after each show, bantering with them in Greek and dining in public. It was all a great success.

Except that one night, during the run of Nero's shows, an earthquake hit the theatre in which he was performing and badly damaged it. Nero himself, pointing to the fact that no one had died, hailed it as a sign of divine approval, and promptly wrote a poem announcing as much. Others were not so sure. To those appalled by Nero's flouting of traditional sensibilities, it seemed as though the foundations of everything that had made Rome great were being violently shaken. Put to the torch as well – for the inferno later that summer was on a scale so patently calamitous as to suggest a fateful disorder in the affairs of gods and men. Although, in the immediate wake of the fire, Nero made efforts to appease the heavens with supplications as showy as he could possibly make them, neither they nor the execution of the sinister and patently seditious Christians prevented whisperings against Caesar himself. No matter how energetic he might show himself in tackling the aftermath of the catastrophe, and no matter how glittering his plans for the reborn city, he could do little to alleviate the immediate misery of people who had lost everything to the fire. Even as the months passed, and the rubble was cleared away, anger continued to fester. Many citizens, nostalgic for the cramped quarters which on Nero's orders were being replaced with sweeping boulevards and low-rise accommodation, complained that in the new city there would be no escaping the sun. Others, even more agonisingly, had to watch as surveyors mapped out the lineaments of lakes and fields over what only a short while before had been their homes. 'An overweening estate has robbed the poor of their dwellings.'[64]

And not only the poor. Senators too had lost properties to the Golden House. Even those whose real estate had not been appropriated knew that Nero, by planting a park in the middle of the city, was placing his foot directly on the corpse of their prestige. For a century and more, the shade of a garden perfumed with exotic blooms had been the ultimate badge of status in Rome. From Maecenas to

Messalina, the elite of the city had hankered after them with slack-jawed longing. Now, though, the game was up. Ringed as it was by hills, the sprawling parkland of the Golden House offered to the gaze of everyone in Rome a glimpse of the pavilions and lawns that previously had been the prerogatives of the super-rich. To the poor, at least, it offered a feel of fresh breezes, a break from the monotony of smoke and brick; to senators only a confirmation that they were as nothing compared to Caesar. 'There stands in the city now only the single house.'[65]

That the familiar sights of central Rome should have been lost to countryside bore witness to what senators found most disorienting about Nero: his ability to dissolve the boundaries of everything that they had always taken for granted. To many it seemed an unnerving power, for it hinted at something more than human. Nero himself, it was true, hardly seemed sprung from a dimension of the supernatural. Bull-necked and podgy, he had never quite lost his baby fat. The image of Caesar, though, was not bound by flesh and blood. Nero, who had transformed a yacht into a death-trap, and the Campus into a brothel, knew how to play tricks with people's expectations. In the workshop of Zenodorus, the world's most famous sculptor, a head almost four metres high was being fashioned out of bronze.[66] Designed to top an immense statue that, when completed, would stand guard over the entrance to the Golden House, it portrayed that golden charioteer of the heavens, the Sun. There was, though, in the contours of the god's face, more than a suggestion of a second charioteer. The Colossus, as the bronze would come to be known, 'was designed to resemble the Princeps'.[67] When completed, the statue was to be crowned by the rays of the sun and portrayed as the guardian of the world. Visible from across the city, it would hint at a status for Nero verging on the divine.

Yet if his face, seen from a certain angle, seemed ablaze with the eeriness of someone more than human, then so also, seen from another, did it seem shadowed by the savagery of a beast. Of the many strange sex games with which Nero was reported to have indulged himself, none was more unsettling than one which had combined a simulation of criminals being torn to pieces with the nauseating practice of oral sex. Men and women – or boys and girls, according to some reports – had supposedly been bound to stakes; Nero, dressed in the skins of a wild animal, had then been released from a cage and pretended to gnaw at their private parts.[68] Scandalous on every level, as his floor-shows were invariably devised to be, the performance had made sinister play with the origins of the Roman people – whose city, as everyone knew, had been founded by a wolf-suckled king. Now, with much of Rome in ruins, it was as though Nero intended to found it anew. It was even claimed that he wished to rename it after himself: 'Neropolis'[69] True or not, such rumours had wide currency. Of a man whose face, seen from a certain angle, might seem that of a god, and from another that of a werewolf, almost anything could be believed. And so it was, in the months that followed the catastrophe of the fire, that a claim was first heard in elite circles so stupefying, so utterly monstrous, that to countenance it was to cast Nero as a criminal without parallel in the history of his city: that he, the heir of Augustus and First Citizen of his people, was the very man who had burned Rome down.

The surest evidence for this appalling charge was, of course, the use to which he had put the calamity; but it was noted as well that the fire, when it began again the second time, had originated on an estate owned by Tigellinus. Flamboyant and murderous, Nero certainly had form when it came to crimes on a mythical scale. What was a spot of arson, after all, to a self-confessed matricide? Just as the guilt he had shown at his mother's murder was as theatrical as it was self-indulgent, so in a similar manner, it was claimed, he had been inspired by the spectacle of Rome burning to play on his lyre and sing of the fall of Troy. Quite where Nero was supposed to have given this performance was much disputed. Some said in his palace, others on its roof, others yet on the tower in Maecenas's gardens. The precise details, to those convinced of his culpability, were unimportant. Rumour, as ever in Rome, had a habit of fuelling itself. That the moon had been full in the sky on the night of the conflagration, rendering it most unsuited to a project of arson; that Nero had thrown himself into the task of fighting the blaze with energy and commitment; that the costs of repairing the damage were crippling: none of these considerations served to extinguish the talk of his guilt.* Instead, just as the fire itself had done, it spread furiously, and it spread fast – and soon enough, come the New Year, it was starting to lick at the foundations of Nero's regime.

'Murderer of mother and wife, a driver of chariots, a performer on the public stage, an arsonist.'[70] The list of charges was long. Few in the upper echelons of Roman society doubted that Nero, if permitted to live, would add to it. To kill a Caesar was, of course, a fearsome thing; but by early 65, enough were convinced of its necessity to start plotting Nero's liquidation. Large numbers of senators and equestrians were recruited to the conspiracy; so too, no less crucially, assorted Praetorians. Most senior of all the officers to join it was Faenius Rufus, who, on the death of Burrus, had been appointed prefect alongside Tigellinus, and whose reputation for honesty was as impressive as his colleague's was shameful. The presence of such a man in the ranks of the plotters helped to boost numbers, steady the waverers, and give to the conspiracy a broader base than any since that against Julius Caesar, more than a century before. Not that the conspirators had any intention of restoring the Republic. Thrasea Paetus, the man who more than any other had come to serve as the conscience of the Senate, and who sedulously marked the birthdays of Brutus and Cassius, was not invited to join the plot. Instead, the intention was to

---

* All the ancient historians of antiquity whose work has survived take Nero's guilt for granted, with the telling exception of Tacitus. 'Whether the disaster was the result of accident or the criminality of the Princeps,' he tells us, 'is uncertain. There are historians who back both points of view.' The same is true today – although with a substantial majority of historians inclined to exonerate Nero. The verdict I would deliver is one of 'not proven' – which is, under the circumstances, more than damning enough.

replace Nero with a new Caesar. Almost half a century after the disgrace and suicide of Gnaeus Calpurnius Piso, it was a scion of the same illustrious family whom the conspirators had fixed upon to serve as their figurehead. Gaius Calpurnius Piso combined a distinguished career of public service with an easy and ready charm: men could imagine him as emperor and not shudder at the prospect. True, he lacked even the vaguest link to the August Family; but that could be overcome. Octavia had not been the only daughter born to Claudius. There was a second, still alive, and in her thirties: Antonia. It was agreed among the conspirators that Piso should divorce his wife and marry her. The link that this would establish to Augustus, although tenuous, would be sufficient — it was hoped — to satisfy the Roman people. Piso's own talent for popularity could then be relied upon to do the rest. Even Seneca, torn between residual loyalty to Nero and horror at what his pupil had become, was prepared to countenance the prospect of a new Caesar. Some among the conspirators went so far as to hope that he might end up emperor himself. Although the ailing philosopher, now in semi-retirement, refused to receive Piso in person, he did not betray the pretender when sounded out. Instead, he temporised. 'Let him know,' he told Piso's emissary with pointed ambivalence, 'that my own security is bound up with his well-being.'[71]

Visions of a universal cataclysm continued to haunt the old man. In his nightmares, he could imagine the sky turning to black, and the whole world lost to darkness. There was, though, in the contemplation of utter calamity, a kind of liberation. When the worst came to the worst, submission could no longer be an option. 'No man is more unhappy than he who never faces adversity. For he is not permitted to prove himself.'[72] Time was when the leading men of the Senate would have demonstrated the truth of this maxim on the line of battle, serving the greatness of their city amid viscera and swarms of thirsty flies, or else perishing in the attempt; but those days were gone. Now, the field of courage open to Rome's most eminent citizens was shrunken and diminished. Not, though, the qualities required to take up position on it. 'No matter how it manifests itself, the measure and value of *virtus* never change.'[73] The courage required to strike at Nero in the Circus, in the full view of the Roman people, as the conspirators planned to do, was a fearsome thing. When it had been suggested to Piso that he invite his victim to Baiae, to the luxurious villa that he owned there, and commit the deed in private, he had refused in tones of contempt. It had to be public, or not done at all. Unless Nero's blood were spilled in the capital, it would never serve to wash clean his crimes. So it was that Flavius Scaevinus, the senator who had laid claim to the honour of striking the first blow, did not trust to his own dagger, but removed one from a temple. The murder was to be nothing squalid. Rather, it was to be a sacrifice.

Yet to live in hope, as Seneca knew, was to live as well with the prospect of failure. 'Those who do so find that the immediate future is forever slipping their grasp, and that desperation then steals in, and the dread of death, that curse which renders everything else a bane.'[74] And so it proved. When news was finally brought to Seneca, waiting anxiously on his estate, of how the conspiracy had fared, it could not have been worse. A freedman in the household of Scaevinus, his suspicions roused after being asked to sharpen his master's dagger, had betrayed the plot. Piso, despite being urged by his backers to launch a coup, had reflected in despair on Nero's popularity with the Roman people, and killed himself. Arrests had been made across the city. Line after line of shackled suspects had been put on trial. Informers had been marshalled, confessions taken, the guilty put to death. 'The origins, progress and suppression of the conspiracy had been fully documented.'[75] There was nowhere left to hide. When Seneca, returning to Rome from Campania, was stopped four miles outside the city by a Praetorian officer and asked to explain the message he had sent to Piso, he knew that nothing he could say, no denials or protestations of innocence, were liable to save him. All his life he had been obsessed by death. The ability to stare it in the face – and if needs be to welcome it – had always been for him the measure of a man. Now at last the moment of his own trial had come. Seneca prepared himself to pass it.

Official confirmation from Nero that he was indeed to kill himself arrived at his villa borne by a squad of Praetorians. His suicide, in the event, was to prove protracted and agonising. First he cut his wrists, then his ankles, and finally behind his knees; but not enough blood would flow. A cup of hemlock, prepared for just such an eventuality, failed in its work as well. Only when Seneca was taken into his bath-house and placed by his slaves in steaming water did he at last feel his life ebb away. He died as he had lived, a philosopher. In his last moments, though, even as he dictated edifying precepts to his atten-dant secretaries, he could not help but linger on the supreme, the scarring failure of his life. Just before slitting his wrists, Seneca had for-mally accused his erstwhile pupil of the crimes that he had been obliged for so long to whitewash. 'After Nero had murdered his mother and brother, what remained for him save to kill his teacher and mentor?'[76] These words, as the dying man had known they would be, were widely bruited, a prosecution from beyond the grave. Nero himself, for all the delight that he reportedly took in the news of Seneca's suicide, could hardly help but be stung. First his mother, now his tutor: both had perished with condemnations of him as a monster on their lips.

Ever since his adoption by Claudius, Nero's longing to bask in the cheers of the Roman people had been at war with his sense of para-noia. It was in the struggle to balance these instincts that he had repeatedly sacrificed those who were closest to him. Now, though, with the revelation of Piso's plot, the full scale of his unpopularity with the Roman elite had been starkly exposed. A stone had been lifted, and hatreds rendered visible to Nero's gaze that seemed to him as contemptible as the scurrying and writhing of a multitude of creep-ing things. That the Senate had turned out to be consumed by its hatred of him came as no great surprise, for Nero had delighted in scandalising it and scorning its ideals. Altogether more of a shock had been his discovery of treason in the camp of the Praetorians. Faenius Rufus, their prefect, had played a desperate double game, torturing and executing his fellow conspirators even as he sought to tip them the wink whenever no one else was watching; but that particular game had been brought to an end when his cover was blown by an indignant Scaevinus. Other officers, though, rather than conceal their role in the conspiracy, had gloried in it. Why, Nero demanded of one, had he broken his oath of loyalty? 'Because,' the centurion replied, 'there was no other way to redeem you from your crimes.'[77] Most, though – so Nero had to reckon – were less fastidious in their morals. Accordingly, in the wake of the conspiracy's suppression, and the execution of the various officers who had proven themselves treacherous, he made sure to throw money at the problem. Massive bonuses, fresh privileges: nothing was too good for the Praetorians. As for prefects, Nero had wearied of men with scruples. Tigellinus's new colleague was a man with a reputation as evil as his own. Nymphidius Sabinus was a tall, grim-faced man, the grandson of Claudius's potent freedman, Callistus. His mother was rumoured to have worked as a whore in the slave quarters on the Palatine. His father, so the rumour had it, was Caligula.

Well might the Senate cower. Nero's boredom with its pretensions, long self-evident, had now patently metastasised. The promotion of Nymphidius, the awarding to Tigellinus of a statue both on the Palatine and in the Forum, the lavishing of honours on henchmen who had helped to secure convictions during the treason trials: all proclaimed it loudly. It was not only Nero's suspicion of the nobility, however, that had been confirmed for him by the exposure of Piso's conspiracy. So too had his need to be loved. Sure enough, barely had the blood of the executed conspirators dried than Nero was readying himself to fulfil at long last a much-cherished ambition and perform on the ultimate public stage: Rome itself.

The background to the occasion was sombre. Plague had struck the city. The streets echoed to mourning and were filled with funeral fires. The crowds, as they filled the theatre, were in a mood to have their spirits raised. Nero duly obliged. To the horror of watching senators, but the delight of his adoring fans, Caesar appeared on stage and recited a poem. He then left the theatre; but the assembled crowds, stamping and applauding, demanded his return, urging him to 'make a public show of all his various talents'.[78] Aulus Vitellius, skilled in the stage-management of such things, promptly hurried after his master. Declaring himself the spokesman of the people, he announced that it was their universal desire to see Caesar enter the contest for best musician. Coyly, Nero allowed his arm to be twisted. Changing into the long flowing robe and platform heels of a *citharode*, he returned to the stage, lyre this time in his hands. His fingers brushed the strings; he cleared his throat; he began to sing. Not even the sweat that was soon pouring down his face could bring him to pause. Only when he was finally done with his performance did he sink to his knees and soak up the ecstatic applause. The verdict of the judges, when it was announced, came as no great surprise. Nero, awarded the palm of victory, had the grace to look relieved; but the true prize was to be heard in the cheering of the crowds. Rhythmic and measured, it echoed to the Roman sky. Nero, as he soaked it up, was able to know himself truly adored.

Which was just as well – for the memory was one that he would soon have all the more reason to cherish. Profoundly though he craved the devotion of the Roman people, there could be no doubting the true love of his life. As glamorous, fashionable and unfeasibly sexy as ever, Poppaea Sabina was now doubly precious to Nero – for she was pregnant too. Already, a couple of years earlier, she had borne her husband a daughter; although the baby had died young, there could be no doubting her ability to give him an heir. It was, then, doubly a calamity when Nero added to the long list of people whose lives he had brought to an end the one that he could least bear to lose. He had never meant to kill Poppaea. It had been foolish of her to nag him, of course, especially when all he had done was to come home late one evening from the races. He had been tired, and pretty much bound to lash out; but even so, he should never have kicked her in her swollen stomach.

Nero's grief, suffused as it was with guilt, was of a suitably titanic order. At Poppaea's funeral, he incinerated an entire year's supply of perfume – and then burned some more, just for good measure.

Rather than watch the body of his beloved turn to ashes, he chose, like a pharaoh of old, to embalm it, before consigning it to the Mausoleum of Augustus. Poppaea herself was declared a goddess, and money extorted from the leading women of Rome to build her a temple. No longer the wife who had died in squalid and miserable circumstances, her swollen belly livid with bruising, she reigned instead eternal in the heavens, the presiding deity of beauty and desire: 'Venus Sabina'.[79]

It was all very Nero. Those who had come to dread and detest him could hardly help but recognise in Poppaea's unhappy fate something of Rome's own. A city too, after all, might be abused, and pummelled, and kicked. Poppaea's death, coming as it did so soon after the suppression of Piso's conspiracy, had done nothing to calm Nero's nerves. 'No matter how many people you put to death,' Seneca had told him in the wake of Agrippina's murder, 'you can never kill your successor.'[80] The warning was one to which Nero, at the time, had been content to pay lip-service; but not now that he had lost his unborn child. With no one of his own blood now to succeed him, his dread of potential rivals had become even greater. He and his mother between them had already done much winnowing, and there remained, with the exception of Nero himself, only a single male descendant of Augustus left alive. Lucius Junius Silanus was young, but he was not naïve. When a posse of soldiers arrived in the remote Italian town to which he had been exiled, he resisted arrest. The attempt was doomed. Strong though he was, he had no sword. The centurion in charge of the death squad cut him down. Other eminent victims soon followed. Some, like Thrasea Paetus, were old enemies of an emperor no longer prepared to tolerate so much as a hint of opposition. Others were men altogether too seasoned in the command of legions for Nero's comfort. Others yet were men famous for their wealth. A year on from the judicial killings that had followed Piso's conspiracy, and it seemed to Rome's elite that the entire nobility was drowning in a superfluity of blood.

Yet the perfumes that Nero had burned in Poppaea's honour and the spices with which he had packed her corpse were reminders that what he could brutalise he could also beautify. The money plundered from senators executed for treason did not just sit in his coffers. Nor did the ever heavier taxes that he had begun to impose on the provinces, nor the income from the fertile estates of Africa that he had moved to appropriate from their owners, nor the treasures that his agents were looting from temples across the entire span of the Roman world. Desperately expensive though it was to rebuild a city as vast as Rome, Nero was hardly the man to stint on the repairs. He had no option but to extract money from whatever source he could – for to economise was unthinkable.

Any lead was worth following up. When an equestrian from Carthage reported a sensational dream, in which he had been shown a great cache of bullion buried under his fields, left there a millennium before by the founder of his city and waiting to be discovered, Nero had dispatched an entire squadron of treasure-hunters to recover it. That a long and increasingly frantic excavation had turned up nothing, and that the Carthaginian himself, mortified in the extreme, had ended up killing himself, was an embarrassment, to be sure; but not a terminal one. Nero remained true to what he saw as his highest responsibility: to delight his fellow citizens. In the early summer of 66, the long-anticipated arrival in Rome of Tiridates, who had at last travelled from Armenia to receive his crown, provided a perfect opportunity to dazzle the Roman people – literally. On the day of the ceremony itself, the sun rose over a Forum crowded with citizens dressed in togas of blinding whiteness, and lined by Praetorians whose armour and standards 'flashed like shafts of lightning'.[81] Once the coronation had been completed, it was staged a second time in the Theatre of Pompey, where the stage, the walls and even the props had been gilded to extravagant effect. There, beneath a rich purple awning which portrayed Nero as a celestial charioteer surrounded by golden stars, Tiridates paid him obeisance. No one could doubt, looking at the king in his barbarous robes prostrating himself before Caesar, that the far ends of the world had come in submission to its centre. It was indeed, as everyone said, 'a golden day'.[82]

What did it matter that shanty towns filled with those made home-less by the fire continued to dot the city's outskirts, or that in close rooms heavy with the sweat of desperation there was no proroguing the treason trials just because the king of Armenia was in town? And later, when Tiridates had gone back home, the gold had been stripped from Pompey's theatre and the rose petals swept up from the Forum, still there was no diminution in the blaze of Nero's glamour. Looming beyond the Forum rose the base of the massive bronze fashioned by Zenodorus, the half-constructed Colossus that, when completed, would brush the stars with the rays of its diadem. Beyond it in turn stretched the lake, the forests and the fields which simulated, in the heart of the capital, all the manifold natural beauties of the world. Meanwhile, gilded and adorned with jewels, the façade of the Golden House extended from the side of the Oppian Hill, and all the summer long seemed lit by fire. It was as though, in the midst of the scorched and nervous city, the Sun himself had built his palace.

Nero could afford to scorn his enemies. For a decade and more he had been straining on the leash, eager to break free from the pre-scriptions of a crabbed and superseded order and to create, as befitted the supreme artist that he was, his own reality. The Senate, wounded and demoralised, appeared powerless to resist him; the people, enrap-tured by his command of fantasy and spectacle, eager to participate in his reconfiguring of what it might mean to be a Roman. There seemed nothing that Nero, if he wished it, could not ultimately bend to his will.

Back to Reality

Early in the autumn of AD 66, a great fleet of ships bearing Caesar and his entourage pulled into the harbour of Corinth.[83] Situated on the narrow isthmus that separated mainland Greece from the Peloponnese to the south, the city was very much Nero's kind of place. Celebrated for its prostitutes and bronzes, it also boasted a

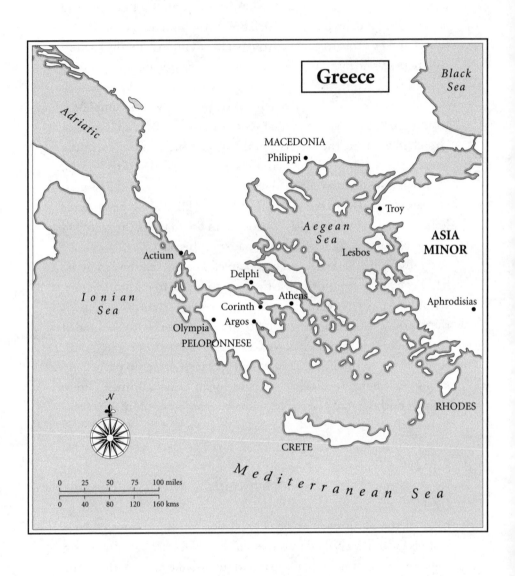

Greece

Black Sea

Adriatic

MACEDONIA

Philippi •

Troy •

Aegean Sea

ASIA MINOR

Actium •

Delphi •

Lesbos

Ionian Sea

Athens •

Corinth •

Aphrodisias •

Olympia •

Argos •

PELOPONNESE

RHODES

N

CRETE

Mediterranean Sea

| 0 | 25 | 50 | 75 | 100 miles |
| 0 | 40 | 80 | 120 | 160 kms |

famous festival: the Isthmian Games. Every two years, huge crowds would gather outside Corinth to gawp at a variety of sporting and artistic contests. 'All of Asia and Greece come together for these games.'[84] Now, though, a visitor from Italy was planning to make his presence felt at the event. Nero, fresh from his triumphs in Naples and Rome, was ready to take the festival circuit of Greece by storm.

Obedient to his orders, organisers of the most prestigious games had rescheduled their events to ensure that they could all be held in the single year. As a result, the Olympics had been postponed for the first time in their history, while other festivals had been specially brought forward. Nero intended to compete in them all. That done, he aimed to continue eastwards, there to win yet further glory by subduing the barbarians who lurked beyond the Caucasus. Not since Claudius's expedition to Britain had a Caesar left for the provinces; and not since Augustus had toured the eastern Mediterranean and won back the eagles from Parthia had quite such an extended absence from Rome been planned by a ruler of the world. The hype, as Nero headed east, was immense. One astrologer foretold that he would make an island of the Peloponnese by cutting a canal through the Isthmus, a second that he would sit on a golden throne in Jerusalem. The whole of Greece was agog.

Meanwhile, back in Rome, there were plenty who regarded Nero's eastern adventure with disgust. The more exclusive the circles, the greater the sense of outrage tended to be. The contempt was, of course, entirely mutual. To watch Nero's travelling companions descend the gangplanks onto Corinthian soil was to know that the Roman elite had been put decisively in the shade. Not since Tiberius's retirement to Capri had access to Caesar been so humiliatingly barred to them. Heading down the Appian Way to take ship for Greece, Nero had been alerted to yet another plot against his life, its exposure confirming him in a suspicion of the Senate that would have done credit to Caligula. 'I detest you, Caesar, for being of senatorial rank.'[85] This joke, often repeated in his presence by a particular henchman of his, a hobbling one-time cobbler named Vatinius, never failed to bring a smile to

Nero's lips. True, not all senators were banned from his presence. Looking ahead to the projected campaigning in the Caucasus, Nero had made sure to bring with him on his travels the odd seasoned campaigner. Typical was a former consul by the name of Vespasian. A veteran of the conquest of Britain, his war record had just about served to compensate for his unfortunate habit of falling asleep during Nero's recitals. Yet in truth, Vespasian was only of marginally better stock than Vatinius, and not all his commands and magistracies could obscure the fact that his grandfather had worked as a debt collector. For those in the Senate who could still trace their ancestry back to the heroic beginnings of Rome, it was a profound humiliation. What was there to choose between a former cobbler and a peasant who had risen to become a consul? That Vatinius was a malicious and disreputable parasite and Vespasian a decorated war hero made barely a difference. Both had the ear of Caesar. The world was turned upside down.

But there was worse. Soldiers and courtiers were not the only people in the retinue of Augustus's heir. There were also to be found in it teeming hordes of musicians, voice coaches and personal trainers – for Nero, as a contender in the Olympic or Isthmian Games, could hardly be expected to function without vast numbers of backroom staff. In Greece, the home of drama and competitive sport, the notion that what happened in a theatre or on a race track might hold up a mirror to the broader world was a familiar one; but never before had anyone thought to blur the boundaries between them to quite such dizzying effect. Nero was not, as most visitors to the province were, a tourist. He had no interest in merely poking around the sights. The Greece that he had come to experience was not the land of art and antiquities, but of still living myth. A games staged in Olympia, or on the Isthmus, or in Argos, where Agamemnon had once reigned, or at Delphi, where Apollo had his most famous shrine, offered communion with the legendary heroes of the past in a way that no corresponding festival in Rome ever could.

It was this that gave to all those who competed in them their glamour; and it was why, despite his status as Caesar, Nero refused to take first place for granted. Without the edge of genuine competition, after all, his victories would be worthless. Hence, just like any other entrant in the games, he was prey to stage-fright, bitched about his rivals behind their backs and lived in dread of the judges. Ruler of the world or no, he could not afford a performance that would make him look a fraud – and everyone knew it. That the judges, at event after event, had little choice but to award him first prize did not diminish the genuine awe felt by many spectators at his feats. The greatest festivals in Greece had all been founded by gods or heroes of royal blood; and now, with the arrival of Caesar to headline at them, the ancient days of song and legend seemed renewed. Across the East, wherever theatres were to be found and sporting contests staged, the glamour of his achievements could hardly help but blaze. Senators in Rome might scoff, but Nero had his eyes fixed, not just on the capital, but on all the lands that he ruled.

In Greece, he could breathe more freely. Visitors to the great festivals there were attuned to his sensibility. Back in Rome, for instance, even Nero had hesitated to perform as an actor. Those who made a show of their bodies before the public gaze, draping themselves in exotic costumes and speaking other people's lines, were regarded by upstanding citizens as little better than whores. It was this that explained their presence alongside adulterers and gladiators among the class of people defined by the law as *infames*. Disapproval of the theatre was a venerable Roman tradition. Moralists had always condemned it as a threat to 'the qualities of manliness for which the Roman people are renowned'.[86] Actors, it was sternly noted, were inclined to effeminacy. They rarely had due respect for the boundary that existed between male and female. Only strictness could serve to patrol it. An actor who had found it amusing to keep a married woman as a page, her hair cut short to look like a boy's, had been whipped and banished from Rome on the personal instructions of Augustus himself. Those who played others in public threatened subversion at every level. Even the most basic fundamentals risked being undermined. Seneca, watching a play in which a slave played

Agamemnon and imperiously threw his weight around, had been prompted to reflect on the illusory nature of rank itself. 'Who is the "Lord of Argos"?' he had mused. 'Why, only a slave!'[87]

No such anxiety, though, was likely to trouble Caesar. That Nero, like so many of the heroes who featured in the repertoire, was descended from a god, and wielded kingly power, gave to his appearance on the stage a quite exceptional heft. Acting came naturally to him. Back in the first days of his rule, addressing the Senate, he had delivered a speech composed for him by Seneca and been roundly mocked for it behind his back: 'for those with long memories noted that he was the first emperor to rely on borrowed eloquence'.[88] Even then, though, Nero had penetrated to the heart of what it meant to be a Princeps. To rule as Caesar was to play a part. The performance was all. Now, arrived in Greece, Nero's aim was to make this apparent to the entire world. Taking to the stage, sometimes his mask would be painted to look like the hero he was playing, sometimes to look like himself. No one could mistake the point that was being made. The events of Nero's life, its many trials and tribulations, were as worthy a subject of drama as anything conjured up from myth. To watch him star as Orestes was to know that the murder of Clytaemnestra had been rivalled by a second, no less terrible act of matricide. When he played the part of a woman giving birth, who could not reflect on the tragedy that had seen him lose his heir? When he wore a mask fashioned after the features of Poppaea, who could not be reminded of the homicidal fits of madness sent by the gods upon many an ancient hero, and pity Nero likewise? It was a bravura act. Vision, audacity, conceit: his performance boasted them all. Only Nero could have attempted it; only Nero could have pulled it off to such stunning effect.

Resurrecting Poppaea on the stage was only a beginning, though. Beyond the theatre too, Nero aimed to bend reality to his will. His sense of bereavement remained unassuaged. In the wake of Poppaea's death, he had briefly considered marrying Antonia, the only surviving child of Claudius; but when she, not surprisingly, had shown herself reluctant to wed her sister's killer, he had opted instead to have her put to death for treason. Tellingly, his choice of a new wife had been a woman very like Poppaea. Statilia Messalina, lately married to a consul executed in the wake of Piso's conspiracy, was stylish, beautiful and clever. Nevertheless, not even the fascination she shared with Nero for training and strengthening her voice could compensate, in her new husband's opinion, for her one abiding drawback: she was not Poppaea.[89] This was why, just as Nero had once delighted in sleeping with a whore who looked like his mother, he had ordered a hunt to be made for a doppelgänger of the wife he had kicked to death. Sure enough, a woman with a close resemblance to Poppaea had been located, and delivered to his bed; but he had soon wearied of her. Then someone else had been tracked down: someone soft-skinned, amber-haired, irresistible. To Nero, brought this prize, it was as though his dead wife had been restored to him. So completely did he imagine himself to be gazing on her face again, caressing her cheeks and taking her in his arms, that Poppaea seemed to him redeemed from the grave. Nevertheless, there was a twist. For all the eeriness of the resemblance, it was not a woman who had been found for Nero – nor even a girl. The lookalike, so perfect as to convince a grieving husband, was not perfect in every detail. The double of Poppaea Sabina, Nero's greatest love, was a boy.

Nothing was more ephemeral than beauty of such a kind. Like the blossoms of spring, it afforded a delight that was all the sweeter for being so fleeting. It was this quality that rendered boys with exquisite looks such luxury items of merchandise. Rather like Lucrine oysters, they were prized highly by those who bought them precisely because they were so quick to go off. A slave-dealer, desperate not to lose value on his merchandise, might use ants' eggs to retard the growth of hair in a boy's armpits, and blood from lambs' testicles to keep his cheeks smooth; an owner, rather than accept that a treasured catamite had hit puberty, might dress him as a girl 'and keep him beardless by smoothing away his hairs, or else plucking them out by the roots'.[90] The grim truth was, though, that there existed only one reliable option for preserving the springtime of a boy's looks; and Nero had duly taken it.

Sporus, he had nicknamed his victim, 'Spunk'. Even when mocking traditional values, Nero remained sufficiently a Roman to find eunuchs a bit of a joke. If not quite as sinister as the *Galli*, whose castration was self-inflicted, boys gelded on the orders of their masters trailed after them the unmistakable perfume of the countercultural. Soft, infertile and indelibly associated with the harems of eastern despots, they could hardly have been less in tune with the stern virtues of Roman manhood – which was, of course, for those with an eye to fashion, precisely the point. Maecenas, while administering Italy during the Actium campaign, had scandalised conservatives by appearing in public with an escort of two eunuchs; Sejanus, confirming moralists in their loathing for him, had owned one called 'Boy Toy', whose record sale-price, even decades later, could still provoke gasps of wonder.[91] Nero, though, as was his invariable habit, had gone just that little bit further in scandalising respectable opinion. Yes, Sporus had been gelded to ensure the preservation of his beauty – but that was not the only reason for castrating him. It was not a eunuch that Nero was interested in taking to bed, after all, but his dead wife. He wanted Poppaea Sabina back.

And so that was the name given to her double. As his instructress in becoming an Augusta, Sporus was assigned a woman of high rank named Calvia Crispinilla, whose qualifications as a wardrobe mistress could hardly have been bettered. Modish and aristocratic, she had also won herself a notorious reputation as 'Nero's instructress in sexual pleasures'.[92] Delivered into Calvia's hands, Sporus was duly arrayed in Poppaea's robes, his hair teased into her favoured style and his face painted with her distinctive range of cosmetics. 'Everything he did, he had to do it as a woman'[93] – and a wife of Caesar's at that. As Nero toured Greece, so Sporus travelled with him, borne in the litter of an Augusta and attended by a bustling train of maids. Only one thing remained to complete the transformation. The nuptials, when they were staged during the course of Nero's sojourn in Greece, positively screamed tradition. The bride, veiled in saffron, was given away by Tigellinus; wild celebrations were held throughout the province; prayers were even raised to the gods that the happy couple would have children. Only one thing prevented the illusion from being complete: the new Poppaea Sabina's lack of a woman's anatomy.

Even that was not for want of trying. Nero, if he could have done, would have excised the maimed remnants of genitals from Sporus altogether, parted the living flesh of the wretched boy's groin and opened up a passageway to an implanted uterus. The blatant impossibility of fulfilling such an ambition did not prevent huge rewards being offered to anyone who might achieve it – whether by surgery, or else by darker means. The cutting of a channel where before there had been none was precisely the kind of project that had always tickled Nero's fancy. Back in Italy, he had ordered the construction of a canal stretching all the way from Puteoli to the Tiber, a distance of some 150 miles. Then in Greece, rising to the challenge set by the oracles, he had no sooner arrived in Corinth than he was giving orders for a canal to be hacked out through the Isthmus. An engineering project designed to facilitate the flow of trade, it was also something much more. The ceremony which inaugurated the project could hardly have made this more explicit. Emerging from a sumptuous tent, Nero kicked things off by singing a hymn about sea nymphs; then, taking a golden pitchfork, he struck the earth with it three times. Snipping the Peloponnese from mainland Greece, he proudly declared, would be on a par with anything achieved by the heroes of legend. Fantasy and a spectacular infrastructure project; golden pitchforks and gangs of toiling prisoners; songs about sea nymphs and the sweat and strain of cutting through hard rock: it was all inimitably Nero.

But what if reality, rather than submitting to the dictates of his imagination, insisted on defying them? Sporus's groin remained without a vagina; the canal that was supposed to link Puteoli to the Tiber appeared stuck in the Bay of Naples; the excavations at the Isthmus prompted dark warnings behind Nero's back that he was trespassing on the affairs of the gods. Meanwhile, beyond the stadia and theatres of Greece, on distant frontiers and in remote provinces, the affairs of the world did not stay still. Reports from the East were particularly ominous. In Judaea, long-simmering tensions had finally exploded into open revolt. News of a failed attempt to restore order in Jerusalem had been reported to Nero shortly after his arrival in Corinth. Rather than abandon his tour of Greece and head to Judaea himself, he had opted to send the best man ready to hand: Vespasian. Meanwhile, back in Rome, rumours that the Senate was to be abolished, and responsibility for the provinces handed over to equestrians and Nero's freedman, were doing nothing to steady nerves. Spies, keeping track of potential conspiracies, noted an alarming increase in correspondence between various governors in Gaul and Spain. Prominent among them was Nero's legate in Lugdunum, a senator descended from one of the Gallic royal families, by the name of Gaius Julius Vindex. 'Physically fit and mentally alert, seasoned in war and bold enough not to shrink from a perilous enterprise, he combined a deep love of liberty with immense ambition.'[94] Such qualities, in the death throes of the Republic, might well have marked him out as a contender in the great game of the civil wars; but those days were long gone. No one now could hope to rule the world who was not a descendant of Augustus. Of that much Nero was confident. Nevertheless, when it was reported to him that Vindex had been in communication with Galba, who for eight years had been serving as a governor in Spain, he did feel a slight fluttering of alarm. Seasoned by now in what it took to nip treachery in the bud, he gave orders to his spymasters. Galba was to be eliminated. Then, having issued those instructions, Nero turned his attentions back to a more important matter: his ongoing tour of Greece.

His boldest and most hair-raising feat was achieved, fittingly enough, on the greatest sporting stage of all. Of the many events staged at Olympia, none could compare for sheer peril and excitement with the chariot race. Reaching back to the origins of the games, it was the festival's ultimate showcase for skill and courage. Nero, by entering it, was taking his life in his hands — and all the more so because, rather than the normal complement of four horses, he intended to race with a team of ten. It was the god-like thing to do, of course; but it also required extremes of practice that no one distracted by the care of the Roman world could possibly have attained. Unsurprisingly, then, amid the dust, the collisions and the hairpin bends, Nero was thrown. Watching as he lay on the baked dirt of the race track, curled up against the lethal passage of the other chariots, inches from being crushed to death, no one would have blamed him for retiring from the contest. But he was Caesar, and made of sterner stuff. Dazed and bruised, Nero insisted on clambering back into his vehicle and renewing the contest. Although it proved beyond him to complete the race, the crowds still rose to applaud him. The judges awarded him first prize.

The seal was set on a remarkable love affair. For the first time, a Caesar had appealed over the heads of the senatorial elite, not simply to the Roman people, but to those without citizenship, to provincials. On 28 November 67, at a grand ceremony in Corinth, Nero made this official. 'Men of Greece, I bestow on you a gift beyond your wildest expectations.' Their taxes, he informed them, were abolished — a magnificent gesture. 'I grant you this favour out of good will, not pity, and as a mark of gratitude to your gods, whose care for me both by land and sea I have always found so constant.'[95]

Meanwhile, though, across the remainder of the Roman world, there was no let-up in the screwing out of taxes. Even as Judaea burned, provincials elsewhere were being bled white to pay for Nero's rebuilding of Rome and his projected campaigns in the East. In Gaul, in Spain and in Africa, resentment of his agents, 'whose exactions were as criminal as they were cruel and oppressive',[96] was steadily mounting. Whereas in Greece and the provinces to the east Nero's achievements were widely bruited, in Spain mockery of him was widespread, and satires against him openly repeated. Galba, who had intercepted the message sent from Greece that he should be put to death, pointedly made no attempt to suppress them. Still, though, he hesitated to make his opposition to Nero's regime public. Other governors too, terrified of provoking their master's suspicions and mistrustful of each other, likewise preferred to lurk and wait, and see what might happen.

Few had any doubts as to the stakes. For a century, the world had been at peace. No one could remember a time when citizen had fought with citizen. Nevertheless, memories of the great blood-letting of the civil wars, when the Roman people had almost destroyed themselves, and the world with them, remained vivid. Seneca, in plighting himself to the service of Nero, had reached for language that he knew his young master would particularly appreciate. Only if kept hitched to the chariot of a Caesar, he had declared, would the Roman people be spared calamity: 'for were they to slip the reins, then all their greatness and power would surely be shattered into splinters'.[97] The conceit was not his own. Maimed horses, splintered wheels, corpses lying broken in the dust: again and again, in the world before the rise to supremacy of Augustus, men had glimpsed in these spectacles an image of much greater ruin. What feeling more terrifying for a people, after all, than to know themselves hurtling out of control, and powerless to stop it? 'As when chariots burst out from the barriers, gathering speed with each lap, and the driver, borne along by the horses, tugs upon the reins in vain, and finds the car does not obey them.'[98] Understandably, therefore, those with legions at their backs hesitated to come out in open insurrection; understandably, too, the news of Nero's crash in the Olympic Games, when reported back in Rome, prompted considerable reflection.

In the event, the freedman he had appointed to administer the capital in his absence had to travel to Greece in person, to persuade his master of the scale of the gathering crisis and the desperate need for his return. Spited of the chance to proceed to the Caucasus and play at being a general, Nero was not the man, of course, to let that stop him making a splash. His entry into Rome was as spectacular as any procession ever witnessed in the city. Indeed, in a conscious echo of the triumphs awarded his great-great-grandfather, he rode in the chariot once used by Augustus. Nero, though, was celebrating victories that no Roman had ever won before. He wore on his head the wreath of wild olive that proclaimed him a winner at the Olympic Games; by his side stood the world's most famous *citharode*, whom he had defeated in open contest. Banners proclaimed Nero's titles, and all the numerous crowns that he had won in Greece were borne before him, for the edification and delight of the Roman people. Meanwhile, along the perfumed procession route, songbirds were released, and ribbons and sweets tossed to the cheering crowds. 'Hail to Nero, our own Apollo!' they cried. 'Augustus! Augustus! O Divine Voice! Blessed are they that hear you!'[99]

No matter the gloomy warnings of his security advisors, Nero could feel confident that he still enjoyed the love of the Roman people. He had always relied upon his incomparable mastery of image to dazzle and confound his enemies, and he had no intention of changing that now. Yet the ultimate test was fast approaching. In Gaul, where Julius Vindex had been biding his time, waiting for the right moment to raise the banner of rebellion, Nero faced an adversary with a mastery of propaganda almost the equal of his own. In March 68, a coin was minted on Vindex's orders which showed two daggers, and a cap of the kind worn by slaves when granted their freedom. It was a pointed illustration. One hundred and twelve years earlier, in the wake of the Ides of March, Brutus had issued a near-identical design; and now it was the Ides of March again.[100] Nero, who had retired to Naples for the spring, received the news of the revolt from Vindex himself. A letter from the rebellious governor reached him on 19 March, the anniversary of his mother's death. The coincidence, once again, was pointed. Vindex had a talent for drawing blood. Not content with addressing Nero as 'Ahenobarbus', he rubbed salt in the wound by deriding the Emperor's ability as a musician. Nero, stung to the quick, could not help but betray his indignation. 'Repeatedly he would corner people, and demand, did they know of anyone who ranked as his equal?'[101]

In general, though, he affected dismissive contempt towards the threat of rebellion. More than a week had passed before he made a formal response to Vindex's insulting letter, and in that time he had made sure to pursue his customary interests with a perfect show of calmness and indifference. Nero knew what he faced in Vindex. The muscle-bound sense of duty, the parading of martial values, the harping on moral codes bred of an age when the Roman people had subsisted on turnips: it was everything he most despised. In his attempt to reach over the heads of the senatorial elite to the masses who cared nothing for their antique pretensions he had deliberately mocked everything that Vindex represented: and he continued to mock it now. Rather than address the Senate in person, he sent them a letter, explaining that he had a sore throat and needed to save his voice for his singing. When he did invite some prominent senators to a consultation, he spent most of the meeting showing them his plans for a new kind of hydraulic organ, and even promised to play it for them in due course – 'just so long as Vindex does not object'.[102] Nero's sarcasm was bred, not of insouciance, but of the very opposite: determination never to respond to his enemies' propaganda on its own terms. Leaving a drunken banquet one evening, he declared his intention to appear before Vindex's legions unarmed and do nothing but weep; 'and then, after he had persuaded the rebels by that means to change their minds, he would the next day rejoice among his rejoicing subjects, and sing hymns of victory – which, indeed, he ought at that very moment to be composing'.[103]

Behind the scenes, though, Nero was taking the threat to his regime very seriously indeed. Although he could not resist commissioning a wagon train to transport his various props to the front, nor arming his concubines like Amazons and giving them all a military short back and sides, he knew better than to rely on theatricals. So it was that he summoned the expeditionary force he had readied for the Caucasus campaign to Italy, conscripted vast numbers of marines, and even slaves, into hurriedly raised legions, and dispatched them northwards, there to patrol the frontier with Gaul. To command them, he chose a former governor of Britain by the name of Petronius

Turpilianus, who had proven his loyalty to Nero's satisfaction by taking a prominent role in the suppression of Piso's conspiracy. Simultaneously, letters were sent to the recently appointed General of the North, a man of noted integrity named Virginius Rufus, with orders to muster the legions of the Rhine and march south against Vindex. So it was, then, even as he chatted away nonchalantly to senators about musical instruments, that Nero could contemplate with satisfaction the pincer movement threatening his foes. The rebels appeared certain to be crushed. For good measure, though, Nero made sure to offer a fortune to whomever could bring him Vindex's head.

But then, in mid-April, the news took a turn for the worse. Galba, showing his hand at last, had declared himself a legate, not of Caesar, but of the Senate and the Roman people. Recognising in the blue-blooded veteran of the German front an altogether more formidable class of adversary than Vindex, Nero promptly fainted. When he came to, and was reassured by his old nurse that many princes in the past had faced similar evils, he brushed aside this well-meaning attempt to console him by informing her, in a tone of some asperity, that his own woes were wholly without precedent. Worse, though, was to come. Galba's rebellion prompted numerous others who had been patiently biding their time to join him. Some familiar names were among their ranks. Otho, erstwhile husband of Poppaea, had leapt at the chance to return from Spain, where he was serving as one of its governors, and had unhesitatingly pledged his loyalty to Galba. Meanwhile, in Africa, the sinister Calvia Crispinilla, tutor to the wretched Sporus in the arts of being an Augusta, had thrown in her lot with the province's governor, and incited him to join the insurrection. Then, in May, came the bitterest blow, a defection all the more cruel because it came garbed in the robes of triumph. The armies of the Rhine, meeting with Vindex's forces, had annihilated their opponents. Vindex himself had committed suicide. Rather than renew their oaths to Nero on the battlefield, though, the victorious legions had hailed their general as emperor. Virginius, true to his reputation for moral probity, had turned them down; but only then to declare his neutrality in the looming struggle for control of the world. Meanwhile, it was reported of Petronius, the general entrusted by Nero with the defence of northern Italy, that he too was wavering in his loyalties. The habit of obedience to the House of Caesar, forged by Augustus and his heirs over a century and more, appeared suddenly on the verge of collapse. The old wolfishness, the savagery that in the earliest days of Rome had seen Remus felled by Romulus, had not, after all, it seemed, been tamed for good. Rushing to meet each other in the ecstasy of mutual slaughter, the legions of Virginius and Vindex had both ignored their commanders' efforts to hold them back. 'The crash of the battle had been terrible – like that of charioteers whose horses refuse to obey them.'[104] As in the terrible days before the rise to supremacy of Augustus, so now. Events were careering madly out of control.

And Nero, seasoned charioteer that he was, knew it. Brought the news of Petronius's defection while he was dining, he tipped over the table in his fury, and dashed a couple of precious goblets to the floor. Then, after making sure to source a supply of poison, he left behind him the sprawling magnificence of the Golden House and headed for one of his estates further out of town. Here, wrestling with his options, he abandoned himself to despair. Even the Praetorians, whose love he had always gone to such extremes to court, appeared to be wavering. When Nero urged their officers to rally to him, they temporised. 'Is it really such a terrible thing to die?'[105] These words, addressed by a Praetorian officer directly to Nero's face, were like a touch of ice. Evidently, the cancer of disloyalty was starting to reach into the very heart of his regime. Were there any so close to him now that they could still be trusted not to switch sides? Certainly, there was no sign either of Tigellinus or of his colleague as Praetorian prefect, Nymphidius Sabinus. Both, Nero had to reckon, had abandoned his cause. Both, in his hour of need, had proven themselves true to their reputations as venal and treacherous.

In a mood of mounting desperation, Nero now began to turn other plans over and over in his mind. Perhaps, come the morning, he should head to the Forum dressed in black and make a direct appeal to the Roman people, employing all his talent for pathos? Or perhaps he should flee to Alexandria? Nero decided to sleep on it. His dreams, though, were fitful. Waking up at midnight, he found to his horror that the villa was almost empty. His guards had gone, and his friends, and even the caretakers – who, to add injury to insult, had stolen his supply of poison. Briefly, Nero wondered whether to hurl himself into the Tiber; but then, after a histrionic dash out into the night, he decided that he was not yet ready to abandon hope altogether, and returned inside. A few loyal companions still remained to him: Sporus, his beautiful woman's face and amber hair a reminder of happier days, and three attendants. One of these, a freedman by the name of Phaon, offered his master the use of a villa to the north of Rome. Unable to think of any better bolt-hole, Nero accepted. Still barefoot, he wrapped himself up in a faded cloak and covered his head, and then, after mounting a horse, held a handkerchief up to his face. As lightning jagged in the sky, and the earth quaked, he and his four companions cantered out into the streets and embarked on their escape from Rome.

The journey was a hair-raising one. Riding past the Praetorian camp, the five horsemen could hear wild slogans being shouted: prophecies of doom for Nero and of success for Galba. A passer-by, seeing the speed at which they were riding, assumed that they were hunting the fugitive emperor, and cheered them on. Most heart-stopping of all, when Nero's horse was startled by the stench of a corpse abandoned in the road, and he let slip the handkerchief covering his face, a retired Praetorian recognised him. The soldier did nothing, though, beyond saluting him; and so Nero, against the odds, was able to make it to Phaon's villa. Yet even here, there were fresh indignities to endure. Because Phaon insisted that they enter by the back, Nero was required to stumble through reeds and brambles, and then, after his companions had dug a tunnel, to squeeze himself under the wall. Shattered and despairing, he tottered into the slave quarters and flung himself down in the first room he came to, a mean and squalid chamber with no furniture for him to rest on beyond a lumpy mattress. Here, mourning the ruin that had overwhelmed him, Nero ordered his companions to prepare him a pyre and dig him a grave. Still, despite the urgings of his companions, he hesitated. The scale of his downfall numbed him. He could not bring himself to take the final step. Instead, he could only weep, and lament the loss to the world that his death would spell.

Then a letter arrived, borne by one of Phaon's couriers.* Nero snatched it from the man's hand. He read it, and as he did so, he turned paler still. The Senate had declared him a public enemy. No mercy was to be shown him. Senators, as though in honour of a time when there had been no Caesars to put them in the shade, had sentenced him to a death as antique as it was savage. He was to be stripped naked, yoked and led through the streets, and beaten to death with rods. Rather than suffer such a fate, Nero knew, he had no choice but to finish things off himself. He picked up a pair of daggers, tested their points, then put them down again. 'The fatal hour,' he cried out, 'has still not come.'[106]

But it had. Even as he was instructing Sporus to mourn him as a wife properly should, by wailing and tearing at her hair and robes, he heard the sound of hoofbeats thundering towards the villa. Again, he reached for his dagger. This time, with the aid of a freedman, he summoned the courage to drive it into his throat. A centurion, rushing into the room, attempted to staunch the flow of blood with his cloak, but it was too late. 'Such loyalty,'[107] the dying man murmured; and then his eyes began to bulge horribly. Nero Claudius Caesar Augustus Germanicus was dead.

And with him the entire dynasty of which he had been the last surviving member. Its extinction came as no surprise to those versed in

---

* An intriguing implication of this letter is that Phaon had tipped people off as to where he was going. The arrival of a death squad soon afterwards implies that agents of Galba would have been among them.

the art of reading omens. In the villa once owned by Livia, in the laurel grove, stood four withered trees. Each one had been planted by a Caesar; and each one, shortly before the Caesar's death, had died. Then, shortly before Nero's suicide, the tree that he too had planted had begun to wither – and with it, from the roots up, the entire laurel grove. The chickens too, bred of the hen dropped miraculously into Livia's lap, had all expired. The meaning could hardly have been any clearer. The line of the Caesars was destined to end with Nero – and so it had proved. To be sure, emperors would follow in his wake, and all would be graced with the title of Caesar. None of them, however, would rule as descendants of Augustus. Galba, too old, too stern and too mean to delight a people still half in love with Nero, did not last long; and sure enough, in January 69, beside the spot in the Forum where Marcus Curtius had once vanished into the abyss, he was hacked to death. Otho followed three months later; eight months after him, Vitellius. Three emperors had perished in the space of a year. In the end, it was left to Vespasian, back from the Jewish war, to establish himself as master of the world. More than that, he succeeded in founding a new dynasty. When he died in his bed a decade later, he was succeeded by his eldest son, who in turn was followed by his younger brother. Like Augustus and Claudius, Vespasian even ended up a god.

Never again, though, would the Roman people be ruled by emperors touched by the sheer mystique and potency that membership of the August Family had bestowed upon the heirs of Augustus. Nero, taking to the stage, had been right to recognise within himself the quality of myth. All his family had possessed it. The blood in their veins had been touched by the supernatural. The dynast who had healed the wounds of civil war, and planted in the midst of a king-hating people an impregnable and enduring autocracy, was justly reckoned a god. The name of Augustus would remain a sacred one for as long as there were men who wore the title of Caesar. It served as an assurance to humanity that a man midway between the earthly and the divine might indeed reign as a universal prince of peace, and ascend triumphant to heaven. Augustus, victorious over his enemies as no man in history had been, had triumphed eventually over death itself. So too had his heirs. Even Caligula had haunted the house where he was murdered, and the gardens where his body was burned. When Nero killed himself, and brought the bloodline of Augustus to extinction, many simply refused to believe it. Decades on, across the Roman world, people were convinced that he would come again. 'Everybody wishes he were still alive.'[108]

Even those who had suffered most terribly at his hands, and had every reason to execrate his memory, could not help but acknowledge the charisma of the House of Caesar. Some three decades after Nero's suicide, a Christian named John recorded a vision of the end days revealed to him by an angel. Out of the sea he had seen a seven-headed beast rise; 'and one of its heads seemed to have a mortal wound'.[109] What was the wound, so many who read John's vision would wonder with dread, if not the sword blow to the throat with which Nero had ended his own life?* The wound, so the angel had revealed to John, was destined to be healed; and the beast, which 'was, and is not',[110] would rise from the bottomless pit. On its back would ride a woman; and the woman would be 'arrayed in purple and scarlet, and bedecked with gold and jewels and pearls, holding in her hand a golden cup full of abominations and the impurities of her fornication'.[111] Rarely before had the Rome ruled by the August Family been made to sound so glamorous.

'What an artist perishes with me.'[112] So Nero, with his customary lack of modesty, had declared as he steeled himself to commit suicide. He had not exaggerated. He had indeed been an artist – he and his predecessors too. Augustus and Tiberius, Caligula and Claudius: each,

---

* Victorinus of Pettau, a bishop from Pannonia who was martyred in AD 303, was the first Christian writer to interpret the wound to the beast's throat as an allusion to Nero's suicide. The Geneva Bible comments on it: 'This may be understood of Nero, who moved the first persecution against the Church, and after slew himself, so that the family of the Caesars ended in him.'

in his own way, had succeeded in fashioning out of his rule of the world a legend that would for ever afterwards mark the House of Caesar as something eerie and more than mortal. Painted in blood and gold, its record would never cease to haunt the Roman people as a thing of mingled wonder and horror. If not necessarily divine, then it had at any rate become immortal.

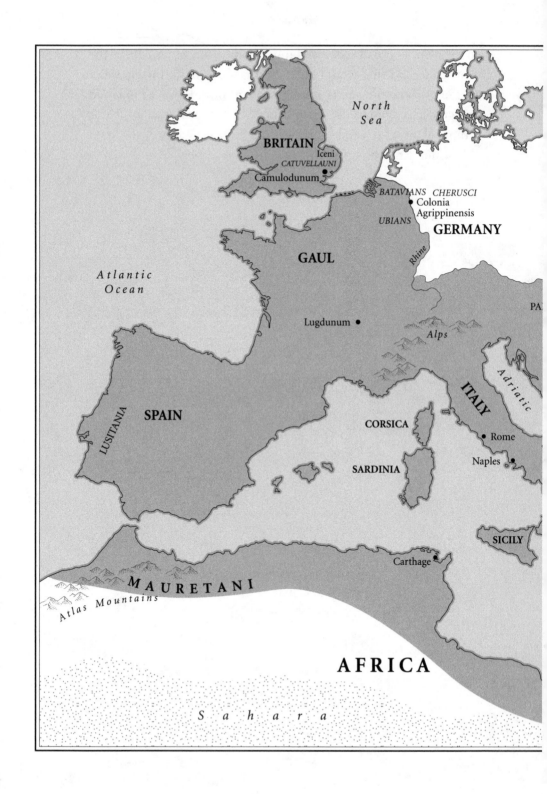

Roman World in AD 69

0   100   200   300   400   500 miles

0   200   400   600   800 km

N

NNONIA

Danube • Tomis

Black Sea

Caucasus Mts.

ILLYRIA

ARMENIA

MACEDONIA
Philippi •

Brundisium •

Tigris

ASIA MINOR

GREECE *Aegean*

• Carrhae

Actium •

Euphrates

• Athens

• Antioch
SYRIA

CRETE

Mediterranean Sea

JUDAEA
• Jerusalem

Alexandria •

EGYPT *Nile*

Red Sea

TIMELINE

38: Marriage of Livia to Caesar *Divi Filius*. Birth of her second son, Drusus. Caesar *Divi Filius* starts to call himself *Imperator Caesar*.

33: Agrippa, as aedile, sluices out Rome's drains.

31: Battle of Actium. Maecenas gives Horace a Sabine farm.

30: The deaths of Antony and Cleopatra. The annexation of Egypt.

29: Imperator Caesar celebrates three triumphs. Crassus defeats the Bastarnians.

28: Completion of the temple of Apollo on the Palatine.

27: Imperator Caesar becomes Augustus. The 'Augustan settlement'.

23: Augustus, seemingly on his deathbed, recovers. He lays down his consulship, and is awarded new powers by the Senate. Death of Marcellus.

22: Augustus leaves Rome on a tour of the East.

21: Agrippa marries Julia.

20: Augustus reclaims the eagles lost by Crassus. Birth of Gaius to Agrippa and Julia.

19: Augustus returns to Rome.

18: Augustus's adultery laws. Birth of Lucius, Gaius's younger brother.

17: Rome celebrates the dawning of a new cycle of time. Augustus adopts Gaius and Lucius. Marcus Lollius loses his eagle to a German raiding party.

15: Birth of Germanicus.

12: Augustus becomes *Pontifex Maximus*. The death of Agrippa. Drusus inaugurates an altar to Rome and Augustus in Lugdunum.

11: The marriage of Tiberius and Julia. The birth of Claudius.

8: The death of Horace.

9: The death of Drusus. Tiberius escorts his body back to Rome.

6: Tiberius retires to Rhodes.

2: Augustus is awarded the title 'Father of his Country'. He dedicates the temple of Mars the Avenger. Julia is engulfed by a sex scandal, and exiled.

1: Gaius sets out for the East.

AD 2: Tiberius returns to Rome. The death of Lucius.

4: Death of Gaius. Augustus adopts Tiberius, who adopts Germanicus.

6: The Pannonian Revolt.

8: The exile of Augustus's granddaughter, Julia. The exile of Ovid.

9: Ovid arrives in Tomis. The battle of the Teutoburg Pass.

10: Tiberius takes command of the German front.

12: Tiberius returns to Rome for his triumph. The birth of Caligula.

14: The death of Augustus. Tiberius becomes *Princeps*. The execution of Agrippa Postumus. Mutiny in Pannonia and on the Rhine.

15: Sejanus becomes sole Praetorian prefect.

16: Tiberius recalls Germanicus to Rome. The capture of Clemens.

17: Germanicus leaves for the East. The death of Ovid.

19: The death of Germanicus. The return of Agrippina to Italy. The death of Arminius.

20: The trial and suicide of Piso.

23: The death of Tiberius's son, Drusus.

25: Sejanus tries, and fails, to marry Livilla. The trial of Cremutius Cordus.

26: Tiberius leaves Rome for Campania.

27: Tiberius settles on Capri. The collapse of the amphitheatre at Fidenae.

28: The trial of Titus Sabinus.

29: The death of Livia. The exile of Germanicus's wife, Agrippina.

31: Caligula is summoned to Capri. The fall of Sejanus.

33: The death of Agrippina.

37: The death of Tiberius. Caligula becomes emperor. He falls ill, then recovers. The birth of Nero.

38: The death and consecration of Drusilla.

39: Caligula denounces the Senate, marries Milonia Caesonia, and leaves for Germany. The execution of Lepidus, and the banishment of Caligula's two surviving sisters, Agrippina and Julia Livilla.

40: Caligula on the shores of the Channel, before returning to Italy. He crosses a bridge of boats at Baiae. He enters Rome, and suppresses a conspiracy.

41: The assassination of Caligula. Claudius becomes emperor. Agrippina and Julia Livilla are recalled from exile. Julia Livilla is promptly sent back into exile. Seneca is exiled to Corsica. The deification of Livia.

42: A coup against Claudius is suppressed. Suetonius Paulinus crosses the Atlas mountains. Work begins on developing Ostia.

43: The invasion of Britain.

47: The trial and suicide of Valerius Asiaticus.

48: The downfall of Messalina.

49: Claudius marries Agrippina. Seneca is recalled from exile.

50: Claudius adopts Nero.

51: The capture of Caratacus.

53: Nero marries Octavia.

54: The death of Claudius. Nero becomes emperor.

55: The death of Britannicus.

58: Nero falls in love with Poppaea Sabina.

59: The murder of Agrippina. Nero celebrates the first shaving of his beard.

60: Boudicca's revolt.

61: The murder of the City Prefect by one of his own slaves.

62: The death of Burrus and promotion of Tigellinus to the Praetorian prefecture. Nero divorces, exiles and executes Octavia. He marries Poppaea Sabina.

64: Nero performs in public for the first time, in Naples. Tigellinus's party on the Campus Martius. The Great Fire of Rome.

65: Piso's conspiracy. Seneca commits suicide. The death of Poppaea Sabina.

66: The visit of Tiridates to Rome. Nero leaves for Greece.

67: Nero competes in the Olympic Games and marries Sporus. He returns to Rome.

68: The rebellion of Julius Vindex. The death of Nero. Galba becomes emperor.

69: The death of Galba. Otho, Vitellius and Vespasian become emperor in succession.

DRAMATIS PERSONAE

Before Augustus

ROMULUS: Founder and first king of Rome.

REMUS: His twin brother. Killed in mysterious circumstances.

TARQUIN THE PROUD: The last king of Rome, expelled in 509 BC.

BRUTUS: Tarquin's cousin, and leader of the revolution that founded the Republic.

CORNELIUS COSSUS: The second Roman general, after Romulus, to win the 'spoils of honour'.

MARCUS CURTIUS: A Roman who sacrificed himself for the good of his city by jumping into a mysterious chasm.

SCIPIO AFRICANUS: The conqueror of Carthage.

MARCELLUS: The third Roman general, after Romulus and Cornelius Cossus, to win the 'spoils of honour'.

TIBERIUS GRACCHUS: Tribune and champion of the plebs. Murdered in 133 BC.

GAIUS GRACCHUS: Younger brother of Tiberius Gracchus. Tribune and champion of the plebs. Murdered in 121 BC.

MARCUS LIVIUS DRUSUS: Champion of the Italians, whose murder in 91 BC helped to prompt their revolt. Livia's adoptive grandfather.

POMPEY 'THE GREAT': The most powerful man in Rome during the last decades of the Republic.

SEXTUS POMPEY: His son. A piratical opponent of the Triumvirs following Julius Caesar's assassination.

CRASSUS: A fabulously wealthy power-broker who died fighting the Parthians in 53 BC.

HORTENSIUS HORTALUS: An orator famous for his brilliance and high living.

HORTENSIA: His daughter.

CASSIUS: Assassin of Julius Caesar.

BRUTUS: Assassin of Julius Caesar. Descended from the Brutus who expelled Tarquin the Proud.

JUNIA: His sister. Long-lived.

ANTONY: Lieutenant of Julius Caesar. Triumvir. *Bon viveur.*

LUCIUS: Antony's brother.

IULLUS ANTONIUS: Antony's son.

CLEOPATRA: The Queen of Egypt. Paramour first of Julius Caesar, then of Antony.

LEPIDUS: Triumvir and Pontifex Maximus.

The Julians

AENEAS: Son of Venus. A Trojan prince who fled the sack of his city for Italy.

JULUS: The son of Aeneas. Ancestor of the Julians.

JULIUS CAESAR: The conqueror of Gaul whose crossing of the Rubicon led to civil war and his own subsequent dictatorship. Assassinated in 44 BC.

OCTAVIUS: Great-nephew and adopted son of Julius Caesar. Triumvir. Ended up as Imperator Caesar Divi Filius Augustus, and ruled as Princeps until his death in AD 14.

SCRIBONIA: His first wife.

JULIA: The daughter of Augustus and Scribonia. Close friends with Iullus Antonius. Exiled in 2 BC.

OCTAVIA: Augustus's sister. Married to Antony, then divorced. Stepmother to Iullus Antonius.

MARCELLUS: Son of Octavia by her first marriage. Descended from the
Marcellus who won the 'spoils of honour'. Died in 23 BC.

ANTONIA THE ELDER: Elder daughter of Octavia and Antony.

ANTONIA THE YOUNGER: Younger daughter of Octavia and Antony.
Mother of Germanicus, Livilla and Claudius.

GAIUS: Oldest son of Julia and Agrippa. Adopted by Augustus. Died in
AD 4 in Asia Minor.

JULIA: Oldest daughter of Julia and Agrippa. Owner of the smallest
dwarf in Rome. Exiled in AD 8.

LUCIUS: Second son of Julia and Agrippa. Adopted by Augustus. Died
in AD 2 in southern Gaul.

AGRIPPINA (I): Second daughter of Julia and Agrippa. Married
Germanicus. Mother of Nero (I), Drusus (III), Caligula, Agrippina
(II), Drusilla and Julia Drusilla. Returned to Rome with her
husband's ashes in an urn. Fell out spectacularly with Tiberius.

AGRIPPA POSTUMUS: Third son of Julia and Agrippa. Adopted by
Augustus, then exiled by him in AD 9.

The Claudians

ATTIUS CLAUSUS: Migrated to Rome in 504 BC. Founder of the
Claudian line.

APPIUS CLAUDIUS THE BLIND: Builder of the Appian Way.

CLAUDIUS PULCHER: Son of Appius Claudius. His descendants, the
Pulchri, constituted the more high-achieving branch of the
Claudians.

CLAUDIUS NERO: Son of Appius Claudius. Ancestor of the Nerones,
whose achievements under the Republic failed to measure up to
those of the Pulchri.

APPIUS CLAUDIUS PULCHER: Notoriously arrogant head of the
Claudians during the last decade of the Republic. A fan of
oracles.

CLODIUS PULCHER: His younger brother. Tribune and paramilitary.

CLODIA METELLI: Eldest of the three sisters of Appius Claudius and
Clodius. Famously *soignée*.

DRUSUS CLAUDIANUS: A partisan of Julius Caesar who then became a
follower of his assassins. Livia's father.

LIVIA DRUSILLA: Mother of Tiberius and wife of Augustus. Ended up a
goddess.

TIBERIUS CLAUDIUS NERO: First husband of Livia. Unsuccessful rebel.

TIBERIUS: The elder son of Livia and Tiberius Claudius Nero.
Son-in-law, then adopted son of Augustus. Rome's most
effective general. Succeeded Augustus as Princeps. Ruled from AD
14–37.

DRUSUS (I): The younger son of Livia and Tiberius Claudius Nero.
Married to Antonia the Younger. Led a Roman army to the Elbe.
Father of Germanicus, Livilla and Claudius.

VIPSANIA: Tiberius's much-loved first wife, until he was obliged by
Augustus to divorce her. Subsequently married to Asinius Gallus.

DRUSUS (II): The son of Tiberius and Vipsania. Married to Livilla.
Father of Gemellus.

GERMANICUS: The elder son of Drusus and Antonia the Younger.
Dashing. Married to Agrippina (I).

LIVILLA: The daughter of Drusus and Antonia the Younger. Bitchy.
Married to Drusus (II).

GEMELLUS: The son of Drusus (II) and Livilla. Tiberius's grandson.

CLAUDIUS: The younger son of Drusus and Antonia the Younger.
Prone to stammering and dribbling. Emperor from AD 41 to 54.

ANTONIA: Daughter of Claudius and his second wife, Aelia Patina.

MESSALINA: Wife of Claudius. A great-grandniece of Augustus.
Notorious for her love-life.

OCTAVIA: Daughter of Claudius and Messalina. Nero's first wife. Their
marriage was not a success.

BRITANNICUS: Son of Claudius and Messalina. The last of the
Claudians.

The Julio-Claudians

NERO (I): Eldest son of Germanicus and Agrippina (I). Came to a sticky end.

DRUSUS (III): Second son of Germanicus and Agrippina (I). Came to a sticky end.

CALIGULA: Youngest son of Germanicus and Agrippina (I). Properly called Gaius, 'Caligula' was a nickname given him as a young boy. Emperor from AD 37 to 41.

LOLLIA PAULINA: Famously rich and beautiful. Caligula married her in AD 38, then divorced her six months later.

MILONIA CAESONIA: Caligula's last wife. Enjoyed dressing up.

JULIA DRUSILLA: The daughter of Caligula and Milonia Caesonia. Reportedly an unpleasant child.

AGRIPPINA (II): Eldest daughter of Germanicus and Agrippina (I). Sister of Caligula, niece and wife of Claudius, mother of the Emperor Nero.

NERO: The son of Agrippina (II) and Gnaeus Domitius Ahenobarbus. Adopted by Claudius in AD 50. Emperor from AD 54 to 68.

DRUSILLA: Second daughter of Germanicus and Agrippina. Caligula's favourite sister. Ended up a goddess.

JULIA LIVILLA: Youngest daughter of Germanicus and Agrippina. Exiled by both Caligula and Claudius.

The Ahenobarbi

LUCIUS DOMITIUS AHENOBARBUS: Married to Antonia the Elder. The first Roman general to cross the Elbe.

GNAEUS DOMITIUS AHENOBARBUS: His son. Married to Agrippina (II). Father of Nero.

DOMITIA: Nero's aunt, who looked after him during his mother's exile.

DOMITIA LEPIDA: Domitia's sister. The mother of Messalina.

Augustus's Rome

MARCUS AGRIPPA: Augustus's *consigliere*. Married to Julia (I).

MAECENAS: Descendant of Etruscan kings. Patron of poets.

HORACE: Poet and – thanks to Maecenas – owner of a Sabine farm.

VEDIUS POLLIO: Financier who flashed his cash too much for Augustus's liking.

EGNATIUS RUFUS: Sponsor of firemen and would-be consul.

HOSTIUS QUADRA: Notorious as the most depraved man in Rome. Fond of mirrors.

OVID: Poet. A *flâneur* who pushed at limits.

TITUS LABIENUS: Historian, whose account of the civil wars was burned on Augustus's orders.

CASSIUS SEVERUS: Sharp-tongued lawyer.

Governors and generals

MARCUS LICINIUS CRASSUS: Grandson of the Crassus killed at Carrhae. Governor of Macedonia, but not as decorated a general as he would have liked to be.

BALBUS: The last citizen from outside the August Family to celebrate a triumph.

LOLLIUS: Governor of Gaul who lost an eagle to a war-band of Germans. Guardian of Gaius on his eastern tour. Grandfather of Lollia Paulina.

VARUS: Governor of Germany. Led three legions into the Teutoburg Pass. Did not lead them back out.

CAECINA: Germanicus's deputy in Germany.

GNAEUS CALPURNIUS PISO: Governor of Syria. Close associate of Tiberius and opponent of Germanicus. Ended up in serious legal difficulties.

PLANCINA: Piso's wife. Friend of Livia.

SENTIUS: Appointed governor of Syria by enemies of Piso.

GALBA: Appointed to the command of the Rhine by Caligula. Appointed to Spain by Nero.

SUETONIUS PAULINUS: As governor of Mauretania he crossed the Atlas mountains, and as governor of Britain suppressed Boudicca's revolt.

Praetorians

SEIUS STRABO: An Etrurian. Appointed Prefect by Augustus. Ended up as Governor of Egypt.

AELIUS SEJANUS: His son. Promoted by Tiberius to the joint command of the Praetorians, then served as sole Prefect. Tiberius's right-hand man.

APICATA: Sejanus's wife. Divorced in AD 23.

MACRO: Prefect in succession to Sejanus.

CASSIUS CHAEREA: A grizzled veteran with a soft voice.

CORNELIUS SABINUS: Praetorian officer. Colleague of Cassius Chaerea.

BURRUS: Agrippina's protégé, appointed as Prefect under Claudius. Famed for his blunt speaking.

TIGELLINUS: Gigolo, racehorse trainer and party animal. Appointed one of two prefects by Nero in succession to Burrus.

FAENIUS RUFUS: Tigellinus's colleague as Prefect.

NYMPHIDIUS SABINUS: Prefect in succession to Faenius Rufus. Rumoured to be Caligula's son.

Victims

CREMUTIUS CORDUS: A historian who named Brutus and Cassius 'the last of the Romans', and paid for it.

ASINIUS GALLUS: Husband of Vipsania, Tiberius's divorced wife. Fatally prone to snideness.

TITIUS SABINUS: An associate of Germanicus. Victim of a sting.

JUNIUS SILANUS: Former consul. Father-in-law of Caligula.

ATANIUS SECUNDUS: Equestrian. Victim of his own hyperbole.

JUNIUS PRISCUS: Not as rich as he was rumoured to be.

PASTOR: Father of a murdered son.

ASPRENAS: A senator spattered with flamingo blood.

SILANUS: The victim of a bad dream.

POPPAEA SABINA (I): Love rival of Messalina.

SUILLIUS RUFUS: Notorious prosecutor. His comeuppance arrived in the end.

RUBELLIUS PLAUTUS: Tiberius's great-grandson. Suspected of having an affair with Agrippina (II).

LUCIUS JUNIUS SILANUS: Nero excepted, the last surviving descendant of Augustus.

THRAESA PAETUS: Famously upright, in the sternest moral tradition of the Senate.

Conspirators

MARCUS AEMILIUS LEPIDUS: Caligula's close friend, and intimate of his sisters.

GAETULICUS: A henchman of Sejanus. Commander of the Rhine under Tiberius and Caligula.

BETILIENUS CAPITO: Father of a murdered son.

MARCUS VINICIUS: Married to Julia Livilla. Would-be emperor in the wake of Caligula's death.

ANNIUS VINICIANUS: Friend of Lepidus. Would-be emperor in the wake of Caligula's death.

PAETUS: Not as brave as his wife.

GAIUS SILIUS: The most handsome man in Rome. Reported to have made an unwise marriage.

GAIUS CALPURNIUS PISO: Distinguished, well-bred and ambitious to reach the top – despite not being related to the August Family.

FLAVIUS SCAEVINUS: A senator in possession of a dagger removed from a temple.

Survivors

MEMMIUS REGULUS: Consul and trusted henchman of Tiberius. Husband of Lollia Paulina, before Caligula obliged him to divorce her.

THRASYLLUS: Tiberius's astrologer. Avoided being thrown off a cliff.

LUCIUS VITELLIUS: Governor of Syria. Returned from his term of office to establish himself in Rome as a trusted agent of both Caligula and Claudius. A smooth operator.

CAECINA LARGUS: An early backer of Claudius to be emperor. Owned a house on the Palatine complete with lotus trees.

Freedmen and Slaves

CLEMENS: Slave and look-alike of Agrippa Postumus – or was he?

PALLAS: Former slave of Antonia the Younger. One of Claudius's most valued freedmen.

CALLISTUS: Powerful freedman under Caligula and Claudius. Died in his bed. The grandfather of Nymphidius Sabinus.

NARCISSUS: The third of Claudius's triumvirate of powerful freedmen. Not an admirer of Messalina.

CALPURNIA: One of Claudius's concubines.

ACTE: Nero's first girlfriend. Presided over his funeral.

SPORUS: A young boy possessed of girlish looks. Castrated, then married, by Nero.

PHAON: Owner of a villa north of Rome.

Actors and Artists

APELLES: Actor, with a tendency to stammer without a script

MNESTER: Actor. Much admired by Caligula.

PARIS: Actor. Much admired by Nero.

ZENODORUS: Sculptor of Nero's Colossus.

Gauls

GAIUS JULIUS VERCONDARIDUBNUS: High priest of Rome and Augustus at Lugdunum.

VALERIUS ASIATICUS: Fabulously wealthy. Would-be emperor in the wake of Caligula's assassination. Owner of expensive gardens.

JULIUS CLASSICIANUS: Appointed by Claudius to restore the administration of Britain after Boudicca's revolt.

JULIUS VINDEX: A descendant of kings with a rebellious instinct.

Barbarians

DELDO: King of the Bastarnians.

PHRAATES: King of Parthia and enthusiast for détente with Augustus.

ARMINIUS: Roman equestrian and chieftain of the Cherusci.

CUNOBELIN: King of the Catuvellauni.

CARATACUS: His son. Leader of British resistance to the Roman invasion.

PRASUTAGAS: King of the Iceni.

BOUDICCA: Queen of the Iceni. Fiery.

TIRIDATES: King of Armenia. Crowned in Rome by Nero.

Friends and Foes of Nero

SENECA: Philosopher, rhetorician and writer. Exiled by Claudius, but brought back to Rome by Agrippina (II). Nero's tutor.

AULUS VITELLIUS: Son of Lucius Vitellius. Friend of Caligula and Nero. Charioteer.

OTHO: Partner of Nero's night-time revels. Husband of Poppaea Sabina (II).

POPPAEA SABINA (II): Amber-haired beauty, and daughter of Messalina's great rival. The love of Nero's life.

VATINIUS: Nero's court jester.

VESPASIAN: Seasoned general of humble background. Fought in Britain and accompanied Nero to Greece.

STATILIA MESSALINA: Nero's third wife. A noted intellectual.

CALVIA CRISPINILLA: Sporus's instructress in the art of being a woman.

PETRONIUS TURPILIANUS: Former governor of Britain. Commander of Nero's troops in Italy.

VIRGINIUS RUFUS: Commander of the Rhine.

NOTES

Unless otherwise stated, 'Tacitus' refers to *The Annals*; Valerius Maximus to *Memorable Doings and Sayings*; Livy, Justin, Florus, Appian, Dionysius of Halicarnassus, Cassius Dio, Velleius Paterculus and Herodotus to their respective Histories; Lucretius to *On the Nature of Things*; Petronius to *The Satyricon*; Lucan to *The Civil War*; Strabo to his *Geography*; Aulus Gellius to *Attic Nights*; Macrobius to *The Saturnalia*; Pliny to Pliny the Elder, and his *Natural History*; Artemidorus to *The Interpretation of Dreams*; Vitruvius to *On Architecture*; and Frontinus to *On Aqueducts*.

Preface

 1 Suetonius. *Caligula*: 46
 2 Ibid: 22
 3 Ibid: 50.2
 4 Seneca. *To Helvia*: 10.4
 5 Eusebius. *The Proof of the Gospel*: 3.139
 6 Philo. *On the Embassy to Gaius*: 146–7
 7 Ovid. *Letters from Pontus*: 4.9.126
 8 Mark 12.17
 9 Cassius Dio: 52.34.2
10 Ibid: 53.19.3
11 Tacitus: 3.19
12 Ibid: 1.1
13 Tacitus: 3.65
14 Valerius Maximus: 3.6. preface
15 Seneca. *Letters*: 57.2
16 Seneca. *On Clemency*: 1.11.2
17 Ovid. *Sorrows*: 4.4.15

1 Children of the Wolf

1 Witness, for instance, a dedication made in the late third or early second century BC by a Greek on the Aegean island of Chios, which showcased Romulus and Remus. 'According to the story,' the inscription read, 'it came about that they were begotten by [the war god himself], which one might well consider to be a true story because of the bravery of the Romans.' Quoted by Wiseman (1995), p. 161.

2 Livy: 31.34

3 Justin: 38.6.7–8

4 Ennius: fragment 156

5 Florus: 1.1.8

6 Sallust. *The Conspiracy of Catiline*: 7.1–2

7 Livy: 7.6.2

8 Lucretius: 3.834

9 Livy: 37.45

10 So, at any rate, reports Valerius Maximus: 2.2.1

11 Livy: 38.53

12 Livy: 38.50

13 Valerius Maximus: 6.2.8

14 Cicero. *On Piso*: 16

15 Cicero. *On his House*: 66

16 Manilius: *Astronomica*: 1.793

17 Petronius: 119

18 Suetonius. *The Deified Julius*: 20

19 Livy. *Periochae*: 103

20 Propertius: 3.4, line 2

21 Appian: 2.31

22 Lucan: 1.109–11

23 Petronius: 121

24 Virgil. *Aeneid*: 2.557. In the poem, the headless corpse is Priam's; the detail that Virgil was echoing a description of Pompey we owe to Servius. The description was almost certainly from Asinius Pollio's history of the civil war. (See Morgan (2000), pp. 52–5.)

25 Dionysius of Halicarnassus: 7.70.1

26 Justin: 28.2.8

27 Suetonius. *The Deified Julius*: 77

28 Cicero. *Philippics*: 6.19

29 Plutarch. *Titus Quinctius Flaminius*: 12.6

30 Livy: 1.3. The observation probably dates to the decade after Caesar's assassination. See Luce.

31 Cicero. *In Defence of Marcellus*: 27

32 Pliny: 8.155

33 Cicero. *Philippics*: 3.12
34 Ovid. *Fasti*: 2.441. Ovid transposes the oracular command to the time of Romulus, but its actual date was 276 BC. See Wiseman (2008), p. 76.
35 Plutarch. *Julius Caesar*: 61.4
36 Cassius Dio: 44.11.3
37 Cicero. *Republic*: 2.30.52
38 Gaius Matius, a businessman whose entire career was marked by a deep suspicion of politics. He is being quoted with deep disapproval by Cicero. *Letters to Atticus*: 14.1
39 Josephus. *Antiquities of the Jews*: 14.309
40 From the *Memoirs* of Augustus, fragment 6. Quoted by Ramsey and Licht, p. 159.

2 Back to the Future

1 Livia was born, almost certainly in Rome, on 30 January 59 – or possibly 58. See Barrett (2002), pp. 309–10
2 Virgil. *Eclogues*: 4:61
3 Plutarch. *Roman Questions*: 102
4 Seneca. *On Mercy*: 1.14.3
5 Barrett (2002: p. 348, n. 18) notes the lack of explicit evidence identifying Livius Drusus as the adoptive father of Drusus Claudianus, but acknowledges the circumstantial evidence to be overwhelming.
6 Dionysius of Halicarnassus: 3.67.5
7 Cicero. *Against Verres*: 5.180
8 Cicero. *On the Responses of the Haruspices*: 13.27
9 Cicero. *For Marcus Caelius*: 21
10 Tacitus: 1.4.3. Scholars are agreed that the darkening of the Claudians' reputation occurred at some point in the first century BC; Wiseman (1979) convincingly dates it to the late 50s and 40s.
11 Valerius Maximus: 1.4.3
12 Lucan: 2.358
13 Cicero. *On his House*: 109
14 For the significance of the crocus stamen as a flower part used 'to promote women's menstrual and reproductive cycles', see Sebasta, p. 540, n. 33.
15 Plutarch. *Romulus*: 15.5
16 Appian: 4.11
17 Velleius Paterculus: 2.71.2
18 Valerius Maximus: 6.8.6
19 Suetonius. *The Deified Augustus*: 2
20 Although according to Dio (47.49.3), it was lost at sea. Another tradition is recorded by Plutarch (*Brutus*: 53.4), who reports that Antony had Brutus's body cremated and the ashes sent home to his mother.
21 Appian: 4.8

22 'In Praise of Turia': the quoted passage comes from a eulogy carved by a mourning husband on the tombstone of his wife. The dead woman has long been identified with a paragon of selfless heroism named Turia, who – according to an anecdote recorded by Valerius Maximus (6.7.2) – risked everything to save her husband from the evils of the Proscriptions. Classicists, as is their way, are now more sceptical than they were of this identification – but not entirely dismissive.

23 Appian: 4.4

24 Suetonius (*Augustus*: 15) says that 200 senators and knights were offered as a literal sacrifice. The story clearly derives from a hostile source – but although much exaggerated, it is clear that that its origin must lie in an authentic episode.

25 Suetonius. *Augustus*: 62.2. Suetonius is quoting Augustus's own words (fragment 14).

26 Ibid

27 By Brunt (1971), pp. 509–12

28 Virgil. *Eclogues*: 1.11–12

29 Propertius: 4.1.130

30 Virgil. *Eclogues*: 9.5

31 Horace. *Satires*: 2.1.37

32 Ibid: 1.6.72–3

33 Virgil. *Georgics*: 1.505

34 Strabo: 6.1.2

35 Propertius: 2.1.29

36 Velleius: 2.88.2

37 Horace. *Epodes*: 7.17–20

38 Horace. *Odes*: 2.13.28

39 Horace. *Satires*: 2.2.126–7

40 Appian: 5.132

41 Ibid: 5.130

42 Plutarch. *Antony*: 24

43 Virgil. *Aeneid*: 4.189–90

44 Seneca. *Letters*: 94.46. The quotation is from Sallust, *The Jugurthine War*: 10.6.

45 Seneca. *On Benefits*: 3.32.4

46 Strabo: 5.3.8

47 Horace. *Epodes*: 9.5

48 Horace. *Satires*: 1.5.29

49 Ibid: 1.6.61–2

50 Ibid: 2.6.58

51 Ibid: 2.6.1–3

52 *Res Gestae*: 25.2

53 Virgil. *Aeneid*: 8.678–9

54 Horace. *Odes*: 1.37.1

55 Ovid. *Fasti*: 1.30
56 Cicero. *On Duties*: 2.26
57 Livy: 1.10
58 Cornelius Nepos. *Life of Atticus*: 20.3
59 Or rather, in accordance with what the young Caesar and his agents claimed to have been venerable custom. Just as likely is that the entire ritual was made up. See Wiedemann, p. 482.
60 The name was stamped on sling-shot. The young Caesar was also accused on the sling-shot of being a 'cocksucker' and having a loose anus. See Hallett (2006), p. 151.
61 The link between the defeat by Sextus and the adoption of the name *Imperator* was first made by Syme in a classic essay (1958).
62 Horace. *Satires*: 2.6.55–6
63 Virgil. *Georgics*: 4.90
64 For the impenetrable nature of the murk that envelops the origins of the triumph, see Beard (2007), pp. 305–18.
65 Dionysius of Halicarnassus: 2.34.2
66 Virgil. *Aeneid*: 8.717
67 Propertius: 2.8.14
68 Virgil. *Aeneid*: 1.291
69 Cassius Dio: 51.24
70 Livy: 4.20
71 An inscription from a recently discovered coin, minted in 28 BC. See Rich and Williams.
72 *Achievements of the Deified Augustus*: 6.1
73 Ibid: 34.1
74 Aulus Gellius: 5.6.13
75 The inscription is from a coin minted in 19 BC. See Dear, p. 322
76 Cassius Dio: 53.6
77 Ibid: 53.20
78 Horace. *Odes*: 3.8.18
79 Ibid: 1.35.29–30
80 Ibid: 3.14.14–16
81 Ovid. *Sorrows*: 4.4.13–16
82 Some scholars dispute whether this temple was in fact built, but the evidence – consisting as it does of both coins and the explicit statement of Dio that it was indeed raised on the Capitol 'in imitation of that of Jupiter' (54.8) – seems to me irrefutable.
83 Ovid. *Fasti*: 1.609–10
84 Macrobius: 2.4.20
85 Ibid: 2.4.12
86 Quoted in Suetonius. *Life of Horace*
87 Suetonius. *The Deified Augustus*: 70.2

88 Servius. *On the* Aeneid: 4.58
89 Velleius Paterculus
90 Plutarch. *Antony*: 75
91 Virgil. *Aeneid*: 8.720
92 Just as the vast temple of Jupiter on the Capitol was dedicated to Juno and Minerva as well, so did Liber share his temple with Ceres and Libera. Wiseman (2004: p. 68) convincingly argues that this was no coincidence, and that the temple of Liber was consciously founded as a counterpoint to the huge temple on the Capitol.
93 Suetonius. *The Deified Augustus*: 79.2
94 Ovid. *Sorrows*: 1.70
95 Suetonius. *The Deified Augustus*: 94.4
96 Ibid: 72.1
97 Cicero. *In Defence of Murena*: 76
98 Horace. *Satires*: 1.8.16
99 Cicero. *On the Agrarian Law*: 2.17
100 Ibid. *To Atticus*: 1.19.4
101 The number of tribunes increased over the succeeding decades. By 449 BC, there were ten.
102 Cassius Dio: 54.10
103 Macrobius: 2.4.18
104 Horace. *Odes*: 3.6.1–2
105 Ibid: 7–8
106 Ovid. *Fasti*: 1.223–4
107 'In Praise of Turia'
108 Horace. '*Carmen Saeculare*': 47–8
109 Ibid: 57–60
110 Ovid. *Fasti*: 6.647
111 From Suetonius's life of Horace
112 Suetonius. *The Deified Augustus*: 58.2
113 Ovid. *Fasti*: 3.709
114 Ibid: 5.553
115 Suetonius reports that all these statues were dressed as though for the celebration of a triumph; but we know from the fragments of them found that in fact some of them were shown wearing togas.
116 Suetonius. *The Deified Augustus*: 31.5
117 Horace. *Odes*: 4.14.6

3 The Exhaustion of Cruelty

1 *Funeral Lament for Drusus*: 351. In *Poetae Latini Minores* 1, ed. E. Baehrens (1879)
2 Plutarch. *Life of Cato the Censor*: 16
3 Ovid. *Loves*: 3.15.6

4 Dionysius of Halicarnassus: 6.13.4

5 Ovid. *The Art of Loving*: 3.121–2

6 Ovid. *Sorrows*: 4.10.35

7 Ibid: 4.10.37–8

8 Ovid. *The Art of Loving*: 3.122

9 Ibid: 1.17

10 Cato the Censor, in Plutarch's life of him: 17

11 Ovid. *Loves*: 1.15.3

12 Ibid: 1.7.38

13 Cicero. *Tusculan Disputations*: 2.53

14 Petronius: 92. The tone is satirical but matter-of-fact.

15 Pliny the Younger. *Letters*: 3.1.2

16 *Priapea*: 25.6–7

17 Valerius Maximus: 6.1. preface

18 Cato the Elder: fragment 222. Later jurists ruled that, although the father of a woman taken *in flagrante* might legally kill her, a husband could not – unless his wife's lover was of low or sordid social standing.

19 Ovid. *Loves*: 3.4.37

20 Ibid: 3.4.17

21 Ibid: 3.4.11

22 Ovid. *On Women's Facials*: 25–6

23 Seneca. *Natural Questions*: 1.16.6

24 Ibid: 1.116.9

25 Ibid: 1.16.7

26 Horace. *Odes*: 3.6.19–20

27 Ibid: 3.24.33–4

28 Pseudo-Acro, scholiast on Horace: 1.2.63. Quoted by McGinn, p. 165

29 Tacitus. *Annals*: 3.28

30 Horace. *Odes*: 4.5.21–2

31 Ovid. *Loves*: 3.4.5–6

32 Cassius Dio: 48.52

33 Ovid. *Sorrows*: 3.1.39–40

34 Velleius Paterculus: 2.79.1

35 Pliny: 15.137

36 Cassius Dio: 54.6

37 Suetonius. *Tiberius*: 51.2

38 Macrobius: 2.5.9

39 Ibid: 2.5.8

40 Ibid: 2.5.4

41 Philo. *Embassy to Gaius*: 167

42 Seneca. *To Polybius, On Consolation*: 15.5

43 Ovid. *The Art of Loving*: 1.184

44 Ibid. 1.177–8

45 Ibid, 1.175
46 Ovid. *Loves*: 1.5.26
47 Pliny: 7.149
48 Seneca. *On Mercy*: 1.10.3
49 Ibid: 1.11.2
50 Ovid. *The Art of Loving*: 2.573
51 Ibid: 2.552–3
52 Ibid: 2.2.599–600
53 Artemidorus: 2.9
54 Velleius Paterculus: 2.91.4
55 Ovid. *Fasti*: 5.145–6
56 Plutarch. *Moralia*: 207e
57 From a Messenian inscription discovered in 1960. Quoted in Zankel, p. 259.
58 From a decree of the town council of Pisa. Reproduced in Lott (2012), p. 72.
59 Ovid. *The Art of Loving*: 1.203
60 Cassius Dio: 55.13.1
61 From a letter written by Augustus to Gaius in AD 1, and quoted by Aulus Gellius: 15.7
62 Tacitus: 6.25
63 Ulpian. *Digest*: 1.15.3
64 Cassius Dio: 55.27.1
65 Confusion surrounds the fate of Julia's husband, since a man of his name who appears on an inscription in a list of priests is described as dying in AD 14. A commentary on the poet Juvenal, though, makes it clear that he was executed. The priest was therefore almost certainly his son.
66 Some scholars (e.g. Claassen, pp. 12–13) date Ovid's exile to AD 9 but internal and external evidence alike seem to me definitively to point to AD 8. Legally speaking, Ovid was not an *exsul*, an exile, but a *relegatus* – someone 'relegated' from Rome, but without the loss of his civic rights. Ovid himself, though, often referred to his loneliness and misery as an '*exsilium*' – as well he might have done.
67 Ovid. *Sorrows*: 2.207
68 Ibid: 6.27
69 Ovid. *Black Sea Letters*: 2.2.19
70 For a survey of the many theories about Ovid's exile, see Thibault. My reading of it follows Green (1989). As Claassen comments (p. 234), 'No other explanation than a political one can make sense of Ovid's exile.'
71 Ovid. *Sorrows*: 1.11.3–4
72 Ibid: 2.195–6
73 Ovid. *Sorrows*: 5.10.37
74 Ovid. *Letters from Pontus*: 1.2.81–2
75 Ovid. *Sorrows*: 5.7.46
76 Ovid. *Fasti*: 2.291

77 Ovid. *Sorrows*: 2.199–200
78 Ibid: 5.10.19–20
79 Valerius Maximus: 6.1.11
80 Velleius Paterculus: 2.115.5
81 Ovid. *Sorrows*: 2.171–2
82 Cicero. *On Duties*: 2.27
83 The opening of Augustus's record of achievements, the *Res Gestae*
84 Virgil. *Aeneid*: 1.279
85 Albinovanus Pedo: 3, quoted in Benario, p. 166. 'The realm of shadow' is specifically a reference to the Wadden Sea. The poem describes a naval expedition in AD 16.
86 Tacitus: 2.24
87 Tacitus. *Germania*: 4
88 Or possibly, on some interpretations, in 10 BC.
89 Strabo: 4.4.2
90 Ovid. *Amores*: 1.14.45–6
91 Tacitus. *Germania*: 19
92 Cassius Dio: 56.18
93 Velleius Paterculus: 2.118.2
94 Florus: 30.3
95 Suetonius. *The Deified Augustus*: 23
96 Ibid. *Tiberius*: 21.3. The phrase was Augustus's own.
97 Ibid. Augustus was quoting – or rather adapting – the poet Ennius.
98 Ovid. *Black Sea Letters*: 2.1.37–8
99 Ibid: 2.1.61–2
100 Seneca. *On Benefits*: 3.38.2
101 *Consolation to Livia*: 356
102 Tacitus: 5.1
103 Ibid
104 Cicero. *On the Republic*: 1.67
105 Ovid. *Black Sea Letters*: 3.1.118
106 Velleius Paterculus: 2.130.5
107 Ovid. *Black Sea Letters*: 3.1.125
108 Suetonius. *The Deified Augustus*: 64.2
109 Such, at any rate, is the evidence of an inscription found at Rhegium, which records a freedwoman of Julia's having a mother who was a freedwoman of Livia's. See Barrett (2002), p. 51.
110 Tacitus: 4.71
111 The inscription is quoted by Flory, p. 318. The temple was that of *Fortuna Muliebris*, 'Female Fortune'. The same inscription can be found on the Arch of Ticinum: '*Drusi f. uxori Caesaris Augusti*'.
112 Livy: 8.18.6
113 Virgil. *Georgics*: 128–30

114 Suetonius. *The Deified Augustus*: 51.3
115 Seneca the Elder. *Controversies*: 10, Preface 5
116 Tacitus: 1.72
117 Velleius Paterculus: 126.3
118 Suetonius. *The Deified Claudius*: 3
119 Ibid: 41.2
120 Cassius Dio: 55.32
121 Tacitus: 1.5
122 Velleius Paterculus: 11.123.1
123 Ibid: 11.123.2
124 Suetonius. *The Deified Augustus*: 99.1
125 Tacitus: 1.6. Pettinger (p. 178, n. 28) convincingly argues that the details of this episode derived from Tacitus's reading of a source unconsulted by other historians: the memoirs of Germanicus's daughter (and the mother of the Emperor Nero), Agrippina. 'Tacitus, in using the private memoirs of the younger Agrippina, has landed a scoop ...'
126 Ibid
127 Suetonius. *Tiberius*: 22
128 Ibid: 23
129 Tacitus: 6

4 The Last Roman

1 The garden had originally belonged to Pompey.
2 Ovid. *Black Sea Letters*: 4.13.27
3 Suetonius. *The Deified Augustus*: 99.1
4 Tacitus: 1.11
5 Suetonius. *Tiberius*: 21.2
6 Velleius: 2.126.3
7 Tacitus: 1.13
8 Cassius Dio: 56.26
9 Velleius: 2.124.2
10 Cassius Dio: 57.1
11 Suetonius. *Tiberius*: 25.1
12 The suggestion is Syme's (1986), p. 300
13 Suetonius. *Tiberius*: 24.1
14 Tacitus: 1.17
15 Luke 7.8
16 Tacitus: 1.23
17 Ibid: 1.51
18 Velleius: 2.125.1–2
19 'Senatus Consultum de Cn. Pisone Patre': line 161
20 Tacitus: 3.33. The words are those of Severus Caecina, Germanicus's

deputy on the Rhine, following his return from the front. The influence of Agrippina on his sentiments can only be surmised.

21 Valerius Maximus: 3.2.2
22 Tacitus: 2.26
23 Velleius: 2.129.2
24 Tacitus: 1.33
25 Suetonius. *Tiberius*: 50.3
26 Tacitus: 1.53
27 Velleius: 2.126.3
28 Tacitus: 2.39
29 Ibid: 2.40
30 Ibid
31 Tacitus: 2.26
32 Valerius Maximus: 5.5
33 See Syme (1980), p. 336: 'the surmise is easy'.
34 Seneca. *On Anger*: 1.18
35 Cicero: *The Republic*: 5.1.2
36 Tacitus: 4.38
37 Cassius Dio: 57.15
38 Tacitus: 2.43
39 Ibid: 2.53
40 Artemon. *Anthologia Graeca*: 12.55
41 Paraphrase of an anecdote in Josephus's *Antiquities of the Jews*: 18.171–6
42 Polybius: 31.4
43 Tacitus: 1.55
44 Ibid: 1.56
45 Philo. *Special Laws*: 3.174
46 Ehrenberg and Jones, p. 138 (320b)
47 *Res Gestae*: 27
48 Tacitus: 2.71
49 'Senatus Consultum de Cn. Pisone Patre': lines 55–6
50 Ibid: line 46
51 Tacitus: 2.83
52 Ibid: 3.4
53 Ibid: 3.15
54 See Versnel, pp. 383–7
55 Ovid. *Fasti*: 2.551
56 Ovid. *Black Sea Letters*: 4.8.49–51
57 Seneca. *On Benefits*: 5.25.2
58 Seneca the Elder. *Controversies*: 10.3.5
59 Statius. *Silvae*: 3.3.200–1
60 'Senatus Consultum de Cn. Pisone Patre': lines 115–16
61 A phrase that appears on a number of Tiberius's coins.

62 Tacitus: 3.34
63 Ibid: 4.8
64 Ibid: 3.65
65 Ibid: 11.21
66 Cicero. *On Duties*: 2.50
67 Tacitus: 4.34
68 Seneca. *To Marcia, On Consolation*: 22.5
69 Tacitus: 6.7
70 Pliny: 26.2
71 For the likelihood that Tiberius coined the word, see Champlin: http://www.princeton.edu/~pswpc/pdfs/champlin/090601.pdf, pp. 5–6
72 Tacitus: 4.52
73 Ibid: 4.54
74 For the rumours linking Gallus to Agrippina, see Shotter (1971), pp. 454–5
75 Tacitus: 4.40
76 Ibid: 4.41
77 Strabo: 5.4.8
78 For the likelihood that Tiberius identified with Ulysses, see Stewart, pp. 87–8. For a fascinating meditation on the broader implications of this self-identification, see Champlin's *Tiberiana* essay, 'Tales of Brave Ulysses'. Juvenal, writing a century later, explicitly compared Tiberius to Ulysses (10.84).
79 Ovid. *Metamorphoses*: 3.158–9
80 Cassius Dio: 58.4
81 I am indebted to Llewelyn Morgan for pointing this out.
82 Pliny: 8.145
83 Suetonius. *Caligula*: 22.2
84 Tacitus: 3.55
85 Cassius Dio: 58.5
86 Tacitus: 4.2.
87 Valerius Maximus: 9.11.ext.4
88 The details of Apicata's suicide are derived from an inscription which records that someone connected to Sejanus – almost certainly his wife – committed suicide eight days after the execution of Sejanus himself. It is possible, though, as Jane Bellemore has argued, that the person referred to in the inscription was not Apicata but Livilla – in which case we would have evidence that the couple had secretly married at some point. The case is open.
89 Tacitus: 6.6
90 Plutarch: fr. 182, in *Plutarch's Moralia*, ed. F. H. Sandbach (1969)
91 Suetonius. *Tiberius*: 60
92 Ovid. *Loves*: 3.4.25
93 Tacitus: 6.1
94 Tacitus: 6.20
95 Suetonius. *Caligula*: 11

96 Philo. *Embassy to Gaius*: 142
97 For the location and height of this lighthouse, see Champlin (*Journal of Roman Studies*, 2011), p.96.
98 Tacitus: 6.46
99 Seneca. *Letters*: 43.3

5 Let Them Hate Me

 1 Suetonius. *Tiberius*: 75.1
 2 Suetonius. *Caligula*: 15.1
 3 Ibid: 14.1
 4 Philo. *On the Embassy to Gaius*: 41
 5 Tacitus: 3.24
 6 Josephus. *Antiquities of the Jews*: 18.256
 7 Cassius Dio: 59.7.4
 8 Augustus's legislation on seating had initially targeted theatres, then amphitheatres – but the precise legal situation of the Circus Maximus is not clear. According to Cassius Dio (55.22), senators and equestrians were allocated seats there by Augustus; but Suetonius describes them as sitting among the rest of the Roman people until the time of Claudius (*Deified Claudius*: 21.3).
 9 Philo. *On the Embassy to Gaius*: 45
10 Suetonius. *Caligula*: 29
11 Petronius: 117
12 Seneca. *On Providence*: 4.4
13 Tacitus. 4.62
14 Seneca. *Letters*: 7.5
15 Cassius Dio: 59.22.7
16 Suetonius. *Caligula*: 24.1
17 Seneca. *To Polybius on Consolation*: 17.5
18 Homer. The *Iliad*: 2.204. Caligula is described as quoting it in Suetonius's biography of him (22.1).
19 Cassius Dio: 59.18.5
20 Ibid: 59.16.5–6
21 Ibid: 59.16.11
22 Ibid: 59.16.6
23 See Winterling (2011), p. 108, for this interpretation of an event that Cassius Dio (59.20.1–3) has badly garbled.
24 See Barrett (1989), pp. 125–6. The clinching evidence for Caligula's recruitment of the two legions is provided by the tombstone of a centurion: Smallwood, p. 278.
25 From an inscription recording the *Acta Fratrum Arvalium* – the protocols of a priestly brotherhood named the Arvals. It appears in Smallwood, p. 14.

26 The link between Gaeticulus and Lepidus is only made specific once, in a throwaway comment by Suetonius (*The Deified Claudius*: 9.1). It is strongly implied, though, by Cassius Dio, who describes the executions of the two men, and the exile of Caligula's two sisters, in consecutive sentences.
27 Tacitus: 12.64. Tacitus muddles the Domitia who looked after Nero with her sister, Domitia Lepida.
28 Suetonius. *Caligula*: 29
29 The attack was probably against a tribe called the Canninefates, who lived on an island in the Rhine delta. It appears to have been, at best, indecisive. See Tacitus, *Histories*: 4.15.3.
30 Persius: 6.46
31 Suetonius. *Caligula*: 49.1
32 Cassius Dio: 59.23.3
33 Or so says Suetonius (*Caligula*: 19.1). Cassius Dio says the bridge went from Puteoli to a place near Baiae named Bauli; Josephus that it went to Misenum, a town on the same promontory where Baiae is located, but too far from Puteoli to be credible.
34 Suetonius. *Caligula*: 19.3
35 Cassius Dio: 59.17.11
36 Suetonius. *Caligula*: 22.1
37 Josephus. *Antiquities of the Jews*: 19.121
38 Philo. *On the Embassy to Gaius*: 263
39 Quoted by Suetonius (*Caligula*: 30.1) from the poet Accius
40 This is nowhere stated specifically, but can be deduced by cross-referencing the account of the conspiracy in Cassius Dio with Tacitus's mention of a senator forced to commit suicide under Nero who, twenty-six years earlier, had betrayed a conspiracy to Caligula. See Barrett (1996, pp. 156–7) and Winterling (2011, pp. 136–7).
41 Seneca. *On Anger*: 3.19.2
42 Suetonius. *Caligula*: 30.1
43 Cassius Dio: 59.26.9
44 Ibid: 59.27.6
45 Josephus. *Antiquities of the Jews*: 19.86
46 Seneca. *On Anger*: 2.33.4
47 Cassius Dio: 59.29.9
48 Ibid
49 Suetonius. *Caligula*: 41.1. The story has been widely doubted, but attempts to explain it away seem to me less plausible than the supposition that it was simultaneously an attack on the prestige of the nobility, a satire on Augustan values, and a typically Caligulan amplification of the sexual fantasies enacted on Capri.
50 Seneca. *On Firmness*: 18.1
51 Ibid: 18.2

52 Cassius Dio: 59.29.2

53 Ibid: 59.25.7

54 Philo. *On the Embassy to Gaius*: 338

55 This account derives principally from Josephus, whose sources for the assassination of Caligula were excellent. Suetonius gives two alternative accounts, which nevertheless differ only slightly in the details. According to one of them, the first blow to hit Caligula was to the chin.

56 Such, at any rate, is the evidence of Seneca (*On Firmness*: 18.3).

57 Cassius Dio: 59.29.7

58 Josephus. *Antiquities of the Jews*: 19.199

59 It is Josephus who tells us that Caesonia was killed several hours after her husband's death. According to Suetonius, she and her daughter were with Caligula when he was attacked, and died alongside him.

6 Io Saturnalia!

1 Josephus. *Antiquities of the Jews*: 19.115

2 Ibid: 19.159

3 Ibid: 19.168

4 Cassius Dio: 60.1.3

5 Suetonius. *The Deified Claudius*: 10.3

6 Ibid: 3.2

7 The phrase is found on a coin of Claudius's, dated AD 41/2. The formula *EX.S.C.* confirms that it was a decree of the Senate's.

8 See Suetonius, *The Deified Claudius*: 10.4. For the finances of Claudius's expenditure on the military, see Campbell (1984), pp. 166–8 and Osgood (2011), pp. 35–7.

9 Tacitus. *Histories*: 4.74

10 Suetonius. *The Deified Augustus*: 101.4

11 Josephus. *Antiquities of the Jews*: 19.64

12 Ibid: 19.65

13 Statius. *Silvae*: 3.3.64–6

14 Dionysius of Halicarnassus: 4.23.2

15 Ovid. *Loves*: 1.8.64

16 Tacitus: 13.27

17 Horace. *Satires*: 1.6.45

18 Horace. *Epodes*: 4.6

19 Seneca. *Letters*: 47.10

20 Dionysius of Halicarnassus: 4.23.2

21 Catullus: 14.15

22 Horace. *Epodes*: 4.5

23 Pliny the Younger. *Letters*: 3.16.6

24 See Bradley (1994), pp. 166–7

25 Herodotus: 4.184
26 Pliny: 5.1.14
27 Vitruvius: 8.2.24
28 Pliny: 30.13
29 The surrender of the king of Orkney to Claudius comes in a late history, that of Eutropius but seems to derive from a reliable source. Tellingly, the detail that the Orkneys are thirty in number comes from a geographer, Pomponius Mela, who was writing even as Claudius was returning from Britain, and bruiting his achievements. See Stevens (1951 (1)). An alternative theory holds that Eutropius had confused Claudius's campaign with a later one, that of Tacitus's father-in-law, Agricola, who in AD 83 sent a fleet which circumnavigated Britain.
30 Suetonius. *The Deified Claudius*: 17.3
31 Seneca. *To Polybius on Consolation*: 14.1
32 Tacitus: 12.38
33 Boatwright convincingly argues that Claudius made the entire tradition up, relying on his reputation for antiquarian scholarship to ensure that the claim would be widely accepted.
34 Frontinus: 16
35 Artemidorus: 2.9
36 Pliny: 36.123
37 Seneca. *On Benefits*: 4.28.2
38 Acts 11.28
39 The estimate of the annual amount of grain imported is Aldrete's (p. 134).
40 Cassius Dio: 60.11.3
41 See Williams (2010), p. 190, for this analogy.
42 Suetonius. *Galba*: 22
43 Seneca. *Trojan Women*: 91
44 Tacitus. 9.2, 'Mollitiam corporis' – literally, 'softness of body'. *Mollitia*, when applied to a man, did not just mean soft, but soft like a woman: the kind of man, in other words, who allowed himself to be fucked.
45 Cassius Dio: 60.2.4
46 Ovid. *Loves*: 2.17.1
47 Cicero. *Republic*: 1.67
48 Suetonius. *Vitellius*: 2.5
49 Ovid. *The Art of Loving*: 3.215–16
50 Seneca. *On Benefits*: 6.32.1
51 Juvenal: 6.129
52 Tacitus: 11.30
53 Ibid: 11.31
54 Ibid: 11.35
55 Ibid: 11.36. See Williams (2010), p. 217, for the strong likelihood, if not absolute certainty, that the Suillius Caesonius mentioned by Tacitus as

'playing the woman's role' was the son of Asiaticus's prosecutor. As
Williams says, 'This is a rare moment in the midst of the innuendoes and
accusations that pervade Roman texts, a moment when we come
temptingly close to being able to ascertain what actually happened.'

56 Tacitus (12.1–2) describes Narcissus, Callistus and Pallas as each pitching a
different woman to their master: a scene so reminiscent of the episode
from Greek mythology in which three goddesses staged a beauty pageant
before the Trojan prince Paris as to be obviously fictional. Nevertheless,
with Pallas a strong partisan of Agrippina's, and Narcissus just as obviously
opposed to her cause, it does provide an entertaining allegory of
Claudius's court.

57 Suetonius. *Claudius*: 39.2
58 Tacitus: 12.6
59 *Octavia*: 142. The play was traditionally, if implausibly, ascribed to Seneca.
Its true authorship remains unknown.
60 Tacitus: 12.7
61 Ibid
62 Suetonius. *Claudius*: 41.2
63 Tacitus: 12.42
64 Seneca. *To Polybius on Consolation*: 12.3
65 Suetonius. *Claudius*: 43
66 Cassius Dio: 61.35.4
67 Suetonius. *Nero*: 9

7 *What an Artist*

1 *Octavia*: 156
2 Tacitus: 12.37
3 Cassius Dio: 61.7.3
4 Suetonius. *Nero*: 10.1
5 Seneca. *On Mercy*: 1.14.2
6 Tacitus: 13.13
7 Ibid: 15.42
8 Suetonius. *Otho*: 3.1
9 Tacitus: 13.14
10 So, at any rate, says Tacitus. Suetonius claims that Britannicus was
cremated the day after his death.
11 *Octavia*: 169–70
12 Seneca. *On Mercy*: 1.16.2
13 Pliny: 16.200
14 It is possible that Nero's successors agreed. Trajan, an emperor in the early
second century AD, and who was consistently rated by the Romans as
their best, is supposed to have declared that 'no emperor had been the

equal of Nero during the first five years of his reign'. Trajan too built a great harbour at Ostia; and it has been credibly suggested that he was paying tribute to Nero's own record there (Thornton, 1989).

15 Calpurnius Siculus: 7.45–6
16 Cassius Dio: 61.12.2
17 Ibid: 61.5.4
18 *Octavia*: 125
19 Pliny: 37.50
20 Cassius Dio: 61.11.4
21 Ibid: 61.2.2
22 Ibid: 61.13.2
23 Horace. *Epistles*: 1.1.83
24 So reports Tacitus, at any rate. According to Cassius Dio, Agrippina made it to the shore unaided. Dio also reports that the ship sank straight away.
25 Tacitus: 14.8
26 Cassius Dio: 61.14.2
27 For the theatricality of Agrippina's murder, see Baldwin and especially the brilliant book on Nero by Champlin (2003), pp. 84–111.
28 Tacitus: 14.10
29 The games were called by Nero *Ludi Maximi*, 'The Greatest Ever Games'.
30 Seneca. *Natural Questions*: 12.3
31 Tacitus: 14.15
32 This was Aelia Catella, cited by Cassius Dio (61.19.2). 'Aelia Catella is assumed a daughter of Sex. Aelius Catus, hence sister of Aelia Patina' (Syme 1986, n. 79). Aelia Patina had been Claudius's second wife. He had married her in 28 and divorced her in 31.
33 Cassius Dio: 19.20.5
34 Seneca. *Letters*: 14.6
35 Tacitus, although our best source for the events of Boudicca's revolt, mistakenly dates it to AD 61.
36 Seneca. *Medea*: 371–2
37 Seneca. *Medea*: 376–9. The play is ostensibly referring to the Greek hero Jason and his voyages with the Argonauts, but it is clear that Seneca has Roman expansion into Britain on his mind as well.
38 Seneca. *On Benefits*: 7.3.2
39 Seneca. *On Benefits*: 7.27.1
40 Tacitus: 14.37
41 Tacitus. *Agricola*: 19
42 Pliny: 3.39
43 Tacitus: 11.23
44 Ibid: 11.24
45 Ibid: 15.44
46 Quoted by Augustine in *The City of God*, 6.10

47 Valerius Maximus: 1.3.3
48 Quoted by Augustine in *The City of God*, 6.11
49 Tacitus: 14.44
50 Ibid: 14.45
51 Seneca. *On the Happy Life*: 7.3
52 Cassius Dio: 62.13.2
53 Ibid: 62.13.4
54 Calpurnius Siculus: 1.49–51
55 Seneca. *Natural Questions*: 3.29.9
56 Cassius Dio: 62.28.1
57 Tacitus: 15.37
58 Ibid
59 According to Chinese records, the comet was visible for seventy-five days, between 3 May and 16 July. See Rogers, p. 1953.
60 Cassius Dio (62.18.2) says that two-thirds of Rome was destroyed, while Tacitus (15.40.2) says of the fourteen districts into which the city was divided, only four were left untouched by the fire. Archaeological evidence suggests that they were both exaggerating. See Newbold, p. 858.
61 Tacitus: 15.44
62 Pliny: 10.2.5
63 Pliny the Younger. *Panegyric in Praise of Trajan*: 46.4
64 Martial. *On Spectacles*: 2.8
65 Ibid: 2.4
66 The estimate is Albertson's, who suggests, based on the various figures given for the height of the statue, that was 31.5 metres tall.
67 Pliny: 34.45
68 For an elucidation of this extraordinary episode, reported by both Suetonius and Cassius Dio, see Champlin (2003), pp. 169–71.
69 Suetonius. *Nero*: 55
70 Tacitus: 15.67
71 Ibid: 15.60
72 Seneca. *On Providence*: 3.3
73 Seneca. *Letters*: 71.21
74 Ibid: 101.10
75 Tacitus: 15.73
76 Ibid: 15.62
77 Ibid: 15.68
78 Ibid: 16.4
79 Cassius Dio: 63.26.3
80 Ibid: 62.18.3. Seneca delivered the warning in the wake of Agrippina's murder.
81 Ibid: 63.4.2
82 Ibid: 63.6.1

83 No chronological account of Nero's sojourn in Greece has survived. Estimates of when precisely he might have arrived in Corinth range from August to November.
84 Livy: 33.32
85 Cassius Dio: 63.15.1
86 Valerius Maximus: 2.4.2
87 Seneca. *Letters*: 80.7
88 Tacitus: 13.3
89 An ancient commentator on the satirist Juvenal tells us that an aristocratic and intimidatingly learned woman who is described by the poet as taking an interest in the arts of oratory was none other than Statilia Messalina. *Scholiast on Juvenal*: 6.434
90 Seneca: 47.7. The details of how to keep boys hairless derive from Pliny: 30.41.
91 The translation of 'Paezon' as 'Boy Toy' is Champlin's (2012), p. 380. The gasps of wonder are Pliny's (7.129).
92 Tacitus. *Histories*: 1.73
93 Dio Chrysostom. *On Beauty*: 11
94 Cassius Dio: 63.22.1
95 From an inscription found in 1887 at Karditza, Greece. Smallwood, p. 64
96 Plutarch. *Galba*: 4.1
97 Seneca. *On Mercy*: 1.4.2
98 Virgil. *Georgics*: 512–14
99 Cassius Dio: 63.20.5
100 Evidence for this having been more than coincidence is circumstantial but strong.
101 Suetonius. *Nero*: 41
102 Ibid
103 Ibid: 43
104 Plutarch. *Galba*: 6.3
105 Suetonius. *Nero*: 47.2. The line is a quotation from Virgil.
106 Suetonius. *Nero*: 49.2
107 Ibid: 49.4
108 Dio Chrysostom. *On Beauty*: 10
109 Revelation 13.3
110 Ibid: 17.8
111 Ibid: 17.4
112 Both Suetonius (*Nero*: 49.1) and Cassius Dio (6.29.2) record it. It was evidently, as Dio says, 'a much quoted saying'.

BIBLIOGRAPHY

Albertson, Fred C., 'Zenodorus's 'Colossus of Nero', *Memoirs of the American Academy in Rome* 46, 2001

Aldrete, Gregory S., *Floods of the Tiber in Ancient Rome* (Baltimore, 2007)

Alston, R., *Aspects of Roman History AD 14–117* (London, 1998)

Andrade, Nathanael J., *Syrian Identity in the Greco-Roman World* (Cambridge, 2013)

Andreau, Jean and Raymond Descat, *The Slave in Greece and Rome*, tr. Marion Leopold (Madison, 2006)

Badel, Christophe, *La Noblesse de l'Empire Romain: Les Masques et la Vertu* (Seyssel, 2005)

Baker, G.P., *Tiberius Caesar* (New York, 1928)

Baldwin, B., 'Nero and his Mother's Corpse', *Mnemosyne* 32, 1979

Ball, Warwick, *Rome in the East: The Transformation of an Empire* (London, 2000)

Balsdon, J.P.V.D., *The Emperor Gaius (Caligula)* (Oxford, 1934)

Barrett, Anthony A., *Caligula: The Corruption of Power* (New Haven, 1989)

——*Agrippina: Sister of Caligula, Wife of Claudius, Mother of Nero* (London, 1996)

——*Livia: First Lady of Imperial Rome* (New Haven, 2002)

Barry, William D., 'Exposure, Mutilation, and Riot: Violence at the 'Scalae Gemoniae' in Early Imperial Rome', *Greece & Rome* 55, 2008

Barton, Carlin A., *Roman Honor: The Fire in the Bones* (Berkeley and Los Angeles, 2001)

Bartsch, Shadi, *Actors in the Audience: Theatricality and Doublespeak from Nero to Hadrian* (Cambridge, Mass., 1994)

Batty, Roger, *Rome and the Nomads: The Pontic-Danubian Realm in Antiquity* (Oxford, 2007)

Bauman, Richard A., *Women and Politics in Ancient Rome* (London, 1992)

Beard, Mary, 'The Sexual Status of Vestal Virgins', *Journal of Roman Studies* 70, 1980

——*The Roman Triumph* (Cambridge, Mass., 2007)

Bellemore, Jane: 'The Wife of Sejanus', *Zeitschrift für Papyrologie und Epigraphik* 109, 1995

Benario, Herbert W., 'The Text of Albinovanus Pedo', *Latomus* 32, 1973

Bergmann, M., 'Der Koloss Neros, die Domus Aurea und der Mentalitätswandel im Rom der frühen Kaiserzeit', *Trierer Winckelmannsprogramme* 13, 1993

Bicknell, P., 'The Emperor Gaius' military activities in AD 40', *Historia* 17, 1968

Bingham, S., 'Life on an island: a brief study of places of exile in the first century AD', *Studies in Latin Literature and Roman History* 11, 2003

Birley, Anthony, 'Sejanus: His Fall' in *Corolla Cosmo Rodewald. Monograph Series Akanthina* 2, ed. Nicholas Sekunda (Gdansk, 2007)

Boatwright, M.T., 'The Pomerial Extension of Augustus', *Historia* 35, 1986

Bradley, Keith, *Suetonius' Life of Nero: An Historical Commentary* (Brussels, 1978)

——'The Chronology of Nero's Visit to Greece A.D. 66/67', *Latomus* 37, 1978

——'Nero's Retinue in Greece, A.D. 66/67', *Illinois Classical Studies* 4, 1979

——*Slavery and Society at Rome* (Cambridge, 1994)

Bradley, Keith and Paul Cartledge (eds), *The Cambridge World History of Slavery: The Ancient Mediterranean World* (Cambridge, 2011)

Brunt, P.A., *Italian Manpower, 225 B.C.–A.D. 14* (Oxford, 1971)

——*Social Conflicts in the Roman Republic* (London, 1971)

——'The Role of the Senate in the Augustan Regime', *Classical Quarterly* 34, 1984

——*The Fall of the Roman Republic, and Related Essays* (Oxford, 1988)

Buckley, Emma and Martin T. Dinter, *A Companion to the Neronian Age* (Chichester, 2013)

Campbell, Brian and Lawrence A. Tritle (eds), *The Oxford Handbook of Warfare in the Classical World* (Oxford, 2013)

Campbell, J.B., *The Emperor and the Roman Army* (Oxford, 1984)

Cancik, Hubert and Helmuth Schneider (eds), *Brill's New Pauly* (Brill, 2009)

Carandini, Andrea, *La Casa di Augusto dai 'Lupercalia' al Natale* (Rome, 2008)

——*Rome: Day One*, tr. Stephen Sartarelli (Princeton, 2011)

Carey, Sorcha, 'A Tradition of Adventures in the Imperial Grotto', *Greece & Rome* 49, 2002

Carlson, Deborah N., 'Caligula's Floating Palaces', *Archaeology* 55, 2002

Cartledge, Paul, 'The Second Thoughts of Augustus on the *res publica* in 28/7 B.C.', *Hermathena* 119, 1975

Chamberland, Guy, 'A Gladiatorial Show Produced *In Sordidam Mercedem* (Tacitus *Ann.* 4.62)', *Phoenix* 61, 2007

Champlin, E., 'Nero Reconsidered', *New England Review* 19, 1998

——*Nero* (Cambridge, Mass., 2003)

——'Nero, Apollo, and the Poets', *Phoenix* 57, 2003

——'God and Man in the Golden House', in Cima and la Rocca

——'Sex on Capri', *TAPA* 141, 2011

——'Tiberius and the Heavenly Twins', *Journal of Roman Studies*, 101, 2011

——'Seianus Augustus', *Chiron* 42, 2012

——*Tiberiana 1–4*, Princeton/Stanford Working Papers in Classics http://www.princeton.edu/~pswpc/papers/authorAL/champlin/champlin.html

Chilver, G.E.F., *A Historical Commentary on Tacitus' Histories I and II* (Oxford, 1979)

Cima, Maddalena and Eugenio la Rocca, *Horti Romani* (Rome, 1995)

Claassen, Jo-Marie, *Ovid Revisited: The Poet in Exile* (London, 2008)

Claridge, Amanda, *Rome: An Oxford Archaeological Guide* (Oxford, 2010)

Bibliography

Coarelli, Filippo, *Rome and Environs: An Archaeological Guide*, tr. James J. Clauss and Daniel P. Harmon (Berkeley and Los Angeles, 2007)

Coates-Stephens, Robert, *Porta Maggiore: Monument and Landscape: Archaeology and Topography of the Southern Esquiline from the Late Republican Period to the Present* (Rome, 2004)

Cohen, Sarah T., 'Augustus, Julia and the Development of Exile *Ad Insulam*', *Classical Quarterly* 58, 2008

Coleman, K.M., 'Fatal Charades: Roman Executions Staged as Mythological Enactments', *Journal of Roman Studies* 80, 1990

Colin, Jean, 'Juvénal et le mariage mystique de Gracchus', *Atti della Accademia delle Scienze di Torino* 90, 1955–6

Commager, Steele, 'Horace, *Carmina* 1.37', *Phoenix* 12, 1958

Cooley, Linda, 'The Moralizing Message of the *Senatus Consultum de Cn. Pisone Patre*', *Greece & Rome* 45, 1998

Corbier, Mireille, 'Child Exposure and Abandonment', in Dixon (2001)

Cornell, T.J., *The Beginnings of Rome: Italy and Rome from the Bronze Age to the Punic Wars (c. 1000–264 BC)* (London, 1995)

Crook, John, *Consilium Principis: Imperial Councils and Counsellors from Augustus to Diocletian* (Cambridge, 1955)

Dalby, Andrew, *Empire of Pleasures: Luxury and Indulgence in the Roman World* (London, 2000)

D'Amato, Raffaele, *Arms and Armour of the Imperial Roman Soldier: From Marius to Commodus, 112 BC–AD 192* (Barnsley, 2009)

D'Arms, John, *Romans on the Bay of Naples: A Social and Cultural Study of the Villas and Their Owners from 150 B.C. to A.D. 400* (Cambridge, Mass., 1970)

Dasen, Véronique and Thomas Späth, *Children, Memory, and Family Identity in Roman Culture* (Oxford, 2010)

Davis, P.J., *Ovid and Augustus: A Political Reading of Ovid's Erotic Poems* (London, 2006)

Dear, David R., *Roman Coins and Their Values: The Republic and the Twelve Caesars 280 BC–AD 96* (London, 2000)

De La Bédoyère, Guy, *Defying Rome: The Rebels of Roman Britain* (Stroud, 2003)

Demougin, S., *L'Ordre Équestre sous les Julio-Claudiens* (Paris, 1988)

Dixon, Suzanne, *The Roman Mother* (London, 1988)

——*The Roman Family* (Baltimore, 1992)

Dixon, Suzanne (ed.), *Childhood, Class and Kin in the Roman World* (London, 2001)

Drogula, Fred K., 'Controlling Travel: Deportation, Islands and the Regulation of Senatorial Mobility in the Augustan Principate', *Classical Quarterly* 61, 2011

Dueck, Daniela, *Strabo of Amasia: A Greek Man of Letters in Augustan Rome* (Abingdon, 2000)

Dupont, Florence, *Daily Life in Ancient Rome*, tr. Christopher Woodall (Oxford, 1992)

Du Quesnay, Ian M. Le M., '*Amicus Certus in Re Incerta Cernitur*: Epode 1', in Woodman and Feeney

Eck, Walter, *The Age of Augustus*, tr. Deborah Lucas Schneider and Robert Daniel (Oxford, 2007)

Edmondson, Jonathan (ed.), *Augustus* (Edinburgh, 2009)

Edwards, Catherine, 'The Truth about Caligula?', *Classical Review* 41, 1991

——*The Politics of Immorality in Ancient Rome* (Cambridge, 1993)

——*Death in Ancient Rome* (New Haven, 2007)

Ehrenberg, V. and A.H.M. Jones, *Documents Illustrating the Reigns of Augustus and Tiberius* (Oxford, 1955)

Elsner, Jás and Jamie Masters, *Reflections of Nero: Culture, History & Representation* (London, 1994)

Erdkamp, Paul (ed.), *A Companion to the Roman Army* (Oxford, 2011)

Evenpoel, Willy, 'Maecenas: A Survey of Recent Literature', *Ancient Society* 21, 1990

Eyben, Emiel, *Restless Youth in Ancient Rome*, tr. Patrick Daly (London, 1993)

Fagan, Garrett G., 'Messalina's Folly', *Classical Quarterly* 52, 2002

——*The Lure of the Arena: Social Psychology and the Crowd at the Roman Games* (Cambridge, 2011)

Fantham, Elaine, *Julia Augusti: The Emperor's Daughter* (Abingdon, 2006)

Favro, Diane, *The Urban Image of Augustan Rome* (Cambridge, 1996)

Fears, J. Rufus, 'The Theology of Victory at Rome: Approaches and Problems', *Aufsteig und Niedergant der römischen Welt* 2, 1981

Ferrill, A., *Caligula: Emperor of Rome* (London, 1991)

Flory, Marleen Boudreau, 'Sic Exempla Parantur: Livia's Shrine to Concordia and the Porticus Liviae', *Historia* 33, 1984

Flower, Harriet I., 'Rethinking "Damnatio Memoriae": The Case of Cn. Calpurnius Piso Pater in AD 20', *Classical Antiquity* 17, 1998

——'Piso in Chicago: A Commentary on the APA/AIA Joint Seminar on the "Senatus Consultum de Cn. Pisone Patre"', *American Journal of Philology* 120, 1999

——'The Tradition of the *Spolia Opima*: M. Claudius Marcellus and Augustus', *Classical Antiquity* 19, 2000

——*The Art of Forgetting: Disgrace & Oblivion in Roman Political Culture* (Chapel Hill, 2006)

Flower, Harriet I. (ed.), *The Cambridge Companion to the Roman Republic* (Cambridge, 2004)

Forsythe, Gary, *A Critical History of Early Rome: From Prehistory to the First Punic War* (Berkeley and Los Angeles, 2005)

Fraenkel, Eduard, *Horace* (Oxford, 1957)

Freudenburg, Kirk, '*Recusatio* as Political Theatre: Horace's Letter to Augustus', *Journal of Roman Studies* 104, 2014

Galinsky, Karl, *Augustan Culture* (Princeton, 1996)

——*The Cambridge Companion to the Age of Augustus* (Cambridge, 2005)

Gambash, Gil, 'To Rule a Ferocious Province: Roman Policy and the Aftermath of the Boudiccan Revolt', *Britannia* 43, 2012

Gibson, A.G.G., *The Julio-Claudian Succession: Reality and Perception of the 'Augustan Model'* (Leiden, 2013)

Ginsburg, Judith, *Representing Agrippina: Constructions of Female Power in the Early Roman Empire* (Oxford, 2006)

Goldsworthy, Adrian, *Antony and Cleopatra* (London, 2010)

Goodman, Martin, *The Roman World: 44 BC–AD 180* (London, 1997)

——*Rome & Jerusalem: The Clash of Ancient Civilizations* (London, 2007)

Goudineau, C. and A. Ferdière (eds), *Les Villes Augustéennes de Gaule* (Autun, 1985)

Gowing, Alain M., *Empire and Memory: The Representation of the Roman Republic in Imperial Culture* (Cambridge, 2005)

Grandazzi, Alexandre, *The Foundation of Rome: Myth and History*, tr. Jane Marie Todd (Ithaca, 1997)

Gray-Fow, Michael J.G., 'Why the Christians? Nero and the Great Fire', *Latomus* 57, 1998

Green, C.M.C., 'Claudius, Kingship, and Incest', *Latomus* 57, 1998

——'The Slayer and the King: 'Rex Nemorensis' and the Sanctuary of Diana', *Arion* 7, 2000

Green, Peter, '*Carmen* et *Error*: The Enigma of Ovid's Exile', in *Classical Bearings: Interpreting Ancient History and Culture* (Berkeley and Los Angeles, 1989)

Grether, Gertrude, 'Livia and the Roman Imperial Cult', *American Journal of Philology* 67, 1946

Griffin, Jasper, 'Augustus and the Poets: "*Caesar qui cogere posset*"', in Miller and Segal

Griffin, Miriam T., *Nero: The End of a Dynasty* (New Haven, 1984)

——*Seneca: A Philosopher in Politics* (Oxford, 1992)

Grossi, Olindo, 'The Forum of Julius Caesar and the Temple of Venus Genetrix', *Memoirs of the American Academy in Rome* 13, 1936

Gruen, Erich S., *The Last Generation of the Roman Republic* (Berkeley and Los Angeles, 1974)

——*Culture and National Identity in Republican Rome* (Ithaca, 1992)

Grüll, Tibor and Lászlo Benke, 'A Hebrew/Aramaic Graffito and Poppaea's Alleged Jewish Sympathy', *Journal of Jewish Studies* 62, 2011

Gurval, Robert Alan, *Actium and Augustus: The Politics and Emotions of Civil War* (Ann Arbor, 1998)

Habinek, Thomas and Alessandro Schiesaro (eds), *The Roman Cultural Revolution* (Cambridge, 1997)

Hallett, Judith P., 'Fulvia, Mother of Iullus Antonius: New Approaches to the Sources on Julia's Adultery at Rome', *Helios* 33, 2006

Hallett, Judith P. and Marilyn B. Skinner, *Roman Sexualities* (Princeton, 1997)

Harrison, S.J., 'Augustus, the Poets, and the Spolia Opima', *Classical Quarterly* 39, 1989

Hekster, O. and J. Rich, 'Octavian and the Thunderbolt: The Temple of Apollo Palatinus and Roman Traditions of Temple Building', *Classical Quarterly* 56, 2006

Henderson, John, 'A Doo-Dah-Doo-Dah-Dey at the Races: Ovid *Amores* 3.2 and the Personal Politics of the *Circus Maximus*', *Classical Antiquity* 21, 2002

Herbert-Brown, Geraldine (ed.), *Ovid's* Fasti: *Historical Readings at its Bimillennium* (Oxford, 2002)

Hersch, Karen K., *The Roman Wedding: Ritual and Meaning in Antiquity* (Cambridge, 2010)

Hind, J.G.F., 'The Middle Years of Nero's Reign', *Historia* 20, 1971

——'The Death of Agrippina and the Finale of the "Oedipus" of Seneca', *Journal of the Australasian Universities Language and Literature Association* 38, 1972

——'Caligula and the Spoils of Ocean: A Rush for Riches in the Far North-West?' *Britannia* 34, 2000

Hopkins, Keith, *Sociological Studies in Roman History,* Volume 1: *Conquerors and Slaves* (Cambridge, 1978)

———*Sociological Studies in Roman History,* Volume 2: *Death and Renewal* (Cambridge, 1983)

Houston, George W., 'Tiberius on Capri', *Greece & Rome* 32, 1985

Humphrey, J., *Roman Circuses: Arenas for Chariot Racing* (London, 1986)

Hurlet, Frédéric, *Les Collègues du Prince sous Auguste et Tibère: de la Légalité Républicaine à la Légitimité Dynastique* (Rome, 1997)

James, Simon, *Rome and the Sword* (London, 2011)

Jenkyns, Richard, *Virgil's Experience: Nature and History: Times, Names, and Places* (Oxford, 1998)

Jeppesen, K.K., '*Grand Camée de France*: Sejanus Reconsidered and Confirmed', *Mitteilungen des Deutschen Archäologischen Institut, Römische Abteilung* 100, 1993

Joshel, Sandra P., 'Female Desire and the Discourse of Empire: Tacitus's Messalina', *Signs: Journal of Women in Culture and Society* 21, 1995

Judge, E. A., '"Res Publica Restituta": A Modern Illusion?', in *Polis and Imperium: Studies in Honour of Edward Togo Salmon,* ed. J.A.S. Evans (Toronto, 1974)

Keppie, Lawrence, '"Guess Who's Coming to Dinner": The Murder of Nero's Mother Agrippina in its Topographical Setting', *Greece & Rome* 58, 2011

Kiernan, V.G., *Horace: Poetics and Politics* (Basingstoke, 1999)

King, Charles W., 'The Roman *Manes*: the Dead as Gods', in *Rethinking Ghosts in World Religions,* ed. Mu-chou Poo (Leiden, 2009)

Kleiner, Fred S., 'The Arch in Honor of C. Octavius and the Fathers of Augustus', *Historia* 37, 1988

Knapp, Robert, *Invisible Romans* (London, 2011)

Knox, Peter E: 'The Poet and the Second Prince: Ovid in the Age of Tiberius', *Memoirs of the American Academy in Rome* 49, 2004

Koortbojian, M., *The Divinization of Caesar and Augustus: Precedents, Consequences, Implications* (Cambridge, 2013)

Kovacs, Judith and Christopher Rowland, *Revelation* (Oxford, 2004)

Kuttner, *Dynasty and Empire in the Age of Augustus: the Case of the Boscoreale Cups* (Berkeley and Los Angeles, 1995)

Lacey, W.K., 'Octavian in the Senate, January 27 B.C.', *Journal of Roman Studies* 64, 1974

Lange, Carsten Hjort, *Res Publica Constituta: Actium, Apollo and the Accomplishment of the Triumviral Assignment* (Leiden, 2009)

Leach, Eleanor Winsor, 'Claudia Quinta (*Pro Caelio* 34) and an altar to Magna Mater', *Dictynna* 4, 2007

Lega, C., 'Il Colosso di Nerone', *Bullettino della Commissione Archeologica Comunale in Roma,* 1989–90

Leitão, David D., 'Senecan Catoptrics and the Passion of Hostius Quadra (Sen. Nat. 1)', *Materiali e Discussioni per l'Analisi dei Testi Classici* 41, 1998

Lendering, Jona and Arjen Bosman, *Edge of Empire: Rome's Frontier on the Lower Rhine* (Rotterdam, 2012)

Levick, Barbara, 'Tiberius' Retirement to Rhodes in 6 BC', *Latomus* 31, 1972

——*Claudius* (Oxford, 1990)

——*Tiberius the Politician* (London, 1999)

——*Augustus: Image and Substance* (Harlow, 2010)

Littlewoood, R.J., 'Ovid among the Family Dead: the Roman Founder Legend and Augustan Iconography in Ovid's *Feralia* and *Lemuria*', *Latomus* 60, 2001

Lobur, John Alexander, Consensus, Concordia *and the Formation of Roman Imperial Ideology* (London, 2008)

Lott, J. Bert, *The Neighbourhoods of Augustan Rome* (Cambridge, 2004)

——*Death and Dynasty in Early Imperial Rome* (Cambridge, 2012)

Luce, T.J., 'The Dating of Livy's First Decade', *TAPA* 96, 1965

Lyne, R.O.A.M., *Horace: Behind the Public Poetry* (New Haven, 1995)

MacMullen, Ramsay, *Enemies of the Roman Order: Treason, Unrest, and Alienation in the Empire* (Cambridge, Mass., 1967)

Malitz, Jürgen, *Nero*, tr. Allison Brown (Oxford, 1999)

Malloch, S.J.V., 'Gaius on the Channel Coast', *Classical Quarterly* 51, 2001

Mattingly, David, *An Imperial Possession: Britain in the Roman Empire* (London, 2006)

——*Imperialism, Power and Identity: Experiencing the Roman Empire* (Princeton, 2011)

Mayor, Adrienne, *The First Fossil Hunters: Paleontology in Greek and Roman Times* (Princeton, 2000)

McGinn, T.A., *Prostitution, Sexuality, and the Law in Ancient Rome* (Oxford, 1998)

McPherson, Catherine, 'Fact and Fiction: Crassus, Augustus and the *Spolia Opima*', *Hirundo* 8, 2009–10

Meiggs, Russell, *Roman Ostia* (Oxford, 1960)

Michels, Agnes Kirsopp, 'The Topography and Interpretation of the Lupercalia', *TAPA* 84, 1953

Miller, Fergus and Erich Segal, *Caesar Augustus: Seven Aspects* (Oxford, 1984)

Miller, J.F., *Apollo, Augustus, and the Poets* (Cambridge, 2009)

Momigliano, Arnaldo, *Claudius: The Emperor and his Achievements* (Oxford, 1961)

Morgan, Llewellyn, 'Tacitus, *Annals* 4.70: An Unappreciated Pun', *Classical Quarterly* 48, 1998

——'The Autopsy of C. Asinius Pollio', *Journal of Roman Studies* 90, 2000

Murdoch, Adrian, *Rome's Greatest Defeat: Massacre in the Teutoburg Forest* (Stroud, 2006)

Murison, C.L., *Galba, Otho and Vitellius: Careers and Controversies* (Hildesheim, 1993)

Nappa, Christopher, *Vergil's* Georgics, Octavian, and Rome (Ann Arbor, 2005)

Newbold, R.F., 'Some Social and Economic Consequences of the A.D. 64 Fire at Rome', *Latomus* 33, 1974

Nicolet, Claude, *The World of the Citizen in Republican Rome*, tr. P.S. Falla (London, 1980)

Oliensis, Ellen, *Horace and the Rhetoric of Authority* (Cambridge, 1998)

Olson, Kelly, *Dress and the Roman Woman: Self-presentation and Society* (Abingdon, 2008)

Oost, Stewart Irvin, 'The Career of M. Antonius Pallas', *American Journal of Philology* 79, 1958

Osgood, Josiah, *Caesar's Legacy: Civil War and the Emergence of the Roman Empire* (Cambridge, 2006)

——*Claudius Caesar: Image and Power in the Early Roman Empire* (Cambridge, 2011)

Parker, Philip, *The Empire Stops Here: A Journey Along the Frontiers of the Roman World* (London, 2009)

Perrin, Y., 'Êtres Mythiques, Êtres Fantastiques et Grotesques de la Domus Aurea de Néron', *Dialogues d'Histoire Ancienne* 8, 1982

Pettinger, Andrew, *The Republic in Danger: Drusus Libo and the Succession of Tiberius* (Oxford, 2012)

Pollini, John, *From Republic to Empire: Rhetoric, Religion, and Power in the Visual Culture of Ancient Rome* (Norman, 2012)

Potter, David S. (ed.), *A Companion to the Roman Empire* (Oxford, 2010)

Potter, D.S. and D.J. Mattingly: *Life, Death, and Entertainment in the Roman Empire* (Ann Arbor, 1999)

Powell, Lindsay, *Eager for Glory: The Untold Story of Drusus the Elder, Conqueror of Germania* (Barnsley, 2011)

Raaflaub, Kurt A. and Mark Toher (eds), *Between Republic and Empire: Interpretations of Augustus and his Principate* (Berkeley and Los Angeles, 1990)

Ramsey, John T. and A. Lewis Licht, *The Comet of 44 B.C. and Caesar's Funeral Games* (Chicago, 1997)

Renucci, Pierre, *Caligula l'Impudent* (Paris, 2007)

Rich, J.W., 'Augustus and the *Spolia Opima*', *Chiron* 26, 1996

——'Augustus's Parthian Honours, the Temple of Mars Ultor and the Arch in the Forum Romanum', *Papers of the British School at Rome* 66, 1998

Rich, J.W. and J.H.C. Williams, '*Leges et iura p. R. restituit*: A New Aureus of Octavian and the Settlement of 28–27 BC', *Numismatic Chronicle* 159, 1999

Rogers, Robert Samuel, 'The Neronian Comets', *Transactions and Proceedings of the American Philological Association* 84, 1953

——'Heirs and rivals to Nero', *TAPA* 86, 1955

Roller, Duane W., *Through the Pillars of Herakles: Greco-Roman Exploration of the Atlantic* (London, 2006)

Roller, Matthew B., *Constructing Autocracy: Aristocrats and Emperors in Julio-Claudian Rome* (Princeton, 2001)

Romm, James, *Dying Every Day: Seneca at the Court of Nero* (New York, 2014)

Rose, C., *Dynastic Commemoration and Imperial Portraiture in the Julio-Claudian Period* (Cambridge, 1997)

Rosenstein, Nathan, *Imperatores Victi: Military Defeat and Aristocratic Competition in the Middle and Late Republic* (Berkeley and Los Angeles, 1990)

Rosenstein, Nathan and Robert Morstein-Marx, *A Companion to the Roman Republic* (Oxford, 2010)

Rousselle, Aline, 'The Family under the Roman Empire: Signs and Gestures', in *A History of the Family*, vol. 1 (Cambridge, 1996)

Rudich, Vasily, *Political Dissidence Under Nero: The Price of Dissimulation* (London, 1993)

Rutledge, Steven H., *Imperial Inquisitions: Prosecutors and Informants from Tiberius to Domitian* (London, 2001)

Saddington, D.B., '"Honouring" Tiberius on Inscriptions and in Valerius Maximus – a Note', *Acta Classica* 43, 2000

Sailor, Dylan, *Writing and Empire in Tacitus* (Cambridge, 2008)

Saller, R., 'Anecdotes as Historical Evidence for the Principate', *Greece & Rome* 27, 1980

Scullard, Howard Hayes, *Scipio Africanus in the Second Punic War* (Cambridge, 1930)

Seager, Robin, *Tiberius* (Oxford, 2005)

Sealey, Paul R., *The Boudiccan Revolt Against Rome* (Oxford, 2004)

Sebasta, J.L., 'Women's Costume and Feminine Civic Morality in Augustan Rome', *Gender and History* 9.3, 1997

Shatzman, Israël, *Senatorial Wealth and Roman Politics* (*Latomus*, 1975)

Shaw, Brent D., 'Raising and Killing Children: Two Roman Myths', *Mnemosyne* 54, 2001

Shotter, D.C.A., 'Tacitus, Tiberius and Germanicus', *Historia* 17, 1968

——'Tiberius and Asinius Gallus', *Historia* 20, 1971

——'The Fall of Sejanus: Two Problems', *Classical Philology* 69, 1974

——'Cnaeus Calpurnius Piso, Legate of Syria', *Historia* 23, 1974

——'Agrippina the Elder – A Woman in a Man's World', *Historia* 49, 2000

Sijpesteijn, P., 'Another *ovaia* of D. Valerius Asiaticus in Egypt', *Zeitschrift für Papyrologie und Epigraphik* 79, 1989

Sinclair, Patrick, 'Tacitus' Presentation of Livia Julia, Wife of Tiberius' Son Drusus', *American Journal of Philology* 111, 1990

Small, Jocelyn Penny, *Cacus and Marsyas in Etrusco-Roman Legend* (Princeton, 1982)

Smallwood, E. Mary, *Documents Illustrating the Principates of Gaius, Claudius and Nero* (Cambridge, 1967)

Speidel, M.A., 'Roman Army Pay Scales', *Journal of Roman Studies* 82, 1992

Stevens, C.E., 'Claudius and the Orcades', *Classical Review* 1, 1951

——'The Will of Q. Veranius', *Classical Review* 1, 1951

Stewart, A.F., 'To Entertain an Emperor: Sperlonga, Laokoön and Tiberius at the Dinner-Table', *Journal of Roman Studies* 67, 1977

Swain, Simon (ed.), *Seeing the Face, Seeing the Soul: Polemon's* Physiognomy *from Classical Antiquity to Medieval Islam* (Oxford, 2007)

Swan, Peter Michael, *The Augustan Succession: An Historical Commentary on Cassius Dio's Roman History*, Books 55–56 *(9 B.C.–A.D. 14)* (Oxford, 2004)

Syme, Ronald, *The Roman Revolution* (Oxford, 1939)

——'Seianus on the Aventine', *Hermes* 84, 1956

——'*Imperator Caesar*: A Study in Nomenclature', *Historia* 7, 1958

——'Livy and Augustus', *Harvard Studies in Classical Philology* 64, 1959

——'Domitius Corbulo', *Journal of Roman Studies* 60, 1970

——'The Crisis of 2 B.C.', *Bayerische Akademie der Wissenschaften*, 1974

——'History or Biography: The Case of Tiberius Caesar', *Historia* 23, 1974

——*History in Ovid* (Oxford, 1978)

——'The Sons of Piso the Pontifex', *American Journal of Philology* 101, 1980

———The Augustan Aristocracy (Oxford, 1986)

Tatum, W. Jeffrey, The Patrician Tribune: Publius Clodius Pulcher (Chapel Hill, 1999)

Taylor, L.R., 'Horace's Equestrian Career', American Journal of Philology 46, 1925

———'New Light on the History of the Secular Games', American Journal of Philology 55, 1934

Thibault, John C. The Mystery of Ovid's Exile (Berkeley and Los Angeles, 1964)

Thomas, Yan, 'À Rome, pères citoyens et cité des pères (IIe siècle av. J.C.-IIe siècle ap. J.C.)' in Aline Rousselle, Giulia Sissa and Yan Thomas, Famille dans la Grèce et à Rome (Paris, 1986)

Thompson, E.A., 'Early Germanic Warfare', Past and Present 14, 1958

Thornton, M.K., 'The Enigma of Nero's Quinquennium', Historia 22, 1973

———'Nero's Quinquennium: The Ostian Connection', Historia 38, 1989

Todd, Malcolm, The Early Germans (Oxford, 2004)

Torelli, Mario, Studies in the Romanization of Italy, tr. Helena Fracchia and Maurizio Gualtieri (Edmonton, 1995)

———Tota Italia: Essays in the Cultural Formation of Roman Italy (Oxford, 1999)

Townend, G.B., 'Calpurnius Siculus and the Munus Neronis', Journal of Roman Studies 70, 1980

Townsley, Jeremy, 'Paul, the Goddess Religions, and Queer Sects: Romans 1:23–28', Journal of Biblical Literature 130, 2011

Treggiari, S., Roman Freedmen During the Late Republic (Oxford, 1969)

Van Voorst, Robert E., Jesus Outside the New Testament: An Introduction to the Ancient Evidence (Grand Rapids, 2000)

Versnel, H.S., 'Two Types of Roman Devotio', Mnemosyne 29, 1976

Vout, Caroline, Power and Eroticism in Imperial Rome (Cambridge, 2007)

Walbank, Frank W., 'The Scipionic Legend', in Selected Papers: Studies in Greek and Roman History and Historiography (Cambridge, 1985)

Wallace-Hadrill, Andrew, 'Civilis Princeps: Between Citizen and King', Journal of Roman Studies 72, 1982

———Rome's Cultural Revolution (Cambridge, 2008)

Warden, P.G., 'The Domus Aurea reconsidered', Journal of the Society of Architectural Historians 40, 1981

Wardle, David, 'Caligula's Bridge of Boats – AD 39 or 40?' (Historia 56, 2007)

Warmington, B. H., Nero: Reality and Legend (London, 1969)

Weaver, P.R.C., Familia Caesaris: A Social Study of the Emperor's Freedmen and Slaves (Cambridge, 1972)

Weinstock, Stefan, 'Victor and Invictus', Harvard Theological Review 50, 1957

Welch, K.F., The Roman Amphitheatre: From its Origins to the Colosseum (Cambridge, 2007)

Welch, Tara S., The Elegaic Cityscape: Propertius and the Meaning of Roman Monuments (Columbus, 2005)

Wells, C.M., The German Policy of Augustus: An Examination of the Archaeological Evidence (Oxford, 1972)

Wells, Peter, *The Barbarians Speak: How the Conquered Peoples Shaped Roman Europe* (Princeton, 1999)

——*The Battle That Stopped Rome: Emperor Augustus, Arminius, and the Slaughter of the Legions in the Teutoburg Forest* (New York, 2003)

Whitmarch, Tim, 'Greek and Roman in Dialogue: the Pseudo-Lucianic *Nero*', *JHS* 119, 1999

Wiedemann, Thomas, 'The Fetiales: A Reconsideration', *Classical Quarterly* 36, 1986

Wilkinson, Sam, *Republicanism During the Early Roman Empire* (London, 2012)

Williams, Craig A., *Roman Homosexuality* (Oxford, 2010)

Williams, G., 'Did Maecenas "Fall from Favor"? Augustan Literary Patronage', in Raaflaub and Toher

Wilson, Emily, *Seneca: A Life* (London, 2015)

Winterling, Aloys, *Politics and Society in Imperial Rome*, tr. Kathrin Lüddecke (Oxford, 2009)

——*Caligula: A Biography*, tr. Deborah Lucas Schneider, Glenn W. Most and Paul Psionos (Berkeley and Los Angeles, 2011)

Wiseman, T.P., *Clio's Cosmetics: Three Studies in Greco-Roman Literature* (Leicester, 1979)

——*Remus: A Roman Myth* (Cambridge, 1995)

——*The Myths of Rome* (Exeter, 2004)

——*Unwritten Rome* (Exeter, 2008)

Wistrand, E., *Horace's Ninth Epode and Its Historical Background* (Göteborg, 1958)

Wood, Susan, '*Memoriae Agrippinae*: Agrippina the Elder in Julio-Claudian Art and Propaganda', *American Journal of Archaeology* 92, 1988

——'Diva Drusilla Panthea and the Sisters of Caligula', *American Journal of Archaeology* 99, 1995

——*Imperial Women: A Study in Public Images, 40 BC–AD 68* (Leiden, 1999)

——'Tacitus' Obituary of Tiberius', *Classical Quarterly* 39, 1989

Woodman, A.J., 'Amateur Dramatics at the Court of Nero: Annals 15.48–74', in *Tacitus and the Tacitean Tradition*, ed. T. J. Luce and A. J. Woodman (Princeton, 1993)

Woodman, A.J. (ed.), *The Cambridge Companion to Tacitus* (Cambridge, 2009)

Woodman, Tony and Dennis Feeney, *Traditions and Contexts in the Poetry of Horace* (Cambridge, 2002)

Woods, David, 'Caligula's Seashells', *Greece & Rome* 47, 2000

——'Caligula, Incitatus, and the Consulship', *Classical Quarterly* 64, 2014

Woolf, Greg, *Becoming Roman: The Origins of Provincial Civilization in Gaul* (Cambridge, 1998)

Yavetz, Z., *Plebs and Princeps* (Oxford, 1969)

——'Seianus and the Plebs. A Note', *Chiron* 28, 1998

Zankel, James E. G., 'New Light on Gaius Caesar's Eastern Campaign', *Greek, Roman and Byzantine Studies* 11, 1970

Zanker, Paul, *The Power of Images in the Age of Augustus*, tr. Alan Shapiro (Ann Arbor, 1990)

INDEX